The Complete
Outdoor Cookbook

BY THE SAME AUTHORS

A Family Guide to Saltwater Fishing

The Pennysaver Cookbook

Family Fun on and around the Water
    by Dan Morris and Norman Strung

The Fisherman's Almanac
    by Dan Morris and Norman Strung

The Savor of the Sea
    by Dan Morris and Matilda Moore

The Hong Kong Cookbook
    by Arthur Lem and Dan Morris

The Mike Douglas Cookbook
    by Mike Douglas and Dan Morris

The Sterling Cookbook
    by Jack Sterling and Dan Morris

The Complete Outdoor Cookbook

by Dan and Inez Morris

With a chapter on
Wilderness Cooking
by Norman Strung
and a chapter on
How to Prepare and Cook Wild Game
by Norman and Priscilla Strung

HAWTHORN BOOKS, INC.   *PUBLISHERS   NEW YORK*

Contents

List of Illustrations   vii

PART I

When, Where, and How to Cook Outdoors

1. Cooking Outdoors at Home   3
2. Camp Cooking   34
   What to Do before Going   34
   After Arrival   74
3. Wilderness Cooking, by Norman Strung   86
   Forest, Lake, and Mountain Country   86
   Desert Camping   112
4. Foraging for Food and Water   116
5. Boat Cooking   136
6. Picnics and Cookouts   166

PART II

Facts Every Outdoor Cook Should Know

7. Meat, Poultry, and Fish   189

8. Other Perishables   199

9. Food Poisoning Is No Accident . . . and It's No Fun!   203

10. Nutrition   206

11. Planning Menus   209

PART III

Yard, Camp, Wilderness, Boat, and Picnic Recipes

12. About the Recipes   215

13. Seasonings and Sauces   217

14. Salads   222

15. Soups   237

16. Meats   248

    Beef   248

    Lamb   261

    Liver   265

    Pork   266

    Veal   272

    Poultry   276

    Frankfurters   282

17. Fish and Shellfish   285

18. Meat and Fish Combinations   302

19. Eggs   310

20. Legumes   315

21. Vegetables   318

22. Desserts and Breads and So Forth   331

23. How to Prepare and Cook Wild Game,
    by Norman and Priscilla Strung   345

Index   357

List of Illustrations

A grill   ix

A reed "wall"   6

An expanded-metal Rid-Jid dining group   9

The Coleman dining fly   10

A cinder-block stove   12

A frame made of coat hangers for a grill hood   14

The grill hood finished with aluminum foil   15

A charcoal cooker with spit attached   16

The Coleman roll-around grill with quick-connect couplings   18

The permanently installed Char-Broil gas cooker   18

The versatile Auto-Fire charcoal starter, cooker, and heater   22

The Coleman three-burner gasoline stove   39

The Thermos two-burner gasoline stove   40

The Coleman two-burner propane stove   41

The Coleman super stove, with lantern, ten-pound propane
      bottle, and five-foot hose   42

Ronson's lightweight butane camp stove   43

The Coleman stove-top camp oven   47

A store-bought reflector oven with shelf, and a homemade aluminum-foil reflector oven   48

Coleman's top-carrying thirty-quart–capacity Poly-Lite cooler   51

Coleman's side-carrying forty-four-quart–capacity Low Boy   51

Coleman's versatile three-way, sixty-eight-quart–capacity cooler   52

Tupperware's all-purpose food containers in camp   57

Fastening a strip of hold-anything tape to a Campanion   70

"Fuzz sticks"   76

The keyhole lay   98

The log-cabin fire   99

The teepee fire   100

The outdoorsman's way of planking a fish steak   107

Water hemlock   130

Variations of poison oak and poison ivy   131

Poison ivy   132

Poison sumac   133

Cypress spurge   134

Tall field buttercup   135

Stinging nettle   135

Wantagh Park and Marina, Nassau County, Long Island, New York   138–139

Homestrand's Mark 218 electric stove and oven for boats   145

The Skippy One wood- and coal-burning stove   146

Homestrand's two-burner alcohol stove for boats   148

A table-foodbox-Thermos kit   171

The Thermos Jet-Air stove   182

Tupperware food containers for waterborne picnics   184

Fish Laulaus   291

Wrapping vegetables for foil-baking   319

 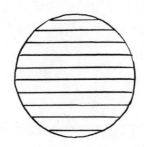 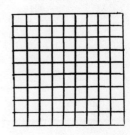

This is a grill.

- Some people spell it *grille*
- Others call it a rack
- Or grate
- Or grid

No matter what you call it, or we call it, this is what we mean.

PART I

When, Where, and How to Cook Outdoors

1—Cooking Outdoors at Home

You, much like Aladdin, can open doors to a new way of life. He did it by rubbing a magic lamp. You can do it by cooking a hamburger over an outdoor fire.

Try it someday, and if you've never done it before, we think you'll then know at least 80 per cent of the reasons why more than half of the homes being built in the United States today combine outdoor living with indoor living.

It makes no difference over what sort of fire you cook that first hamburger: driftwood, scraps of lumber, leaves and twigs, old-fashioned charcoal, or new-fangled briquettes. It will kick off an aroma, a delectable aroma, quite like nothing you've ever smelled before. It will taste quite like nothing you've ever tasted before.

The wind will rustle, the birds will sing, and you'll lean back with a sigh of content.

It will perhaps be your first encounter with nature in more years than you care to remember. But you'll be hooked. From the hamburger you'll progress to a steak and from there to barbecue sauces and chops and fish and crunchy-skinned roasts.

You'll discover that being alive is a little better than you thought it could be. You won't want it to end, not that kind of living. So you'll fix up whatever outdoor space you have around your house for outdoor cooking and outdoor eating. Or if you do not have room for both, you'll do your cooking outdoors and your eating indoors.

Apartment-house dwellers would be the ones most likely to fall into

3

that category. For them, outdoor living might be a tiny terrace towering high above a city street. But outdoors is outdoors, and the hamburgers they cook there can taste just as delectable as the ones cooked beside a mountain stream or on an ocean beach.

Instead of a picnic fire, which could mean scrounging for wood, all they need is some sort of a charcoal stove. They come in all sizes, shapes, and forms. Some are good; some are excellent. None of them is bad.

The thing to do is get the one that fits the terrace, fire up, start cooking, sit back, and enjoy the spring, summer, autumn, and the winter—yes, even the winter breezes—while the folks next door slave over what, in apartment houses, passes for a kitchen stove.

Apartment-house terraces, which more aptly might be called balconies, are easily enclosed and furnished for year-round use. You know what storm windows are: two or three aluminum tracks on which either window panes or screens can slide up and down. Well, all it takes to enclose a terrace is a series of them. Presto, you have an all-weather enclosure. Open the windows when it's sunny and warm; close them when it's cold. Furnish it as fancy and pocketbook dictate. Perhaps with wicker, perhaps with bamboo, aluminum, redwood, or wrought-iron furniture (any or all of them with waterproof, weather-resistant cushions, of course), indoor-outdoor lamps, and—most important of all—a stove that is meant to give all that you cook the taste and tang of the outdoors.

You'll spend long hours there no matter what the season of the year. In the summer, with all the windows wide open, cook and eat outdoors. In the winter, open the windows (dress warmly for the occasion, of course) while cooking, extinguish your fire when whatever it is that you're cooking is done, and eat indoors.

That's all it takes to combine outdoor and indoor living, cooking, and eating if you live in an apartment house. It's not quite so simple, though, for folks who live in one- or two-family houses located in congested areas where homes have little or no yard space. They have to put their imaginations to work, unless their houses are blessed with porches or sun decks. Then, in all likelihood, all they have to do is what the apartment-house dwellers did, only a bit more so.

For example, they may have to provide a roof, a circumstance that did not confront the apartment-house dweller, whose terrace roof is the terrace on the floor above. A visit to almost any department store, outdoor shop, lumber yard, or nursery takes care of this problem. You'll discover that you have quite a wide choice of easy-to-erect overhangs to choose from: awnings, either roll-up or stationary; sheets of durable, decorative aluminum; nonbreakable sheets of ersatz glass, some corrugated, some not, which permit sunlight to filter through. A good man around the house can install any of them, or the seller can provide for installation. Or if you have a mind to, you can hire a carpenter. Screen it or glass it in, furnish it, and you have brought outdoor living into your house come rain, sunshine, or snow—winter, summer, spring, and fall.

Now comes the real test of neighborliness. You live in a two-family house. Neither you nor the other occupant has a porch or sundeck. But you do have a yard. Here's where you must put more than just imagination to work. Diplomacy, tact, and compatibility are needed, too. Luckily, though, such close neighbors can get along and usually do get along, doing things together but always respecting the other family's need for privacy.

If their yard is big enough, they can, if they desire, easily and inexpensively divide it in two. If their yard is too small for that, they'll have to share and share alike, not only in facilities but also in time and in use. So on the assumption that two families who share the same house also will be able to share the same yard amicably, we'll say no more about it and speak now only as if all homes are one-family homes.

What you do with your yard is dictated by the amount of space you have. But, small or large, you should make the most of it. If it's very small, you can do what the apartment-house resident does: cook outside and eat inside. If it's very big, in part of it you can build an indoor-outdoor room by using screening and sliding glass walls. Then you can use your yard all year round, day or night, for everything—not only cooking and eating, relaxing and playing, but for sleeping, too (if you have heat or sleeping bags).

People with average-size yards must put their imaginations and their creative and artistic talents to work. Just to give you an idea of how simply this can be done: Our yard measures exactly 30 feet by 60 feet. A bit to one side stands a willow tree, allowing just enough space for our son David to lay out an extremely miniature baseball diamond. Yet we have an outdoor living, playing, cooking-dining room, sheltered from winds and eyes of curious passersby (they stream in by the thousands in the seaside resort town where we live), which adds three or four months to our summers in addition to giving us the privacy of a desert retreat.

Inez did it through the imaginative use of easily and cheaply purchased roll-up reed fencing, held in place by flower boxes that I, though I know little of carpentry, built in one afternoon. Most of the time one side of our reed wall cuts through David's infield because it provides us the most protection from the wind. But if David and his friends want to play ball or if the wind shifts, in a matter of minutes our outdoor room can take on new shape and dimension.

Here's a rundown of what to use and how to use it if you should want to adapt the same idea for your yard:

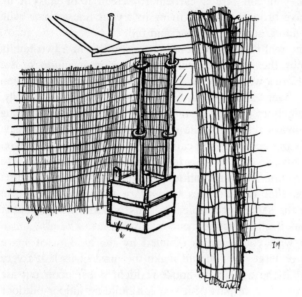

A reed "wall"

Fencing

Roll-up reed fencing comes in 8-foot to 15-foot lengths, from 3 to 6 feet high. We use the 6-foot heights. They can be purchased from gardening shops, nurseries, lumber yards, and department stores for about $5 to $15 per roll.

Flower Boxes

The number you'll have to make will be determined by the size of your yard, the number of rolls of fencing you use, and the velocity of the wind where you live. You'll need the following materials to make each box:

    2 lengths of 2 x 2, each 24 inches long, for front corner posts
    2 lengths of 2 x 2, each 6 feet long, for rear corner posts
    3 lengths of 1 x 6, each 18 inches long, for each side, making 12 in all
    3 lengths of 1 x 6, each 18 inches long, for the bottom
    8-penny nails

Nail four sides of the flower box to the corner posts, allowing 1 inch of space between each length of 1 x 6. Nail bottom pieces of 1 x 6 to box, again allowing 1 inch of space between each length.

That's all there is to it.

Roll the fencing out into roughly the position you want it to be in, space the boxes as needed, and tie the fencing to the 6-foot uprights with short lengths of flexible wire that can easily be poked between the reeds. You might set the boxes back to back with the fencing sandwiched in between, or you might checkerboard the boxes, one on one side of the fencing, the next on the other side. Let the wind and your personal preferences be the deciding factors.

The job is now done, except for one thing: If there should come a big blow, the winds would knock everything for a loop. That's the reason for the oversize flower boxes. Fill large cans with dirt (5-gallon pretzel cans are perfect), plant flowers in the dirt, and set the cans inside the boxes. The weight now will anchor the fence in place, come just about anything that nature has to offer.

That's all there is to it—at a cost to us of no more than $50 or $60. What it will cost you will depend upon the size of your yard and how much of it you want to enclose.

Such an arrangement has great versatility. In fact, it's as easy to give your outdoor all-purpose room a new look as it is to rearrange your living-room furniture. What you do is change the shape and the dimensions of the walls. It's very simple. A half-hour's work and the job is done. Simply lift out the dirt and flower-filled pretzel cans, untie the wire, move the now very light boxes and fencing to wherever you want them, retie the wire, and restore the pretzel cans.

A word to remember: The reed fencing will not last forever. Just how long it survives depends pretty much on what section of the country you live in, how cold and how windy it gets there, whether you take it down and store it in winter or let it stand in place, how often the kids bang into it. But, no matter what, it should last from three to five years, and after that it's easily replaced.

There is nothing to stop you from having a more permanent stay-in-one-place enclosure. It might be made of wood in a variety of shapes and styles, masonry, canvas, shrubbery, color-impregnated cinder block, wire, glass (real or imitation), screening, plastics, glass brick, and heaven only knows what else. You can spend a little, or you can spend a lot. You can hire a landscape architect or a gardener, or you can design it and build it yourself. But before you do anything, check your local building codes and find out what is permissible and what is not.

The important thing is to get the perimeter structure. Once you have that, you have your outdoor all-purpose room. Now all you need to do is furnish it. Once again imagination is called for.

We have in our outdoor all-purpose room an outdoor all-purpose table. It's made of a 5-foot by 9-foot sheet of ¾-inch outdoor plywood cut in half crosswise, with each half sitting on two wooden sawhorses. One side of the table top is painted green, the other is redwood-stained. Most of the time, it's in place, green side up, as though it had never been sawed in two, with a net stretched across for a fast (or slow) game of table tennis. Remove the net and, presto, it's a dining table big enough for a Henry VIII–size party. Separate the two halves, and you have two tables, one for grown-ups, the other for kids.

Redwood benches usually serve as dining chairs but sometimes, particularly when we are in the mood for a Dar Bin Loo (recipe on pages 302–303) and dining Oriental style, the benches replace the sawhorses, and we sit around the now low-slung table on plastic-covered pillows. To give you an idea of just how versatile our all-purpose table can be, once or twice when rains suddenly hit us we've moved that arrangement into our living room.

It takes two tablecloths to cover our table, sedately matching ones whose combined length make it possible for them to hang low enough to hide the sawhorses. They're stainproof and soil resistant, yet they're elegant enough for candlesticks and stemware. But they can be checkered and informal enough to fit any cut-up mood.

Surround so versatile a table with a few metal-and-plastic lounge chairs to supplement the redwood benches, and you have all the outdoor furniture you'll ever need. But again you needn't stop there. A visit to the right stores and shops will trigger all sorts of ideas.

In redoing your yard, you may have laid brick or flagstone. You may have covered it over with a roof, one end of which is attached to your house. If so, then you'll surely want to look at wrought-iron tables and chairs. They go beautifully with flagstone or brick. They'll be expensive to buy, but if they're good quality, they should last a lifetime.

There are much less expensive metal yard and patio furnishings, though. If you don't want to spend much money or if you think wrought iron is a bit too Early American, there now is on the market fold-away expanded-steel furniture that has the aura of wrought iron but is more sleek, more modern, and, between you and us, more comfortable, too.

So you shop around. You see redwood, bamboo, aluminum, fiberglass, and whatever the manufacturers, aided and abetted by their test-tube departments, will have added to the marketplace between the time this is written by us and read by you. You make your choice, and the salesman, in case it had slipped your mind, reminds you of the sun. Then you look at yard umbrellas by the yard, and maybe you find one that you like. But if we were looking for something to shelter us from the sun, we'd look at dining flies such as those shown in the illustration on page 10. We think they are far more sturdy than an umbrella can ever be and lots more adaptable for other uses, too. Did you ever try taking a yard umbrella along on a picnic or a camping trip? Well, if you haven't, don't start now.

This expanded-metal Rid-Jid dining group folds for compact storage. It is manufactured by General Housewares Corporation, Spring Park, Minnesota. (*Summer & Casual Furniture Manufacturers Association*)

Instead, take along your dining fly. It's easily knocked down and erected again in any sort of soil; it's light; and it doesn't take up nearly so much storage space en route to wherever it is that you're going.

Now let us have light because, after all, there are more hours to the day than merely the sunlit ones. Here, too, you have a wide choice. In our yard we have two sources: for good vision we have floodlights installed according to UL safety standards by a licensed electrician who

The Coleman dining fly (*Coleman Company, Inc.*)

at the same time ran some heavy-duty lines, complete with outlets, into our yard; for atmosphere we have inexpensive citronella candles set inside inexpensive clear plastic chimneys that are set atop inexpensive aluminum rods, which poke easily into the ground wherever we choose to have them. The complete assembly—candle, chimney, and rod—costs about $2.

In lighting fixtures too, you have a wide choice, not only in sizes, shapes, and styles but also in price. There are gas lights that burn gas, some of them styled very much like the gaslights of yore, and gas lights so strictly ersatz that they burn electricity. Some of them stand tall, some of them are slung low to the ground, so you'll be sure to see where you're stepping. Look them over and take your pick. It's your money. Just stay away from low, open-flame fixtures against which women's skirts might brush.

You now have the makings of an all-purpose outdoor room, except for facilities for what this book is mainly about—cooking, a subject we'll come to in a moment. Put them all together and it's beautiful, it's comfortable, it's inviting.

But you may want additional decorations, perhaps a variety of decorations, each to create a certain mood for a certain occasion:

- You can fasten travel posters to the walls.
- You can add a row of potted plants where they'll be most effective.
- You can hang balloons and paper streamers from your trees and shrubs.
- You can decorate with driftwood and seashells and fish netting.
- You can set out wine and other varicolored bottles.
- You can hang windbells and mobiles galore.
- You can make lovely transparent plastic forms, using materials and instructions that come in kits.
- You can string Japanese lanterns, but be sure that they are flameproof and won't catch fire from the heat of an electric bulb.
- You and your family and guests may don beachcomber togs or grass skirts and such (please, not the men!) if the party you're planning warrants it.

Whatever you do, it is almost certain to look pretty, provided you keep it simple. Don't put everything out at once; just those things suitable to a particular occasion.

The Different Types of Outdoor Stoves and Fireplaces

Do-It-Yourself Masonry

There are so many different sorts of appliances designed to be used for outdoor cooking that we're afraid mere mortals such as we cannot possibly keep up with them all. And the number is growing all the time.

So be it. The more outdoor stoves, the more outdoor cooks, and the more people who are discovering how good it is to take this first step toward living more in tune with nature.

Whether you cook in a yard, on a penthouse patio, on a porch or a sun deck, or on a tiny apartment-house terrace, there's a stove or a fireplace waiting for you to take home from whatever store or outdoor shop you care to visit.

But it's not necessary to buy ready-made equipment in order to cook outdoors. The Indians didn't. They built their fireplaces out of whatever was on hand. You can, too.

If you have a supply of wood and live where local ordinances permit, you can build the sort of fire described in "Camp Cooking" and "Wilderness Cooking," chapters 2 and 3. Or you can use charcoal laid on aluminum foil in a shallow slit trench, which you can dig in two minutes. Or dig either an oblong or square pit about 6 to 10 inches deep and line the sides with fireproof red brick and the bottom with gravel. You'll be able to cook by day and burn logs by night. Or vice versa. Our friend Arthur Lem, a great Chinese caterer-chef with whom Dan wrote *The Hong Kong Cookbook,* swears by pit cooking. Sometimes he tops the pit with a large wire rack, sometimes nothing at all. It depends on what he is barbecuing. In short, there are many ways you can build an outdoor stove. You can be as primitive or as modern as the material you use.

Look around your premises to see what you have on hand. A few red bricks? Cinder blocks? Fine. With them and a rack you borrow from your kitchen stove you can have a fireplace as good as almost any stove that you can buy and probably much better than most. The holes in the cinder blocks permit you to have a good draft blowing onto the coals from whatever direction the wind is coming at the moment. The knock-down fireplace is that easy to put together again. Lay a bed of sand or gravel or broken shells between them, and that's where you build your fire. Add or subtract red bricks to regulate the cooking distance from the coals. Adjust the draft through placement of other bricks, and you have a fireplace that many store-bought charcoal stoves can't compete with.

You can convert it into a smoke-cooker by adding enough bricks or blocks to hold a sheet of heavy canvas over it like a tent, well out of reach of the fire. Secure it well so that it won't blow away, making sure to leave air vents on both bottom and top. Whatever it is you're cooking will take on new dimensions. But don't take our word for it. Look at the

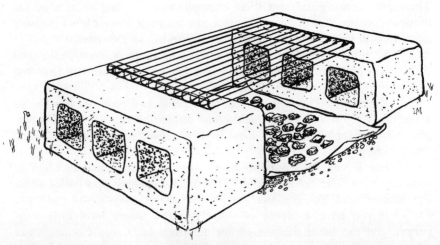

Cinder-block stove

newest charcoal cookers on the market, and you'll note that many of them have been built using variations of this principle.

This type of take-down-and-put-up-again fireplace is the only kind of masonry cooker that you should ever build, no matter how great the urge to do something with your hands. Rigidly fixed, immovable fireplaces long ago proved to be far more ornamental than practical, if for no other reason than that once erected there they stay, no matter from whence comes the wind, and, with them, about the only thing you can be sure of is this: no matter how they are positioned, the smoke will always blow in your face.

The Charcoal Grill

Realistically, however, rather than build a masonry fireplace—makeshift or permanent—you'll more likely shop around for a ready-made charcoal or (a fairly recent development) gas stove. Whether you intend to spend $5 or $500, these are the things to look for:

- It should be made of material that won't succumb to the elements.
- Moving parts should move easily. This applies especially to the grill on which your foods will cook.
- The grill should have a wide range of heights above the coals.
- You should be able to get at the coals easily in case your fire goes out or needs replenishing after you've started to cook.
- The legs should be very sturdy.
- It should have some sort of workable damper built in so that you have a draft, without which the fire will not burn, and so that you can control the draft.

The simplest charcoal stove, the one most of us are familiar with, has a round metal bed, 3 or 4 inches deep, with a flat or rounded bottom on which the fire is laid. Over this is a removable wire grill (also known as rack, grate, and grid), on which we place the food. The grill usually can be cranked up or down, but some models come with notched braces on each side. Either way, the food can cook at from an inch to about 5 inches from the coals. The legs generally are either fold-up or removable. The less you pay for this basic charcoal stove, the more likely it is that it won't last more than a year or, if you're lucky, two.

There are more elaborate versions of it. Most are on wheels, some have sideboards, some have upper-story shelf space, others have warming drawers, and some have hoods. Some are oblong, many have spits, and some are equipped with built-in thermometers.

It's not difficult to improvise a hood for the simple charcoal grill that does not provide its own. There are two ways to do this. Loosely arrange two or three thicknesses of heavy-duty aluminum foil over whatever you may be cooking and, wearing insulated gloves, gather the edges of the foil and tuck them under the edges of the grill. Or, you can fashion a hood from coat hangers and aluminum foil as shown in the sketch details. Here's how:

1. Clip off hooks of six or seven coat hangers with wire cutters; straighten wire with pliers.

2. Form two or more lengths into a firm circle, using picture wire to bind ends together. This is the base of hood and should fit just inside grill.

3. Loop remaining wires umbrella-fashion and attach to base circle, using pliers to twist ends. Fasten together with picture wire at top.

4. Cover with heavy-duty aluminum foil. Leave small portion of foil loose at top to open for draft.

Place your hood over a simple round charcoal stove. Keep the cooking coals replenished as needed with fresh ones, and you can barbecue

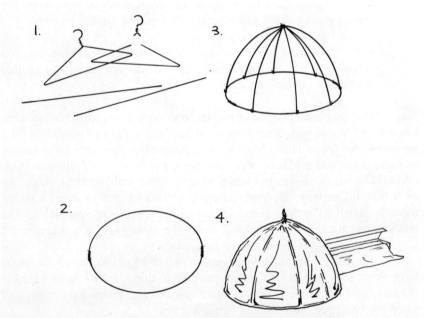

A frame made of coat hangers for a grill hood (*Reynolds Wrap*)

a whole chicken or even a very small turkey. See the recipe for roast turkey on pages 280–281 for detailed instructions.

Then there is the charcoal stove that the Japanese did not, so far as we know, copy from anybody. They created it themselves, and their word for it is *hibachi*. Its popularity is growing in the United States, and for good reason, because: (1) it has a small, deep fire box, which results in economical use of fuel; (2) its heat is concentrated; and (3) it is made of iron, a heavier, more durable material than that used in all but our better charcoal stoves. Some hibachis have one fire box; others have two. Most are oblong, but now that they're also being made in America, some are also oval. That is, we suppose, styling.

The Japanese do their charcoal cooking on low tables, close to the ground, so make sure that any hibachi you buy comes mounted on solid slabs of wood. Some of the American versions are mounted on long legs. We don't recommend them because we think they're inclined to be top-heavy and are easily knocked over, especially by kids. Don't buy the cheapest hibachi you can find. It's likely to be made of easily broken pot

The grill hood finished with aluminum foil (*Reynolds Wrap*)

metal and is therefore less likely to withstand the test of time and rough use. The hibachi is perfect for broiling steaks, burgers, chops, and fish.

It is mainly the newer, larger, heavier models of the more conventional outdoor stove which have hoods, spits, good thermometers, and draft control so good that, with hood lowered, they are quite a bit akin to the oven in your kitchen range. And, in addition to the round ones and the oblong ones, there is also one that resembles a kettle drum more than it does a stove. It's quite versatile, quite popular, quite expensive, and it will do just about all that its manufacturer says it will. It comes in a variety of models for use in yard, porch, or patio, and there is also one with detachable legs that's good for packing along on picnic or camping trips. There is still another kettle stove that's made to fit inside your fireplace. Quite a handy item, that, if ever your cookout is suddenly called off because of rain.

Charcoal cooker with spit attached. Coals are raked to back of cooker, and aluminum-foil pan is placed under spit to catch drippings. (*Reynolds Wrap*)

In buying a charcoal cooker with a spit attachment, make sure the grill area is large enough to permit the coals to be at the back of the revolving roast, not directly under it. You should be able to place a flat, shallow pan directly under the roast to catch the drippings.

The Auto-Fire Cooker-Lighter-Heater

This, we think, is the greatest invention ever to come on the charcoal cooking scene. We'll tell all about it in the "Starting Your Charcoal Fire" section (see pages 21–23).

The Gas Stove

The latest stove on the marketplace does not burn charcoal at all. It burns gas, but the food that is cooked on it has the taste of charcoal. That's because, the manufacturers point out, charcoal itself has no flavor; it's the drippings that fall on the embers that impart the flavor of charcoal. You know, they're right, and they ought to be, because the two makers of gas stoves that we know of are highly reputable and well known. One is the Coleman Company, the same people who have been making Cadillac-type camping equipment since what seems to be the year 1; the other is the Columbus Iron Works, which has long manufactured just about the best line of charcoal-burning outdoor stoves we've ever seen.

The Coleman gas cooker and the Columbus gas cooker operate in just about the same way. Lay a bed of volcanic fire rock on top of the gas heating unit, and light it as you would your kitchen range. The lava briquettes convert the gas flame to radiant heat, giving you just about the finest "charcoal" cooking you've ever tasted. The volcanic rock is long-lasting and self-cleaning, thus sparing you quite a bit of mess.

Both cookers give you a choice of gases to burn. Either hook into the household supply of gas or into a tank of bottled liquid petroleum gas (LPG) through the use of a flexible hose and coupling that clips into place as easily as the gas line on an outboard motorboat does.

For movability, there are three models to choose from: fixed post; pedestal mounting, which enables you to carry the cooker from one place to another; and, obviously the most easily mobile of all, a model that rolls around on wheels. They have large cooking surfaces, full-circle rotation (the wind need never be a problem), hood, spits, smoking units, cutting boards, and temperature-control units that permit you to roast a bird or a choice chunk of beef just as you would in the kitchen.

The permanently installed Char-Broil gas cooker (*Columbus Iron Works*)

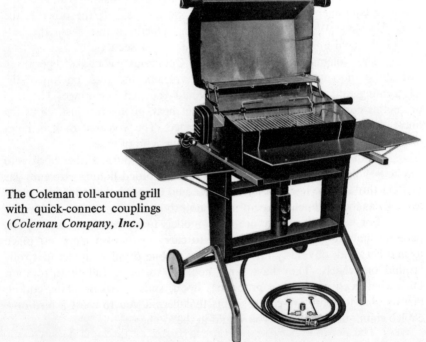

The Coleman roll-around grill with quick-connect couplings (*Coleman Company, Inc.*)

Paper Burner

If you're old-fashioned enough to get your news from newspapers and not from television, you'll never lack fuel if you ever want to broil a steak over the Safari Grill. Just roll up a wad and put a match to it and you're in business. It's really not a yard or patio item, though.

Other Sources of Cooking Heat

There are many set-on-the-table stoves that can be used outdoors as supplementary sources of cooking heat: any of the traditional chafing dishes; Ronson's Table Chef, which is fueled with an easy-to-handle butane injector that comes with it; Sterno (canned heat) table stoves; electric plates; and electric skillets. They all have their special uses and special occasions. Want to serve a wonderful buffet outdoors but with all the indoor comforts? That's what they're for.

A word of caution about using electric cookers outdoors. Inside the house, in all likelihood, you're wired for them. But how about outside? So, before plugging one into an outdoor socket, make sure you have heavy-duty lines. Any electrical equipment you use outside should carry an Underwriter's Laboratory (UL) label certifying that it has passed a safety test. It should have a three-wire power cord ending in a three-way plug, which requires using a three-way outlet. The third wire is a grounding wire to protect you from shock. *So don't cut one of the prongs off your cord in order to fit it into the standard two-hole outlet.* Call an electrician instead.

There you have it—a summation of the stoves, stoves, stoves, and still more stoves available to you, the outdoor cook. Now we'll talk about that peskiest of all peskies.

Starting Your Charcoal Fire

Here now, we'll tell you all that we can about the many, many ways of starting a charcoal fire—the bane of all outdoor chefs' existences—but we'll also tell you right now that so far as we are concerned the *only* way to start one is with the Auto-Fire Cooker-Lighter. So, as people do with desserts, we'll save the best for last. We'll start with what we believe is the worst.

Fluids and Jellies

We think they're all bad. They are uncertain. If you don't follow directions exactly, they can taint the taste of food. They can be dangerous.

You needn't take our word for it. Just read the label on any can of the stuff that you lay your hands on. They'll warn you of just about everything but taste-tainting. That you'll have to find out by eating.

The National Fire Protection Association, whose warnings count the most, warn against the use of gasoline, benzene, paint thinners, and similar liquids. Kerosene, which has the same flash point as most commercially prepared liquid charcoal-fire starters, is less hazardous than gasoline, benzene, and others, but it must be handled with care.

The lower the flash point of a liquid or jelly starter, the more readily it will vaporize and the more the vapors may spread over the whole area of grill or (and here is one of the dangers) beyond. The person who uses a low flashpoint starter risks getting a hand, arm, or clothing caught in the flarcup.

How do you know what the flash point of a starter is? You have to read the fine print on the labels, and no two manufacturers' contents of the can are necessarily the same. So you have to look for these indications:

- The least dangerous starters are those with flash points above 80°, which approaches the kerosene range. Such cans will be labeled "*Caution! Combustible.*"
- Those with flash points between 20° and 80° will be labeled "*Warning! Flammable.*"
- Those with flash points at or below 20°, which approaches the gasoline range, will be labeled "*Danger! Extremely Flammable.*"

Then, as if all that is not bad enough, there is still another extremely important precaution that you must never forget. Use liquid and jelly starters *only as starters*. Regardless of the type or brand uses, adding any of them to liven up a poorly burning fire is extremely perilous. The stuff has to hit only one live coal, and you may have a flash fire on your hands, if not also in your hair, face, and clothes.

In addition to all these precautions, the NFPA also warns you to keep liquid and jelly starters away from children. These starters are poisonous. Our advice is: don't use them. Don't allow them anywhere near your home or loved ones.

If you think we're being overly cautious, read the label on any can. Here's what it says on the first can that we picked up (the capitalized words are theirs, not ours): "DANGER vapor harmful—flammable. May be fatal or cause blindness if swallowed. Read back label carefully." And the back label starts out with big letters printed in red:

DANGER—POISON. Contains methyl alcohol. Vapor harmful. May be fatal or cause blindness if swallowed. Induce vomiting. Call physician. Cannot be made nonpoisonous. KEEP AWAY FROM CHILDREN.

CAUTION—FLAMMABLE MIXTURE. DO NOT USE NEAR FIRE OR FLAME.

CAUTION: Never sprinkle directly from can or add to going fire. Wipe up any spilled fuel and re-cover can before igniting. Use caution. No responsibility assumed by seller other than value of cans and contents.

We hope that convinces you.

Electric Igniters

These are long-handled rods on which are mounted metal heating elements, some of them straight, some of them bent into an oblong shape. The element is buried in the charcoal, the electric wire is plugged into an outlet, and you're in business—but only if you have an electric outlet. If you do, these igniters are fast and good. When using one, make sure that you remove it from the coals when they catch fire. Pull the plug and set the igniter well out of the reach of children or, for that matter, adults, too. Electric igniters hold their heat a long while and can cause serious burns.

Tinder, Kindling, Newspapers, Milk Cartons, Candles, and Such

A charcoal fire can be started in the same manner as any outdoorsman's wood fire (see page 77)—first with some tinder, then with some kindling and the charcoal. Or you can try piling briquettes into a pyramid over loosely wadded balls of newspaper. Flame should be applied to paper at two or three points at the same time. Or try using broken up and loosely crumbled milk cartons.

There are people who swear by a piece of candle judiciously placed in the middle of whatever it is they choose to use as tinder. They put a match to the wick, settle back and have a beer, and swear that it works every time.

Then there are the vast majority of charcoal chefs who just swear that, no matter what they try, their fires don't start. For them and all others we recommend the following.

The Auto-Fire Cooker-Lighter-Heater

This versatile little contraption looks like a short length of stovepipe. You apply a match to it and, presto, you're cooking over charcoal in minutes! It's the handiest gadget we've ever seen. It's not only a sure-fire charcoal

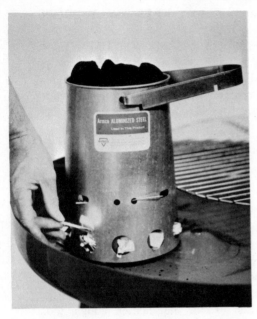

The versatile Auto-Fire charcoal starter, cooker, and heater. (*Upper left*) For grill coals, light paper and when coals begin to glow, lift by handle; coals will fall into grill. (*Upper right and lower left*) For cooking, set skillet or coffee pot on movable handle. (*Lower right*) For heating. (*Auto-Fire Corporation*)

lighter; it's also a camp cooking stove and an ice fisherman's heater and heaven only knows what else.

The Auto-Fire's secret of success is nothing more than a few holes, which provide a controlled fixed draft no matter where the wind is blowing from, and a swinging grate.

All you do is this: Wad a sheet of newspaper up loosely and poke it under the grate, set the Auto-Fire in your charcoal stove, place as much charcoal as you think you'll need on top of the grate, and light the paper with a match. The Auto-Fire will hold up to three pounds of charcoal, which will then ignite in about ninety seconds and be cooking hot in from six to ten minutes, depending upon how much coal you're using. Pick up the Auto-Fire by the handle, the grate swings down, the coals fall into your stove, and you're in business!

The Auto-Fire is small and light and can easily be taken with you wherever you go. In fact, Ross McCluskey, *Field & Stream*'s auto camping editor, has this to say about it:

> Well, I'm convinced. I've seen the Auto-Fire in operation . . . three different units on three different kinds of days, muggy, brisk and average. And each did exactly what you said it would: produced searing-hot charcoal in six minutes. And within twenty minutes it broiled perfectly done steaks.
>
> You can't really blame me for being skeptical. I've been suffering from charcoal frustration for twenty-five years. I've squirted liquid fluid and alcohol on the charcoal, I've used chemical starters . . . liquids, pellets and cakes. I've huffed and I've puffed, and I inevitably came to the conclusion that charcoal will only burn when it is damn good and ready to.
>
> But your little stove, in six minutes, produced a bed of coals so hot they immediately seared the meat, keeping the juices inside and producing a beautiful, tender crust.

Quite a testimonial, especially for an item that sells in the stores for only $3.95, if you can find a store that sells them. If you can't, send your check or money order to the man who invented it: G. B. Byars, President, Auto-Fire Corporation, Post Office Box 487, Corinth, Mississippi 38834.

Where charcoal cooking is concerned it will be the best $3.95 you ever spent.

Instant-Starting Briquettes

These are so good that we rate them immediately behind the Auto-Fire as a foolproof way to start your fire quickly and surely. They have three faults, however: (1) There are several brands on the market, and all of them that we know of cost more than most people care to pay; (2) they are not completely safe, and so precautions have to be taken; (3) most brands are good, but some brands are not. The only way to learn which to use is by trial and error.

Using them is child's play. Just touch a match to the package they come in, wait about fifteen minutes, and you're in business. But don't let a child do it because of the dangers that may be involved. The labels will tell you what they are.

Extinguishing a Charcoal Fire

Don't let a charcoal fire burn needlessly once you're through cooking on it. You'll be busy eating and won't give it the attention all outdoor fires should have.

If you have a stove with a hood, shut the dampers and close the cover, and the fire will swiftly smother from lack of oxygen. If your cooker has no hood, obtain somewhere, somehow, some fireproof contraption or other that you can set over or around it. If you have no such gizmo that you can keep handy, resort to the old reliable: water. Just flood the fire box with water, then, when you're sure the coals are extinguished, dump them onto a screen, set it in the sun and let the coals dry out for use another day. If you have no hood, no substitute, and no water, use sand or dirt.

No matter how you've extinguished them, save the cold coals. They can be used a second and sometimes even a third time, each time becoming easier to light.

No one expects a charcoal cooking fire to get out of control. But accidents do happen—a grease-fed flareup into a low-hanging tree branch, a spark shooting to the roof of your house. Once in a while these things happen. So plan ahead. Turn on the water tap on your garden outlet, shut the water off at the hose nozzle and stretch the hose back to the stove with you. Then, and only then, should you start your fire. If you have no water, at the very least keep a bucket of dirt or sand close at hand. You never know.

Accessory Equipment and Storage

There is a long list of things that you'll need if you're going to make outdoor cooking and eating a new way of life for you and your family. Some of them will be things that you can borrow from your kitchen, true, but your barbecue will move along much more smoothly and efficiently if you have a special set of accessories that are for use outdoors and nowhere else.

That way, hopefully, they'll be where you can quickly find them when you need them. Besides, many of the tools that you'll need for cooking over coals will have to be long-handled, and all of them will have to be fireproof.

Here's a rundown:

- One or two extra grills for various needs that occasionally will arise.
- Long-handled hinged grills that work something like a sandwich and into which you can put hamburgers, hot dogs, pieces of fish, and whatever else you may be cooking that might otherwise slide into the fire while turning.
- Skewers for kabobs.
- Heavy-duty aluminum foil to line the bottom of your firebox, with holes cut over the draft openings to save you a messy cleanup job every time you cook. Use it, too, to fashion a hood for your stove.
- Gravel or a commercial fire base if yours is a barbecue grill that calls for it.
- Charcoal briquettes, of course.
- Matches and a fire starter.
- Water-repellent tablecloths.
- A water bulb, sprinkler, or hose for dousing a flaming coal or worse.
- Tongs, fork, and spatula for turning.
- Fire-resistant gloves and pads.
- Roast meat and grill thermometers.
- Basting brush.
- Cutting board.
- Carving set.
- Salt and pepper shakers—filled, we hope.
- Paring knife.
- Pliers for adjusting your rotisserie if you have a spit.
- Paper towels.
- A garbage can, preferably one made of colorful plastic.
- But that's not all. Because you'll need some pots and pans from time to time and plates and platters and cups and saucers just about all the time.

If you're like us, you believe that preparing and eating good food is one of life's great joys. And if that good food is prepared and eaten outdoors, then it becomes one of life's greatest joys.

Which means that everything has to look right, taste right, and *feel* right. Which means, please, *no* paper dishes no matter how much of a work-saver they may be. Far better to eat a finely done steak off an honest-to-gosh plate and drink coffee out of an honest-to-goodness cup and consider doing dishes a small price to pay than to have them served up on paper and wish you were dead. We don't mean the dishes should be expensive; we do mean that they should be attractive and styled for eating, not for throwing away.

Luckily, paper is no problem when it comes to pots and pans, because science has not invented any paper ones that can be used for cooking. Not that we know of. And whether or not you need a special set of pots and pans exclusively for outdoor use will depend on how and what you cook.

It may be that the things you cook outdoors will mainly be things that are barbecued over the coals either on a spit or directly on the grill, leaving the accompanying dishes—vegetables, for example—to be cooked indoors and carried out when it's time to eat. So if the day comes when you plan to cook everything on your outdoor cooker, you can use your regular kitchen ware.

On the other hand, if you like to stay out of your indoor kitchen almost entirely, it's quite possible to cook your vegetables, wrapped securely in foil bundles, either in the coals or on top of the grill. And for that you don't need pots. You'll find a number of recipes in Part III describing just how to do it.

If you do a lot of camp and boat cooking, you can use the same pots and pans that you would use there. The appropriate sections beginning on pages 54 and 151 will tell you all about it. Or you can go to a store and look over a wide range of pots and pans that are just as colorful and decorative and expensive as can be. Most of them are good, and since it's your money, we will say no more.

Except this: You can fashion pots and pans for one-time use out of heavy-duty aluminum foil.

But, when you do, or if you do, use a pot or pan over an outdoor fire, be sure to first coat the outside with a film of soap. It's a great help when it comes time to wash the smoke-black away.

Storage

You now have everything you need in order to cook and to eat outdoors. Now comes a problem. What to do with all the equipment when you're not using it? Obviously, the answer is to put it someplace. A place that is free of dust. A place that will be ever dry no matter how hard it rains. A place that the young'uns can't raid. A place that will withstand the rigors of winter.

The answer, or rather one of the answers, is this: a storage shed.

You can build your own, but don't begin unless you're sure you are a skill-ful enough carpenter to meet all of the aforementioned musts. Because if you are not, this is what you're letting yourself in for: a charcoal stove suddenly eaten away by rust; a very angry wife when she reaches into the shed to start cooking (everything else is ready: the marinated steak, the corn, the potatoes, the popcorn; there is not a second to be wasted), but everything that's in the shed that she needs is covered with dust. Brother, you had better start running!

So unless you're sure you can build a good storage shed, either have one built for you or buy one. They come in all sizes, shapes, and colors, and they're priced accordingly.

For folks who live in apartments it's not quite so easy because big sheds don't go well on small terraces. So they'll have to use their imagina-tions. Perhaps a chest on which they can set cushions and also use as a seat. Perhaps a footlocker that they can slide out of sight. Perhaps plastic covers with which they can cover their stove and a host of other things. Perhaps a "Campanion" like the one described on pages 70–71, which our Montana friends and colleagues, Norman and Priscilla Strung, invented to pack with them into places like the Spanish Peaks Wilderness. If one is not enough, then two or three.

Perhaps apartment dwellers will store everything inside the apart-ment, something that householders with limited space might do too, and tote out as much of it as they need whenever the urge for a barbecue meal hits them.

Everybody Gets into the Act

Hopefully, all the cookout-and-eatout utensils can be stored in one place. If not, use a series of small dustproof, easily carried boxes or cartons or Campanions, because it's much easier to carry one carton out than for a number of people to run in, gather up, and run out with a lot of individual items.

It's pretty hard to include in such carriers all the extras you'll need when you have guests. It behooves you, then, to keep some well-constructed spare cartons available for use when you are going to entertain. Pack all the dishes, silverware, glassware, and so on into them the day before the big event, and put them near a door leading to your outdoor dining room.

Avoiding Serious Traffic Problems

Long before you do much outdoor cooking and eating, study your layout, both indoor and outdoor, for potential bottlenecks. You might—here we're talking mainly to folks who don't have the necessary weatherproofed stor-age space—build some shelves or cupboards near the most convenient house-to-yard doorway. You can place your containers there, ready to be moved outside, and there need not be a constant stream of people in and out and through your indoor kitchen.

Even if there is only one door in and out of the kitchen, perhaps you have a window in the kitchen or some other room that looks out on your outdoor all-purpose room. If so, you could put tables (permanent, folding, or rollaway) both inside and outside it. Stack things on the former, and hand them out to someone tending the latter.

When you're entertaining a crowd that includes young children, let them set up their own bar if they're big enough, if not do it for them, filling spigot-type camp jugs with ice water, pink lemonade, and punch. Be sure to include a stack of paper cups and to have that colorful plastic garbage can handy to receive used cups. This will help keep an endless stream of thirsty young traffic out from under foot.

Father, in all likelihood, is a guy who can't be held back when it's barbecue time. Let him get into the act early. Very early. Be sure he has on hand all the things that bartenders and meat cooks need:

- Ice bucket. Filled with ice, of course.
- Glasses (but not paper; they're for kids).
- Hard liquors.
- Seltzer and club soda and ginger ale.
- Sliced lemons and oranges.
- Cherries.
- Wine.
- Beer.
- A camp or picnic cooler containing the meat he's going to broil.
- Barbecue sauces.

We repeat. Make sure he has them all in place outdoors long before zero hour. Otherwise you'll have him under foot, and fathers (so Inez tells me) can be worse nuisances than kids.

When all else is in place, have father bring out all the tools he'll need, including the hose and cleanup equipment. That should keep him busy for a time. Then, when that chore is done, have him run down to the ice machine eighteen miles away for a spare supply of cubes just in case your refrigerator-freezer should run out. And, if things have gotten to that state, take the kids with him.

Oh, yes, while he's out, have him pick up fresh bread and extra milk and cream.

One or two camp or picnic coolers are fine for bottled or canned soft drinks and to keep creamy desserts and salads from incubating harmful bacteria that can cause serious illness (see pages 203–205). Place such foods first in storage containers such as Tupperware, which are moisture-proof yet look nice enough for company serving; then place the containers in the coolers, where they can stay until it is time to place them on the table.

Another way to beat the heat when serving perishables is to freeze a 2-inch layer of water in the bottom of foil-lined pans on which to set covered serving dishes containing the perishables. Putting food coloring in the water will create some very interesting effects and is a chore, incidentally, that children love to do.

Just one idea to show you how versatile, yet practical, this can be:

We often line a 2-inch-deep serving dish with alternating green and blue ice cubes. On it we set an aluminum wire rack. On the rack we set aluminum-foil dishes filled with individual servings of frozen fish salad (recipe on page 225) unmolded onto a lettuce-leaves garnish, and then, while one of us, who shall remain nameless, sweats over a hot charcoal stove, Inez passes the serving dish around for guests to help themselves.

You can, of course, buy thermos types of both eating and serving dishes that keep food either hot or cold. Some of them have clear bubble tops through which beautifully arranged foods can be seen easily.

You also can construct food coverings from heavy clear plastic, or you can buy rolls of the thinner and more flexible stuff and wrap it around dishes of food or a fruit-ball–filled watermelon shell (recipe on page 229) so that you can have them not only to eat but also to decorate your table, secure in the knowledge that they'll be safe from dust and insects if not from people who can't wait for you to tell them to come and get it.

For sandwich-, hamburger-, and hot dog–type eating or for any snack or light lunch kind of dining, you should be able to put everything into one or two containers and let the kids or someone else lug them out of the kitchen. Ditto with fresh fruit and cherry tomatoes and anything else that can be eaten with the fingers.

Your family probably will accept a routine for helping cook and eat outdoors much more readily than for indoor eating. It may even develop without anyone ever needing to say: "You do this. You do that," and then having to stand there to see, and to hope, that it gets done. The odds are good that Dad will take over the meat cooking and potato and corn-roasting departments (heaven help you if you try to stop him) as well as starting the fire and watching it burn down from flame to gray-and-red–flecked coals.

He can do these things while cozying up with a drink in a comfortable chair. Which is another way of saying that it almost goes without saying that he'll automatically take charge of what goes on outside the house while Mother is putting the finishing touches to indoor chores. If you stick to a safe way of building and starting a fire—no liquids and no jellies of any kind—he might even let older children take over the fire-building and tending for him, as he watches them constantly, of course.

Once the aroma of barbecuing meats starts to fill the air, getting volunteers to set the table shouldn't be difficult. That leaves you—the Mother, the Chief Cook, the Menu Planner—free to handle any inside cooking that may be called for, culminating your indoor chores by carrying washed salad vegetables outside to prepare while sitting down and joining Dad in a drink. Goldbrick!

When you have guests who want to help, just expand this routine. Let the men—they will anyhow—help Dad in the yard. Meantime back in the kitchen, have some things laid out for the girls to work on while they chat with you. Planning ahead so that guests who want to can actually help without feeling they're getting in the way is an important part of outdoor dining.

Children, especially someone else's, can be a big help. They like to set tables, make center pieces, scrub clams (see the backyard clambake recipe on pages 305–306), decorate, and do anything at all that involves getting their hands into soft mushy food. We once kept three of our youngest guests busy for over an hour shaping aluminum-foil fish-salad dishes.

Most very young children are uninhibited hams. So we sometimes take advantage of that fact very early in the day by assigning them an un-used room to plan and practice a "play" that they will be able to perform for the adults after the meal is over. If they have a box of old clothes for costumes and the promise of the use of the clothesline with a sheet hung on it for a stage curtain, they're likely to stay out of the main line of traffic from kitchen to yard for quite a while. This also means that they won't be bumping into the outdoor stove and otherwise getting in Papa Chef's way.

Cleaning up can become an easy part of the everybody-helps routine if you keep extra paper napkins, paper towels, and a sponge handy, in addition to that plastic garbage can we've spoken of several times before (perhaps lined with a plastic bag for easy disposal). If the meal is informal, everyone can wipe off his dishes right into the can when he finishes eating. Then over to the outdoor faucet where a large plastic dishpan is ready and waiting for a quick rinsing. Then stack them up for transportation into the kitchen and a hot-suds final going-over. Then into their proper storage places.

Meantime, Dad and his cronies have extinguished the embers, polished up and cleaned up the grill with steel wool or soap pads, cleaned up the plastic tablecloths and furniture with a sponge and water from the hose.

Presto! The job is done.

Indoors it would have been work. Outdoors it was fun.

And now it is the children's hour.

Hang the stage curtain over the clothesline, settle back blissfully with coffee or after-dinner drink.

It's curtain time.

It's time for the show!

A perfect ending for a perfect day.

Menus

Here now is a listing of some of the menus that we've found to be most successful in our yard. (The recipes are given further on in the book.) They range from simple family fare—but, oh so delicious—to elaborate menus we've used when entertaining. Augment these with some of the menus we've listed in the chapter on picnicking and you'll never wonder what to serve when company is coming.

The most important thing to remember, in fact the most important advice we can give you for entertaining outdoors is this: don't try out new dishes; use only those you've cooked and served outdoors before. Try them out on your family first. They'll enjoy being this sort of guinea pig.

The more you cook and serve the same things, the more casual, relaxed, and flexible you'll be when you prepare and offer them to guests. Which means the more fun everyone will have. Including you.

ANYTIME MENUS

Meal in a Burger
Ice Cream from the Good Humor Man
Fruit Punch

Manhattan Clam Chowder
Bread and Butter or Margarine
Apple Pie with Cheese or Ice Cream
Beverage

Avocado and Orange Salad
Fish Steaks in Zesty Sauce
Instant Cooking Rice with Cheddar Cheese Soup as a Sauce
Bread and Butter or Margarine
Strawberry Shortcake
Beverage

SUMMER–SUPPER–WITH–THE–FAMILY MENUS

Liver and Bacon Kabobs
Carrot-Mushroom Soup Mold
Fried Chicken
Potato Salad
Lemonade and Cookies

Steak Barbecued in Vinegar and Olive Oil
Easy Baked Beans
Many-Colored Cole Slaw
Bread and Butter or Margarine
Fresh Fruit in Season
Beverage

Lamb Shanks, Simmered then Barbecued
Boiled Vegetables in Celery Sauce
Bread and Butter or Margarine
Fruit Salad Gelatin, with the Meal or as a Dessert
Beverage

LIVING IT UP A LITTLE

Chicken Soup with Dill Matzoh Balls
Tossed Salad with Vinegar and Oil Dressing
Corn on the Cob Cooked in the Coals
Potatoes Cooked in the Coals
Barbecued Chicken Marinara
Bread and Butter or Margarine
Grapefruit Halves Baked in Honey
Beverage

Chopped Chicken Liver in Shape of Chicken with Crackers
Stuffed Celery à la Waldorf
Caesar Salad
Whole, Unstuffed Chickens in Orange-Lemon Sauce
Foil-Baked Potatoes
Bread and Butter or Margarine
Canned Pears with Cream Cheese
Beverage

*EVERYBODY GATHER ROUND, COOK YOUR OWN,
AND LOVE IT!*

The Outdoor Dar Bin Loo
Fresh Fruit in Season

*ENTERTAINING OUTDOORS THE TWO–IN–A–ROW,
QUICK–GOURMET WAY*

Clambake on Saturday
Paella on Sunday
Lettuce and Onion Salad
Watermelon Fruit Basket Salad
Beverage

2—Camp Cooking

WHAT TO DO BEFORE GOING

Gone are the days when a camping trip was a for-men-only adventure that involved hours of work clearing a campsite, pitching a tent, building a fireplace, and chopping wood to feed into it.

All that, of course, after the rut-road ordeal of getting there in a Reo or some similar, but not-so-antique, vehicle was over with, that is.

But times have changed.

Now the roads are good, transportation is good, campsites complete with everything but hot and cold running bourbon are waiting. Some even including sandboxes for toddlers.

Today, camping can be—and more and more is—a family affair.

Do you want to enjoy all the comforts of home while communing with nature in the Great Outdoors? Do you want a bit of rugged living thrown in? Do you want to really rough it from beginning to end? If the latter, turn now to "Wilderness Cooking," Chapter 3, starting on page 86. There Norman Strung, our friend and Dan's coauthor on several outdoor books, college teacher, widely read outdoor-magazine writer, and —most important of all—a licensed hunting and fishing guide in Montana, will tell you all about roughing it. The Spanish Peaks Wilderness country is his proving ground. But if one of the former is your choice, read on.

Commercial Campgrounds

It is at one of these, generally speaking, where you can expect to find the most modern conveniences. Much more so than in public camps. They charge a fee, either nightly or weekly and somewhat sizable, and in exchange provide a maximum of services: electrical and sanitary facilities, either hooked up directly to your camper or trailer or available in a central, modern, building for folks who prefer to pitch tents; picnic tables; grill-type fireplaces and barbecuers; wood; water and bathing facilities; and garbage service.

Some also have coin-operated laundry machines and general stores that stock everything from foodstuffs and cooking and eating utensils and stove fuels to suntan lotions, mosquito repellents, and paperback books. If a commercial campground does not have all these conveniences on the premises, it's very likely that such camp-follower adjuncts are located close by.

Some even have highly modern cabins. But we don't call that camping, at least not for the purposes of this outdoor cookbook.

If extensive facilities are your primary consideration, a commercial campground such as those operated by Kampgrounds of America (KOA) would be your best choice. Most such chains are nationwide and offer a directory of all their locations and facilities. If your local library doesn't have one, check the Yellow Pages or a travel agency. KOA's address is P.O. Box 1138, Billings, Montana 59103.

One last word about such pay-to-play campgrounds:

While they certainly do offer more modern conveniences than do the public camps, they're more likely to be crowded and located on unimaginative sites chosen not so much for their closeness to nature as for their proximity to highways.

Perhaps recognizing this shortcoming, in 1969 KOA introduced something new, albeit a takeoff on an old idea, in the way of outdoor living:

KOA Ranch Kamps

All we can tell you about them is what the KOA catalog says: "Starting this year, KOA is offering a dude ranch vacation, tailored to the pleasures of today's camper . . . a bit of the Old West set aside just for your camping enjoyment. There's horseback riding . . . hiking along rustic trails, angling for tail-walking trout, hunting in season, and lots of elbow room. . . ."

It sounds good, well worth looking into. But be quick, because there aren't very many KOA Ranch Kamps to go around: just two, one in Chugwater, Wyoming, and the other in Swan Valley, Montana.

Improved Public Campgrounds

These are still the best bets for people who really love the outdoors and are willing to rough it a very little bit. Constructed by either state or federal agencies, these campgrounds usually are found in the middle of large tracts of public land, tastefully located in an outdoor setting. They offer such facilities as a grill fireplace, picnic tables, wood, cold water, garbage service, and modern sanitary facilities. Such amenities as showers, hot water, laundry service, and stores are usually not available.

The public agency that oversees such campsites often charges a small token fee or requires the Department of the Interior's "Golden Eagle Passport" (which costs less than $10) for entry.

The location of improved public campgrounds can be learned by writing to the Department of the Interior in Washington, D.C., or to the state in which you plan to camp. The names of the appropriate agencies vary from state to state, so address your letter to State Department of Parks and Recreation, State House, Capital City, and it will be sure to filter over to the right people.

But do your mailing very early, because these campsites usually have a long list of takers, and it's always a case of first come, first served.

There are, though, campsites available to you that seldom have waiting lists.

Unimproved Public Campgrounds

The name means just what it implies: very few improvements beyond the natural state. But, oh, what a lovely state that usually is! Here you're most likely to see nature as it was meant to be seen.

Civilized facilities are virtually nil. Essentially they consist of nothing much more than a place to park, a crude fireplace, and a garbage can. However, the scenic splendor, the pure water, the unpolluted air, more than compensate for the lack of conveniences.

Although the populated East has few such campgrounds and the number of those remaining shrinks in direct relationship to the apathy of the public, there is no shortage in the areas of the West not conveniently accessible to land "developers" who destroy, usually with the aid of public officials, and call it progress.

Short on facilities they may be. Located on seldom-traveled back roads they are. But the scenery is magnificent and untouched, the smell of pine or sage is breathtaking, and the feeling of being in truly primitive and wild country is no farther than a few steps from camp.

Information on such campsites usually will be included in literature describing improved public campgrounds. If not, write and ask specifically for data on the unimproved variety.

An Important Thing to Remember

No matter where and how you plan to camp out and cook out, be sure to include a check of local fire regulations high on your list. In many areas, you may have to have a permit to build a charcoal fire. And regulations may change from week to week and day to day, depending upon rainfall and the aridity of the land and foliage around you.

How to Get There

Unless you're backpacking or horsebacking or canoeing into the wilderness (Chapter 3), the main method of getting to where you're going is by automotive vehicle or, ever increasingly, by boat (Chapter 5).

What kind of automotive vehicle?

Well, once upon a time it was only the family jalopy with camping and cooking gear hanging from every ear. Now, though, you pays your money and you takes your choice, right up to a land-roving palace on wheels.

There are trailers that consist of homes that you pull behind cars, trailers that look like boxes but open into complete camping units, miniature houses that fit onto pickup trucks and which are called campers, and— if that is not enough to choose from—there are mobile homes and motor homes and cruisers and travel cruisers and van-a-homes, etc., etc., etc.— all of which are just about one and the same thing: a house on wheels. They look like buses—some are large, some are small—and the one you choose depends on how much money you care to spend and how comfy and cozy you want to be whilst pursuing the rugged life.

Virtually all of these vehicles are fitted with all of the equipment you'll need, including of course cooking gear for an extended vacation trip. Most of them include refrigerators, tables, cupboards or shelving for cooking and eating utensils, ample storage space for dry, boxed, and canned foodstuffs. And, of course, stoves. Most are table-top two-burners, but many are built-in ranges. Usually they burn a liquefied petroleum gas, but some may call for white, also known as unleaded, gasoline. The fancier vehicles may even have electric ranges that operate off of batteries or a generator.

The outdoor life is not quite so simple for folks who travel by car or station wagon. Not only do they have to start from scratch, buying this and that and that and that and that and combining it all into a well-blended camping unit, but also they have to figure where to carry it all.

So we'll look now at the cooking and eating apparatus that they'll have to buy.

Stoves

When off on a camping trip, especially the first one, a person's mind fills with the thrill, the adventure, the romance, the joy, of cooking over an open campfire.

But then comes the awakening:

- You get to where you're going only to learn that it hasn't rained in a month. The woods are tinder dry. The ranger will not let you start a fire.
- It is very early in the morning and you can't wait for that eye-opener cup of coffee. However, wait you must because the fire that was burning brightly when off to bed you went has gone out. So, before you can brew a pot of coffee, you first must build and start a fire.
- You are not so famished that you can't wait to eat, the weather is fine, the woods are wet, you plan a meal that's not only fit for a king but also for the ranger you've invited to be your dinner guest. Repasts like that take time. Campfires are built smack down on the ground. So you have to cook your banquet feast and tend it haunched on your heels. The aches, the pains, the muscle cramps are killing you. Then the wind shifts, smoke fills your eyes, sparks fall on countless things that burn, including your skin and clothes.

For any or all of these reasons you are, to say the very least, slightly disillusioned about Life in the Great Outdoors.

So if you're a novice fire-builder, your camping trip will be much more pleasant if you use your fire—when local conditions permit you to build one, that is—mainly for sitting around, for gazing into, for singing to, for toasting marshmallows and maybe roasting hot dogs.

Eventually there will come the day when you have mastered the fine art of building a campfire, and the fire warden or the park ranger will tell you that there's nothing to stop you. You'll then be able to produce a bed of coals in a reasonable length of time. Over them you cook your meats and fish, and you begin to learn what camp cooking and camp eating are really all about—as delightful as a backyard barbecue. You find out one of the big reasons why more and more people every year join the outdoor ranks. You find out that life is a joy.

Although you cook your meat and your fish over camp coals—which, of course, can be charcoal just as at home—rely mainly on a store-bought stove of some sort for cooking not only that morning pot of coffee but also vegetables and rice and things like that.

This means that first on the list of things that you take with you on a camping trip must be a camp stove. Those that have proved the most popular over the years and therefore the most practical and best burn white gasoline, liquefied petroleum gas, or wood. Next come stoves that burn jellied alcohol (Sterno) and charcoal cookers.

Let's look at them one at a time. If we seem to go overboard about Coleman stoves, it is only because they've been around for seventy years and their manufacturer takes pride in their craftsmanship.

Gasoline Stoves

Ed Hardy, of the Coleman Company, tells us that these are the most widely used camp stoves on the market today, perhaps outselling all others combined by two to one.

They can burn either leaded or unleaded (white) gasoline, but the latter is preferred because it is much freer of impurities, thus minimizing the possibility of clogged generators. It is a clear gasoline and burns with a clean blue flame.

The Coleman three-burner gasoline stove (*Coleman Company, Inc.*)

They come in one-, two-, and three-burner models. The one for you depends on how many people you'll be cooking for and how many pots you'll want on the fire at once. The two-burner, which is the most popular, weighs only eighteen pounds. It folds up to look something like an attaché case when not in use and takes up very little storage space. Set up and ready for use, the top becomes a backside windshield, and two wings swing into place to block the wind from either side.

The gas tank, carried inside the stove when not in use, is easily fitted into position. Fill it with fuel, pump it a couple of times to build up pressure, light it as you would a kitchen stove, and start cooking.

The stove can be used anywhere that's practical: the tailgate of a station wagon, atop a table, or on foldaway legs beneath a dining fly. Even in a tent, provided you make sure it is well ventilated.

White gasoline is available just about anywhere that you'll go to camp, so you need not carry more than an emergency supply with you. But carry it only in a can that is made for the purpose. Be sure to always keep it well away from open flame.

Thermos, another fine old name when it comes to equipping people with what it takes to make for the good outdoor life, is moving up fast with its line of camp stoves. The feature that makes them a strong contender is a filter built into the generators. This keeps the gasoline feed

The Thermos two-burner stove uses either leaded or unleaded gasoline. (*King-Seeley Thermos Co.*)

lines and burners free of impurities, thus preventing them from clogging up and permitting the camper who owns a Thermos stove to burn *any* gasoline, white (unleaded) or leaded.

Liquefied Petroleum Gas Stoves

Let's start by finding out what liquefied petroleum gases (LPG or LP Gases) are. So over to the bookshelf to learn what our encyclopedia (Collier's) has to say on the subject. Here it is:

> These gases are composed chiefly of propane and butane hydro-carbons which are recovered from natural gas at the wells. They are also produced at petroleum refineries where they are known as liquefied refinery gases. The liquefied petroleum gases of commerce may be from either source and are transported and stored under pressure in the liquid state. The largest market for LP-gases in 1960 [our encyclopedia was published in 1962] was for use as a fuel for cooking, space heating, hot water and refrigeration in residences where it is the familiar bottled gas.

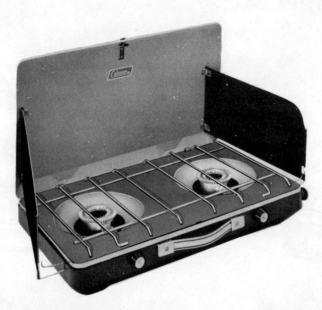

The Coleman two-burner propane stove (*Coleman Company, Inc.*)

So now we know.

LPG is a liquid only while being held in storage. Once it is hooked up to a stove and readied for use, it reverts to its natural state.

Liquefied petroleum gas stoves look almost exactly like gasoline stoves, and they're becoming increasingly popular, particularly among women campers, probably because there is no pumping, no priming, no pouring of fuel. The tank of bottled gas screws right to the stove, and usually no tools are needed.

There are shortcomings, however:

- If gasoline leaks, you'll see it, because it is a liquid, and be able to do something about the dangerous vapors. Not so, however, with LPG. You can't see it, because it is a gas. It can puddle without your ever knowing it—that is, until it explodes.
- LPG is more expensive than white gasoline.
- To be on the safe side you have to carry an ample supply of filled LPG tanks with you. This is because the connecting links are not standardized, and one manufacturer's tank will not necessarily fit another manufacturer's stove. Camp stores do not

The Coleman super stove, with lantern, ten-pound propane bottle, and five-foot hose (*Coleman Company, Inc.*)

stock all tanks of all makers, so there you may be, left with a cold stove to cook on.
- The tanks are not refillable. Therefore you must dispose of them as emptied. But never, never, never in a fire, because they can explode.

To offset these disadvantages, Coleman and some other manufacturers have recently added to their line what is called a propane super stove. It is fed, according to Coleman's Mr. Hardy, not by a 1-pound container that has to be thrown away once it is empty but by a 10-pound refillable bottle of fuel that is hooked up to the stove by a 5-foot or 10-foot length of leakproof hose. Additionally, says Hardy, a Coleman lantern can operate off of the tank while the stove is in use. And, he tells us, it costs about 80 per cent less per hour to use fuel from the 10-pound refillable bottle than it does to use fuel from the use-it-only-once container. The price of the latter varies from about $1 to $1.50 a can, depending on where in the country you buy it. It costs only about $1.50 to fill the 10-pound bottle with about a month's supply of fuel.

While Coleman has been the outstanding name in American-made camp stoves for many years, the increased interest in outdoor living is

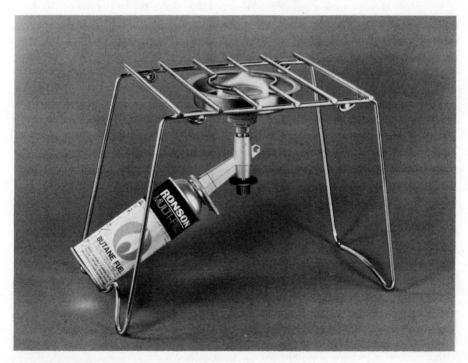

Ronson's lightweight butane camp stove (*Ronson Corporation*)

having its effect on other manufacturers. You'll find many brands of stove in the marketplace. Most you won't recognize, which does not necessarily reflect upon their product, but some you will.

Ronson, for instance, well known for things like cigarette lighters and food blenders, has brought out a self-cleaning butane-fueled Camp 'n' Cook one-burner stove complete with foldaway stand. It's light and easily packed, fine for morning coffee or a quickie lunch.

Precautions

Whether you cook with gasoline or liquefied petroleum, there are dangers that only you can avoid. Here is a rundown of precautionary measures that, if adhered to, can prevent your camping vacation from ending in tragedy:

- Look for the UL, or some other nationally recognized testing service, label on the stove that you buy.
- Chances are that even though you're cooking with gas a camp-fire will be burning at the same time. Make sure that they are a safe distance from each other.
- Don't throw empty LPG containers into an open fire.
- If your tank runs dry while cooking, don't try to detach or hook up a full one while the campfire is burning or until you have removed your stove to a completely safe distance downwind from it.
- Don't try to put out a gasoline fire with water. Always keep an approved fire extinguisher handy.
- Check your stove often for leaks.
- Make sure your stove is always in excellent working condition.
- Don't light a stove inside a tent until you've first made sure there is plenty of ventilation. Ditto for any other enclosure, because LPG fumes sink and can be trapped in low nooks and crannies unless the breeze has a clear passage to sweep them away.
- Follow the manufacturer's operating instructions to the letter.
- Best of all, try your stove out at home before embarking upon a camping trip. See how long a disposable cannister of LPG fuel will last. Try your pots and pans on the burners for size.

Wood Stoves

Some folks are firmly convinced that the best time of the year to go camp-ing is when the frost is on the pumpkin—late fall and early winter, when there is an honest-to-goodness nip in the air. They are right out there, in the center of where it's happening, when the leaves and the grasses, the bushes and the shrubs, are changing from green to red and gold and russet and brown and all of the other colors in nature's paintbox. For these people, nothing can beat a wood fire and the smells that the blazing embers put forth.

These mainly are the people who use wood stoves. They and shepherds and such who spend most of their lives outdoors. Rugged folk, such as these, need more than a stove that cooks. Their stove must warm, too. A wood stove, solidly built out of solid metals and large enough to cook on, is quite a load to carry around. Probably the best of them is the time-tested Sheepherder. It has everything that anyone would ever expect a wood-burning stove to have, including an oven for baking pies and bread and everything else. It weighs about thirty-five pounds. The Sims stove rates right up there with it.

Smaller wood stoves scale down to about five pounds in weight, and, obviously, the smaller they are the easier they are to carry.

So if cold-weather camping is for you, the wood stove may also be for you. But make sure there is plenty of firewood available where you're going. And, in setting one up inside your tent, make sure that it is about two feet from the walls and that the stovepipe is well insulated where it pokes through the tent top.

Wood stoves also, obviously, can be set up outside a tent, thus making them ideal for warm-weather outdoor cooking, particularly if you're going to camp in one place for a long time.

For many campers, antique hunting in country barns is part of camp life. If you haven't joined the ranks, try it sometime, and it very well may be that you'll be lucky enough to find an old-fashioned cast-iron stove rusting away somewhere. By all means buy it if you can and you'll probably have a better wood-burning stove than has been manufactured in the last fifty years.

Remove the rust and then take simple measures to preserve the finish, as you must also do with new wood stoves, and its finding, purchase, and use well might be the high spot of your trip.

Rust removers are available in all hardware stores, and you can keep new rust from accumulating just as you would on an iron pot—by keeping it dry and rubbing a little oil into the surface. There's a product called lampblack—as old as America but not in wide use these days—that also can be helpful in keeping iron stoves in shape.

When purchasing a new stove, ask the dealer and read the instructions in order to learn how best to preserve the finish. And be sure to find out the length and possibly the angle of stovepipe you'll need to make the stove draw properly. Be sure, too, that the stove has a workable damper, because, just as with an open fire, air and its movement are an important part of fire building and fire control.

Charcoal Stoves

Some of the charcoal cookers described in Chapter 1 are fine for camping. Whether you take yours with you will depend on its size and your experiences with it at home. However, you can purchase one with removable legs and take it with you whenever camping or picnicking you do go.

A twin-firebox hibachi is an ideal camping and picnicking companion. But whether it is an ideal traveling companion depends on how heavy a total load you can carry. The hibachi is, you know, probably the weightiest of all portable charcoal cookers.

If you plan to cook over charcoal, the Auto-Fire also is an excellent friend to have along. In Chapter 1 we described how it is used as a charcoal-fire–starter. Now we'll tell you how to use it as a cooker. It's very simple.

Set the pin in place to keep the grate from springing open. Detach the handle and clip it to the notches in the top rim. That's where you set your pot or pan or small wire grill. Fill the Auto-Fire with only as much charcoal as you'll think you'll need. Wad your paper into place, light it, wait a few minutes, and start cooking. That's all there is to it.

The Auto-Fire isn't large enough for more than one thing to be cooked on it at a time. But it's ideal for breakfast bacon and eggs and for broiling a steak or a fresh-caught fish.

Jellied Alcohol

Despite all the new developments in camp cookery, not to be overlooked is that old faithful, the uncomplicated little Sterno stove, which still provides campers with a quick and easy way of heating up a can of beans.

Stove-Top Oven

A highly handy thing is this, enabling you to cook in camp dishes that you might otherwise only get to eat at home. There are many models to choose from. Some are collapsible, most have heat indicators. Just set the stove-top oven atop a burner of your gasoline, butane, or propane stove and pop in whatever it is that you intend to roast, bake, or otherwise oven-cook.

Today, thanks to the vast improvement in camp refrigeration (which we discuss later in this chapter), one of the stove-top oven's best functions is for heating up casseroles and putting the finishing touches on the two-step recipes you'll find in Part III. The casseroles and the first step of the partially do-ahead recipes—which you do at home, freeze, and

The Coleman stove-top camp oven (*Coleman Company, Inc.*)

plop into your portable refrigerator—make for simple-as-a-breeze camp dinners, thanks to the top-of-the-stove oven.

Reflector Oven

This is a great gizmo to have along for making pies and biscuits and some of the simpler dishes that have to be baked. Kind of romantic, too, because the flames from a glowing—and perhaps roaring—campfire are what make it tick.

The reflector oven is made of bright metal. It's about fifteen inches long, open on one of its broad sides, its other sloping downward from the opening. Reflector ovens can be purchased either permanently assembled or foldaway. Buy whichever you have room to carry. You also can make one, either out of galvanized metal or heavy aluminum foil. But, no matter what anybody tells you, don't try to make your own unless you are skillful with your hands.

Use it like this:

Build your campfire against a large rock or some other big background off of which the heat will bounce. Place your reflector across the fire from the rock—on a flat, nontippable surface, of course. Slide the food to be cooked into the oven and you're cooking, not with gas, not with charcoal, not with wood, but with the heat that radiates from the flames and bounces from the reflector's sloping sides and top and maybe slightly off the bottom, too.

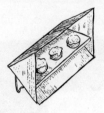

(*Top*) Store-bought reflector oven with shelf. (*Bottom*) Homemade aluminum-foil reflector oven.

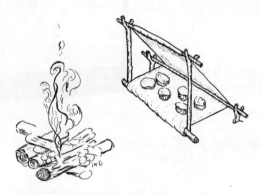

Several things to remember in cooking with a reflector oven:

- Keep the inside of it clean and free of grease and, therefore, bright.
- Position it so that the wind will not smother your cooking food with unwanted smoke.
- Don't move it or touch it while in use without thick gloves or pot holders.
- Don't poke your fist inside the oven to see if the biscuits are done—not even a little finger, because the radiated heat can be fierce.
- Keep your flames reasonably high because without them you'll have no radiant heat. And keep them as even as you can because any time the fire flickers down for an instant, cold air will rush into your oven and chill its contents.

If you are preparing more than a one-dish meal, you can cook part of it in your reflector oven and the rest over your campfire. Or rather, in a small area just beside your campfire into which you rake your embers as the wood burns down. What you do is lay your fireplace stones in a keyhole shape (see Chapter 3). The big end of the keyhole is for reflecting

—meaning both into the oven and deep thoughts—the small end is for cooking.

Summing up:

The compact, easy to carry, reasonably easy to construct reflector oven can be a great boon to a camper once he's learned its intricacies and has become a competent fire builder. Or it can be a worse headache than a bear in camp looking for honey.

Do-It-Yourself Oven

Now hear this!

It's easy to have an oven along with you wherever you go without ever lugging an oven along with you!

You do it simply by using pots or skillets that you always pack along on camping trips.

Here's how:

- Take a fairly large, deep pot or skillet.
- Place a bowl in it upside down.
- Place a pie plate or cookie tin atop the topsy-turvy bowl.
- Place simple things that you want to bake, such as biscuits, in the tin.
- Place a pot or skillet of equal size or slightly smaller upside down atop the one you're already using.

Presto! Just like that you have an oven. Place it atop a stove burner or on a rack over your campfire keyhole and you're in the baking business.

So much for stoves and making foods hot. Let's talk now about keeping foods cool and, therefore, free from illness-breeding bacteria, from the moment you leave home until you head back again.

Camp Refrigeration

With today's modern ice chests, it's possible to keep foods frozen or cool for days without adding ice. This means that meats, fresh eggs, salads, mayonnaise, dairy products, and fresh vegetables can all be part of camp menus.

The determining factor in the success you have keeping perishable foods unspoiled lies not only in the quality of your cooler but also in how often you open the door, how long it stays open, how much ice it will hold, and how you pack it.

Start by remembering that cold settles, heat rises.

To keep your entire ice chest cold you should put your ice on the top and foods that must be kept near freezing on the bottom. The more things you are keeping cold, the quicker your ice will melt. So to help preserve the life of your ice, try putting it midway in your chest with less perishable items like vegetables, eggs, bacon, butter, and cheese on top. (Wrapping the ice in newspaper may help preserve it, but it also keeps cold from circulating, so you shouldn't do it.) The topmost foods will be cool, the bottom cold, and your ice will last longer.

Freezer jells, a jelly-like substance that is packaged in plastic bags and can be used over and over again, hold the cold well. They also eliminate another bugaboo of campers: melted ice water in the bottom of their coolers.

The amount of ice you'll need can't be determined by any rule of thumb, but you can increase the length of time it will last by freezing any foods that won't be harmed by the process. An added benefit: Not only will frozen foods give ice a longer life span, they'll also help to keep other foods cold, thus lessening the need for ice.

Another great space- and ice-saver is this: Fill milk containers or jars about seven-eighths full with fruit juice, plop them into your home freezer, and then use them instead of ice in your cooler. When they melt, you don't discard; you drink.

If you have a regular camp vehicle, most likely you have an icebox built into it and in some cases, perhaps even an electric refrigerator. For the auto and station wagon set, however, there is a wide variety of ice chests or coolers (call them what you will) to choose from. Visit any store that has a well-stocked selection of outdoor supplies, and you'll see just about all that there is to see.

They'll all look pretty. Most will have exteriors made of a modern synthetic, but some will be made of aluminum or wood. They'll be multicolored. Most will be longer than they are high. A few will be higher than they are long. You'll be able to see all that. But what you won't be able to see is what counts the most—the insulation.

So ask questions. And insist upon straightforward answers. If a beautiful box is lined with sawdust or cork, it's not the box for you, because it won't seal in the cold as well as do coolers whose walls are lined with one of the many polyester synthetics now being produced under a variety of scientific-sounding trade names.

Our advice therefore is this: When in doubt, buy only a cooler made by a reputable manufacturer.

Look, too, for these things and be sure that the box you buy has them:

- Tops or doors that seal tightly when closed.
- Rounded interior corners for easy cleaning.
- Seamless, too.

Coleman's top-carrying thirty-quart–capacity Poly-Lite cooler (*Coleman Company, Inc.*)

Coleman's side-carrying forty-four-quart–capacity **Low Boy** (*Coleman Company, Inc.*)

- Drain-cocks to run off water from melted ice.
- An upper compartment of some sort (it could be no more than a tray or a shelf) on which to set ice. Cold, you'll recall, settles, so you want your ice to be up high.
- Stainproof and rustproof interiors.

In choosing your cooler, you will have to bear in mind the space limitations of your car or station wagon. Ditto the frequency with which you'll have to open the door to get a bottle for the baby or a soda for a kid.

Maybe you'll decide that you're better off with two small boxes instead of one that's on the large side. Not only will they possibly fit better into your vehicle but you can use one exclusively for the kinds of food and drink that icebox raiders are always on the prowl for. Human ones, we mean.

Coleman, we think, makes the daddy of all coolers—a box that both outside and inside looks like a household refrigerator scaled down to camp size. It has an ice compartment that holds a twenty-five-pound block of ice and three shelves on which you can store sixty-eight quarts of food, yet its dimensions are only about 27 x 16 x 17 inches and it weighs less than twenty-three pounds.

It has quite a unique space-utilizing factor: By a simple couple of abracadabra motions it can be switched from vertical upright to horizontal chest and its door made to swing from left to right and vice versa. It's called (as though you hadn't guessed) the Coleman Convertible Cooler.

Food stored in a properly constructed, properly insulated, and properly iced cooler should stay cold about three days even if you run low on ice, but since replenishment supplies of ice are fairly readily available just about anywhere you might go to camp you therefore should have no food-preservation problems. Especially if you take these precautions:

- Chill your cooler well before loading it at home. You can do this either by filling it with ice and letting it stand for at least a day or, if you have a freezer that's large enough, by setting your cooler inside it, leaving the cooler door ajar, for twenty-four hours.

Coleman's versatile three-way, sixty-eight-quart–capacity cooler (*Coleman Company, Inc.*)

• When in camp, keep your cooler in the shade of a tree or a dining fly, moving it as the sun moves if necessary.

We don't recommend it, because we think the stuff is too hazardous to handle and it shouldn't ever be permitted in places where children might poke their hands, but some people add to the longevity of their wet ice by setting it upon a layer of dry ice. If you want to join their ranks, be sure to wear gloves while handling the stuff.

There are ways, too, of cooling foods without using ice. The best is by simply putting your perishables into a watertight container and totally submerging it in a cold-running stream or ever-bubbling spring. Or you might resort to an old and proven standby of prospectors and other desert-rat types: Build a desert cooler.

It's nothing more than a box, say 3 x 2 x 2 feet in diameter, made of heavy screening and with one or two wooden shelves.

The frame is made of 1 x 2-inch boards to which are nailed two layers of screening. On the inside of the screening you nail strips of 1 x 2, which serve a dual purpose: as ledges on which to set your shelves and as double protection against the prying and probings of any predatory animals trying to get at the goodies inside. The door is made in the same way and hinged and latched on.

You set it somewhere in the shade, as high off the ground as possible, and exposed to the wind. Now you drape water-soaked burlap over the top so that it hangs down about eight or ten inches on all four sides.

Nature does the rest. The wind blows through the wet burlap; the cool breeze fans your food so that it keeps. Butter, for example, will remain at an easily spreadable consistency but will never get mushy.

The desert cooler, as we said, proved itself long ago in the Mojave. But it can be used anywhere in the open. We don't advise it in wild country, however, where the smell of edibles will waft downwind and attract certainly destructive, and perhaps dangerous, animals to your camp.

One important thing to remember:

Keep that burlap wet. Not soaking but slightly more than damp. The best way, if tap water is available, is to hook up a hose and keep water constantly dripping on the cloth.

How to Load Your Cooler for the Trip to Camp

First of all, you have to begin by doing certain things long before anything goes into the cooler. They are:

• Freeze all foods that can be frozen, whether cooked or raw. This includes many two-step recipes to be found in Part III.
• Thoroughly chill all foods, especially drinks, that require chilling.

- Thoroughly chill your cooler as described a few pages back. If it won't fit into your home freezer, perhaps your butcher will let it stand in his walk-in box for a day.
- Wrap everything that does not come in self-wrappers. Or, better still perhaps, put everything in plastic bags or icebox containers. (We'll discuss the wonders of Tupperware later.)
- Make menus for each meal you plan to eat in camp and label each wrapper accordingly. You then will be able to tell at a glance what packages to take from your cooler when the time to prepare each particular meal rolls around, thus minimizing the time you will have to keep your cooler door open.

Once these preliminaries are taken care of, this is what to do:

- Place your frozen foods in a cluster around the center of your cooler, keeping the packages you will use last in the center of the cluster.
- Pack around the cluster your other foods, putting in first, as much as possible, those that are the most perishable and that you are going to use last.
- Put your least perishable items (eggs, bacon, butter, and cheese) on top.
- Fill whatever space is left, perhaps only nooks and crannies by now, with raw vegetables. If you have to leave some tomatoes or lettuce or carrots or string beans or such out, no great harm done. A cautionary word though: take very few, if any, such vegetables from home with you. Far better to buy them fresh along the road or at the farm stand nearest your camp.
- If there is still any available space, fill it with well-chilled canned or bottled drinks. Or, better still, fill it with ice and stow such things as drinks and nosebag lunches (see pages 72–73) in a smaller cooler or in an insulated plastic zipper bag.

Cooking and Eating Utensils

Camp cooking and eating require the same basic things you would need and use were you cooking and eating at home. So before you rush out and buy anything, check what you have that can stand a bit of battering around. Check how much space you have in which to stow it, so you will be better able to decide what to take along with you. Measure your heavy lids. It's amazing how many tops of one thing will fit over the tops of other things. Once that is done, you'll be better able to decide what to buy.

High on your list should be a good-sized Dutch oven, preferably one with short legs and made of iron. It easily may turn out to be the most important pot in camp because of its tremendous versatility. Make sure that the one you buy has a tight-fitting cover and a handle that's solidly implanted.

Other than that, just about all the utensils you'll need can be purchased in nested sets designed for compact storage. This includes not only pots and pans but also knives, forks, spoons, and dishes.

One such set comes in service for up to six. It includes plates, two pots, a coffee pot, cups, and a frying pan—all of them neatly contained in a kettle. It is constructed of aluminum and weighs little. Some of the newer models have plastic cups for people like us who don't like to burn our lips on hot metal. And some have plastic instead of aluminum plates, for those, we suppose, who don't like the sound and the feel of metal spoons and forks scraping against metal plates. They're prettier, too.

Owners and users of nesting sets usually supplement them with one or two other cooking utensils. How many extra pots and pans you take along will depend on three things: (1) how much storage space you have to spare, (2) how important weight is, and (3) what kind of recipes you plan to use.

Remember, you'll only be able to cook as many dishes as you have pots for. Ingenuity, plus the one-pot recipes in Part III, will help you solve any problems you run into.

A camping trip is no time to experiment. If at all possible, use utensils that you've used at home. In cooking, the old saying "Familiarity breeds contempt" does not apply. You can probably cook a much better omelet in a heavy iron skillet you are familiar with than in a bright and shiny—and thin—aluminum one that came out of a nest.

So when you do buy, buy only good-quality material and brand names you know. Buy square-cornered, moistureproof utensils that nest well together. When purchasing plastics, try to get the kind you can pack either hot or cold food in.

Buy just the bare necessities at first. On your maiden camping trip go no farther than your own back yard. Or if you feel that that is not far enough, make it no more than a one-night stand in which you have to plan and prepare no more than three or four meals away from home.

Next, try a three-day weekend, using our sample menus and food list. Then you'll have a much better idea what extras your family, with its particular needs and interests in food, will require.

You'll also need, of course, outdoors tools of the cooking trade. On your list, therefore, be sure to include such necessities as a long-handled fork, dipper, ladle, slotted spoon, long-handled tongs, spatula, and skewers for kabobs.

A word about the skewers. Someone might suggest that you don't need them because green pieces of tree branches are there for breaking off and taking.

Well, maybe they are.

But please don't join the ranks of those thoughtless people who are fast stripping our beautiful land of its greenery. Far better that you lug store-bought skewers along than that you damage a tree.

Furniture for Cooking and Eating in Camp

Once you've decided upon the one big basic thing—the kind of heat source you want for your cooking—the next step is to round up appropriate furniture.

The height of the stove you'll be using . . . Does it or does it not have legs to stand upon? The state of your joints . . . Do you or do you not suffer from arthritic pains and leg cramps when you remain stooped too long? The equipment you expect to find waiting when you get to your campgrounds . . . Does it or does it not have picnic tables and benches? The answers to all these questions will determine whether you should bring one or two sturdy folding tables with you—one to set a stove on, the other on which to set and prepare foods for the fire.

And those aching joints. If you're over thirty-five, you'll almost surely want to have at least one folding chair. If you don't sit in it while tending to your fire, you certainly will while eating and relaxing. But you can't take one chair along for yourself and none for other members of your family. So maybe you'll want a couple more folding chairs. After all, kids—in this case, kids are anyone under the age of thirty-five—are entitled to their comforts, too.

But tables and chairs can take up precious storage space in your family jalopy.

What to do about it?

Well, many if not most campgrounds have decidedly limited shelving space. One thing you can do is pack all your packable paraphernalia in wooden boxes. Not only do they store well while in transit, but you can use them: (1) in place of shelves when you get to camp merely by setting one atop the other, open side out, in sort of a bureau effect; (2) as a table upon which to set the stove; (3) as a work surface while preparing a meal; (4) as a chair. Not very comfortable but still better than stooping or otherwise crouching on your heels.

Package Now, Eat Later

It's a great boon for any camp cook, male or female, to have foods clearly marked and labeled. Do that and you'll save an awful lot of time and motion looking for this, that, or the other thing. We needn't tell you—we're sure you know—that nothing can be worse than not being able to lay your hands on something at just the moment it should go into the pot or onto the fire.

So before you leave home, pack all that you possibly can in individual wrappings and label it and date it for the camp meal for which it is intended. Plastic bags and Tupperware are ideal for this. We're sure you know all about plastic bags. But Tupperware: if you don't know it, hurry up and get acquainted. Just as we think of Coleman products as the campers' Cadillac, so we think of Tupperware when it comes to food packaging, carrying, and storage.

What Tupperware does is lock in the flavor and freshness of foods, whether raw or cooked, frozen or unfrozen. When we say "lock in," we mean just that. It's not only the craftsmanship and the materials that go into the making of Tupperware products, it's also the way the cover seals down tight yet snaps off in a jiffy. And Tupperware is unbreakable, which makes it just about perfect for camp use.

Tupperware's all-purpose food containers make this homey camp scene easy to duplicate. (*Tupperware*)

There is a Tupperware container to fit just about every cook's every need—from freezing a large roast to storing salt and pepper. The line can't be seen in stores. Its salespeople are neighborhood ladies who have Tupperware parties in private homes. If there is no such person near where you live, we suggest that you check the Yellow Pages or write to Tupperware International Headquarters, Orlando, Florida 32802.

The preplanned use of plastic bags and Tupperware in your home kitchen certainly will add to your preliminary chores. But, conversely, it will add immeasurably to your free time at camp. So since a camping trip is, or should be, a vacation trip, do as much as you can at home:

- Premeasure ingredients, put them in the smallest possible containers, and seal them tightly (with wire twists made for this purpose if you use plastic bags).
- Each meal's bundle of ingredients can be tied together and stored together. If only in a paper bag, that will do.
- Label each bundle clearly: Friday dinner, Sunday lunch, and so on.
- Perhaps write down the recipe, too, and pack it with each set of ingredients. At least note the number of the page on which it appears in this book and be sure you take the book to camp with you.

Camp Aids

Gas Lanterns

They're indispensable in camp, especially if you're going to do any cooking and eating after dark. Of them all, we think that a propane lantern is the best because it requires no preliminary pumping. It's ready for instant use at the touch of a match and takes up less space than white-gasoline models. It throws as much light as a 100-watt bulb, and a tank of fuel will last many evenings.

Dining Fly

See pages 8–10.

Insect Repellent

There are many new and effective insect repellents on the market for the individual camper and, more important, for the entire camping area. They come in spray cans and bottles for people—meaning you, the cook, so that you need not be plagued while at work—and in strips or aerosol bombs for camp areas. They are incredibly effective and a real blessing if your camping country is plagued by biting bugs. And, we ask, whose camping country isn't? A good brand name to look for is Cutters. Not only does it do the job, it is not offensive to the nose.

Shovels

Every camp should have one, but it need not be a long-handled thing. An Army surplus shovel that folds is ideal, and this type has caught on with campers the country over. It's both pick and shovel and folds into a twenty-inch package, perfect for stowing.

Cutting Tools

No camp should be without a cutting tool of some sort because no camp should be without a campfire. In fact, a campfire is very much part of what camping is all about. There is nothing so soothing, so restful, so thought-provoking, so reverie-provoking, as a fire, which needs wood. And where there is wood, there has to be something to cut it with.

Mention woodcutting, and almost automatically people think of an ax or hatchet, because they are the traditional tools of the camper. But our advice to you is this: Until you become proficient in their use, far better that you don't take either of them with you. You may have been a good Boy Scout or Girl Scout, but that doesn't necessarily make you a good woodsman. An ax or a hatchet can be not only inefficient in the hands of a tenderfoot, it can be downright dangerous. We suggest that, until such time as you become proficient in their use, get a saw. Camping outfitters now have folding saws for sale that cut through wood twice as fast as an ax and require about half the energy. There are also models on the market that incorporate a shovel, pick, saw, and ax in one package, thus saving weight as well as space.

However, the best saw that we know of is meant to do only one thing: saw. Shaped roughly like a triangle, it enables you to saw with two hands, and, all to the good, its blade is easily replaced. One substitute blade, in fact, is meant to cut bones, not wood. This is an asset because there may come a time when you'll have a bone-in chunk of camp meat to contend with.

As for ax and hatchet, when the day comes that you consider it safe to have them around, a Boy Scout hatchet and a short-handled ax will fill the bill perfectly.

Hooks

Many things used in camping are best hung up and out of the way. Pots and pans, for example. You'll need hooks. They're easily obtained.

Just walk over to your nearest clothes closet and grab a handful of wire coat hangers and you've got the makings. Now all you need is a pair of wire cutters. With it you cut the hangers into a variety of lengths, bend each into an S shape, and you've got hooks.

When you get to camp, you'll need something to hang them from. Drive nails into trees, some might say. But not *us*. Not *you*.

Instead, take a shank of store-bought clothesline with you, measure the distance between two trees, cut off as much rope as you think you'll need, tie knots in it about every six to ten inches, wrap and tie each end around a tree, and then poke one end of an S hook through each knot. Now all you need to do is hang your pots and pans and such from the other ends.

Simple, isn't it?

It's also a good animal chaser. Especially when the wind sets the pots and pans to clanging.

Sample List of Camp Cooking and Eating Equipment Needs

Here is a list of things that you may need in order for the cooking and eating end of your camping trip to be as memorably successful and enjoyable as you want it to be. This rundown is purely a sample. There surely are things on it that you won't want to take to camp with you. Almost as certainly there will be things that you will want to take along that we haven't included.

Many things on the list we spoke of earlier; many things speak now for themselves. Therefore use this list purely as a guide:

> Aluminum foil, both light and heavy
> Auto-Fire charcoal lighter and cooker
> Ax, short-handled
> Band-aids
> Beer-can opener
> Bottle opener
> Bucket (at least one but better two), preferably plastic
> Can openers, preferably the kind with screw handles to assure a
>   smooth edge
> Chairs that fold
> Chapsticks
> Clam opener

Clothespins
Coffee pot
Cooler
Cups
Cutting board
Dining fly
Dish drainer
Dish towels
Dishes
Dishpan
Dutch oven
Face towels
Fire extinguisher
First-aid kit
Fly swatter
Fork, long-handled for cooking
Forks for eating
Garbage can
Gasoline can
Grill to set atop your wood or charcoal fire
Hammer and nails
Hatchet
Insect repellent
Iodine for water purification (see Chapter 4, "Foraging for Food
    and Water")
Knives for eating
Knives for food preparation
Ladle
Lantern
Liquid petroleum fuel canisters, as many extras as you think
    you'll need
Mantles, extra ones for your lantern
Matches (dip heads in nail polish or paraffin or buy Diamond
    waterproof variety or metal ones that work something like
    flint)
Mesh bags for rinsing dishes
Needle and thread
Newspapers, old ones for a variety of purposes
Nutcracker
Paper towels
Plastic bags, small and large ones meant for heavy duty, also
    twist fasteners
Pliers

Pot holders (you may call them pot lifters)
Potato peeler
Rope
S-hooks
Safety pins
Saw
Screwdrivers, both for regular and for Phillips screws
Shovel
Slotted spoon
Snakebite kit
Soap, for yourself and dishes
Soap pads
Spatula
Sponges
Spoons for eating and cooking
Steel wool
Stove
Tablecloths, preferably plastic
Tables, preferably the folding kind
Tarpaulin, preferably plastic
Thermometers, for oven and meat
Tongs, long-handled
Water storage containers, metal, plastic, or canvas

Sample List of Food Staple Needs

This list is also a guide to the staples that ought to accompany you on camping trips. Add or subtract from it as you will.

Bacon, preferably in cans or in one piece
Baking soda
Biscuit mix
Bouillon powder or cubes
Bread
Butter
Candy bars
Canned milk
Catsup
Coffee Mate
Cookies
Crackers
Dehydrated soups, vegetables, and gravies

Eggs
Flour
Jelly
Lemon juice, packaged
Lemons
Milk powder
Margarine
Nosebag lunches (see pages 72–73)
Nuts
Onions
Pancake mix
Peanut butter
Pepper
Potatoes
Prunes and other dried fruits
Raisins
Salt
Spices and seasonings, including packets of seasonings made at
home for use in specific recipes

Planning Your Meals While Still at Home

Now we begin to get down to the nitty gritty of what this chapter is all
about: camp cooking. Yet there you are, still surrounded by four familiar
walls, doing the one thing that all good campers should do—planning your
camp meals while still at home.

So read on, because we have some helpful pointers.

Whether you take every bit of food with you and plan each menu
down to the last crumb depends on a number of things. For instance:

- Is baby going along?
- How much of your camp time do you plan to spend doing things
  far removed from a cooking fire, such as swimming and fishing
  and nature walking and browsing and drowsing?
- Do you look forward with anticipation to making dishes you've
  never made or eaten before?
- What, in fact, is the most interesting part of a camping trip
  for you?

Well, then, if you want to forget about food but still enjoy eating,
if you have a brood of children along who are in the habit of eating at
regular times, you'll enjoy yourself a lot more if you plan in detail and

then organize each meal's ingredients for easy and quick unpacking that won't disturb the rest of your food supply.

One of the most important things to do is to precook and freeze as much as you can carry in a frozen state. Package everything only into one-meal lots.

If you can't carry everything you will need, at least plan so that you don't have to shop in dibs and dabs. If you plan to camp out in different places, try to plan each move so that you will arrive at a good shopping stopover at the time your main stock of food is running low.

Then stay there for a day. Maybe ship the kids off to a movie or to the local swimming pool. And have yourself an orgy of menu-planning according to what's available in the stopover stores. Take the time to restock and reorganize your traveling larder. The results will be well worthwhile. Especially when you cap the day by insisting that you be taken out to dinner that night.

Good Nutrition: Good Trip

Nobody wants to get sick far removed from the family doctor. Nobody wants to waste a vacation nursing children laid low with bellyaches. Nobody wants to feel droopy when there's a mountain to be climbed.

So everybody should observe a few simple rules for good nutrition. You'll find them beginning on page 206. Read them over as often as necessary to refresh your memory.

Probably the most important rule is this: Don't ever make the mistake of forgetting the importance of eating right while away from home.

Perishable Foods

We thoroughly go into the buying and storing of perishable foods in Part II. So here we'll hit only the highlights of things you should bear in mind when taking perishables on a camping trip:

- First, and perhaps most important, is to plan meals so that those items that otherwise would spoil first be used first.
- Both cooked and uncooked meat, poultry and fish that you transport frozen in your camp cooler should either be reheated or cooked as soon as it thaws and while still icy cold.
- Ground meat is far more perishable than meat in one solid chunk because so much more surface is exposed to contamination. So use it quickly.
- Fresh milk and cream that you carry with you should be used up in the first few meals.

- Although fresh vegetables don't spoil quickly, they wilt and gradually lose their flavor and nutritional value if not kept cold.
- Foods such as uncut bacon, smoked meats, salted butter, and margarine will keep for more than a week so long as they remain cool and provided they were very fresh when they came from the store and your home refrigerator.
- Canned foods (some require refrigeration, so check all labels) will keep indefinitely, as will most of those that are dried. However, powdered whole milk and powdered eggs are an exception. Buy only those that bear a U.S. Department of Agriculture label attesting to their wholesomeness and store them according to instructions on the package.

The first point cautioned you to use up your most perishable foods first. Conversely, you should plan to use your least perishable foods last. But do this along with foods you can forage or catch.

Two more observances and then we'll get off this subject and treat you to some sample menus:

- Proper storage, care, and cleanliness usually are all it takes to avoid the discomforts of food poisoning (discussed on pages 203–205).
- If you are going to be camping in a hot, desert area, you obviously will have to plan more exactly than for a trip to high, cool mountainous country with emergency refrigeration provided by ice-cold lakes and streams, a choice of shady storage places, and perhaps even snow.

Write Down Your Menus

So that you'll avoid the burden of food you'll never use, so that you'll be sure to take along everything you'll need: write out a full menu for each day in the field. Write down the approximate amount of ingredients each dish will require. Prepare as much of each menu as you can in your home kitchen. Wrap it and label it.

Planning meals for camp cooking doesn't differ too much from the way you'd do it for home cooking. Try not to overestimate the amount needed for each meal, because this will mean that you'll either have to throw food away or repack the leftovers and lug them home. Chapter 11, pages 209–212, will help you determine how much you'll need for a given number of servings of different foods. The sample menus and needed-ingredient list that follow will give you an idea of how preplanning can help. The two-day sample menus on pages 160–163 of Chapter 5, "Boat Cooking," may also have some ideas you can adapt to camp cooking.

SAMPLE MENUS FOR FOUR ON A THREE–DAY WEEKEND CAMPING TRIP

Thursday Dinner
Two-Step Camp and Galley Stew Number 1 (page 260)
Bread and Butter or Margarine
Tomato Soup Spice Cake (pages 341–342)
Coffee or Tea
Milk or Juice

Friday Breakfast
Orange Juice (Frozen)
Stir-Fried Eggs with Leftover Stew (page 314)
Toast and Butter or Margarine
Coffee or Tea
Milk

Friday Lunch
Two-Day Tossed Camp Salad (page 229)
Quick New England Clam Chowder (page 245)
Bread and Butter or Margarine
Hard-Boiled Eggs
Packaged Cup Cakes
Coffee or Tea
Milk, Juice, or Punch

Friday Dinner
Remaining Two-Day Tossed Camp Salad
Barbecued or Fried Steak with Blue Cheese Butter
(page 218)
Bread and Butter or Margarine
Foil-Baked or Boiled Potato
Tomato Soup Spice Cake
Coffee or Tea
Milk

Saturday Breakfast

Orange Juice (Frozen)
Berry Pancakes (page 333)
Butter or Margarine and Syrup
Fried Canned Spam
Coffee or Tea
Milk

Saturday Lunch

Leftover Steak and Peppers (page 258)
Bread and Butter or Margarine
Packaged Fruit Cake Slices
Coffee or Tea
Milk

Saturday Dinner

Fish with Caraway Seeds (page 292)
(Take along a 2-pound canned, smoked ham as insurance and serve
fried ham slices if you don't catch any fish.)
Succotash and Potatoes Cooked in the Coals (page 328)
Bread and Butter or Margarine
Instant Pudding
Toasted Marshmallows
Coffee or Tea
Juice

Sunday Breakfast

Tang
Clean-Out-Your-Cooler Omelet (page 312)
Toast and Butter or Margarine and Jam
Coffee or Tea
Milk

Sunday Lunch

Dandelion Fish Soup (page 242)
(Take along a spare can of soup in case you catch no fish.)
Canned Meat Sandwiches
Real Fruit Juice Gelatin (pages 233–234) or
Fruit Salad Gelatin (page 234)
Coffee or Tea
Milk

The Foods You'll Need to Prepare Our Sample Menus for
Four on a Three-Day Weekend Camping Trip

1. Frozen foods and liquids: pack them close together so they'll share each other's cold. Put things to be used first on the outside of the cluster:

   2 2-cup containers frozen base for Camp and Galley Stew No. 1
   2 6-ounce cans frozen orange juice concentrate
   4 quarts juice other than orange (pour into plastic jars, leave expansion space at top, freeze, cover with leakproof tops, and carry in cooler as supplemental ice)
   3 pounds steak

2. Foods that should be cold, but not frozen, when they go in cooler or icebox:

   4 slices lean bacon for chowder
   1¼ pounds butter or margarine
   1 2-tablespoon plastic package of blue cheese butter
   15 eggs, fresh, or equivalent amount dried
   4 hard-boiled eggs
   Fresh-caught fish
   1 can smoked ham, about 2 pounds
   10 quarts milk (12 cups per day would meet the basic needs of two adults and two children and provide the necessary amount for cooking; any amount of this 10 quarts can be provided by powdered dry skim milk)
   1 bag of Two-Step, Two-Day Tossed Camp Salad
   Tomato Soup Spice Cake (make this at home)
   1 container sliced vegetables to be used with Leftover Steak and Peppers

3. Foods that do not need to be packed in cooler or ice box:

   1 3-ounce package slivered almonds
   Berries, foraged (take along 1 small can of fruit cocktail as insurance)
   2 beef or chicken bouillon cubes
   About 60 slices of bread
   1 8-ounce can or jar clam broth
   2 7½-ounce cans minced clams

1 16-ounce can dry, whole kernel corn
1 16-ounce can baby lima beans
1 can meat of your choice (6–8 ounces)
1 small can milk
3 10½-ounce cans mushroom soup
3 1-pound cans small whole white potatoes
1 tablespoon caraway seeds
1–2 pounds coffee or tea
1 tablespoon cornstarch
1 package of 4 to 6 cupcakes
3 or 4 young dandelion leaves, foraged fresh
½ teaspoon dried dill weed
4 individually packaged slices of fruit cake
1 clove garlic
1 large bag marshmallows for toasting
½ cup mashed potato flakes
1 3-ounce package lemon gelatin dessert
Small jar cooking oil
2 onions or onion flakes
1 small container onion powder
1 box pancake mix (preferably Krusteaz)
1 tablespoon parsley flakes, dried
4 medium potatoes
1 box instant pudding for 4
1 can Spam (about 1 pound)
1 pinch saffron
Salt and pepper
1 small bottle sherry
1 bottle of syrup
1 small bottle soy sauce
Tang or other citrus-fruit crystals to use when frozen juice is gone
Dessert topping mix (optional) for Tomato Spice Cake
1 pinch sage

Pack Up and Away You Go!

At last—well, almost at last—you can load all your assorted gear and food supplies into the family jalopy and away you go.

But wait! How are you going to pack all those things in that little car?

Well, first we suggest that you make yourself a carrying kit like the one Norman and Priscilla Strung devised.

Campanion

Norman and Sil, those rugged Montanans who would rather camp out than stay home, were constantly plagued by pack rats who seemed to always run off with a knife or a fork or some such thing when it was needed most. Until one bright day they woke to the realization that they'd either lost or misplaced—or simply forgotten to take along—those AWOL items for which the poor rat was taking the rap.

So they invented the Campanion.

Says Norman: "Nothing more than a small suitcase with built-in compartments and elastic bands to secure equipment in place, the Campanion saves at least an hour's time for each camping trip; an hour nor-

Sil Strung fastens a strip of hold-anything tape to her Campanion.

mally spent scouting through drawers and raiding kitchen cabinets for cooking gear.

"To build a Campanion, start with an old suitcase and take each small item you would normally bring on a camping trip and lay it out in plain view. For boxes or cans of equipment, construct compartments in the bottom of the suitcase with plywood or plastic, or secure them in place with elastic bands. Knives, forks, can openers, and cooking utensils, as well as small boxes of spices, fit best in the top of the suitcase, held in place by elastic bands.

"To keep the elastic tied down, you can use the services of a shoe-maker should your suitcase be leather, or you can do it yourself with a 'Pop' riveter if you can locate a metal case. If you use a riveter, put a washer on the elastic side of each rivet so the cloth doesn't pull free.

"After making a place for each item, outline forks, knives, and boxes with a marking pencil, and write in what is supposed to be there, and how many pieces each space holds. For example: '4 knives,' '4 forks,' 'mustard,' 'salt,' etc.

"Although you can take your equipment from the kitchen and fill up each hole before every trip, it's a lot less work if you make up a complete set of spices and a set of eating and small cooking utensils and keep them at all times in your Campanion or whatever container you may devise. That way, everything is ready to be packed in car or camper (or boat) at a minute's notice."

How to Stow and Load

It's no more difficult to intelligently pack your camping gear than it is to throw everything together helter-skelter and wish later that you hadn't.

There are just a few basic things to remember:

- Keep different kinds of gear apart. For the cook, that means there should be a reserved section in the trunk of the car, the bed of the pickup or station wagon, or the cabinet of the camper for cooking utensils and foodstuffs only. This eliminates waiting until sleeping bags are unrolled before you can get at your pots and pans. It also makes everything easier to keep track of, thus cutting down the chance of loss.
- Use every available space. Neatness and compactness is a necessity not only in camp cooking but also in camp transportation. For example, a portable propane stove has plenty of empty space inside it. Use it to carry canned goods, pancake flour or—since it has a steel case—foods that can break or crumble such as

cakes, cookies, and bread and perhaps even eggs. The bread can help cushion them. If you've loaded your cooler with all the perishable items you intend to bring and still have space, wonderful! Fill up that empty space with other foodstuffs and utensils. The cooler is going along anyway, so put its roominess to 100 per cent good use. Do the same with your pots and pans. Use them to stow things while in transit. For example, a plastic bag filled with paper napkins might go well in a coffee pot.

- Only after every nook and cranny in the equipment you have to take with you is utilized should you resort to boxes, preferably wooden, because you're highly likely to have use for them in camp and you'll have them for the trip home again. Don't use paper bags because one of them is sure to break long before you get to where you're going. Besides, square boxes make better use of vehicle space.

- Pack cooking gear and food into your vehicle last. It will be the first thing you, the cook, will want to get at, thus enabling you to start whipping up a meal while the rest of the hungry horde is pitching camp. Packing food last also makes it eminently available should your trip be such a long one that you'll have to—or want to—cook a meal or two beside the road before getting to where you're going.

Nosebag Lunches

For the short haul, and for the unexpected, we recommend nosebag lunches. You cannot possibly know for sure what conditions you will run into while on the road. Maybe you'll be stuck in a long line of unmoving cars. Then comes the moment you've dreaded. It's time, perhaps past the time, for the children's lunch. Or maybe you're moving along nicely, and suddenly it's lunch time.

And, in either case, the kids let you know it.

So what to do about it, because you don't want your brood to go hungry and you wish they'd shut up?

Well, you do about it what the Girl Scouts do. You plan ahead and prepare ahead because you know that things will be a lot more pleasant if there's something always available for children to eat and to drink. Something which, in order to get at, doesn't require the unpacking of carefully stowed equipment.

Therefore, like a good Girl Scout leader, you pack nosebag lunches for each of your children. This should also include husbands and yourself. A nosebag lunch, in case you didn't know, consists of individual bags of food, each of them clearly marked with the name of the person who will be its ultimate consumer. And heaven help the one who gets his hands on someone else's!

You should include in nosebag lunches only such foods as nuts, raisins, dried or fresh fruits that are not messy to peel and to eat, carrot and celery sticks, and tiny unsalted crackers that are popped whole into the mouth, thus eliminating a shower of crumbs at every bite. Animal crackers are perfect. Apples are excellent because, in addition to all their other fine qualities, they also are good thirst quenchers.

Glass bottles aren't too safe in the car, and cans that have to be emptied once they are opened are worse than none at all. Screw-top cans or individual small Tupperware bottles—something that really seals when closed—filled to about seven-eighths of capacity (to allow for expansion) with water, fruit juice, or iced tea or coffee and then frozen are great for everyone.

All the nosebag lunches and drinks can be stowed in an inexpensive insulated plastic zipper bag and kept handy in case an emergency arises. If you don't need the lunches along the way, you may be very glad to have them when you get to camp.

Always remember this: A little quick-energy food can turn a carload of irritable people into happy car unpackers, tent putter-uppers, and firewood gatherers.

AFTER ARRIVAL

At long last you're in camp. Everything is unpacked and in place. It's time now to start cooking. Over a portable gas stove, a charcoal stove, or a campfire.

You know by now, we're sure, how to use the first two, so we'll talk now only about the campfire—specifically the campfire over which you should cook.

It's a sad fact of present-day living that despite man's involvement with fire in the past, few people know how to build a fire that will most quickly and efficiently get a particular job done, be that job to give light, to take the chill off a damp August evening, or to cook a delicious meal.

You can build many different kinds of fire, each of them serving a different purpose. The best place to build a fire for cooking is in the permanent fireplace available at the site you've chosen for a camp. But look first to see how high above the firebed the grill is. If it measures more than eight inches, about all it's probably good for is roasting hot dogs or keeping things warm. There are two things you can do: you can build a rock platform in the bottom of the fireplace, thereby raising the level of the firebed, or, you can forget it and build yourself a new fireplace. It's quite easy.

Begin by digging a shallow hole about three inches deep and slightly smaller than the grill you brought from home, saving the dirt to fill the hole up again when you break camp. Then line three sides of the pit with rocks that will hold the grill level at about four inches above ground level. The open side should be the windward side; reposition the stones as the wind changes direction.

That's all there is to it. Your cooking fireplace is built. There are other ways, but since this is all you'll need for all-round camp cooking, we'll hold their descriptions for the chapter on wilderness cooking, which comes next.

Now you have your fireplace. But don't build, much less light, a fire in it until you have gathered all the materials you will need to start it and keep it going until you are through cooking over it because, once started, you must never leave it alone.

Wood for Your Fire

Your firelay will be the same whether you're using a permanent campground fireplace or one that you've built yourself.

Tinder comes first. You don't need a lot. Just enough very quick-to-catch, hot flaming material that will start the kindling (which comes next) burning. Tinder can be loosely wadded paper, very dry leaves or grasses, pine needles, pine cones, very small and very dry twigs, fallen tree bark (birch is best), or bits of wood taken from dead but still standing trees or from stumps.

Kindling is a bit larger than tinder. It can be small, dry branches or wood shavings whittled with a small knife. Very effective is the woodsman's "fuzz stick," which is nothing more than a core of dry wood with porcupine-like shavings still attached.

Firewood comes last. Although there has been long debate among woodsmen as to the best wood for a cooking fire, we've found few woods to be undesirable, because you don't begin to cook with any of them, hard or soft, until all the tars, pitch, and smoke have burned away. It is true, though, that hardwood makes longer-lasting coals. Which means, then, that if only softwood is available, you'll need more of it.

In case you don't know softwood from hardwood when you see it, a simple but somewhat uncertain way to tell one from the other is by hefting. A piece of dry hardwood feels heavier than the same-size piece of dry softwood.

Don't use resinous woods to build any fire unless you absolutely have to, because they pose a constant danger of sparks. So do paper, leaves, pine needles, and tiny twigs—but only when added to a well-established fire.

A good grill, one with crisscross wiring, helps dissipate sparks

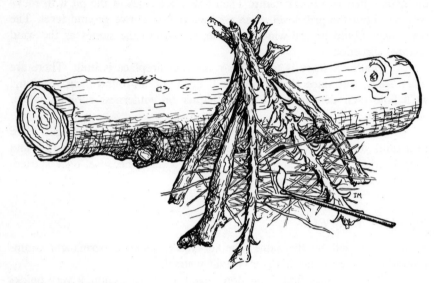

Flames can easily lick up "fuzz sticks," which makes starting a campfire easy.

before they can make contact with tree, tent, or whatever. The best possible protection, however, is to be on the alert at all times.

The most satisfactory size for cooking is a chunk of dry wood that can be cut in two with two swipes of a small hatchet. This smaller wood burns hot and fast, reducing itself to cooking coals in a quarter of the time it would take a three-inch or four-inch log. Gather plenty of this kind of fuel and chop it in advance, because it will take at least enough to fill an average-size wooden box to cook a full meal.

Where to Find Wood

Go into the forest, primeval or otherwise, and look for standing dead trees, preferably saplings. Also dead hangers, a hanger being a sapling that started to fall over only to get hung up in a fork of a live tree. Hangers usually make better firewood than do dead trees that have fallen to earth because the latter may have soaked up too much ground moisture.

Dead stumps and stubs—a stub being a standing dead tree whose top has long since fallen away—are also good sources of firewood.

So, with all that to choose from, there is no need to in any way lay hand or ax to a tree that is still alive and green and growing and bursting with life.

Laying and Starting Your Fire

Lay a piece of firewood in the firebed of your fireplace. Against it, in about its center, arrange your tinder. Stand your kindling, including your fuzz stick, around the tinder in sort of a crisscross pattern and leaning against the piece of firewood. It should look something like half a tepee.

Now stand with your back to the wind, strike a match—plain, paraffined, metal, or whatever—and set the light to the tinder. First the tinder will flare, then the kindling will catch.

That's your starter fire. When you're sure it really has caught, feed sticks of firewood to it in a crosshatch or log-cabin fashion, never over-loading, because good combustion needs plenty of air, but never underloading either.

Remember always that air is one of the most important components of a blazing fire, so pile your wood on loosely, leaving plenty of empty spaces. It's important, too, that the ashes and coals are evenly distributed —a matter that will take care of itself if you crisscross the wood properly.

Your Cooking Fire

Once it gets under way, blazing cheerily, your fire may look just right to start boiling potatoes or making coffee.

But, unless you like a lot of extra work, it is not.

Cooking over a yellow flame means soot. And soot not only can get into food, thereby spoiling its taste if not making it downright inedible, it also gets onto pots and pans and hands and arms and often even clothes.

The only time you should cook with a yellow flame is when using a reflector oven.

Don't start cooking until your bed of ash and coals is about four inches deep and the only flames are small and flickering. Then and only then is your fire ready for cooking.

Lay the grill over the rocks that line the pit, making sure that it sets level. The foods that you are going to cook now should be from four to six inches above the coals. This is an ideal height for broiling meats. Ditto for just about anything else. When the four-inch bed of coals thins down to about two inches and still there is something on the fire that requires longer cooking, you should be able to carefully lift up one side of the grill at a time—wearing fire gloves, of course—and push the stones out from under with a piece of firewood, thus enabling you to lower the grill to ground level.

Prepare a Place to Set Things

At home, this problem takes care of itself because every kitchen has counter or table-top areas on which to set the tools of every cook's trade, up to and including hot pots.

But not so in camp. There you have to think ahead. In fact, that's one of the reasons you brought an extra folding table and those wooden boxes along. Set one or more of them close by your cooking fire and see to it that everyone keeps his cotton-pickin' hands and other odds and ends off it. That especially includes things that might catch fire. Like children's sweaters, for instance.

Even so, keep a pail of water handy, because even though there are no sweaters left around, the boxes and the table are made of wood, and wood does burn.

How to Time Food Cooked over an Open Fire

Timing is one of the keys to every good cook's success. So, rather than go into it here, far removed from the recipe section, we've placed these vital statistics back where they belong. So please turn to page 194 for general timing instructions and to page 104 for high-altitude timing.

Charcoal Cooking

If you prefer this to other forms of camp cooking, just apply the pointers included in Chapter 1, and you've got it made.

Oven Cooking

If you intend to do much oven cooking, portable or Dutch, over a campfire, you'll need a fireplace that will permit you to rake additional coals under it when and if needed or, conversely, to rake them away in order to maintain the proper temperature while cooking, for example, a roast.

For this kind of cooking, some variation of the keyhole fireplace will best serve your purposes. So we refer you to page 99 in Chapter 3.

Adding Variety to Camp Cooking

No one can deny the appetizing appeal of fresh-caught fish fried to a crunchy golden brown, but outdoor chefs are missing some real eating pleasure if all they think of is fried and unimaginatively boiled foods while in camp. Taste isn't the full story either. Nor is time, because there are many other ways of cooking in camp that not only are quick and easy and highly flavorsome but also as healthful as can be.

Diet-conscious Americans shouldn't overlook the fact that one of the built-in benefits of outdoor cooking is that it can be nonfattening and still taste great. Then, too, if the cook also does the dishes she, or he, will be glad to try the many cooking methods that don't involve pots, pans, or cleanup afterward.

Foil Cooking

One of the biggest work-savers and mealtime helpmates a camp chef can have is a roll of aluminum foil. Foil-wrapped meats and vegetables mean no pots and pans. Or, if you do have to use a pot or a pan, a layer of foil on the outside of the utensil means no messy fireblack to wash off. Just throw away the layer of foil. If you need a certain utensil and you haven't got one, two layers of heavy-duty foil can be bent into any shape you want.

Foil-wrapped foods may be either buried in coals or laid on top of the grill to cook, with pretty much the same end result—a packet filled with culinary marvels steaming in their own delectable juices.

Whether you bury them is a matter of choice, but there is this to be said: (1) foods buried in coals will cook faster, which mainly is all to the good but sometimes may be not so good; (2) burial leaves you with more grill space on which to cook other things; but (3) foil packages cooked on top of the grill are more easily tested for doneness.

But whichever way, you first must wrap your fish or meat or vegetables or combination thereof securely in heavy-duty foil. Then, if burial is your way, use a stick or some such thing to make a nest of your coals, drop the packet into the nest, and rake the coals back over it, making sure that it is completely covered. Anything cooked in this way should be done in half the normal cooking time so take care that you don't overdo it.

Many interesting variations in taste can be incorporated in your main dish by adding vegetables, spices, sauces, or wine as you wrap the meat or fish.

Foil cooking, baking, roasting—call it what you will, the results are the savory same—works extremely well on potatoes and corn on the cob. And, yes, if you're an onion lover, on onions, too! If you like your vegetables moist, add a few drops of water before you seal them up.

Broiling

Do we need say more about this great cooking method other than that it's a great pot-and-pan saver and a marvelous flavor producer? Just place your meat or fish on a hot grill, sit back, and lick your chops in anticipation.

Some camp cooks sear steaks or chops for about thirty seconds on each side in a hot frying pan and then transfer them from pan to grill. They do this, they say, to seal in the natural juices and to either eliminate or retard evaporation.

Other cooks would rather sacrifice a little juice than sear the meat.

Still others sear them by holding them briefly just over the coals with a fork or tongs or hinged grill.

We belong to the second school. As for you, try them all and make up your own mind.

Steaming

If by chance you should run into a recipe, in this book or elsewhere, that calls for boiling something or other, try steaming it instead and be prepared for a taste treat such as you've never had before. It's easy, doesn't take long, and it retains a lot of the food's natural health values because none of its goodness is boiled away.

All you need is a pot, with cover, that's large enough to hold whatever it is that you're going to cook, a small wire rack that will fit into the bottom of the pot and—no kidding—four spring-type clothespins. Clip the clothespins to the rack on what roughly might be called its four corners so that they serve as legs; stand the rack in the pot on its clothespin legs; pour a couple of inches of water into the pot; place your food on the rack; place the cover on the pot; and place the pot on the stove. That's all there is to it.

It will take about five minutes for the water to start steaming, and it's then that you must begin your timing. An uncooked lobster should be ready for eating in about twenty minutes; fish and vegetables, in from five to fifteen minutes, depending on what they are and how thick they are.

The best, and only, way to tell for sure when what you're cooking is done is to remove the cover and see for yourself. Feel free to do it, but be quick.

Smoke Cooking in Camp

The unique flavor of smoked fish and meats adds still another dimension to the art of outdoor cooking. So much so that whole books are now being written on the subject, and the first and the best of them, called simply *Smoke Cooking,* by Matt Kramer and Roger Sheppard, contains hundreds of recipes and is replete with directions and diagrams for making a vast variety of smoke ovens.

If you've taken a charcoal cooker to camp with you and if it has a hood on it and good draft control, that is all the oven you need to smoke your way to new culinary horizons.

But if you've taken no smoke oven with you, don't fret. Do this instead:

- Dig a fire pit about eight inches deep and small enough to support your wire grill.
- Dig a channel that slopes gently from a point about eighteen inches to windward into the pit. This will provide your draft.
- Obtain somewhere a cardboard box large enough to straddle your grill with plenty of room to spare. The bigger the box the better. Cut away and discard the bottom flaps but only loosen the top ones so that they can be manipulated to regulate the air flow.
- Collect or whittle a good supply of hardwood chips. Hickory is probably best, but other woods are equally good, especially ash, apple, cherry, maple, aspen, and oak.
- Many people will tell you merely to gather small branches of green wood. But we don't know where you will be sure to find them (barring an act of God—that is, lightning or gale-force winds) without harming a growing, living tree, so we urge you instead to use dry wood.
- Dry wood chips must be soaked in water, the longer the better but certainly no less than an hour, depending on the size and the quantity of the meat or fish you intend to smoke. Jim Martenhoff, Dan's former pen pal, who writes the "Galley Proof" fish cookery column in the fine fishing magazine, *The Salt Water Sportsman,* insists that hickory chips should be soaked overnight, and we don't disagree.
- Go fishing and come back to camp with a mess of fish. Clean them, split them, steak them, or fillet them. Unless of course you're planning to smoke hamburger or steak or some other chunk of beef now reposing in your cooler.
- Fetch a bucket of water and keep it handy, just in case that cardboard box catches fire.
- Build a standard cooking fire, as described a few pages back, in your pit and let it burn down to a four-inch bed of coals.
- Place your fish or meat on the grill, place the cardboard box over the grill, and just like that you're cooking with smoke.
- But wait! Do you see smoke escaping because the box flaps are fixed too widely apart? Okay, cover them with wet newspaper or anything else that you have handy.

Fish smoked in such a cardboard-box oven should be done in about half an hour, allowing about fifteen minutes to each side. A piece of meat about two inches thick should take about a half-hour per side. Pry into it with a knife tip to make sure it's done the way you like it.

Some points to bear in mind in this kind of smoke cookery:

- The oven, or cover, need not be a cardboard box. It can be a large kettle, a wooden box, or a properly propped piece of canvas.
- If you have none of these things, so be it. Just cook on your open grill. But keep feeding the coals with wet chips and keep the smoke rising.
- Brining is not necessary, but it can be helpful, and it does give a slightly different flavor to smoked fish. If you care to brine, simply add a cup of salt, preferably the Kosher variety, to a gallon of water, add the fish and let it soak for thirty minutes, then pat thoroughly dry with a lint-free paper towel. Your fish is now ready for the smoker.

It's Cleanup Time

You've all eaten. You're all content.

Except for the guy or gal who now has to do the dishes.

Well, they need not fret too much, because gone are the camping days of yore when there were no hardwater soaps or soap pads to cut through layers of grease and soot.

Today fast-lathering soaps cut grease in a wink, even in cold water. Sponge-backed steel wool pads act as both dishcloth and abrasive, and hardwater hand soaps work themselves into a cleaning lather in a jiffy.

In short, camp cleanup now is a breeze. It may seem silly to tell anyone how to wash dishes; we'll do so nevertheless, because dysentery or diarrhea can ruin a camping trip, and poorly washed dishes most often are the cause. So!

- Anytime you have a fire going, make room somewhere, somehow, to heat some water. Use a pot, a pail, a coffee can— whatever you have room for.
- Pour that water as it accumulates into some sort of storage container in which you can at least keep it warm.
- When it comes time to do the dishes, have at least a bucket of water boiling hot. Not only does heat help cut dish dirt, it also kills germs.

- Before wetting them, wipe every dish, pot, pan, and piece of cutlery with a paper towel to remove as much grease and food scraps as possible.
- Dunk them in hot water and scrub them with a soap pad, preferably Brillo, with a sponge back, not only because they are loaded with soap but also because the foam rubber can double as a dishrag and they're easily disposed of.
- Transfer them to clean hot rinse water and scrub them again with a wet paper towel. This second scrubbing is important because it helps to remove any soap that might be left.
- One more quick rinse in clean hot water and the job is done.

There can be, of course, variations of the basic techniques. Such as:

- If you have a dish-drying rack, set it off a short way from the main camp area on a raised flat surface—maybe a wooden box or a square of stones—place your dishes in it, pour boiling water over them, and let them dry in the air.
- Place your knives and forks and spoons in a mesh bag as you finish washing them, tie up the end, dunk them in boiling water and hang the bag up with a S-hook to dry.

Garbage Disposal

Garbage not only is unsanitary if left around loose or uncovered, it also attracts pesky insects and wild animals. Therefore:

- If your campsite provides garbage and rubbish cans use them. If not, burn all combustible garbage and scorch the noncombustibles, including cans, because the heat will kill marauder-attracting food odors.
- Dig a pit somewhere out of camp and bury all of the noncombustibles, including the cans. But first cut off both ends and flatten them.

Policing the Area

Dinner is over, the dishes are done, the sun is fading fast, and soon it will be time to sit around the campfire luxuriating in thoughts of the day that's been and in anticipation of the day to come.

It would be a shame to spoil so nice a night.

So while there is still some light to see by, make it a habit of checking that no potential booby traps are left around loose.

An ax stuck in a log, a low clothesline, even a stray bucket can be a real hazard after nightfall. Put them, and everything else that someone might stumble into or over, away for the night. And try to keep them there during the day when they're not in use.

Putting Out the Fire

Fire has been a great friend to man, but it also can be a devastating enemy when it gets out of hand. To insure enjoyment of forests, fields, and dunes for yourself next year and for future generations in the years to come, always build your fire in a safe place, never leave it unattended, and make sure it's dead out when you break camp.

Since cooking coals don't require much oxygen and smoke little, supposedly dead fires have a nasty habit of coming back to life hours and sometimes days after being doused with water. To make sure you won't be responsible for a holocaust, slowly pour at least two full buckets of water on the fire and have someone stir it with a stick as you do so. Make sure that every ember, every spark, is thoroughly saturated.

If you're moving on, fill your fire pit with the dirt you dug from it and pat it down firmly with a shovel. This not only is a fire safety measure, it also eliminates a hole in which someone later might break a leg.

Remember the Next Guy

Filling in that fire pit not only eliminates a hazard, it also helps leave the campsite clean and neat for the next guy, gal, or camping family.

Always leave your camp ground cleaner than when you found it. Take a last look around and pick up any papers, cans, or other trash scraps you find. Gather enough tinder, kindling, and firewood for at least a first campfire, cover it, or put it in as rainproof a place as you can find. The folks who follow you will appreciate it.

Last (and First) on the List: Constantly Check Equipment

Equipment can wear out or become lost; spices and condiments have a habit of allowing themselves to be used up; cooking and eating utensils can break. A wise camper carries a complete list of gear and regularly checks on everything not only before but also after a camping trip. By keeping abreast of what equipment and supplies need repair or replacement, the camp cook can cut short half his or her troubles before they start.

And please, whether or not you're a member of the National Campers and Hikers Association, abide by their Campers' Creed:

Be clean in your outdoor manners. Keep trash and garbage out of fields, water, and roadways.

Be considerate of the rights of others and treat both public and private property with respect.

Prevent fire. Build yours in a safe place and be sure it is out before you leave.

Preserve and teach others to preserve our natural resources, forests, wild life, and waters by practicing conservation.

3—Wilderness Cooking

by Norman Strung*

FOREST, LAKE, AND MOUNTAIN COUNTRY

A trip into truly primitive country is the kind of adventure that has enchanted outdoorsmen since the days of Davy Crockett and Daniel Boone. A crackling campfire at dusk, the sound of trout gulping flies from a mirror-calm lake, crisp mornings and brilliant days, and the matchless taste of good food laced with woodsmoke are just a few of the many priceless memories offered by America's wilderness.

Hiking or riding through mountain trails, canoeing along lonely waterways, or hunting rocks in the desert (see "Desert Camping," pages 112–115) are not sports for tot or tenderfoot. But for the man—and woman and level-headed teen-ager—in good shape it's undoubtedly the most absorbing and challenging of all outdoor activities.

No matter how splendid your physical condition, walking, horse-backing, and canoeing through rugged terrain are real exercises that bring unexpected and unused muscles into play and require untapped and untested sources of energy and stamina.

That calls for practice, planning, and, yes, training, too.

---

* NORMAN STRUNG is a good friend, outdoor writer, college English teacher, coauthor with Dan of *The Fisherman's Almanac* and *Family Fun on and around the Water*, and—most important as far as this book is concerned—Montana fishing and hunting guide to whom the Spanish Peaks Wilderness country is practically a second home.

It also calls for good nutrition.

You have to know how to put together well-balanced, well-cooked meals under any conditions that might develop. Don't depend upon a guide to do this for you; he might fall off a horse and crack his skull and suddenly you have become his keeper.

Because men, in spite of technology's every effort, don't dominate nature, visitors to her home must be prepared to co-exist with her in a partnership where she is the dominant member. She must always be considered first.

The wilderness cook, meaning you, can't count on the luxury of a gas stove and cooler or the convenience of a grocery store a few miles away. You have to be able and ready to build a fire with wet wood, you have to know how to improvise both utensils and meals, how to pack frugally yet wisely. You have to be able to plan meals for your party with precision and accuracy. More than in any other kind of cooking, the wilderness cook is tied part and parcel to where he'll be going and what he'll be doing and how long he'll be there.

Long before thinking about food and meals, if you're the bull cook (that's what wilderness cooks are called, be they male or female), you'll have to familiarize yourself with the geographical, biological, and climatic conditions you'll be up against. You can't change them to suit yourself, but, by knowing what to expect, you can plan your meals around them.

Good contour maps are an absolute necessity to everyone in the party, the cook included. Not only do they give you some idea of the terrain and number of miles you'll be covering in a day, they also have accurate descriptions of suitable campsites that are close to a source of water. You can obtain them by writing to the U.S. Geological Survey, Washington, D.C.

The weather you can expect to experience is another important factor, especially since it varies not only from coast to coast but also from low country to high country in the same state. June, an ideal month for camping in the East or Southwest, is cold, wet, soup-and-hot-dish weather in the Rockies, to say nothing of the fact that it is also a time when snows still lie deep and forage food is scarce in the high country of Montana, Idaho, and Wyoming.

Biological conditions are perhaps the most important to a camp cook because they indicate availability of supplemental food—that is, fish, game, and berries that are in season—as well as where to start looking for it.

In short, the bull cook should ask a lot of questions before preparing a list of foodstuffs to pack into the wilderness. The best way to get the answers is by writing to the U.S. Forest Service, Department of Agriculture, Washington, D.C. If it can't give you detailed information, including pinpoint maps, about the area you'll be venturing through, it can direct you to an agency that can. Another good information source is the Chamber of Commerce of the town closest to where you're going.

Once you have obtained reliable information and familiarized yourself with any unusual conditions or limitations you'll have as a cook, figure out how many days you'll be in the back country and roughly approximate where and when you'll be making camp. Not only is this necessary for your meal planning but for your safety as well.

After you arrive at the gateway to the wilderness you'll be entering, stop by the nearest ranger station or sheriff's office and tell them your plans. It's important that they know when you're going in, when you're coming out, and where you expect to camp. Not only will they then be able to more expeditiously rush to your aid in case of trouble, they'll also be able to tell your campfire smoke from a possible forest fire.

Additionally, in case dry-woods conditions require it, they'll issue you a fire permit.

District rangers are always familiar with the present conditions in their immediate region. They can warn you of hazards like trail washouts and tell you if there will be any other parties in your vicinity, should you require assistance or like to borrow a cup of sugar from the bull cook on the next mountain.

What to Bring

Deciding on the items that will be absolutely necessary to back-country cooking and those that are convenience items and can be eliminated should your gear be too heavy is a tricky business, particularly if this is your first trip into the wilderness. One man's luxury is another man's necessity, and until you have the assurance of experience, predicting how this or that will fit into your brand of cooking is an educated guess at best.

The primary consideration, be you canoeing, back-packing, or horseback riding, is weight, so you first should have some idea of what each mode of transportation will handle.

A man of average build—with a modern, light aluminum frame-and-rayon pack on his back—can carry up to forty-five pounds comfortably, pack included, and cover as much as ten miles a day. But five miles is a more sensible goal.

A sixteen-foot, two-man canoe has a payload capacity of around 500 pounds. Assuming the combined weight of the two canoeists to be 350 pounds, that leaves 150 pounds for gear.

A pack horse, properly loaded, can handle about 150 pounds. Great if just one person is trekking into the wilderness, but figure on never going alone. At least one person should always be with you. That means a pack horse can carry only 75 pounds per camper.

That sounds like quite a lot—between forty-five and seventy-five pounds per person. But it isn't once you take other necessities besides food and cooking and eating utensils into consideration. Sleeping bags weigh at least six pounds. Air mattresses another two or three pounds. Shelter, meaning pup tent or tarp, six pounds more. Plus ten pounds of fishing or hunting gear and five pounds for a change of clothes.

So subtract thirty pounds from the total pay load—and you still haven't allowed for such niceties as slicker and heavy jacket (musts on extended trips), a few nails, a pair of comfortable shoes to wear around camp, and a pillowcase which, when stuffed with your extra clothes, gives you something on which to rest your head come beddy-bye.

Put them all together and you find that they don't exactly leave the bull cook with unlimited space for either food or utensils. Both therefore must be culled to the barest essentials.

An ax, grill, mess kit, knives and forks, matches, aluminum foil, and flashlight should be the cook's core items. Plus first-aid kit and snakebite remedy, because the camp cook is usually also the camp doctor.

By now you've got your pay-load area pretty well filled up, except for a few unfilled holes here and there. So those you fill, and the order of importance is yours to decide, with such things as spatula, ladle, folding shovel and saw, and dish-washing soaps and pads.

Meals, foodstuffs, and menus for every day that you will be in camp must be selected, therefore, with two important factors in mind: which minimum-weight ingredients will give the maximum amount of high-nutrition energy.

For example: Baked beans are a fine food for the wilderness camper. But a medium-size can weighs in the neighborhood of a pound, far too much weight for the food values it contains. Especially since most of that weight is water. Far better that you carry a half-pound of dry beans in a plastic bag and add the water when you're ready to cook.

That's the packing principle never to forget when wilderness wandering you would go. Carry nothing with you that can be added by using an ingredient that will be waiting for you when you get to where you're going.

Such as water.

There are many foodstuffs available in supermarkets and camping-goods stores that function in just that manner: all of them either dried, dehydrated, or otherwise concentrated; all of them able to provide well-balanced, different, and delicious meals three times a day, particularly when combined with things you can forage or catch.

The list of suitable foods for the camper who has to travel light is long and varied. It includes such staples as the aforementioned beans, dried fruits, noodles, powdered milk and eggs, dehydrated potatoes, and whole meals that come dried in a box, like macaroni and cheese, spaghetti, beef stew, Rice-a-Roni, and soups by the score.

By applying a bit of ingenuity and originality such as you'll find incorporated into some recipes in Part III you'll add new dimensions to such otherwise strictly standard fare. For example: wild berries in a pancake batter made only with water (page 333), or quick home-fried potatoes (page 327).

Bernard's Kamp Pack, of San Jose, California, makes entire meals —meats included—all sealed in moistureproof envelopes. And there are always the old military standbys: K and C rations. [To that, I, Dan Morris, who for several years had to suffer through them, can say only one thing— ugh! However, come to think of it, our Seabee outfit had a mess chief who once served us Baked Virginia Spam. That's what we mean by originality and ingenuity.]

Check in at your nearest camp-supply store, and you're sure to find other things to trigger your culinary impulses. The choice seems countless, endless, and so there is no reason why the light-traveling bull cook can't whip up meals with variety and real gourmet appeal. See the sample list of what to bring and foods for the wilderness later on in this chapter.

Planning Your Meals

No matter where you camp, wild country or tame country, the same basics of balance and nutrition hold true. But because steaks, fresh eggs, salad vegetables, and such niceties as mayonnaise aren't practical items for the trail pack, they have to be replaced by other sources of good value and variety.

Bacon, though heavy, is welcome at any back-country meal. Not only is it a meat but also it is an oil to replace butter, margarine, and salad oil. It is quite a flavoring agent, too. Fry it to a crisp, crumble it to bits, add it to an otherwise blah packaged food, and your meal acquires new dimensions. Get slab, not sliced, bacon. Canned bacon is also a practical pack-in item because there is no water; the can contains nothing but meat. It also keeps well in warm weather.

Fish is one of the best foods you can eat. So healthful, in fact, that nutritionists recommend that everyone eat it at least four times a week. And fish will be waiting to be caught in just about any forest or high-country area anyone would ever venture into. In fact, in many cases fishing is man's main reason for venturing into the wilderness. So catch them and eat them while they're still fresh from the water and at their flavorsome best.

Salad greens, though impossible to bring with you, can be foraged from many a grassy field once you've learned to identify edible plants.

So you see, meal planning for the wilderness cook is a combination of knowing what to expect in the way of food consumption, how to find fresh supplemental foods in nature's bountiful larder, plus four big ingredients that good chefs are never without—originality, ingenuity, imagination, experimentation.

Although each trip will have its own special requirements and each individual his own likes and dislikes, there are some general assumptions that can be made about what a group will be eating in a day that will help immeasurably when writing out a grub list.

Breakfast

Although the trend in America is toward light breakfasts, the wilderness outdoorsman needs a hearty first meal to sustain him through the day. Breakfast dishes should be as complete and well rounded as the evening meal and can be planned around three groups:

- Fruits (raisins, dried apples, peaches, apricots, and foraged berries)
- Meats (bacon, ham, fish, powdered eggs, nuts either shelled and packaged or foraged)
- Cereals (grains and flours like pancakes, biscuits, and oatmeal)

Mix them up for variety. Raisins cooked with oatmeal give it a sweetness that does away with the need for sugar. Bacon and pancakes really stick to the ribs, and so also do powdered eggs and fish. As for taste, there is nothing that can beat the flavor of fresh-caught fish broiled over a wood fire.

One more word of advice: If you get complaints about no one's being hungry in the morning, wait an hour or two before cooking breakfast; everyone will be hungry by then. In fact, some of them may even go forth to catch that breakfast fish! And if your party still includes a no-breakfast-for-me diehard, pack his meat-and-pancake portion into a plastic bag and let him stow it in his pocket. He'll have eaten it long before the sun is high in the sky!

Lunch

If you're traveling during the day or just busy fishing or hunting or exploring, chances are you won't want to take time out to cook. With a big breakfast under your belt, lunch can be on the light side. A few strips of jerky (page 348) or a small can of potted meat, some dried fruit, and a candy bar usually are plenty.

Dinner

This is the main meal of the day. You've moved on from where you camped the night before. You've arrived at your campsite for the night to come. But you've planned the move so you'd have plenty of time to prepare a big meal. And, you may be sure, everyone will have the appetite to eat it, probably especially the guy who said he couldn't eat breakfast.

So here is your, the bull cook's, chance to show off quite a little bit, to use your built-in ingredients—originality, ingenuity, imagination, experimentation—to display your skill with a skillet.

Now is the time, much more so than at breakfast and lunch, to incorporate foods you've found with what you lugged with you from the last outposts of civilization. A foraged salad, fresh-caught fish, or stew and potatoes, biscuits, a perhaps-wild vegetable, maybe scones laced with wild berries for dessert; they all combine, they all help, to turn a wilderness dinner into a wilderness feast.

There is one word of warning for the meal-planner always to bear in mind: Don't ever make any specific plans for forage foods in your diet. Chances are there will be plenty around, but you can't depend on their availability. So use them as windfalls, welcome supplements to preplanned well-balanced meals. Don't ever organize your meals around them unless you have already foraged for them and you have them right there in camp with you.

Whenever travel, terrain, and daily itinerary permit, it's a good idea to carry with you something in which to put any nice berries, salad makings, or cooking vegetables that you may chance upon. Plastic bags to which you've added some damp moss to serve as a cushion for ripe berries make good forage containers.

If you stay in one campsite for any length of time—with consequent degrees of boredom—organize a food-forage hunt. There are those for whom such pastime can be a welcome change of pace from fishing for trophy-size cutthroat trout!

SAMPLE MENUS FOR BACK-PACKERS ON A THREE-DAY TRIP

Thursday Night

Dehydrated Beef Stew
Ready-Mix Corn Cakes
Dried Fruit
Kool-Aid

Friday Morning
Tang
Stick-to-the-Ribs Oatmeal (page 335)
Leftover Corn Cakes
Coffee

Friday Noon
Strung's Jerky (pages 348–349)
Leftover Corn Cakes and Jelly
Candy Bar
Water or Reconstituted Powdered Milk

Friday Night
Poached Whole Fish (page 296)
Potatoes and Onions in Butter Herb Sauce (page 326)
Wilderness Salad (page 230) or Dehydrated Vegetables
Kool-Aid
Toasted Marshmallows

Saturday Morning
Tang
Coffee
Quick-Mix Pancakes (page 332) or Berry Pancakes (page 333)
Bacon

Saturday Noon
Cheese and Leftover Bacon Rolled in Leftover Pancakes
Peanuts
Water or Reconstituted Powdered Milk

Saturday Night
Dehydrated Vegetables
Dehydrated Macaroni and Cheese
Bouillon (Cubes or Powder)
Biscuit-Mix Bread (page 331)
Instant Pudding from Mix

Sunday Morning
Tang
Scrambled Eggs (Powdered) and Bacon
Leftover Biscuit-Mix Bread
Hot Chocolate or Coffee

———

Sunday Noon
Pemmican (page 349)
Raisins
Candy Bar
Water or Reconstituted Powdered Milk

Packing

The intelligent use of available space is a prime requirement for any kind of wilderness travel, not only because you'll be able to carry more than if you had stuffed your gear helter-skelter wherever it happened to fit, but, more important, canoeing, back-packing, and horse-packing require precise placement and distribution of weight both for safety and comfort:

- An improperly packed rucksack will bite into your shoulders and give you blisters and backache after the first couple of miles.
- Unevenly weighted and poorly balanced panniers on a pack horse are cruel and dangerous on a steep trail.
- A canoe with weight too high or too far forward will handle like a truck and tip with the first mis-move.

A good rule to remember when packing is to keep the heaviest items on the bottom, be it the bottom of your rucksack, canoe, or pannier. If heavy gear rolls easily, it should be lashed down or wedged in place. This not only keeps the center of gravity low, it prevents sudden shifts in balance.

When packing a horse, you must keep the weight even on both sides of the packsaddle. And—this is important though it may seem incongruous—as you use up grub on the trail, you must replace the weight you remove with rocks. You might think you're doing the horse a favor by lightening his load. But you're not. Without weight, the panniers and harness sway and bounce as the horse jogs along, thus creating burns, blisters, and open sores.

Admittedly, it looks a bit strange at the end of a trip to see a packstring dumping out a big load of rock, but you'll be doing your horses a big favor. Besides, who's there to see you?

A canoe has its peculiarities, too. Not only must the weight be low, but its center of gravity should be moved one or two feet behind the middle of the craft. This raises the bow and digs in the stern, allowing for greater control and maneuverability.

Once fully loaded, equipment must be lashed to the canoe, both to prevent weight from shifting and loss of gear should the craft tip. The best way to lash gear is to first cover it with a waterproof plastic tarp. It not only keeps all your gear neatly tucked in, it can be used in camp later either as a dining fly or as shelter, the latter doing away with need for the luxury of a tent.

When loading a back pack, try to think of it as a seesaw with the place where the shoulder straps join the frame as the fulcrum. Heaviest gear should go in the bottom, light but space-taking gear like sleeping bags and clothes at the top. Pack it high on top and thin in the back.

With a properly loaded pack you should be able to bend slightly at the waist and feel the weight shift from your chest and shoulders to your back. This is precisely what happens as you walk; instead of the weight constantly resting on one part of your body, it will be distributed between two parts.

It makes hiking a lot more comfortable.

When packing actual foodstuffs, make sure they take up as little space as possible. If they're boxed when you buy them, transfer them from their containers to the smallest possible plastic bags, drop identifying labels and cooking instructions inside, and tie each opening tight shut with a wire twist or rubber band.

Repackaging foods in plastic bags instead of boxes allows them to conform to the spaces available in your pack. Additionally, the plastic eliminates any possibility of dry foods becoming wet either through rain or perspiration.

Even dry foods weigh a lot when all of them are in one place. So unless you can scatter them a lot, it's best to figure on stowing them in the bottom of your pack, pannier, or canoe. And so, since hikers and horses ford streams and canoes can take water, it's a good safeguard to put all the little plastic bags in one big waterproof plastic bag.

All, that is, except what you'll want to eat if your plans call for a meal while en route to where you're going. Make that one meal a cold one, a lunch-type repast, pack the things that will go into it in a separate bag, and stow it near the top of your gear.

The Cook and the Campsite

The wilderness cook's first consideration in choosing a campsite should be water. It isn't until you pitch camp a quarter-mile from the nearest stream that you realize just how much you depend upon it. Not only do thirst and cooking cause you to hit the bottom of the bucket in a hurry, there also are dishes, clothes, and hands to be washed. And, a cardinal rule of camping, there always must be plenty of water on hand in case the fire gets out of hand.

A camp close to running water is better than one close to a lake because the latter, being either slow or standing water, is a sure bet for insects. Getting away from the bugs will make cooking and eating a lot more enjoyable, even for the guy who has to lug the water. So, if a lake or pool is all that's available, look for a slight rise or hill and camp on top of it. If there is none, pitch camp at least twenty yards from shore.

The bull cook, being also camp doctor, will have to be sure the water used is fit to cook with and to drink. If not, he'll have to purify it (see page 117).

Food Storage

Most foodstuffs that you pack into the wilderness should require no refrigeration, but, whether they do or they don't, they all require some care. Cooked or uncooked, all foods give off odors that attract wild animals and insect pests. Some unrefrigerated foods will spoil if left in the path of the sun's rays.

So to solve both problems at once, place all your foodstuffs in plastic bags, seal them tight as can be, and hoist them as high in the air as you can, making sure that they're out of reach of a bear standing on its hind legs and that a tree-climbing animal can't get at them from above. In other words, let them swing high and free. This you can do either by stretching rope between trees and using it as you would a clothesline or by dangling the food bags from a tree limb via a short length of line.

Food should never be stored in a tent or on the ground or eaten in the former either, unless you want to risk having animals come in to do your housework for you, cleaning up not only spots where something spilled but everything else including clothes and canvas and what-have-you.

As for food and the containers that you're finished with, burn them and bury them. If they won't burn, at least scorch them. Do your dishes and housework immediately, not later, and you'll stay ahead of the marauders, thus keeping both food and campsite fresh and intact.

Keeping It Cool

You should bring nothing with you that requires refrigeration. However, you will make such acquisitions while in camp—for example, leftovers from the evening meal that you want to save for breakfast, fish that is caught in the morning but is not to be eaten until evening. What to do?

Don't fret. Nature has provided all that you'll need in the way of refrigeration.

Many high-country wilderness areas have snow fields—patches of snow that last from year to year and never completely melt. So, if you're near such a field, dig a hole in the ground or find a hollow log, fill it with snow, and, lo, you have an icebox. Place in it your perishables, cover the opening tightly so odors can't escape and to retard melting. A sheet of plastic under an insulating sleeping bag makes a perfect cover.

Another natural refrigerator is a mountain stream. Make a protective pool out of rocks where the current isn't so strong as to float your food and drink away, then immerse your foodstuffs. Bottles and cans may go in as is, but unprotected foods should be wrapped securely in a sealed plastic bag to prevent them from becoming waterlogged and flavorless.

Cooling by evaporation is a third standby. Water in a wet cloth doesn't really dry up, it breaks into tiny steam-like particles and mixes with air. Science calls this evaporation, a process that uses up heat for energy. So a wet cloth that's drying in a breeze will always be cool. You'll recall this is what makes the desert cooler described in Chapter 2 tick. You can't carry all the makings into the wilderness with you, but you can carry one—a burlap bag—because it's light and takes up little space. Wet it when you get to camp, put your food in it and hang it in a shady spot where the breeze can get at it. Douse it with more water whenever it starts to feel dry and your perishables will keep cool.

The Cooking Fire

Cooking over coals is standard procedure (and what this book is all about), whether you're at a backyard barbecue or deep in the primitive areas of the Northwest, Canada, or Alaska. But in the wilderness a cooking fire also has to provide heat and light. It's important, therefore, that you build it right.

But, most important, you must build it in a place that will not set the woods afire. If at all possible, build it on rock or sand, because what appears to be dirt may be humus several feet deep, and humus is like punk, like a wick on a candle. Light a fire on humus, and it can travel underground, popping up fifteen or twenty feet away to shoot flame up the hollow trunk of a dead tree.

If you must build your fire on soil, first clear a spot at least ten feet in diameter and as deep as necessary of all flammable material. Never build it in a stand of high, dry grass, or any grass for that matter if you can avoid it. Never build it either against a tree or the roots of a tree, a log, a stump, near a bush, or under overhanging branches.

No matter how many lovely, alluring illustrations you've seen on television, in books, and in magazines of fires laid in such picturesque places, they're all dangerous. Chances are they were set up purely for picture-taking purposes by a camera crew composed of experts on everything except woodsmanship.

And while we're on the subject of pretty pictures, you'll also see photos of Rube Goldberg–like arrangements of branches from which pots hang over the fire. Well, there are two things wrong with such pictures: (1) The branches would have to be green, thereby making it necessary to harm a tree in order to collect them, and (2) nine times out of ten the whole contraption, including dinner, will wind up in the fire. These exercises may be fun for photographers and Boy Scouts but not for hungry adults who have been stretching unused muscles all day.

Another attractive—and highly practical-appearing picture—is that of two logs, leveled off on the top, laid parallel to each other. Between them is a fire, and across them are a variety of pots and pans. Very pretty, very practical, but again we must ask: From whence came the green logs? Dig a slit trench instead or use rocks.

Now the various types of campfires, starting with the best (you'll find most of the basic, beginning steps in Chapter 2, "Camp Cooking"):

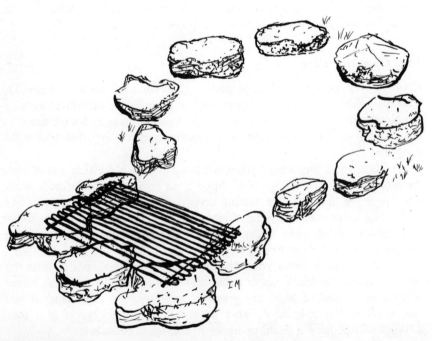

The keyhole lay

The Keyhole Lay

This undoubtedly is the most ingenious fireplace ever designed for the camp cook. Basically nothing more than a hole in the ground or wall of rocks in the shape of a keyhole, this fire provides light and cooking heat at the same time.

Using a keyhole lay is simple. Build a log-cabin or tepee fire in the large round part of the keyhole; then, as this feeder fire burns on, scrape the coals into the narrow part of the keyhole. In a short time you'll have plenty of coals for cooking and an ever-ready source of new coals should you require more. Feed fresh wood into the feeder fire only, never onto the coals.

The Log-Cabin Fire

This is the quickest way to get good cooking coals. Build your starter fire (see page 77) in the wide end of the keyhole lay and arrange your firewood in a crosshatch pattern, much like the construction of a log cabin.

The log-cabin fire

This arrangement assures good draft, and so the fire burns all at once, resulting in evenly distributed, evenly cured coals, which are moved into the cooking end of the keyhole.

The Tepee Fire

So called because the firewood is arranged in a conical shape, like an Indian tepee, this is a very efficient lay for a night fire, but it is not desirable as a cooking fire. The bright, hot flames soot up utensils and burn food, and the fire uses up wood too quickly.

The Winter Fire

If you are unable to clear snow away from the area in which you intend to build a fire, don't fret. Instead, build your fire above it simply by criss-crossing logs as if you were building a cabin or by stacking rocks until high

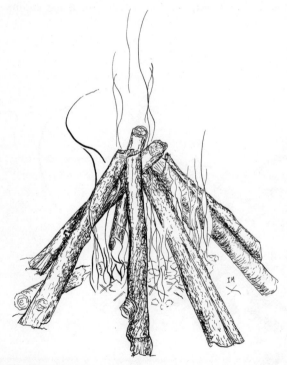

The teepee fire

enough to clear the snow. Fashion a platform atop it with wet branches, cover it with dirt or sand, and build your fire there.

Wind in the winter may be your worst enemy. Block it by erecting a tarp or snow wall to the windward side of your fire.

The Holding Fire

If for some reason you want to keep a fire going for a long time without the addition of more wood, dig a slit trench, line it with wet wood, then use a log-cabin fire to get it started.

The Squaw Fire

Those are the fires that will serve the bull cook's purposes in the most efficient and safest possible way. Unfortunately, however, too many novice campers build what the Indians, quite disparagingly, call the squaw fire. Just dropping a bundle of twigs and sticks in a random fashion is called that because Indian braves were skeptical of a squaw's ability to build a decent fire. The unarranged wood can either fall packed tightly, resulting in a slow, smoky fire, or fall loosely, in which case it burns hot, quick, and bright. In other words, the squaw fire is unpredictable and not really good for anything but trouble.

We tell you how to make it only so that you never will.

The Reflector Oven

What can be an important addition to the wilderness cook's bag of tricks is the reflector oven, especially since he can make one as needed instead of lugging a prefabricated one along.

Simply stretch heavy-duty aluminum foil over a tentlike frame of green willows.

Follow the directions for using it on pages 47–49, and you can bake bread, cookies, and biscuits just as easily as can the cook who uses a store-bought reflector oven.

Small Stoves

There are a number of different styles and weights—from a few ounces to a few pounds—of small stoves designed for carrying on wilderness trips. One, weighing a pound and a quarter, holds one pint of gas, naphtha, or benzene and will boil water very quickly, even at a high elevation. These little stoves carry too little fuel to be considered as anything more than a quick means of getting a pot of hot coffee or cooking an emergency meal when traveling for a day through a treeless, fuelless country.

The best of them, we think, is a one-burner alcohol stove that was developed for Arctic survival. It can be much more than just a convenience item on a journey into the wilderness. If you possibly can, pack one along with you.

Woodcutting

The use of an ax around the campsite makes for great reading in outdoor stories, but the truth of the matter is that the smart man uses it as little as possible.

Most wilderness campsites have plenty of firewood nearby that is small enough to be broken over your knee, thus doing away with the need of an ax, especially since this size wood makes the best cooking coals.

Don't get the idea that an ax isn't necessary around camp, because it is. But there are do's and don'ts that you have to abide by:

- Use only a single-bitted ax and make sure it's well sharpened.
- Always keep the ax out of the hands of an inexperienced camper, because his mistakes can be downright dangerous. The wilderness, miles from any doctor, is no place for him to gain experience.
- If wood has to be cut—for a night fire, for example—select logs no more than three or four inches in diameter and cut them to size with four swipes of a sharp ax, two swipes to a side. If you have to hack more than that, your ax isn't sharp enough.
- Check the edge occasionally to make sure the ax is as sharp as it ought to be—that is, sharp enough to bite into wood with every swing and never bounce or glance off into your shinbone.
- When using an ax, always wear tough shoes or hiking boots, keep a firm grip on the handle with both hands, and never let its head drop in back of you on your backswing. If you go beyond the twelve-o'clock position on your backswing, you're not only wasting energy, you're also losing valuable accuracy, which can be dangerous.
- Keep the ax sheathed whenever it is not in use. An ounce of prevention, you know.

And, last but not least, the best rule of all. By far the most sensible woodcutting tool is a collapsible saw. If you have room, take one along and use your ax mainly for driving stakes, clearing brush and such.

Starting a Fire on a Wet Day

How do you start a cooking fire no matter how wet or soggy the day? Exactly as you would on any other day, except that you must gather your tinder and kindling in slightly different ways:

- Small "sucker" branches grow on every tree, protected from the elements by the trunk itself and by an umbrella of larger upper branches. They always are dry enough and small enough to quickly catch fire.
- Birds and squirrels purposely build their homes in the driest spots possible, lining them with grasses, wood chips, and pine needles. So find an abandoned nest—the woods are full of them—and raid it. The interior will hold the quickest-burning material.
- If you are in pine country, gather up a supply of pine cones. They are full of pitch and burn hot and fast.
- The pure pitch that flows from wounds in a conifer, then hardens in drips that somewhat resemble candlewax, is another source of ready flame.
- Gather together lots of twigs no bigger around than a pencil. Wet or not, they will dry quickly in even a modest flame and quickly catch fire.

Now to build your fire. Wad a paper towel or a little bit of toilet paper loosely in the center of your fireplace. Surround it with a healthy handful of sucker branches, nest-makings, pine cones, or conifer pitch. Touch a lighted match to the paper. As soon as the tinder catches well, begin adding the pencil-sized kindling and keep adding them until you have a sizable bed of coals.

The job is done. Add your firewood, wet or dry, as you always would. It should catch fire no matter how wet it is.

One word of caution: Don't use resinous woods to build any fire unless you absolutely have to, because they pose a constant danger of sparks. So do paper, leaves, pine needles, and tiny twigs, but only when added to a well-established fire.

A good grill, one with crisscross wiring, helps dissipate sparks before they can make contact with tree, tent, or whatever. But the best possible protection is to be on the alert at all times.

Wet-Weather Shelter

If at all possible, no wilderness camp should be without a plastic tarpaulin. It is light, inexpensive, and can do many jobs. Its presence will be most appreciated in wet weather, when it can be used as a welcome cover for your dining area by day and for shelter at night.

The best weight to get is from six to ten mill. Six mill is light, ideal for back-packing, but won't withstand much of a wind. Ten mill will withstand the Four Horsemen of the Apocalypse if pitched right, but it's a little on the bulky side for carrying.

The standard size is 8 x 12 feet, enough to make a good dining or kitchen fly (see pages 8–10) or a comfortable shelter for two or three campers. Properly pitched and properly ventilated, such a shelter can be heated with a candle.

There are a number of ways to pitch a tarp. The lay of the land, wind direction, and location of your cooking fire will determine how and where you position it.

To erect it for shelter purposes follow these steps:

- Stretch a length of line between two trees that stand at least fifteen feet apart, first tying four knots in it: two of them where one edge of the tarp will meet the line, two on the other.
- In choosing the trees to which the supporting line will be fastened, if possible one of them should be a supple sapling. Pull it down a bit when fastening the line to it and thus eliminate any sagging that might take place when and if the line stretches since the tree will slowly move back to an upright position, thus taking up the slack.
- Pull your tarp over the line so that half hangs on each side, with the edges between the knots.
- Fasten the tarp to the line with spring-type clothespins, placing two of them between the knots. This will keep the tarp from bunching up on the line in a high wind.
- Place a smooth pebble in each of the four corners and centers of the tarp and wrap the plastic around them. Tie your supporting lines around the resultant knobs and then lash the other ends to pegs positioned to open the tarp into a V-shaped tent. Using pebbles in this way will make it unnecessary for you to puncture the plastic.

High-Altitude Cooking

Camp cooks who are unaware of the problems incurred in high altitudes— for example, it takes five minutes to cook a three-minute egg at 6,000 feet —can do a lot of cussing before figuring out why it is that their culinary masterpieces are getting to the table half-done.

But once you, the cook, recognize the problem, you'll have little trouble getting the knack of high-country cooking.

So, some things for you to always bear in mind when to mountain country you would go:

- The higher you are, the lower the temperature at which water will boil. Sea-level boiling temperature is 212 degrees Fahrenheit. A mile (5,280 feet) in the air, it drops to 201 degrees; at 10,000 feet, to 194 degrees.
- Lower boiling temperatures mean cooler cooking water; therefore boiled, steamed, and baked foods will cook more slowly and thus will need more water.
- Cakes and biscuits at 6,000 feet require nearly twice as much water as a recipe would call for at sea level.
- A two-pound fish that would take about fifteen minutes to steam in hot coals at sea level will take at least twenty minutes at 6,000 feet.
- When boiling food, make sure to replace the water as it boils away.
- Dehydrated foods (especially freeze-dried) that have to be soaked before cooking should be left in water longer than recommended, then cooked slowly.

Food for Free

One of the most enjoyable aspects of creative outdoor cooking is finding and using foods that you can catch or forage. Plant, animal, fin fish, and shellfish identification are interesting pastimes in themselves, but the quest takes on added meaning when you incorporate foods thus acquired into the camp menu.

They truly can turn an otherwise so-so outdoor meal into a culinary delight. Then, too, wild, fresh foods are always a welcome change from packaged and preserved camp fare, especially since they may add some valuable nutrition by providing variety and vitamins lacking in your regular fare.

It would be impossible to list every available wild food in the United States and Canada without compiling a separate book of huge proportions. But there are some general observations about forage foods available to the camper and camp cook, and they are in Chapter 4, "Foraging for Food and Water."

Emergency Cooking Measures

Three of the easiest things to do in the wilderness are to forget, break, and lose equipment. But there are many ways to improvise needed utensils. Among them, these:

- A green forked stick, its ends sharpened, makes a fine meat fork and a serviceable spatula.

- A piece of meat speared to the end of a pointed green stick will enable you to spit it (just as you would toast marshmallows) exactly as you like your wood-broiled meat to be.
- Three flat triangular rocks fitted against each other on a bed of coals more than make up for an AWOL grill. Be sure there is enough of a gap between them to allow air to circulate, wait a few minutes for them to get hot, then set your pots on them and start cooking. (Always take care in adding rocks to a fire that they are not porous and water-soaked. Such rocks are inclined to break up or explode.)
- The rock triangle also makes a good emergency griddle for steaks and fish, much better than the Indian method of placing them directly on the coals—something that you can do, too, if you don't mind a coating of ashes on your food.
- Collect some rocks, each of them about the size of a silver dollar, and build a log-cabin fire, interspersing the rocks with layers of wood. By the time the fire has burned down to coals, the rocks will be red hot. Pick them up by using two green forked sticks as you would chopsticks and drop them in any water-filled container. The water will quickly come to a boil and continue to boil with the addition of more rocks.
- Rocks heated in this manner are ideal for a number of cooking methods, not all of them emergency measures by any means. By burying hot rocks with a loosely sealed container of food you have an oven that keeps flavor where it belongs: in the food.
- Hot rocks in a shallow hole are just the ticket for a meal that must be simmered for a long period of time.
- Find a piece of dry hardwood and shape it into as flat and large a board as possible. Preheat it alongside your fire while steaking or splitting a fish that you've just caught. Grease the heated board well, fasten the fish to it with a couple of lengths of wire (or green vine if you have no wire), prop the board up close alongside the fire with sticks or stones, check it for doneness after about five minutes with a fork (if it flakes easily it's done), draw the wire away sideways so as not to break the flesh, and you have broiled fish that's guaranteed to be better than any you can buy in any gourmet restaurant.* You can have a planked steak this way, too, but you'll have to take the wire off and turn it.
- Pat a thin layer of clay or mud around a fish without bothering to remove the scales, making sure they're completely covered. Allow that first layer to dry enough to handle, then pack a heavy

* From *The Savor of the Sea,* by Dan Morris and Matilda Moore.

The outdoorsman's way of planking a fish steak—or any other kind of steak

coating of clay or mud around every inch of the package. Set it before the fire to dry, then bury it in hot coals. Figure on seven minutes to the pound, then take it from the ashes and break away the clay or mud. The skin and scales will come away with the wrapper.* Do the same with a bird and watch the feathers disappear.

• Some foodstuffs make good cooking utensils. For example, you can split a fairly large onion in two, remove the center, break an egg into the hole, set the onion on the coals and let it be for a minute or two. Then you eat both egg and utensil—a grand dish!

* From *The Savor of the Sea.*

- Anything that's hollow or that can be shaped into a container that does not leak will serve as a pot in which to make soup or boil water: a hole in a log, birch bark, even the skin of an animal.

In addition to all these emergency alternatives nature has given the wild-country camper to choose from, there is one that is the contribution of man—aluminum foil. If you have a roll of it with you, preferably heavy duty, your troubles are over.

Chapter 2 told of many ways of using it. Here are others:

- If a pot springs a leak, line it with foil and continue to use it for everything from boiling to frying.
- Turn up the edges of a piece of foil slightly, place it on a heated thin, flat rock, and you have a griddle.
- Wrap foods in foil and place them in a hole lined on the bottom and sides with hot silver-dollar–size rocks, heap more rocks on top of the package, and you're baking.

Cleaning Up

Camp cleanup in the wilderness is even more important than in tame country for many reasons, of which we need mention only one: bears.

The chance of trouble from these food-scrounging creatures increases the farther you get from civilization. So though we've said it before, we'll say it again: Wash your dishes immediately after every meal, burn your garbage thoroughly, and scorch and bury all noncombustibles deep.

Soap, of course, is the easiest and best thing to use for washing dishes. But if your supply has run out or if you didn't have room to bring any along, once again nature has provided two good abrasives—ash and sand.

Pure white, powdery wood ash contains the same chemical that is the base for every soap on the market. Use it with warm water and a handful of grass for a dishrag. For jobs that require scouring, a handful of sand does as good a job as any steel wool. Remember that any washing job will be easier if you first wipe grease off utensils. If you're traveling and haven't time to wash the dishes after a midday meal, at least wipe them clean.

When you break camp, clean the area thoroughly, pick up every scrap of debris, don't leave until everything looks as natural and untouched as the day you arrived.

And, of course, your fire should be dead out and thoroughly buried. (See page 84.)

What to Bring

The items that follow constitute an ideal list of the foodstuffs, utensils, and other camp aids that the wilderness camper should pack with him. However, you can take along only what you have room for. So it is for you and you only to decide what might be eliminated. We hope everything that we've said before will help you make the right decisions.

Foodstuffs

Bacon (slab)
Bouillon cubes or powder
Biscuit mix
Candy bars
Canned meats
Cheese
Coffee
Corn cake mix
Dehydrated baked beans
Dehydrated beef stew
Dehydrated gravy mix
Dehydrated macaroni and cheese
Dried fruits (be sure to include apricots and prunes)
Dried vegetables, including minced onions
Garlic powder
Hot chocolate mix
Jelly (individual plastic packages)
Jerky (pages 348–349)
Kool-Aid
Kraft dehydrated potato slices
Krusteaz pancake mix
Margarine
Maple syrup mix
Marshmallows
Oatmeal (instant)
Pemmican (page 349)
Pepper
Powdered eggs
Powdered milk
Pudding mix (instant)
Raisins
Salt

Shelled nuts, including peanuts
Sugar
Tang
Tea
Vinegar

Utensils and Camp Aids

Aluminum foil (heavy-duty)
Ax (single-bit)
Brillo soap pads
Burlap bag
Can opener
Candles
Canteen
Clothespins (spring-type)
Coffee pot (wide-bottomed)
Chapstick
Dishes
Eating tools (knives, forks, spoons)
First-aid kit
Fishing rod
Fishing-tackle kit (pocket-size)
Flashlight
Frying pan
Grill
Insect repellent
Iodine
Matches (see page 61)
Mess kit
Needle and thread
Paper towels or tissue
Plastic tarp
Pots and pans
Rope
Saw (collapsible)
Snake-bite remedy
Soap
Spatula
Swiss army knife

Camping-goods stores have mess kits that include knives, forks, and spoons, and they also have nesting sets of pots, pans, and frying pans.

A trail rod is best for the back-packing fisherman. It breaks down into a foot-long package that will stow neatly anywhere. A fishing rod on a camping trip is more than a sporting instrument, it's also necessary to the catching of a major food supply.

Rope is always needed around camp. For the packer, the rope that is unbeatable is parachute cord, because of its lightness and tremendous strength.

The Swiss army knife is ideal for the camper who wants to reduce carrying weight. It not only has standard items like knives, awls, and screwdrivers, it also manages to squeeze spoons, forks, and even a toothpick into its compact frame.

DESERT CAMPING

If you like camping and if you've never camped in the deserts of the Southwest, by all means try it. But make your first expedition only for a day. Then you will know if you want to stay for a few days or a few weeks or not at all. It will take you only that long—twenty-four hours—to either love or hate the desert.

The moving sun, the changing light, and the force of the wind may transform what at first appeared to be a dull, barren waste into a kaleidoscopic sea of enchantment, and you will want to stay forever. Or the shifting sun, light, and wind may change painted cliffs, sculptured rocks, and budding flowers into a glaring blob of shimmering oppressive heat, and you will not be able to get away fast enough. The beauty of the desert, like all beauty, is only in the eye of the beholder.

So go there for the first time only for a day. And you will know then if you love it or hate it.

Make that maiden one-day trip into the desert a picnic-cookout (see Chapter 6); take an extra supply of water with you and an emergency can of gasoline, too. Stick to the paved or hard-traveled roads but—just in case you should foolishly wander or otherwise go astray—also pack a man-sized round-bladed shovel. The chances are excellent that you'll need it to dig out of the sand.

There are campgrounds and picnic grounds in the desert, just as there are everywhere in the country. Make inquiries through the usual channels; select the one most convenient for you; head straight for it, resisting all temptations to explore side roads; and when you get there, stay there. Then do whatever exploring you may want to do on foot, but never out of sight of the road, the picnic area, and your car.

For that kind of toe-dipping voyage into the land of sand and sage, your family car will do fine—but only if you keep the wheels on a hard road, if not all of them, at least the two rear ones.

Protect yourself well from the sun—full, wide-brimmed hat; jeans or levis, not skirts or shorts; shoes at least ankle-high; sleeves rolled down.

Pitch a dining fly if you like and do during the day whatever the spirit moves you to do. But be sure to stay and see the sunsets. Both of them! The one to the West with the sky ablaze with flaming gold, red, brown, silver, purple, and bronze. The reflection to the East with the sky a pastel pasture of pink and blue and lavender and cream. Or go early and see the sunrise.

Then go home, either never again to return or so excited, so enthralled, so eager that you will count the minutes until you do.

It is the next trip—the camping trip that may last for days or weeks—for which you really must plan.

There are two kinds of desert in the United States: low desert, mainly sand at sea level or below; high desert, rugged, rocky, rising terrain that not only has sand but sometimes also snow.

Both have their attractions, both have their campgrounds. Which to choose is up to you. Or, better still, camp in one and take day trips from there into the other.

The fundamentals of camping in the desert are, generally speaking, the same as anywhere else. But there are some important aspects that are different. Let's look at them one at a time.

Choosing a Campground and a Campsite

Consider yourself a tenderfoot when planning your first few desert camping trips. Don't venture off the beaten path until you are sure you are ready. Consider that wilderness, which it is. Beautiful but dangerous wilderness.

Commercial and government-supervised improved campgrounds are steadily increasing in number throughout the deserts of southern California, New Mexico, Texas, Arizona, and parts of Nevada, Utah, and Colorado. Plan on camping in one of them instead of risking your life wandering around on your own.

As for the selection of the exact site on which you will make camp, be sure that it is on the highest possible spot of ground. Stay away from gullies, arroyos, dry riverbeds, washes, and other depressions; it does not rain often on the desert, but when it does, the rains come down in torrents, and flash flooding will fill them with raging waters, often more than twenty feet deep.

Vehicle and Gasoline

The family car, station wagon, camper, or trailer is okay, so long as you stay on hard roads. When you wander off you invite trouble because you will be driving on sand. So, unless you are certain you will drive only to an improved campground and nowhere else, you should embark upon a desert journey only in a high-axle, four-wheel-drive vehicle.

Gasoline stations are few and often very far between on the desert. So never venture into the desert without a full or almost full tank of gas, always carry a five-gallon jerry can of gasoline with you, and try always to know where the nearest gas station is, marking it in your mind or on your map just as the old-time desert rats did water holes.

Always carry a round-bladed shovel with at least a three-foot handle in your desert vehicle to help dig you out of the sand if you should bog down.

Water

Water must be every desert voyager's prime consideration. Water is never easy to find, and often the supply will be limited even in improved camp-grounds.

You must, therefore, always plan on bringing your own and then using it sparsely, wisely. The next chapter will tell you how to find water, but regard what you will learn there as only measures to be resorted to in case of emergency.

Better still, always do this:

- Carry as much water as you possibly can with you, using con-tainers in which it will retain its maximum sweetness and coolness.
- If possible, when you get to camp, transfer it to a large canvas bag that you can hang in the breeze.
- When traveling by car, fill a couple of desert water bags—they're made of canvas and somewhat resemble a Basque shepherd's wine bag—and sling it on the outside of your vehicle to keep it cool.
- At camp, learn not only where the nearest watertaps are but also where the nearest gasoline station is and find out if it has water that you can use if necessary.

- Do what seasoned desert dwellers have always done: Include lots of canned tomatoes in your larder. The liquid in them is water. Use it as such. Drink it from the can if need be. Never drain it off.
- Take little or no dehydrated foods into the desert with you. Include them only if you are sure there will be enough water available to reconstitute them.

Refrigeration

Since ice is made of water, ice is therefore also in short supply on the desert. Therefore:

- Take as much as you can with you in your camp coolers. Take it frozen in containers from which you can drink it when it melts.
- Take with you as much hard-frozen food as possible.
- Learn immediately upon arrival if and where ice can be easily obtained.
- If necessary, build a desert cooler as described on page 53.
- If you pack any dried foods along, remember that some of them will not keep well in a hot climate and must be refrigerated: powdered eggs and dried whole milk, for example. Carefully read the labels on all packages of dehydrated foods before packing them along.

Wood and the Cooking Fire

Wood also is in short supply in the desert. Don't count on it for cooking. You must pack to camp with you one of the good cooking stoves discussed in Chapter 2.

4—Foraging for Food and Water

Are you one of those millions of Americans longing to rediscover the comforting outdoor world of Thoreau and Huck Finn? Well, if so, you need not dream nostalgically about the barefoot boy whose lips were redder still, kissed by strawberries from the hill, because you, too, can reach into nature's larder and help yourself.

You, too, can be a food forager.

There are foods that are easy for anyone to seek, to find, to cook (if they need cooking), and to eat. But there also are those, which, if you are to take and eat them safely, require that you be on close speaking terms with old Mother Nature.

We'll tell you in this chapter mostly about some of the easy ones. But we'll also point out some of the precautions that you should take if ever you're stranded or lost in a wilderness area and must eat what is growing around you in order to survive.

Water

Don't laugh. We're starting with water because it is unquestionably the most important element of all those you someday might be searching for, whether you're on a wilderness hunting trip, lost in the desert or adrift at sea. In fact, the U.S. Air Force Survival Manual has this to say about it:

> You can get along for weeks without food, but you can't live long without water, especially in hot areas where you lose large quantities of water through sweating.

Even in cold areas your body needs two quarts of water a day to maintain efficiency. Any lower intake results in loss of efficiency. If you delay drinking, you will have to make it up later on.

Your system demands it. So it is important that you find water quickly, bearing in mind these pointers:

- Generally, but not always, the farther you are from man and his civilized pollution, the safer the water will be to drink. However, domestic animals, wild animals, or a putrefying carcass lying just out of sight can contaminate clear-looking water without your ever knowing it.
- The safest water you can drink if you are in strange country is often the clear, cold spring water that bubbles up from deep down in the earth.
- Rainwater collected directly in clean containers generally is safe to drink.
- If you're in doubt about the purity of water, boil it for five minutes and thereby kill any disease germs that might make you sick. Boiling might cause an objectionable taste. If so, aerate the water by pouring it back and forth from one clean container to another for a couple of minutes to get rid of the flat taste. A pinch of salt added to a gallon of water will also help make it more palatable.
- If for some reason you cannot or will not build a fire, three drops of 2 per cent tincture of iodine (six drops if water is cloudy) added to a quart of water will make it safe to drink in an hour.
- Cloudy or muddy water can be cleaned of foreign particles by filtering it through layers of cloth or by pouring it through a foot of clean sand. Or just letting muddy water sit for an hour or so will settle out a good deal of the suspended dirt.

If you're camping in arid or semiarid country, locating water can be a difficult but not insurmountable problem. Water means life for both animals and vegetation, so look for lush stands of brush, grass, and trees, particularly willow and cottonwood, and watch for game trails. Animals go to water twice a day; therefore, the paths to their water supply are always well worn.

Once you locate water in dry country, it's always a good idea to purify it no matter how far you may be from civilization. The sheer volume of wild animals that are bound to be using the waterhole guarantees some degree of pollution.

Even if there is no water visible at the surface, trees and green grass always mean water nearby. So feel for a spot where subsurface soil is damp to the touch, then dig a hole two or three feet deep. If it doesn't fill with water naturally, place a can or kettle in the bottom and stretch a plastic tarp over the top of the hole, securely anchoring the edges with rock or mounds of soil. Now take a flat-sized rock, lay it in the center of the tarp so that it forms an inverted cone over the kettle, and wait.

The heat of the sun will leech the water from the soil, the evaporated water will condense and bead on the underside of the plastic, the beads will become droplets that run down the plastic to the lowest point—under the rock—and then drop into the can or kettle. This evaporation method will not by any means produce an instant deluge, but it can provide enough water to keep a man from dying of thirst.

A word to remember: Don't dig needlessly or too fast, because the more you exert yourself the more you'll sweat, thereby losing what you're working so hard to find.

Another good place to dig for water is in the lowest spot you can find in the bottom of a dry stream bed. Dig slowly and feel the soil every six or eight inches. Chances are that by the time you get down about two feet it will begin to feel damp to the touch. So dig some more. By another couple of feet the odds are good that by now you'll have exposed a trickle. If, in another foot or so, the trickle doesn't become more of a rush, hollow out a hole just big enough around to fit a can or kettle into. Wait long enough, and it should fill up with water.

Other emergency sources of water:

- Look for wet spots at the foot of bluffs; if there is going to be any water around, this is where it will be, since water runs downhill.
- Whenever there is a bend in a dry riverbed, look for signs of moisture against the base of the inner—or concave—bank.
- If at sea in a boat, apply the same evaporation principle described a few paragraphs back: the kettle at the low spot, the tarp over the top, a rock or some other weight to form a cone in its center. Sea water thus condensed will turn sweet.
- Chew or mash the flesh of cactus plants and thus obtain enough moisture to save your life.

Animals and Birds

At one time, game was considered the main source of camp meat, but increased destruction of the American outdoors by greedy men has severely limited popular and familiar edible birds and mammals that can be considered available camp food the year round.

As for the animals that most people consider good eating, they all now come, and rightly so, under the aegis of state fish and game departments and are protected by seasons and limits. You can help yourself, unless it is a matter of life and death, only at specified times of the year.

There are, however, many less familiar, less popular sources of meat. Some are not covered by game laws in any state; others are protected in some states but not in all. People who know consider these creatures edible and even delicious, while others protest they'd rather die than eat them. We suspect, however, that if it came to a matter of survival they'd taste good to anyone.

So if you don't know where your next meal is going to come from, set a trap for one of these generally unprotected creatures and live to camp another day. In the following list the italicized animals are those we, or people whose judgment we trust, have sampled and considered better eating: coyote, bobcat, *porcupine,* fox, *raccoon, rabbit, possum, squirrel, frogs* (don't eat toads), some *snakes, turtles,* lizards, and birds like crow, *starling,* magpie, and *sparrow.*

Wherever you go, you'll find people who can fill you in on exactly what's to be had locally in the way of both game and nongame animals, birds, and so on, where to go to get them, and what the hunting laws are in that particular area. Game wardens are an excellent source for all-round hunting information, as are federal, state, and local park officials and owners or clerks in sporting-goods stores. Not only will they tell you what good-eating creatures can be taken without permit, but if you're friendly, lots of them will gladly give you their favorite recipe.

As a matter of fact, there are some excellent recipes of this type included in the recipe section of this book, all of them tested in the field by Norman Strung.

Some Sensible Precautions

All wild game should be cooked for safety, but that doesn't mean over-cooking or cooking at too high a heat. That will destroy flavor, texture and —most important—vitamins. However, just as with certain domestic meats, there are wild meats that must be cooked until they are well done:

- Cook the meat of all rodents—particularly hares, rabbits, and squirrels—until it is well done, just as you would cook pork. These animals might carry a disease called tularemia, to which man is susceptible, but cooking their meat until it is well done makes it safe to eat. Thoroughly cleanse your hands, knife, and utensils after cleaning these creatures.
- Play it safe and do not eat any small game, either animal or bird,

that is listless and too easily caught or if it has spotted or otherwise unhealthy-looking liver.

- Bears may have trichinosis, so cook their meat as you would
cook pork.
- Bear liver has too strong a concentration of Vitamin A for man
to tolerate, so dispose of it along with the entrails and any other
discards.

Poisonous Creatures to Avoid

Whether you're foraging for food either for fun or for survival, camping,
hiking, or picnicking, there are only a very few of nature's creatures you
are in any danger of being poisoned by.

To make sure that you won't run afoul of one of them, observe this
one simple rule: Steer clear!

These creatures don't attack out of malice, only in self-defense.
If you don't cause a situation where they have to defend themselves, you'll
be safe. People who live where there are snakes and spiders and other
similarly poisonous creatures quickly acquire the habit and the knack of
avoiding them, of not getting too close to them, of not accidentally touching them. Acquire the habit, too, and you won't have to spoil your fun
worrying. Here's how:

- Never reach into a hole with your bare hand or foot. As far as a
spider or scorpion is concerned, your shoe is a hole. So shake it
out before putting it on.
- Never turn over a board or a rock with your hand. Use a stick
or a well-booted foot.
- Look before you leap, whether it's over a log, a rock, a fence,
or into a stand of deep grass.
- Don't go swimming or wading in waters infested with poisonous
snakes (or alligators or crocodiles).

Probably the best way of learning to identify snakes, spiders, *et al.*
is at a zoo or museum of natural history, but taking the proper precautions
is far more important than being able to identify what bit you. Remember
that!

And remember this, too. You're in much greater danger of being
hit by a car, breaking your back in the bathtub, getting mugged on a city
street, and getting cancer from smoking cigarettes than you are of being
poisoned while enjoying the outdoors. So don't, for goodness sake, let fear
of snakes or what-have-you spoil your fun or scare you away from the
relaxation of outdoor, away-from-it-all living.

Fish and Shellfish

Fishing is a sport, a fine sport, but it is also the easiest, the nicest, the best way of foraging for food.

You'll fare well, too, if you carry with you a fishing rod and tackle on every trip that you take into the outdoors. Not only will you never go hungry, you'll eat well, because fish, besides being marvelously healthy, is also a joy to the taste if fresh-caught and properly cooked.

Almost everywhere there is water, there are fish. How you catch them is up to you. Many books have been written telling all the techniques. In fact, Dan has written a couple of them, too. But if the truth be known, for every man armed with the latest in rod and reel and lure and hook, there is a small boy who catches just as many fish with cane pole and a bent pin. Maybe not so big a fish, maybe not so fighting a fish, but still a fish that's fun to catch and good to eat.

Almost anything will do for bait—a worm, a grasshopper, a bug. If you cannot find one of them, use a small bread ball, a bright bit of cloth, even a Green or Plaid trading stamp! Fish are curious creatures; they'll bite on anything that attracts their attention.

So if you're in wilderness country and there is the slightest possibility that somehow, sometime, you will find yourself lost, carry always in your pocket with you nothing more than about a twenty-foot length of mason's line and a small fish hook, and you'll never go hungry.

Even easier to come by in case of emergency than fin fish are two very common and very tasty species of shellfish: clams, where there is salt water, and crayfish, where the water is fresh.

To locate clams, just wade around barefooted in shallow salt water. When you feel a hard lump under foot, reach down quickly and root it out with your fingers. If it is not a clam, it may be an oyster, or if you're foraging in what we know as civilized country, it may be a beer can. About that, you and we can see to it that local authorities really crack down on litterbugs while not contributing to the litterbug mess ourselves, either on land or in the water.

If the water is too cold for wading, walk along the shore a few feet above the waterline, tapping the hard sand with a piece of driftwood as you go. The thud will start the clams, if there are any, scurrying for the water, and small air holes will mark their trail. Place yourself between the holes and the water and start digging, but be quick. Clams may be silent, but they are not slow.

Discard any clams that aren't tightly closed or that don't shut tight when you tap them. Scrub the shells clean, and they're ready to be either cooked or eaten raw.

Because of pollution, foraging for clams in strange country poses a threat of hepatitis. But the chances of its presence is lessened the farther you get from its causes, which mainly are industries and municipalities that regard the waters around them as dumping grounds for waste.

Crayfish are almost everywhere in the United States. If you don't know them by that name, you may know them as crawdad, crawfish, freshwater crab, or freshwater lobster. You'll recognize them easily. They're usually grayish green, they're from three to six inches long, they look quite a bit like a lobster but are mostly all tail, and they can be found in from a few inches to a foot or two of water and sometimes in no water at all.

Look sharply for them, and you'll spot them in drainage ditches, in mud, under rocks, and under logs. Then it's just a matter of picking them up—by the back to avoid the claws. If they're in wading water you can catch them with a makeshift net of any kind that's baited with almost anything at all that, to a crayfish, would be considered edible. Just hold the net still, and they'll come crawling in. Or if you have no net, use that mason's line and hook we suggested you always carry with you.

The meat of the crayfish is mainly in the tail. You cook it as you would lobster.

Scallops, crabs, abalones, oysters, and mussels also are good forage foods, though perhaps not so plentiful or so widely distributed around the country as are clams and crayfish. Scallops and oysters can be taken as you would clams. Crabs are obtained by lowering a baited net or hook and line to the water bottom and waiting. Look for mussels clinging to rocks and other matter. At certain times of the year, mussels that are taken from Pacific waters should not be eaten because they have fed on poisonous substances. Abalone, which can be found mainly in California, must be pried loose from the rocks to which it clings.

Avoiding Trouble

You have little to worry about in the way of food poisoning when eating fish caught in the temperate waters of the continental United States and Canada. However, there are precautions to take in tropical waters, a subject we'll come to in a moment.

Shellfish, however, are susceptible to pollution, mainly man-made, and the best way to avoid trouble is by not eating shellfish taken from waters that surround highly populated and highly industrialized areas and, for that matter, isolated waters that the federal government uses as dumping grounds for poison gases and nuclear waste.

A good rule to go by: If the water is biologically safe enough to swim in, then its shellfish generally is safe enough to eat.

Always observe these dos and don'ts:

- Eat only shellfish that is alive until the moment it is cooked. It should look healthy and smell fresh. The shells of bivalves should be tightly closed.
- On the Pacific coast, make local inquiry as to when to avoid eating mussels.
- Put mussels in a pail of water and discard any that float.
- Pry abalone loose from rocks only at low tide, unless you're a really good swimmer and diver, and then only with a tire iron, heavy screwdriver, or some such instrument. Never attempt to use only your hands, because the abalone's powerful muscles can clamp down on your fingers and pin you while the tide comes in.
- Gut fish the moment you catch them. Keep them cool and out of the sun until it is time to cook them; then give them a more thorough cleaning, scale them, and rinse them.
- Don't handle jellyfish. Some of them sting.

Avoiding Trouble in Tropical Waters

Generally speaking, such a heading as this would automatically rule out waters surrounding the continental United States. But we include it because (1) through some strange quirks of nature, the waters around Florida and states that border the Gulf of Mexico, though always warm, sometimes suddenly turn tropical; (2) tropical fish sometimes stray far north of their native bailiwicks; (3) Hawaii is part of the United States; and (4) boatmen can and do set forth for such places as Baja California and the Caribbean.

We'll tell you how to avoid trouble by quoting from a highly reliable source, the U.S. Air Force Survival Manual:

> There are no simple rules for telling undesirable [poisonous] fish from the desirable ones. Often those considered edible in one locality may be unwholesome elsewhere, depending on the place, their food, or even the season of the year. Cooking does not destroy the poison.
> Large barracudas can cause serious digestive illness; yet those less than three feet long have been eaten with safety. The oilfish has a white, flaky, rather tasty flesh which is very poisonous. This fish of the Southwest Pacific and all great sea eels should be carefully avoided. Never eat entrails or eggs of any tropical fish.
> Undesirable fish have certain characteristics:
> Almost all have round or box-like bodies with hard, shell-like skins covered with bony plates or spines. They have small, parrot-like

mouths, small gill openings; and the belly fins are small or absent. Their names suggest their shapes—puller fish, file fish, globe fish, trigger fish, trunk fish.

.   .   .

Reefs are no place for bare feet. Coral, dead or alive, can cut them to ribbons. Seemingly harmless sponges and sea urchins can slip fine needles of lime or silica into your skin, and they will break off and fester. Don't dig them out; use lime juice, if available, to dissolve them. The almost invisible stonefish will not move from your path. It has thirteen poisoned spines that will cause you agony and death. Treat as for snakebite.

Don't probe with your hands into dark holes; use a stick. Don't step freely over muddy or sandy bottoms of rivers and seashores; slide your feet along the bottom. In this way you will avoid stepping on sting rays or other sharp-spined animals. If you step on a sting ray, you push its body down, giving it leverage to throw its tail up and stab you with its stinging spine. A sting ray's broken-off spine can be removed only by cutting it out.

Cone shell and long, slender, pointed terebra snails have poison teeth and can bite. Cone snails have smooth, colorful mottled shells with elongate, narrow openings. They live under rocks, in crevices of coral reefs, and along rocky shores of protected bays. They are shy and are most active at night. They have a long mouth and a snout or proboscis which is used to jab or inject their teeth. These teeth are actually tiny hypodermic needles, with a tiny poison gland on the back end of each. This action is swift, producing acute pain, swelling, paralysis, blindness, and possible death in four hours. Avoid handling all cone snails.

Handle the big conchs with caution. These snails have razor-sharp trap doors, which they may suddenly jab out, puncturing your skin in their effort to get away. Don't use your hands to gather large abalones and clams. Pry them loose with bars or wedges; they will hold you if they clamp down on your fingers.

.   .   .

In crossing deeper portions of a reef, check the reef edge shadows for sharks, barracudas, and moray eels. Morays are angry, vicious, and aggressive when disturbed. They hide in dark holes among the reefs.

In saltwater estuaries, bays, or lagoons, man-eating sharks may come in very close to shore. Many sharks have attacked in shallow water on bathing beaches in the tropic seas. Barracudas have also made such attacks. Usually sharks four feet long and shorter are timid. Beware, however, of all larger ones, including hammerheads. They are potentially dangerous. Not all sharks show fins above the water.

Edible Wild Plants

Many books have been written on the romantic subject of the gathering and the eating of wild mushrooms. Therefore it should be high on this book's list, too. And it is. But not on a list of wild plants to forage and to eat. Wild mushrooms are first on our list of plants to avoid, to shun like the plague.

More than a hundred Americans die every year from mushroom poisoning. Sure, they thought the mushrooms they'd picked were safe to eat. And most of them probably were. But even among stands of definitely nonpoisonous mushrooms there may very easily be just one poisonous one.

And, far worse than the one rotten apple in the barrel, which can only make you sick, sometimes just one poisonous wild mushroom will kill.

It would take an entire book to tell you how to positively, absolutely identify that one poisonous wild mushroom from all those nonpoisonous ones. So, since this book's intent is only to tell you how to more fully enjoy food cooked and, in this chapter, found in the outdoors, we repeat: Leave wild mushrooms where you find them, in the ground. Avoid them. Shun them.

And we'll get on to the definitely good things to be found in our fields and forests.

Thousands of different wild plants are known to have been used by American Indians for foods, beverages, medicines, clothing, fibers, and many other essentials to life and health.

Even in the absence of wheat—a grain not native to the United States—the Indians still had bread. Never having heard of wheat, they never missed it. Rather, one of their most important foods was the nut (acorn) from a number of different kinds of oak trees still abundant today. Indians removed the kernels from the shells, ground them into meal, soaked it for days in a running stream to purge it of its bitter tannic taste, then baked it into a form of bread.

So, too, they did with many other of nature's wild-growing things, in the process creating the forerunners of many well-known and delicious recipes still much eaten in America today, although to most of us their origins are quite unknown.

It would take many books to tell you all you would need to know to safely forage and cook many of those early-American wild plants that, like the acorn, still grow today. So rather than try, here now is a rundown of some of the growing things you can forage for without running the risk of being poisoned—as with wild mushrooms. These things are familiar to all of us, either because many of them grow in our own yards or because we buy their similar-appearing domestic counterparts and sometimes even the wild plants themselves in our stores every day.

Blackberries, Raspberries, Strawberries

There are a number of different species of blackberries, raspberries, and strawberries growing wild. They resemble the domestic varieties you have been buying so closely that you will recognize them at once. Use them just as you would the domestic berries. And be prepared for a flavor treat.

Rose Berries (Rose Hips)

The wild rose is much plainer than is her domesticated cousin with her multitudes of petals. But the thorny stem and the shape of the leaves are quite similar. The berry is the round pod that forms after the blossom dies. You do not have to go into the wilderness to find them because the roses in your garden may also have these pods. These little fruits are red-colored when ripe. They are an excellent supplement for survival fare because they are very high in Vitamin C. Just break open the round pod, discard the inner seeds, and eat the outer covering.

Dandelions

Instead of cursing the dandelions that start poking up through the soil in your yard in the early spring, you should consider them a vitamin-rich volunteer vegetable garden that requires no work at all on your part. Except to pick them and cook them.

Dandelions are so nourishing that the ancients thought of them as lifesavers. Today they are still considered an excellent survival food and a tasty supplement for wilderness camp fare, not only because of their goodness but also because they have a long season and are found throughout the entire country.

If you've had the misfortune of, at one time or another, foraging and finding wild greens only to have them taste tough and somewhat blah, try very young dandelion leaves and unopened flowers, don't overcook them, and we're sure you'll change your mind. (The unopened flowers are sort of a crown nestled down in the root, waiting to spring up at the right moment.) That is when dandelions are at their tastiest best. But if they are older and the leaves are starting to get bitter, you can still enjoy them merely by changing the cooking water once or twice.

Nourishing dandelion roots are well known as a survival food. But also, and this is not quite so well known, they brew up an excellent cup of tea. Here's how. Dig deep around the root to take them out of the ground; wash them and chop them into tiny bits; roast them in a pan or can directly over a fire until dark brown; transfer half a teaspoon of the nuggets to a pot; cover with a cup of warm water and simmer until it acquires the flavor you like, weak or strong. It makes a very warming, a very nutritious, drink.

Experiment with dandelions. And talk to people, both young and old, about ways to use them.

Old-timers will tell you how to make excellent dandelion wine.

Wild Asparagus

You'll have to look closely to discover young, tender, wild asparagus shoots sticking up from well-drained, loose soil in river bottoms, beside irrigation ditches, in fence corners and hedgerows. If and when you see them, you'll recognize them at once because they look like the domestic variety you pay so much for at the grocery store.

Cut them off right down at the ground, wash them, and cook them immediately.

As wild asparagus grows older, the plant surrounds itself with a lovely, feathery foliage that's very easy to spot; but by then the stalk is too tough to be good eating, although it is palatable.

Cattails

Cattails are found standing tall almost everywhere there is water. The cattail is a wild plant but, because of its unique and striking appearance, we are all familiar with it, although perhaps by another name: cossack asparagus, wild corn, flag, cat-o'-nine tails, rush, and bullrush. Whatever the name, it is a treasure trove of delicious food for both the camper and the lost. And in every season it is a different dish and has a different taste.

In the spring, when they are young, the first foot or more of the stem is good eating. Just peel and eat raw or cook as you would asparagus.

In the early summer, gather the yellow-green flower spikes before they become heavy with pollen, husk them as you would corn, and cook them in the same way. For survival, eat them plain; in camp, load them with butter or margarine and have a feast.

Later, when they're pollen-laden, harvest the spikes, rub them through a fine sieve, and use the powder as you would flour for biscuits and pancakes. Some people like it best with regular flour added in a 1-to-1 proportion.

In the fall and winter, dig up the roots, wash and peel, dry well, and grind into a meal or—better still—just add the peeled root to boiling water and serve as a vegetable.

Watercress

Wherever there is cold, clean water you will find watercress—there and in any vegetable store or supermarket. In the latter, you pick a bunch from the display and pay the price. In the former, you pick it from a far nicer display, floating and swaying in the water as gracefully as a ballet dancer, and the price you pay at the most is a pair of wet feet.

All of us know watercress mainly as a garnish or as a salad green, but it also is quite good made into a soup or cooked as a vegetable.

A word of caution: In gathering watercress, don't confuse it with water hemlock, which often grows nearby and is poisonous. The hemlock is taller and very roughly resembles the carrot. The base of its stem is swollen, and several tuberous, irregularly surfaced taproots are attached to it in a cluster. Each fleshy root is an inch or two long. The leaves have toothed edges.

Seaweed

Oriental peoples use nourishing seaweed in many ways. Cook it and eat it as you would spinach. Since some seaweeds are violent purgatives, however, we suggest that you do your first foraging in an Oriental food shop until you learn about the different kinds and how to prepare and rate them.

Nuts

Edible wild nuts include black walnuts, pecans, hazel nuts, and pine nuts. You're probably familiar with all of them. Pine nuts, also called piñon nuts and sold in candy stores as Indian nuts, are among the most flavorful of all available wild nuts and are quite easily gathered. First, of course, you must find a pine tree. Then round up ripe cones and shake them. The nuts will come falling out.

Although most nuts can be eaten raw, boiling or roasting makes them more digestible. They are a high-energy, delicious food and a mighty welcome addition to camp fare because they add nutrition and flavor to so many dishes: desserts, stuffing, bread, vegetables and cereals. They are also an excellent meat substitute.

Precautions against Poisons

When foraging for edible wild plants, it's most important that you know all that you possibly can about not only those you are seeking but also about those you may encounter that are poisonous either internally or externally.

Not only must you know about the *whole* plant but also about its parts, because sometimes one part will be perfectly safe to eat while another part of the same plant will not be. (This is true of domestic plants, too. The stem of the rhubarb plant, for instance, is delicious when baked in a pie, but the rhubarb leaf, according to the Cornell University Extension Bulletin *Common Poisonous Plants,* can be deadly.)

Quite often, too, poisonous plants will grow side by side with the edible ones. For example, water hemlock may be found near watercress.

The safest thing that you, the first-time forager, can do is to stick to the common plants that we've described in this chapter. Then, if the foraging bug gets you and you want to enlarge your repertoire, do your homework.

It can be a great family hobby—starting with a warning to children never to pick or eat anything without first showing the plant, berries, or roots to you. Buy sets of nature identification cards and take them camping with you. Let the children see how many trees and shrubs they can identify right around your campsite while you put the finishing touches on dinner. Available for the asking at most state agricultural colleges are illustrated pamphlets describing the common poisonous plants of an area.

Hopefully, you'll avail yourself of such background information before venturing forth on a food-foraging expedition. But, if you are lost and your survival depends on eating plants you are unfamiliar with, remember these things:

Internally Poisonous

- Many grasses and their seeds can be safely eaten (wild rice, for example, is a grass seed) except when the seeds are infected with poisonous ergot, a black or purplish growth that somewhat resembles an elongated seed.
- When picking unfamiliar nuts or berries, first try to discover whether or not other creatures have dined on them. If they have, you'll be reasonably safe if you eat them too. Birds and bears love berries, and generally, if they can eat them, so can you.

Water hemlock (*New York State College of Agriculture, Cornell Extension Bulletin #538,* Common Poisonous Plants, *by John M. Kingsbury*)

Two ways to tell: partially eaten berries still on the stem; berries or berry coloring in bird or bear droppings.

- Boiling most plants and discarding the water makes them edible. Try eating a tiny bit of the cooked plant. Hold it in your mouth for a few minutes. If it tastes strong or bitter or burns or stings your mouth, don't swallow it.
- *Boiling does not destroy poison in mushrooms. Be on the safe side. Don't eat wild mushrooms.*
- Don't eat any plant that oozes a milky substance when you break it open unless you are certain from past experience that it is harmless.

Externally Poisonous

Whether you forage for foods or not, you should learn to recognize plants that are poisonous to the touch before you ever venture anywhere on an outing. Nationally famed Fire Island and parts of Jones Beach, for example, are covered with poison ivy, which, around the country, runs neck and neck with poison oak as a skin irritant.

Other names for these most common of all poisonous plants include poison creeper, climbing sumac, and three-leaved ivy. Read and heed what a New York State College of Agriculture booklet (Cornell Extension Bulletin 1154), by John M. Kingsbury, has to say about them:

Poison ivy and poison oak differ mainly in the degree of lobing of leaflets. Both are woody plants showing tremendous variation in

Variations of poison oak and poison ivy (*New York State College of Agriculture, Cornell Extension Bulletin #1154, by John M. Kingsbury*)

Poison ivy (*New York State College of Agriculture, Cornell Extension Bulletin #1154, by John M. Kingsbury*)

growth pattern and leaf characteristics (particularly size and waviness or toothing of the edge of the leaflet). Growth may be either as an erect shrub or as a vine climbing by aerial rootlets on fences, walls, or trees, or the plant may lie prostrate on the ground. Leaves are arranged alternately (one at a node) and are compound, with three leaflets.

The leaves may have a glossy or dull surface or may be even somewhat hairy, especially on the lower surface. . . . Under conditions that are poor for its growth, poison ivy may form small, spindly, trailing branches which are well hidden in the other vegetation. Be especially watchful of these.

The alternate leaves, each with three leaflets, will help you to identify poison ivy and poison oak. In autumn and winter the clusters of white berry-like fruits make identification certain.

Other names for poison sumac include swamp sumac, poison elder, poison dogwood, poison ash, thunderwood. During the first year, poison

Poison sumac (*New York State College of Agriculture, Cornell Extension Bulletin #1154, by John M. Kingsbury*)

sumac seedlings have leaves that resemble poison ivy, with three leaflets instead of the seven to thirteen characteristic of the adult plant. Poison sumac grows into a tall, erect shrub or small tree with gray bark and smooth leaflets that have indentations on their edges. They are brilliantly colored in late summer and early autumn.

Poison ivy, oak, and sumac are the most prevalent and therefore the worst of the wild plants that can cause some mighty unpleasant skin conditions. But there are many others that you also must be on the lookout for. Although certain individuals may be allergic to this plant or that, the ones most of us must watch out for are the so-called primary irritants. Some of these plants are more dangerous when it's wet than when dry, others do more damage when they're young than when old. Some of the most common offenders are cypress spurge, the tall field buttercup, and the stinging nettle.

Cypress spurge (*New York State College of Agriculture, Cornell Extension Bulletin #1154, by John M. Kingsbury*)

Tall field buttercup (*New York State College of Agriculture, Cornell Extension Bulletin #1154, by John M. Kingsbury*)

Stinging nettle (*New York State College of Agriculture, Cornell Extension Bulletin #1154, by John M. Kingsbury*)

135

5—Boat Cooking

There was a time not so long ago when a pleasure boat was mainly meant to be a fishing platform for *men*. It is that way no longer, though.

Today the waters are filled with boats, and the boats are filled with women and children as well as men—people who must eat.

So, many of the larger boats today come complete with kitchen or, as they say in nautical circles, complete with galley. As for the smaller craft, they're made to order for nosing up to beach or river bank to put ashore all the things that make a meal—including, of course, something on which to cook it—or if it is an isolated, idyllic spot that lends itself to camping, to transfer to land all that's needed for an extended stay.

Big boat or small boat, cooking aboard or cooking ashore, there are some basic things that—as in all other phases of outdoor cooking— nautical folk must bear in mind if their voyage is going to be a pleasure.

Perhaps the most important is this: *You must plan ahead.*

In many ways, planning ahead will be the same as for camp, wilderness, and desert cooking. But not quite. We'll point out the pertinent similarities and explain the differences:

- You'll have to know beforehand whether you'll be cooking and eating aboard, on the move, at a marina, or at a campground and, if one of the latter, what supplies and facilities will be available to you when you get there. For example, does the marina have electric outlets you can use to juice up power for your electric appliances?

- If you'll be taking a cruise and living aboard, you'll have to know for how long—one day or one month—so you can lay in the supplies necessary to hold you until you arrive at the next port of call where they can be replenished.
- You'll have to plan a voyage and chart a course that will give you the necessary layovers where and when you'll need them.
- You'll have to study reliable charts—landlubbers call them maps —of the waters on which you will be sailing.

There are thousands of miles of navigable waterways available to recreational boaters in the United States today. You could, in fact, set sail from almost any of our inland states on an open-ended cruise that could lead around the world. In case you're not aware of the possibilities, that's not a far-fetched statement because, at the rate new waterways are being opened through government projects, there soon will be only six states without direct, navigable access to the sea. One lifetime is no longer enough to explore all the waterways available to you. All you need, in addition to a seaworthy boat, are time, money, and sailsmanship.

Planning Ahead

How do you amass the welter of facts you'll need to have before putting out from your home port?

Simple. You get the information in much the same way you find out about the campgrounds and picnic grounds available to the land sailor who uses a car instead of a boat for moving about the Great Outdoors. Available are all sorts of charts and maps showing just about every facility for the traveling boatman anywhere in the United States:

- In urban areas, visit any good map store—Rand-McNally has such outlets—and you'll see them on display. The same goes for any good marine-supply store.
- Write to gasoline companies. Boat fuels are big business with them now, and they have highly informative charts for every section of the country where their products are sold.
- Write to the U.S. Department of Commerce in Washington, D.C., and ask for Coast and Geodetic Survey charts of the areas in which you are interested.
- Other similarly good Washington-based pen pals are the National Park Service, the Army Corps of Engineers, the Forest Service, the Bureau of Reclamation.

WANTAGH PARK GUIDE

NOT TO SCALE

N ◊

A - LIGHTED TENNIS COURTS

B - COURT GAMES AREA

C - MARINE PLAYGROUND

D - LIGHTHOUSE AND COMFORT STATION

E - ADMINISTRATION BUILDING

F - LITTLE LEAGUE FIELD

G - SOFTBALL AND FOOTBALL FIELD

H - BASEBALL

I - BASEBALL AND FOOTBALL (LIGHTED FIELD)

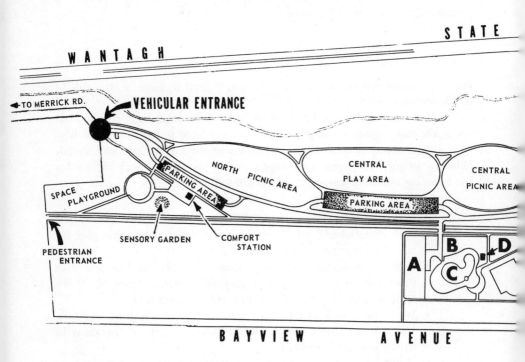

Wantagh Park and Marina, Nassau County, Long Island, New York

138

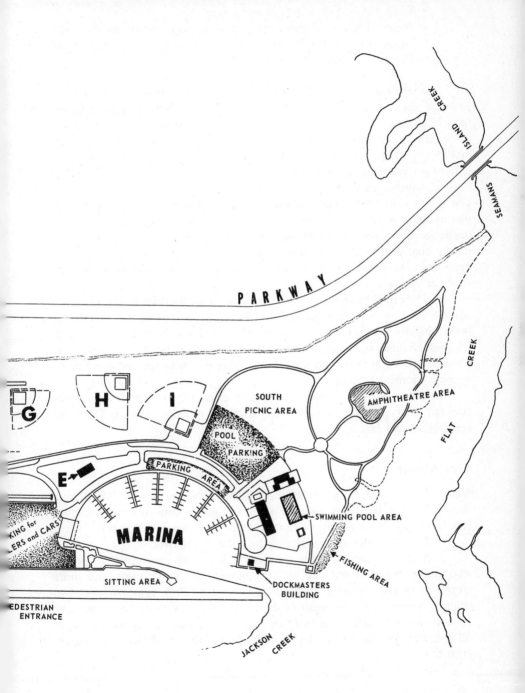

CREEK

ISLAND

SEAMANS

PARKWAY

FLAT CREEK

AMPHITHEATRE AREA

SOUTH
PICNIC AREA

POOL
PARKING

G

H

I

E

PARKING AREA

MARINA

SITTING AREA

SWIMMING POOL AREA

FISHING AREA

DOCKMASTERS
BUILDING

KING for
LERS and CARS

EDESTRIAN
ENTRANCE

JACKSON CREEK

139

- Write to state, county, and municipal governments.
- Write to local chambers of commerce.
- Write to Peter Wilson, executive vice president of the National Association of Engine and Boat Manufacturers, 537 Steamboat Road, Greenwich, Conn. 06830.

Back from any or all of these will come just about all you'll have to know about camping and picnic areas, water depths, channel markings, launching ramps (if you're a trailer-sailor this is important), public docks and marinas and their facilities, access roads, and heaven knows what else, including perhaps a rundown of what sort of public transportation is available to get you from boat to marketplace.

Another excellent place to find such facts is at the marina where you tie up your boat. There's a friendly helpfulness among boating people, just as there is (perhaps more so) among camping people—a true neighborliness that is one of the nicest aspects of the sport. Tell the guy or gal on the boat next door where you're thinking of going. Chances are, they've been there, and they'll invite you aboard for a cup of coffee or something stronger and tell you all they know.

They might even give you a site map of such places as the Wantagh Marine Park in Nassau County, New York, which shows the location of everything from marina to picnic areas. At such public facilities, you can let your children run and play and swim and fish in safety while you plug your electric equipment into a dockside outlet and take care of many boat-keeping chores.

Cap it all off by toting a bag of charcoal to one of the picnic-cookout areas for an evening meal that's a welcome change from the seafarer's usual fare.

Fire Afloat

Many things must be considered in planning ahead for a cruise; high among them is the thing without which the galley cook obviously cannot function—a stove, a source of heat, another word for which is *fire.*

Fire. The dread of seafaring folk the world over.

Year by year, as more and more boats are purchased by people who never owned a boat before, the newspapers carry more and more stories of pleasure craft suddenly being swept by flash fires "of unknown origin." Subsequent investigation shows that most of them have the same causes: human carelessness or ignorance, volatile fumes, a spark. Put them all together, and the result can be an explosion that might blow a pleasure craft to bits.

Gasoline and oil fumes, being heavier than air, settle to the bottom of a boat into the bilge. There they stay. Someone flips an electric switch or flicks the ash from a cigarette or strikes a match to light a stove or spatters hot grease. The spark, the heat, hits the fumes. Boom comes the explosion, the fire, almost certainly the loss of the boat, and possibly the loss of life.

Yet all of this could be prevented if you:

- Adequately ventilate all closed places in a boat, including the galley, before flipping that switch or striking that match.
- Have the right kind of stove.
- Never use gasoline for cooking or to prime a stove.
- Keep the galley well ventilated while the stove is in use.
- Keep the boat—especially the galley—immaculate. Create no pockets, either by an overturned box or fallen rag, under which grease and fuel can collect. Wipe up fuel or grease the moment it hits the deck.
- Don't have curtains, drop cloths, or anything else where it can come in contact with the stove in the event of a sudden pitch, roll, or lurch.
- Don't overfill fuel tanks, whether boat tanks or stove tanks. The overflow is one of the main causes of fumes.
- Don't overfill certain stoves' priming cups with liquid starters. It's much better to use solidified canned heat for this purpose.
- Don't refuel either the boat or the stove while the stove is on or the burners are still hot from recent use.
- Don't do any deep-fat frying aboard a boat.
- Don't store fuel in unmarked containers.
- Preheat stove burners long enough to fully dissipate vapors, otherwise liquid fuel may drip into priming cups and cause flare-ups.
- Keep your burners clean and unclogged. Using good quality fuel is one of the best ways of doing this.
- Keep a Coast Guard or Underwriters Laboratories–approved fire extinguisher within fingertip reach in the galley as well as elsewhere around the boat.
- Write to the National Fire Protection Association, 60 Battery-march Street, Boston, Mass., or the Yacht Safety Bureau, 21 West Street, New York, N.Y., for literature on fire prevention aboard boats. The cost will be nominal—probably less than a dollar—but the savings both in life and property may be great, provided that you read and heed what the pamphlets say.

Observe all these rules, not sometimes but all the time, and there is little likelihood that you'll ever have a fire aboard your boat. But if you do, here is what you should do:

- Maneuver your boat so the wind doesn't fan the fire into a bigger blaze; head into the wind if the fire is aft; head downwind if the fire is at the bow.
- Throw any loose or unattached burning material overboard.
- If the fire is below decks, close all hatches, portholes, doors.
- Put your fire extinguishers to swift use. Today's best extinguishers for oil, grease, and gasoline fires are dry chemical, carbon dioxide, and foam. But keep abreast of new technical developments in this ever improving field.
- Water is best for putting out fires on alcohol stoves, wood, and clothing.
- Keep calm. Even though there might come a time when you cannot control a fire, you always must control yourself. Hysteria may well be far more dangerous to you and others aboard your boat than the fire is.
- Don life preservers the moment fire breaks out in case you have to abandon ship or an explosion should blast you overboard.
- Don't swim far from the fire, because it will be a signal that will bring help.

Stoves

You should never attempt to use a stove on any boat that doesn't have built into it facilities to which you can safely, surely, permanently, attach it. This automatically rules out not only such obvious craft as canoes, rowboats, and inflatable boats but also about 98 per cent of the outboard motorboats plying our waterways, most of our inboard-outboards, and a great many of our inboard cruisers and sailboats.

No matter what kind of boat you may have, if it didn't come from the dealer equipped with a stove, don't try to add one. Instead, carry a camp stove or a charcoal grill, and when it comes time to cook, nose into shore and have a picnic on dry land. Some not quite scrupulous manufacturers circulate literature that say it's perfectly safe to use them aboard a boat. Don't you believe it. If you can't have an underwriter-approved marine stove, do your cooking ashore.

Most new boats large enough to include a galley come from the manufacturer with a complete cooking unit—stove, sink, and icebox—already built in. This can pose quite a family problem: Husband may opt for a boat with an engine or a certain fit of the jib; wife may want a boat with a stove.

Instead of engaging in pitched battle, you might do better to ask yourselves and others questions, the answers to which will help you develop a set of helpful guidelines. Start with this cardinal rule: *only stoves designed for marine use should be installed on boats, and only boats with space to attach a stove in a fixed position where it won't interfere with boat operation should have one.*

Now take it from there. Do you prefer the leisurely life of motorboating or the silence of sailing with nature's breezes providing your power of movement? There is a big difference in the way the two types of boats are used and, therefore, a big difference in the approach to furnishing a galley.

Sailing is a far more active participation sport than is motorboat cruising—a fact of a sailing family's life that makes the providing of hearty meals both mandatory and more difficult for the cook. More difficult because of the dipping and rolling which are so much a part of sailing. There is, however, a way of offsetting the roll and dip of a sailboat in order to hold the stovetop level enough for the chef to function. That's the use of a handy invention called *gimbals.*

Gimbals are socket-type gizmos on the two ends of a galley stove that hold it to a sort of outer casing, thus enabling the stove to swing like a baby's cradle. As the boat rolls toward one side or the other, everything in it may be tilted by as much as forty-five degrees, thus making gimbals a necessity.

Gimbal-hung stoves must be installed on what landlubbers would refer to as the "side" of the boat parallel to an imaginary line (the keel, which, though out of sight, is not imaginary) running down the center from front to back (fore and aft).

Your sailboat galley, in order to have a stove on gimbals, must be long enough for it to be installed fore and aft and wide enough (beam) so that it will have enough space to swing freely without bumping the wall (bulkhead) and without people having to brush against it while trying to pass by. If your sailboat is not large enough for that, then you must have a stove or charcoal grill that you can haul ashore for cooking.

All pleasure boats, by the way, should have gimbal-attached stoves, but on a sailboat the gimbals are mandatory.

Where are you going to be using your boat? Are you planning on long ocean voyages? If so, your boat should be large enough and well-enough built so that you'll have considerable flexibility of choice, thus enabling you to pick with care your stove and other galley equipment and then have it installed, just as you would do with the kitchen of a new house.

Are you going to be in out-of-the-way places? If so, the stove that you choose must have an assured fuel supply available, no matter how remote, how isolated, your wanderings. For the nautical family that uses its boat only for short voyages—never, let's say, more than three days from home—this is no problem. But if you explore faraway places, make sure you pick a stove whose fuel supply can be replenished no matter where you are.

What is the climate where you do your boating? If it's cold, a galley stove that can also double as a source of warmth is great. If it's hot, you need a stove that throws out as little heat as possible.

The Various Types of Fuels

What kinds of fuel do what best? What fuels are safe? What fuels are dangerous? Let's answer the last two questions first. In order of safety, here they are: (1) electricity; (2) coal, coke, or wood; (3) canned heat; (4) alcohol; (5) kerosene; (6) liquefied petroleum gas (LPG). You'll note that gasoline is nowhere on the list. Reason: It's so dangerous that it must never be used for cooking aboard a boat.

Repeat: NEVER.

Now let's look at these fuels one by one and discuss their pros and cons.

Electricity. In choosing a boat with an electric stove, you must know two things. Is its generator good enough to keep you amply supplied? Can it be plugged into a shoreside outlet to replenish power? On most of the newer, larger boats, electric power is no problem. In fact, many of them have completely electric galleys, not only stove but also refrigerator and even freezer. Small boat owners, because of limited power supply, won't find electricity a practical fuel for cooking. At the pace new pleasure-craft conveniences are being developed, however, this may change soon. Already on the market are stoves that range from top burners only to ones complete with ovens and see-through doors.

Although electricity is at the very top of the safe-fuel list, its position there depends greatly on you. It is safe only if installed by experts and if all the lines, switches and other equipment are properly maintained. All it takes is one spark to start a fire.

Coal, Coke, or Wood. It might surprise you to learn that the old iron stove that burns both wood and coal is not nearly so extinct as grandpa's red flannel drawers. Not only is it in use by land-based outdoorsmen as pointed out in Chapter 2, it also has a place aboard fairly stable boats that ply the waters of the world during cold weather.

Homestrand's Mark 218 electric stove and oven comes in a variey of colors—for the boat that has everything. (*Homestrand, Inc.*)

Not only do such stoves give off heat galore, they also are excellent for cooking and thus serve two purposes at once. Be warned: a wood-burner or coal-burner can heat up a galley unbearably in hot weather. Don't go out and buy a boat in which you can install one purely because you have a sentimental, nostalgic attachment to pot-bellied stoves.

Not all of them are made of iron. Other suitable materials are used, too. But they're all much too heavy to be mounted on gimbals, and so they must be installed where they will be affected as little as possible by pitch and roll.

As with all galley stoves that have ovens, the doors must have secure fasteners that will prevent them from swinging open and disgorging hot, and therefore potentially dangerous, foodstuffs on the deck.

There must be adequate insulation behind, under, over, and—depending on where in the galley a wood-burner is located—perhaps on both sides, too.

Such stoves must also have chimneys that draw well, and the chimneys too must be well-insulated.

The Washington Stove Works, P.O. Box 687, Everett, Washington, makes small iron wood- and coal-burning stoves that sell for as little as $50 and weigh less than fifty pounds. They're popular as supplemental stoves on large boats, which use them for heating the cabin and a pot of coffee or to cook a one-pot or two-pot dinner. They're ideal, too, for transfer

The Skippy One wood- and coal-burning stove heats as well as cooks. (*Washington Stove Works*)

to a summer shack on some sandy hideaway where there is an abundance of driftwood to burn. Then, at summer's end, move it back aboard your boat to take the chill off the air and thus extend your boating season by many months.

If you're in the market for a good-quality, hand-assembled marine stove, the Washington Works has them for just about any amount of money you want to pay. And if you don't like any they have in stock, they'll custom-build just what you want for your sailboat, power cruiser, tugboat, commercial fishing boat, or ocean liner.

Canned Heat.   It is not a fast fuel, but it is a safe fuel for use aboard boats. Another nice thing about it, as anyone who has ever used Sterno (its marketing name) knows, a stove that operates on canned (jellied) fuel takes up little space.

There is a small gimbal-mounted canned-heat stove on the market that small boat owners swear by. Called the Sea Swing, it weighs less than five pounds, costs less than $25, takes up only about one cubic foot of space—and not permanent space. All you do is screw a metal plate to the bulkhead, attach the Sea Swing to the plate, cook your meal, take the Sea Swing down, and stow it away.

To help overcome the slowness of canned heat, the Sea Swing has an accessory heat intensifying gizmo that speeds up cooking considerably. It's a grand little stove for the cramped-quarters boating family. If your marine-supply store doesn't stock it, write to the maker: Bremer Manufacturing Company, Inc., 4937 North 32nd Street, Milwaukee, Wisconsin 53209.

Alcohol.   For many years, this fuel has been the favorite of sea cooks for a number of reasons: (1) An alcohol fire can be put out with water; (2) an alcohol stove is easy to light; (3) alcohol evaporates when spilled; (4) it has less odor than does kerosene, which also is popular; (5) its heat is less intense; (6) it cooks quickly.

Alcohol stoves (as do kerosene stoves) have to be preheated, and there are priming cups under each burner for this purpose. They are filled with either alcohol or canned heat, lighted, and when the burner reaches the proper temperature—which does not take very long—the stove is ready for use. Sterno is the safer of the two.

Fuel tanks for both alcohol and kerosene stoves—they are quite similar—can be installed to permit operation either by pressure feed or by gravity flow, but the installation should be done by professionals. Gravity tanks must be placed outside the galley where they can be filled and vented at a safe distance from the stove. Pressure tanks can be inside the galley, but they must be well separated from the heat of stove burners.

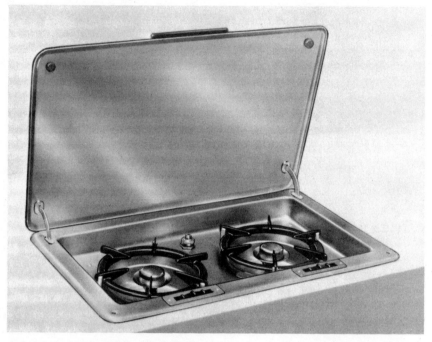

Homestrand's two-burner alcohol stove for a galley (gimbals not shown) (*Homestrand, Inc.*)

The NFPA recommends only a gravity or pressure fuel system and says a definite no to any fuel-feed system that can be affected by the motion of the boat.

Kerosene.   Here are the two best things that this fuel has going for it: (1) It's cheaper than alcohol; (2) it is the one fuel for marine stoves that can be purchased just about anywhere. Of course, the quality of the kerosene you find in many out-of-the-way places may make you regret your discovery.

The Sea Swing comes with a conversion unit (for which, of course, you must pay extra), which permits the use of kerosene instead of a jellied fuel.

Liquefied Petroleum Gas.   We told you all about this fuel in Chapter 2, and there is no need now to repeat. But there is need to tell why

LPG rates on the bottom of the list when it comes to boat cooking. LPG vapors sink. Spring a leak, down into your bilges go the fumes, flip a switch or flick a cigarette ash, and—poof!—you've had it.

Take our advice. No matter how much you may swear by an LPG stove in a dry-land camp, leave it at home when afloat. And don't let anybody tout you onto an LPG marine stove no matter how pretty it may look.

This Is Versatility!   A stove is available that permits you to switch burners from alcohol to electricity and vice versa. At sea you use the former; at dockside you plug into an outlet and use the latter. Write to the Princess Manufacturing Corporation, 741 South Fremont Avenue, Alhambra, California, and they'll tell you all about their several models.

The Stove Top

Keeping pots from slipping from the top of the stove is no problem in camp or at home. Not so, however, at sea. There they can slip and slide and go plop on the deck. So, to guard against such disaster, all good marine stoves come equipped with pot holders to anchor them in place. Some have rails around the burners; some have adjustable tong-like contraptions that grip utensils; some stoves have burners that are sunken.

Whichever stove, whichever device, you choose, make sure it works to your satisfaction. Make sure your pots will fit on the burners when the holding gizmos are in place. Make sure a sudden lurch won't spring them loose. Make sure of all this before buying. At sea it is too late.

Another thing to make sure of: *that your stove is securely mounted; that it can't shift, no matter how rough the weather or the sea, except, of course, for the cradle-like swing provided by gimbals.*

And remember this, girls: *A boat galley has a lot more pitch and roll than your kitchen at home. So don't put up frilly curtains or any combustible material that might suddenly dip down into your fired burners. Far better to use your decorating ingenuity to fit an appropriate fire extinguisher into the color scheme. By appropriate, we mean able to put out a fire caused by the type of fuel your stove burns. Position it far enough away so that a fire on or near your stove won't prevent you from getting to it.*

Be prepared for less efficiency in your galley stove than in your kitchen stove. Some burners, for example, may have a fixed heat that you can't regulate—a very embarrassing situation when trying to slow-cook something. Always have with you some asbestos flame regulators that you can slip between fire and pot or pan when necessary. You'll also have fewer burners to work with. Most marine stoves have only from one to three, so your meals will have to be planned accordingly.

Ovens

Stoves on bigger boats usually boast ovens; those on smaller boats usually
do not. You need never regret being in the latter category, however.

An oven is nice to have, but who really wants to roast a turkey or
a standing rib roast while at sea? Far better, if you have an oven, that you
use it mainly for warming up carried-aboard casseroles or for baking premixed rolls or small loaves of bread.

But be prepared also for an oppressively warmed-up galley—a hor-
rible thought to contemplate when the sun is hot and going below to escape
deck heat is tantamount to going from frying pan to fire.

So shed no tear if you have no oven. There are substitutes:

- Set a pie tin upside down in a heavy pot or skillet. Set another
  tin right-side up atop that. Set your premixed rolls or biscuits
  into it. Put a cover on the pot or skillet. You now have an oven.
  Set it on a burner and bake away at medium heat.
- Set a flame regulator on your burner. Set a pan containing whatever it is that requires oven cooking on top of it. Fit a larger
  pot, upside down, over the ingredient pan. You now have an
  oven.
- For warming things, simply use a double boiler. Or place a large
  pot containing a half to an inch of water on a burner; set a soup
  bowl up side down in the water; set the dish containing the food
  to be warmed on the inverted bowl. Cover the pot. You now have
  a steamer.

Refrigeration

We could repeat just about everything that we said in Chapter 2, but we
won't. We'll be brief:

- If your boat has a fuel-powered refrigerator, check carefully all
  feed lines and connecting links.
- Transport frozen and chilled foods to boat from home in camp
  coolers.
- Use the cooler when aboard as an auxiliary icebox.
- If your boat has no refrigerator, use as many coolers as you
  need.
- If you'd like to dangle perishables in the water to keep cold,
  make sure that they're packed not only in a water-tight con-

tainer but also in one that can resist water motion. Make sure that the lines from which they hang are firmly tied.
• Only do such dangling while at anchor. When under way, haul your food aboard.

Pots and Pans and Such

What kinds of pots and pans are best for cooking aboard a boat? Aluminum? Stainless steel? Enamel? Cast iron? Copper? Stainless steel with copper bottom? Are they heavy enough? Or light enough?

Ask twelve galley cooks and get twelve different answers.

We suggest that you start out by trying the utensils that you already use at home. Not all of them, because too many could turn a pleasure cruise into a chore. Just take along the bare minimum: frying pan, one or two pots, coffee pot. See how well they fulfill all these nautical needs:

• Do they fit your stove's burners when the utensil holders are in place?
• How fast, or slow, do foods cook in them on your boat's stove?
• How well do they store away when not in use? Do they fit inside your galley's storage area?
• How badly do they rust? Is it hard to remove rust from them?
• Find out if they in any way affect the ship's compass. It would be awful to end up in Tampa instead of Tacoma because of a pot.

Once you have all the answers, you'll know what cooking utensils to buy.

Cast iron, for example, cooks beautifully but rusts terribly. You can overcome that easily by coating cast-iron pots with a thin film of oil after each washing. But cast iron is heavy. Is the better flavor of your cooked foods worth the extra weight? Only you can decide.

Copper-bottomed stainless steel withstands the weather wonderfully. But such utensils don't hold the heat as well as heavy aluminum or iron. Simmering may sometimes be well-nigh impossible in them; often the type of stove will be the determining factor. Only you can decide.

Vegetables cooked in heavy aluminum require less water, thus they pack more vitamins and flavor to the table. But aluminum can pit badly, especially in salt air. Is the extra goodness worth it? Only you can decide.

Enamelware cooks well, on the water as at home. But enamel chips quite easily, and so a sudden roll of the boat can produce a spot that easily rusts. Can you guard your pots against such bumps? Only you can decide.

There are many such factors that you and you alone must find the answers to before making a final decision on how to equip your galley. But we can tell you this:

- Plan on menus that require only the bare minimum in the way of cooking and eating utensils. Try to make do with no more than two pots, a coffee pot, and a frying pan.
- Use only pots and pans that are deep enough to minimize the possibility of foods sloshing out.
- Consider well having one of your two pots have an eight-quart or ten-quart capacity. It can double for many things: stew pot, steamer, dishpan. But forget the idea if such a pot won't fit inside your stove's utensil holders.
- If space permits, include a colander and a dish drainer in your galley gear.
- Because every boat's storage space is limited, as much as possible choose utensils that have interchangeable uses: storing, mixing, cooking, serving.
- When you decide to buy new galley utensils, visit a good marine-supply store. You'll find many conveniences that may fit your needs perfectly—for example, nesting sets of pots and pans or pots that stack one atop the other while in use, a great space-saver when it comes to keeping things warm on the stove.

Oven Utensils

If your galley stove has an oven:

- Plan on using square-cornered baking utensils as much as possible. They take up much less space.
- Remember that two small meat loafs or loaves of bread will cook more quickly than one large one, thereby conserving fuel and adding less heat to the galley.
- Bake pies, biscuits, and premixed rolls in pie pans that can also be used for serving.
- If you bring ready-prepared frozen casseroles from home, Corning Ware or some such multipurpose utensil is perfect because it can go from freezer to oven to table.

Eating Utensils

If you plan on being mainly a dockside sailor—folks with lace-curtained boats that never move more than one cocktail length away from their anchorage—then by all means outfit your galley with the finest tableware: china dishes, silver cutlery, and shiny stemware.

But if you plan on using your boat for boating, here's what to get:

- Unbreakable dishes. Melmac and others are quite attractive.
- Stainless-steel knives, forks, and spoons.
- Heavy coffee mugs that don't tip easily but, if they do fall, don't chip easily either.
- Unbreakable glasses for water and milk.
- Heavy-duty glasses, which, we think, are the only kind that do justice to more potent drinks.

Space limitations will dictate how much of each you will have. Wherever possible, use multipurpose utensils. If there are four in your family, carry only utensils enough to feed four. Keep a small supply of paper plates on hand in case of company.

Paper dishes also are good for snacks because they eliminate the need for washing dishes and thus conserve water.

Good Housekeeping

Aboard a boat, where safety is so all-important, cleanliness and orderliness are mandatory in the galley as well as everywhere else. Every bit of spilled food must be wiped up instantly to prevent skids that could result in broken bones while far-removed from medical aid. Ditto for spilled grease, which poses an additional hazard—fire. Cooking and eating utensils must be washed immediately and stowed away in their proper places. Left around loose, many things could go wrong. Everything must have its proper place and be kept there when not in use.

Storage

Any boat with a galley worthy of its name has built-in storage space. This can be anything from open shelves to closets or cupboards (lockers) and pull drawers.

Become acquainted with your craft's storage space and don't bring more aboard than you safely have room for. With one exception: You can pack additional things in nonbreakable containers such as wooden boxes, which can be stowed where they will not interfere with the boat's operation.

Food storage on a small boat without a galley will be about the same as for a camping trip, except that you must not attempt to load as much into a boat as you would into a station wagon. Wooden boxes are best. Stow your light things, as well as those that need the most shelter from the weather, below your foredeck; your heavy things, just aft of amidships. Keep everything well below the height of your gunwales.

All shelves and work counters, including your table top, should be fitted with fiddleboards, a raised edging that prevents loose objects from sliding and spilling.

Other supply and stowage pointers to remember:

- Don't take anything along, particularly perishables, that you can just as conveniently and cheaply procure at some future port of call. This practice can be a money- and space-saver, and a dry-land shopping trip can also be a welcome change of pace.
- Lay in a supply of foam rubber, which can be purchased in most variety and dry-goods stores, and use strips of it as bumper guards for bottles. Speaking of bottles, alcohol should be taken only for medicinal purposes (a shot of brandy might help to settle a seasick-prone stomach) while under way, but it's always nice to have something aboard for the quiet moments.
- All ingredients that come in rust-prone containers should be transferred to ones that won't rust. Heavy plastic bags and containers such as Tupperware are excellent. Label the contents plainly with waterproof crayon and secure tightly.
- Powdered things such as seasonings and dehydrated mixes can get lumpy and difficult to work with. If their original containers are not water- and weather-resistant, transfer them to Tupperware.
- If you're going to be at sea for more than a week or so, it's a good idea to remove all paper labels from cans before the weather does it for you. Label the contents with crayon and then varnish the cans to guard against rust.
- If cans rust in spite of all your efforts, the food in them will be safe to eat if no leaks have developed. Cans with bulged ends should be discarded unopened.
- Avoid large boxes of cereal because of dampness. It's best to take aboard only boxes containing individual servings. Store them in a cool, dry place. If necessary to restore crispness of dry cereals, heat them for five minutes in a medium oven or heavy pot.
- Most breads, if well wrapped, will stay fresh for a week. Canned bread is a good idea, too.
- Take along canned or one-piece slabs of bacon.
- Like bacon, all meats keep best when uncut. So don't cut them until absolutely necessary for cooking or serving.
- Don't take fresh fish along. Far better to catch or buy it—just enough for a meal at a time.
- Smoked ham will keep best in cans. Check the label to see if it must be refrigerated.
- Try to figure out before leaving home how much you'll be using in the way of spices while afloat. Then transfer the needed

amounts from their store-bought containers to plastic pill bottles, label them, and fit them into any small metal or wooden box that can double as a sea-going spice rack. A cigar box is perfect.
- After you've assembled all your foodstuffs and stowed them in their proper places, take inventory. Prepare a list showing where each is stowed and the quantity. Hang the list somewhere, perhaps on the back of a locker door, so that you can tell at a glance how your supplies are holding out. Reduce the quantities on the list as things are used.
- Before stowing anything away, thoroughly clean and disinfect your storage areas. Do the same at the end of a voyage.
- When buying anything anywhere, especially in strange ports, thoroughly check for roaches before carrying it aboard.

Water

One of your biggest storage problems for any voyage that will last for more than two or three days will be water.

At first it will seem that there never is enough room for all you feel you must have along. But that feeling will change as you learn to conserve. For example, you can wash dishes in clean water, whether fresh or salt, that you bucket up from over the side; then you need touch your supply only for rinse water.

Most cruisers have one or more fresh-water tanks built into them. How many and how large depends on the size of the boat.

Small-boat owners must resort to jugs, which is no problem because there are so many good ones to choose from. We think those with a five-gallon capacity are best for a couple of reasons: They're easy to carry; you can have several and reserve just one of them for cooking and drinking, thus keeping its contents fresher and better-tasting.

Many jugs that you'll see in the stores come with spigots built in. Just turn and out comes water. Very handy. Very convenient. But think twice before buying one, because they can drip precious water away and someone just might forget to shut the spigot after using. So, although it may be more inconvenient, it could be best that you use only jugs with wide-mouthed screw-on caps. Keep them tightly closed, and your water will stay fresh.

Emergency Rations

If ever you're going to be sailing or cruising out of sight of land or in waters where you seldom will see other boats—in other words, if ever you venture where you will be out of touch with quick help if the need arises—you'll be wise to have an emergency supply of rations aboard.

In fact, this is also a good idea for small-boat men who ply only well-traveled waterways. You may be riding blissfully at anchor, almost literally surrounded by other boats, when suddenly for some unknown reason your anchor slowly starts to slip.

You don't know it until you're hard aground with an outgoing tide and no other boat can get close enough to help. So there you are with nothing to do but sit and wait until the tide turns and rises sufficiently once again to float you out of so embarrassing a predicament. It may be as long as six hours—a mighty long time to wait. A mighty long time in which to get thirsty and hungry.

So set aside a shelf or a box, consider its contents inviolate except in case of emergency, and fill it with such things as canned fish, canned water, canned fruit juice, unsalted crackers, and dried fruits that have been repackaged in watertight containers. Plus a can opener. And, always before leaving your home anchorage, check to be sure they're still intact and dry.

Garbage Disposal

Along with all the others who use America's waterways, you must be many things: garbageman, policeman, conservationist. *And you must not be one thing: a polluter.*

Keep aboard a plastic garbage can with tight-fitting cover—as large a can as possible. Keep it lined with a plastic bag. Put *all* garbage and refuse into it as fast as it accumulates. The next time you pull up to shore dispose of them, but only if there is an incinerator or receptacles that will be emptied by competent garbage collectors. Keep *all* garbage aboard until you arrive at such a disposal place. If one plastic bag fills up, tie the top securely, stow it away somewhere, and line the can with another.

In other words . . . *Never throw anything overboard—not a can, not a paper plate, not a scrap of food, not anything.*

This is one of the main ways in which we can keep our waterways clean and help to restore them. Besides, it's illegal to dump garbage overboard.

You'll also help combat pollution by never using a detergent for scrubbing decks or doing dishes. It's one of the worst water pollutants known to man or fish. Use old-fashioned yellow or Ivory soap instead.

Galley Equipment

Here is a list of things handy to have in a galley. Use it as a guide to what you should take along. Let your personal cooking habits, the size of your boat, and the amount of storage space available to you be the final determining factors:

Aluminum foil, heavy-duty
Aluminum skillet liners
Baking soda
Bottle opener
Bowls, large, that can double for mixing, serving, and storing
Bowls, small, that can double for mixing, soup serving, and icebox
    storage
Can openers, both beer type and one with screw handle
Canvas carrying bags
Cheesecloth
Chopping board (unnecessary if your stove has a cutting-board top)
Coffee pot
Corkscrew
Dishes, including coffee mugs and drinking glasses
Dish drainer
Dishpan
Dish towels
Double boiler
Dutch oven
Egg beater
Fiddle boards (if not built in)
Fire extinguisher (two in the galley are better than one)
Flame regulators (asbestos pads) for stove burners
Funnels, one for fuel, another for water
Garbage can, plastic with lock-top cover
Grater
Hot-pot holders and lifters
Ice chest or coolers
Ice pick
Ice tongs
Iodine for water purification (see page 117)
Knife sharpener
Knives, forks, and spoons (preferably stainless steel)
Knives: butcher, paring, peeling
Ladle
Lids, interchangeable
Mallet
Matches, waterproofed
Measuring spoons and cups
Oven, folding
Oven thermometer
Pail (two are better than one aboard a boat)
Paper bags
Paper plates, towels, and napkins
Plastic bags, heavy-duty, in a variety of sizes for food storage

Plastic garbage-can liners
Pots and pans, including baking pans and casseroles if you have an
    oven, also a large kettle
Salt and pepper shakers
Scouring pads and cleaners
Scrub brushes
Shopping cart, folding
Skillets, two with covers
Slotted spoon
Soap for dishes
Sponges
Strainers, both small (three inches) and large (eight inches)
Tea kettle
Thermos jug for coffee
Toaster
Tupperware food storage containers
Wax paper to wipe top of cast-iron stove and restore shine
Wire whisk

There it is, a mighty long list. Frankly, it's far more than we would carry. But if your boat is large enough and roomy enough, and if you like to lug along all the conveniences of home (well, almost), it is an ideal list.

It also is a handy checklist to guide you when fitting out your galley.

Use it wisely. Be selective. Take along only what you will surely need and use.

Meal Planning

If you are a typical boat owner, you'll seldom be planning meals to last through a period of more than three or four days. In all likelihood you'll average out at two.

This is good, because for such menus the bulk of the preparation can be done at home, thus relieving you of a galley slave's chains, to say nothing of also relieving the strain on your water and cooking-fuel supplies.

Sometimes it might mean carrying an extra cooler aboard. So what? Just pack each meal's component parts in reverse order of use (the last goes into the cooler first; the first goes in last), each of them handily packaged in its own large plastic bag. Or if you like, pack the first meal into a separate, easily carried, soft insulated bag.

When using Part III, look first for the recipes marked B. The B-recipes are ideally suited for boat use. Pay particular heed to the two-step, prepare-ahead B-recipes. We think you'll find them far easier to fix and that they'll give you better fare than if you did all your cooking and meal preparation in your boat's galley. The one-pot B-recipes also will make your life afloat much more pleasant.

Some sample menus to guide you in your nautical meal planning follow, but we can't overstress the need for including good nutrition. You'll find detailed suggestions for determining the correct amounts to buy for a given number of meals on pages 209–212. We also suggest that you read the chapter on food foraging (Chapter 4), as wonderful a pastime afloat as it is ashore.

It's probably more important on a boat to be sure you're taking along food supplies your family will enjoy eating than it is on any other type of camping trip. It's rather difficult to make an emergency stop to pick up some additional rations if Johnny—or his father—refuses to eat what you brought along.

Another thing to also always bear in mind: *No one but you knows what size portions will satisfy your family. There probably will be a greater variation in the sizes of meat servings than for any other food.*

Check your buying carefully. Far better to lay in too much than to have a cranky crew. You may overload on your first couple of overnight cruises, but you'll get the knack of knowing just how much is enough.

Remember, too, that recommended quantities in recipes in this or any other cookbook are not necessarily the amounts the bodies of you and your seafaring family will crave. Appetites are always greater on water than on land—probably half again as great. In other words, if your husband likes two lamb chops for dinner at home, figure he'll eat three at sea.

Which all adds up to this: Don't prepare menus in advance for more than a day at a time until you've had several cruises under your lifebelts.

This brings us to a couple of other don'ts.

Don't deep fry aboard a boat. It's too dangerous. A sudden roll can spill hot grease all over you (the cook) and maybe also on the stovetop, starting a fire.

Don't keep children waiting too long for meals if you want them to be safely quiet and out of your way while you cook in a galley that may seem to have been designed for a midget. Be ready with snacks—ones that don't provoke thirst, which means that potato chips and salted peanuts are taboo, and that take up no refrigerator space and require no cooking. The nosebag lunches discussed on pages 72–73 are ideal for boating as well as for camping.

So too (not for snacking but for amusement) are the usual things that children like: games, paper, crayons, and such. Felt pens can produce marvelous seascapes. Nature identification cards take up little space and can keep kids content by the hour.

Don't make the mistake of thinking you can plan ahead for everything. No matter what, the time will come when you will want to eat something you hadn't counted on. So, along with everything that you definitely will eat, take along some nonperishables such as dehydrated foods, freeze-dried foods, and canned foods. They'll never go to waste, and they just might fill a sudden need.

SAMPLE BOAT COOKING MENUS FOR A
TWO-DAY WEEKEND FOR FOUR

Friday Dinner

Barbecued Chicken in Oriental Sauce Cooked in Galley (pages 276–277)
Mashed Potatoes (Dehydrated) with Butter or Margarine
Canned Peas
Bread and Butter or Margarine
Cantaloupe (or Other Fresh Fruit from Vitamin A List)
Coffee or Tea
Milk or Juice

Saturday Breakfast

Orange Juice (Frozen)
Shrimp Omelet (page 314)
Toast and Butter or Margarine and Marmalade or Jam
Coffee or Tea
Milk

Saturday Lunch

Creamed Chicken, Mushrooms, and Peas (page 278)
Toast
Fruit-Filled Bakery Cookies
Coffee or Tea
Juice or Punch

Saturday Dinner

Carrot Sticks
Lettuce Wedges with Vinegar and Oil Dressing (page 221)
Veal Parmesan (page 274)
Bread and Butter or Margarine
Nut and Raisin Rice Pudding (page 338)
Coffee or Tea
Milk, Juice, or Punch

Sunday Breakfast
Orange Juice (Frozen)
Matzoh Brie (page 313)
Bacon
Coffee or Tea
Milk

Sunday Lunch
Leftover Veal Parmesan Sandwiches
Coffee or Tea
Milk
Apples, Grapes, and Cheese

When making up your own menus, write them down as we did the foregoing samples. Then write down a list showing each food item you'll need to use in preparing your menus. Pattern your list after the sample that follows. We put all the details into this sample food list (which shows what you'll need to take with you if you prepare our sample menus) so you'd see what we consider the best way to avoid forgetting anything—extra butter in which to fry the Matzoh Brie, for instance, or enough slivered almonds to turn the creamed chicken into a gourmet dish. When writing your own lists of food to take cruising, remember to refer to the recipes you expect to prepare and include each ingredient. *Unless* you plan to use two-step recipes, in which case many of the ingredients will already have been used in the preliminary step 1, which can usually be prepared a day or more ahead of the time you pack for the trip.

The Food You'll Need to Prepare Our Sample Boat Cooking Menus for Four People on a Two-Day Cruise

1. Frozen foods and liquids: Pack them close together so they'll share each other's cold. Put things to be used first on outside of cluster:

> Precooked frozen packages of Barbecued Chicken in Oriental Sauce for 6 to 8. Use leftovers for Saturday Lunch.
> Precooked frozen packages of Veal Parmesan for 6 to 8. Use leftovers for Sunday Lunch.
> 2 6-ounce cans frozen orange juice concentrate. Use 4 cups for Saturday Breakfast, 4 cups for Sunday Breakfast.
> 3 quarts other juice or fruit punch. Use 4 cups for Friday Dinner, 2 cups for Saturday Dinner. Use the extra juice in between meals. (Pour juice or punch into plastic jars, leaving expansion space at

the top. Freeze, cover so containers can't leak, and carry in cooler as supplemental ice.)

2. Foods that should be cold, but not frozen, when they go in cooler or icebox:

8 slices bacon. Use for Sunday Breakfast.

1 pound butter or margarine. Use 4 tablespoons for Friday Dinner, 5 tablespoons for Saturday Breakfast, 5 tablespoons for Saturday Lunch, 2 tablespoons for Saturday Dinner, 3 tablespoons for Sunday Breakfast, 2 tablespoons for Sunday Lunch.

½ pound cheddar cheese. Use half for Saturday Breakfast and half for Sunday Lunch.

1 cantaloupe. Use for Friday Dinner.

1 dozen eggs. Use 6 for Saturday Breakfast, 4 for Sunday Breakfast.

1 medium-size bunch of grapes. Use for Sunday Lunch.

1 head lettuce. Use for Saturday Dinner.

6 quarts milk. Twelve cups per day would meet the basic needs of two adults and two children; skim powdered milk can supplement this amount.

½ pound Mozzarella cheese. Don't use the presliced variety. Use for Saturday Dinner.

2 carrots. Use for Saturday Dinner. Leave out of cooler or icebox if it is crowded.

3. Foods that do not need to be packed in cooler or icebox:

1½ cups slivered almonds. Use 1 cup for Saturday Lunch, ½ cup for Saturday Dinner.

4 apples. Use for Sunday Lunch. Put in cooler or icebox if there's room.

48 slices of bread. Use 6 for Friday Dinner, 6 for Saturday Breakfast, 8 for Saturday Lunch, 8 for Saturday Dinner, 10 for Sunday Lunch. Use extra for snacks.

1 can powdered chocolate to add to milk

1–2 pounds coffee (or tea)

1 5-ounce can boned chicken meat. Hold in reserve for Saturday Lunch in case there's no leftover chicken meat from Friday Dinner.

1 1-pound 15-ounce can or jar of marinara sauce. Use for Saturday Dinner.

1 16-ounce can evaporated milk. Use ¼ cup for Saturday Lunch, 1 cup for Saturday Dinner.

1 3-ounce can sliced mushrooms. Optional for Saturday Lunch.

1 10½-ounce can condensed cream of mushroom soup. Use for Saturday Lunch.

1 16-ounce can of peas. Use for Friday Dinner and Saturday Lunch.

1 15-ounce can rice pudding. Use for Saturday Dinner.

1 4½-ounce can small shrimp. Use for Saturday Breakfast.

8 fruit-filled bakery cookies. Use for Saturday Lunch.

1 box matzoh crackers. Use 1½ cups crumbled for Sunday Breakfast.

1 small jar marmalade or jam. Use ¼ cup for Saturday Breakfast, ¼ cup for Sunday Breakfast.

1 box dry skim-milk powder to supply any extra milk that may be needed.

1 dash nutmeg. Use for Saturday Lunch.

1 small jar olive oil. Use 2 tablespoons for Saturday Dinner.

1 small box dehydrated mashed-potato flakes (Vitamin C–enriched). Use for Friday Dinner.

Salt and pepper.

1 box seedless raisins. Use 1 cup for Saturday Dinner.

1 small jar vinegar. Use 2 tablespoons for Saturday Dinner.

Water for washing, cleaning, drinking, dishwashing, and cooking.

Cooking in Wet and Rough Weather

You must be prepared to alter your menus any time the weather turns foul. So keep abreast of the marine weather reports and, long before your boat is tossing badly, make up pots of hot nourishing soups, coffee, and plain hot water for mixing cocoa or other powdered drinks. Fill your Thermos jugs with these.

Make up lots of sandwiches and then put everything you won't need safely away and fasten all galley and cupboard doors securely. Or, as old salts would say, batten down the hatches.

Dig cans of plain, satisfying stews and such out of their hideaways and put them in the galley, together with can opener and pot, in a place where they can't be thrown about. But don't heat them unless it becomes an absolute necessity.

Get by on the sandwiches, hot soups, and drinks for as long as you can. Don't use the stove if you possibly can avoid it. If eventually you should have to heat a can of stew, *do not* open it and dump the contents into a pot as you normally would do. Instead, pour only a couple of inches of water into the pot, lay the can in it, cover the pot, secure it firmly to the burner, secure the lid to the pot so water can't slosh out, bring the water to a boil, and let it simmer for five or ten minutes, depending upon the size of the can.

Seasickness

Don't apologize if occasionally you come down with a case of *mal de mer*. You're not alone. One of every five sailors does.

Some ways of minimizing such occasions:

- Take a prescribed seasickness pill at least a half-hour before leaving port. Take another every six hours, but only if absolutely necessary.
- Don't eat a heavy meal before setting sail.
- Nip a bit of iced brandy or gin and bitters every now and then.
- Stay away from all other alcoholic drinks, including beer.
- Don't drink tea or coffee on an empty stomach.
- Don't eat fried foods.
- Avoid eyestrain.
- Stay topside as much as possible.

Then, after all that, if the bug still bites you, lie down and be still until it goes away.

Entertaining Aboard

Get-togethers are very much a part of boating and sailing life, but you defeat the relaxing benefits if you let entertaining become complicated. Much of your standard nautical fare will taste just great to your guests.

Or you can dress it up a little by developing your own particular seaboard specialty and always seeing to it that you have the ingredients for making it aboard.

If you're wise, you'll make it a dish that can be eaten in a soup bowl. There's nothing like a hearty, rib-sticking chowder for making guests sit up and take notice. Besides, it's easy to pack a few extra unbreakable soup bowls along.

The Boatman's Bouillabaisse recipe on page 237 is a perfect base on which to build your own special creation. Just add to it or subtract from it as the spirit, and the day's catch of fish, moves you.

An Orange Snapper Punch goes well with anything and will give your guests the same exhilarating surprise a fisherman gets when he hooks into a red snapper. You'll almost surely have the necessary ingredients aboard: sherry and orange juice. Here's how you put them together:

ORANGE SNAPPER PUNCH

4 glasses of ice-cold orange juice
¼ glass sherry
Ice

Combine and shake. Taste. If there's not enough sherry in your drink, add more, ⅛ glass at a time, until it's just right, then serve at once before ice dilutes it too much. Serves 4 to 6, depending on the size of serving glasses.

6—Picnics and Cookouts

Gone are the days of yesteryear. Gone are the days of wilted lettuce and egg salad turned slightly rancid; gone are the days when a picnic meant hours of preparing everything at home and hoping that it would still be edible when you got to where you were going. Today a picnic is a cookout, a clambake, a luau, a barbecue, a turkey roasting on the coals, a hot dog or hamburger broiling on a portable charcoal grill. A picnic is anything you want it to be.

Today you do at the picnic grounds what on other days you do in your own backyard, but with slightly fewer conveniences. You do what you would do on a camping trip, but with slightly more of the creature comforts.

New developments in portable refrigeration make it possible to carry an increasing number of foods away from home to cook and to keep for ever increasing lengths of time without spoiling.

Just pack your ingredients into coolers—perhaps counting on adding some for which you plan to forage—pack your cooler into car or boat, and head for the hills or the dunes.

Your picnic may be fancy, with easy chairs that fold, candlelight, and wine. It can be casual, with a tuft of grass or a log on which to sit. It may be just a couple of kids walking to the beach with surfboards on their heads, sandwiches in their pockets, and matches to light a driftwood fire. It may be all your friends and their families, all the members of your bridge or service club, all the folks who tie up their boats where you do.

Look about you as you travel. You'll notice that an increasing number of parks and wayside rests are springing up with picnic tables, benches, and fireplaces; some even with swimming pools and dressing rooms; virtually all of them with facilities for cleaning up. They're to be found in every conceivable kind of country: seaside, lake, and riverside, mountain and meadow, woodland and desert.

Picnicking need no longer know any seasons. Fifty years ago, when the annual Sunday-school picnic helped usher in the annual summer season, no one would dream of such a thing in any months but July and August.

But today those months, the dog days of summer, are the worst months of all for a picnic. The roads are jammed with traffic. The beaches are jammed with people. The picnic grounds are jammed with picnickers.

So be smart. Confine your outdoor eating and cooking to backyard and campground during July and August. Have your picnic cookouts any other months of the year (the further removed from those two dog-day months the better), unless, of course, you have some easy way of getting to an isolated picnic spot. Then summer probably is best of all.

All off-season picnic-cookouts require are changes of clothing in keeping with the temperature and a closer check on advance weather reports. Consider seriously, therefore, spreading your picnics over twelve months of the year. And, as much as possible, do your summertime picnic cooking at night. Cool evening breezes make a fire welcome. The stars and the flicker of the flames add breath-taking beauty, and food somehow tastes so much better.

Even the dead of winter has days that lend themselves to picnicking. And, of one thing you can be sure, you'll have plenty of room in which to spread your things. Try it.

Take along a tarp or something that you can string up for a windbreak if need be. Take along a hearty, warmth-giving two-step recipe— something like the Camp and Galley Stew recipes on pages 260–261. Take along a coffee pot and all the fixings. Take along lots of wood for a fire.

Head for a picnic area, the more sheltered the better, and if it has a decent fireplace use it. Or, perhaps nicer still, lay a keyhole fire (see pages 98–99). Build a roaring fire in the big end for warmth, rake down the coals for cooking in the little end, enjoy the unforgettable aroma, enjoy the unforgettable flavor, enjoy the bleak browns of winter foliage, enjoy the wonderful whiteness of winter snows, enjoy the solitude. And count your blessings: in the dead of winter you don't have to lug along such excess baggage as sunburn lotions and mosquito repellents.

Equipment and Supplies

What you'll take picnicking in the way of cooking and eating equipment and supplies will be much too varied and dependent upon too many factors for us to try to give you a specific list.

It will depend on where you go, when you go, how long it takes to get there, your mode of transportation, whether it's just your family or a whole lot of families, how many young children, how many teen-agers, and many, many other things. Suffice it to say, practices to which you've grown accustomed on your patio or in camp will do very nicely in helping you to decide what you'll need for a picnic-cookout.

So we'll just discuss some general areas in a way we hope will be helpful and will prevent you from overlooking things that may be important.

Most public picnic grounds are equipped with the same types of wooden tables and benches (and often inefficient fireplaces) found in public campgrounds. So if that is where you're going, take along a camp stove, portable grill or hibachi, plus, of course, fuel.

The farther you get from such places, the more isolated the country-side will grow, the lovelier the surroundings will be—and the fewer the facilities.

Which, we think, is all to the good.

Take along, then, not only something to cook on but also something to eat from and to sit on. Folding tables and lawn chairs are perfect.

No matter where you go, take along a plastic tablecloth and inexpensive cloth napkins—not paper, because they blow all over the place. The tablecloth is handy particularly in places where there is no table to cover. Just spread it on the ground. In such cases small roll-up reed mats are fine for sitting. On a beach, pile up damp sand to make a table-like platform and spread your plastic cloth on that. Even wooden boxes in which you carry your picnic supplies, pushed together, can make a table.

In other words, you need buy nothing. Just take inventory of what not only you but also your picnic companions own. While doing so, don't overlook the fact that station-wagon tailgates make fine tables.

The table service can be as elegant as you like, provided you have the necessary room to carry it. After all, why not use your prettiest dishes in what could often be the prettiest possible background for them? Few of us have dining rooms as attractive as a woodland setting. But if you're worried about breakage or if packing space is limited, you can use your camp gear.

Whatever you decide, you'll need Brillo pads for the pots and soap for the tableware. Plus a dishpan. Unless, of course, you use paper plates, a thought to which we can say only one word—Ugh!

What Food Should You Take?

Teen Picnics

Our two teen-agers are more interested in food than they've been for a long, long time—in fact, since their Cub Scout and Brownie days. Not just food to eat, but also food to fix to look pretty and to talk about. They've sud-

denly become sensitively aware of food as one of life's little pleasures.
Not to be gulped down but to be lingered over.

Eating and communing with nature, we'd say, have been rediscov-
ered by America's young, and this means picnics, no matter what their
word for it may be.

They like to plan their own menus. Sometimes it will be an elaborate meal, done up in a psychedelically decorated box. Sometimes it will
just be peanut-butter sandwiches with lettuce on rolls, maybe with some
crumbled salty bacon mixed in.

All sandwiches that are not going to be protected by a cooler will
be much safer to eat if no mayonnaise is used. Peanut butter is just about
as good a filling as you can use. It keeps much better than meat, and it's
high in satisfying protein.

Plastic bags, tightly closed, will keep out dirt and keep in moisture,
so be sure you have plenty always easily available if your children are in
the habit of whipping up a lunch to take to the beach or the park or the
swimming pool or wherever they may go.

There are many good-quality sandwich spreads that require the
addition of no mayonnaise or anything else that's spoilable in order to taste
good. Stock up on small cans containing the spreads that your children like
best. Keep them where they can easily find them, whenever the picnic
urge hits.

Since fish of all kinds are among the most healthful of all foods, you
might even try to introduce your young ones to sardines that can be carried
in the unopened can and added to a roll or bread when it's time to eat.
Buy the good-quality, boneless types as an introductory offer. Apples,
believe it or not, go well with sardines. So do onion slices. Cherry tomatoes,
if packed so they can't be crushed, are good cooler-less picnic fare that
most kids of all ages like.

We, you might have gathered, are stressing foods that require no
refrigeration. But why, you might ask, since you own a cooler?

Answer: We haven't yet heard of a kid—high teens or low teens—
who always remembers to bring back home things that he or she should
bring back home. So why send valuable containers, such as Thermos jugs
and coolers, off on missions from which they're almost certain never to
return?

However, here is a way that your picnic-bent offspring can have the
finer things in foods. Their only requirement is the availability of drinking
water where they are going, and all you need is an empty two-pound
coffee can.

Wrap pieces of, let's say, fried chicken (it should be ice-cold)
individually; place a layer in the bottom of the can; place a can of frozen
fruit juice concentrate (a kind that needs no can opener) on it; place the
remaining chicken pieces around it; crown it all with a couple of lettuce

sandwiches; put the plastic cover on the can. There you have a cooler that you don't care if you never see again. But one that serves still another purpose. After they've emptied it and rinsed it out, into it goes the contents of the fruit juice can plus water with which to dilute it, and now they have something to drink. And, if they've saved the juice concentrate tin, something to drink out of.

If one coffee can isn't large enough for all the food they're going to take along, let them use two or three. Not too much to carry, because it will take more than four kids to eat all that food.

Here is a menu particularly suited for teen-agers, but people of all ages will also like it. The raw hamburger meat will keep if it is frozen solid and wrapped in aluminum foil. It and the frozen juice will keep things cold if they were cold to begin with.

TEEN PICNIC MENU

Beans with Prunes and Celery (page 316)
Tacos Filled with Guacamole (pages 234–235)
Deviled Eggs (page 311)
Hamburgers on Toasted Buns (page 250) with Relish,
Catsup, and Sliced Onions
Corn Chips and Potato Chips
Fruit Juice (from Frozen Concentrate)

Winter Picnic

A winter outing can be anything that you want it to be:

- A drive to a picturesque hilltop overlook where you can remain in your car with the window open a bit and heater off, of course, and enjoy sandwiches, a Thermos jug of hot soup or coffee, and a juicy apple.
- A ride to a sheltered glen where you can leave the car and open up a carrying case, which—presto!—becomes a small table inside which not only coffee and sandwiches are packed away but a Thermos jug of hot soup, too.
- A hike to an isolated Eden with, on your back, a pack made up of Sterno stove and just enough precooked food to heat thereon.
- A jalopy jaunt to your favorite iced-over fishing hole, car laden with all the fixings for a roaring fire to keep you warm—and to provide coals for broiling steak or chicken or, best of all, a fish fresh-caught through the ice.
- A Barnegat sneakboat voyage to your favorite duck blind, Auto-Fire stove along (see pages 21–23), not only to keep you warm

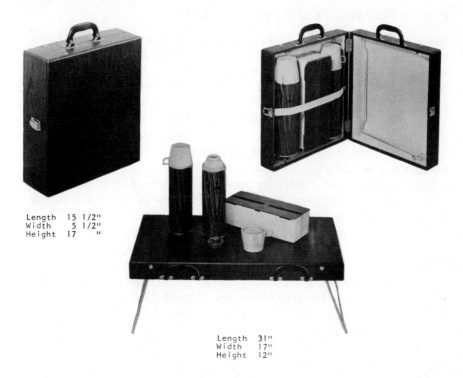

Length   15 1/2"
Width   5 1/2"
Height   17   "

Length   31"
Width   17"
Height   12"

Ideal for an all-weather picnic is this table-foodbox-Thermos kit. (*King-Seeley Thermos Co.*)

> but also to make coffee and bacon and eggs for a soon-after-sunrise breakfast.
> - A snowmobile chute across the fields, your child's fully laden school lunch bucket strapped somewhere thereon.
> - A station-wagon safari to wherever the spirit moves you for a tailgate repast of two-step recipes (see Part III), the first step of which is prepared at home.

Here's a good, yet simple, menu to guide you:

WINTER PICNIC MENU

Tuna Soup (page 247) Made at Home and Carried in a Thermos
Packaged Toast
Barbecued Steak Sandwiches (page 259)
Packaged Cookies
Hot Chocolate in a Thermos

Picnics That Helped Make America Great

Every section of the United States has regional picnicking specialties. In the Middle West, perhaps a fish fry. Down South, hush puppies and fried chicken. In cattle country, a beef barbecue. In tall-corn country, no cook-out is complete without fresh-picked corn on the cob.

They all can form the basis for fabulous feasts.

But, if there lives an American who feels life will never be complete until he has eaten everything at least once, he must travel to the eastern and western extremities of this great land for picnic fare that is practically a way of life.

To Hawaii for a luau. To New England for a clambake.

Since, however, there is small possibility that all of you will be able to do that, we'll bring them to you.

The Luau

Hawaii, you might say, is America's melting pot of the Orient. There live in harmony people from everywhere, but particularly from China, Japan, Korea, and the Philippines. Hawaiian foods have the touch, the tang, the flavor of the East.

Since Hawaii is a tropical state, much of the eating there is done outdoors—not only at home, but also in lovely public Oriental gardens and at the beach, which is no more than a half-hour's drive from every Hawaiian home, or on the mountaintops that overlook the beaches.

Hawaiians have luaus everywhere.

You can, too. In your backyard. In any public park or picnic ground. On any beach or on any mountain, whether the beach is in Georgia or the mountain is in Montana.

Plan an outdoor meal, just as you always do, make all or most of the dishes Oriental, and you have a luau. A little one in your yard for just your family. Or, better still, because the word *luau* is so exotic, make it a really festive occasion. Gather together all your friends, all your relatives, all your co-workers, all your club members. Gather together any congenial group of people and choose a locale that is large, isolated, picturesque, and there have your luau.

In planning a luau, the gathering of ingredients could pose quite a problem. Ideally, you should do your shopping in a city's so-called Chinatown area or in an Oriental specialty shop, of which, surprisingly, there are quite a few scattered around the United States.

If that's impossible, try specialty-food stores, gourmet shops, the food sections of large department stores, and even your own friendly neighborhood supermarket.

If all that fails and if there is a Chinese laundryman in your town or a Japanese farmer just down the road—well, that might be the happiest break of all. Approach them nicely, warmly, politely. Ask them if they can help you obtain the ingredients you'll need.

Don't be surprised if they not only cooperate but also—after you've sincerely invited them—if they become part of your luau group.

However, despite all these alternatives, in the luau menu that follows we've included only dishes that can be made with few or no Oriental ingredients.

LUAU MENU

Assorted Canned Oriental Appetizers*
Canned Smoked Oysters
Marinated Fish (page 236)
Radishes, Green Onions, Sliced Cucumbers, Cherry Tomatoes
Fish Laulaus (page 290)
Barbecued Spareribs (page 267) with
Hawaiian-Style Sweet and Sour Barbecue Sauce (page 220)
Sweet Potatoes Baked in Coals (page 329)
Bread and Butter
Assorted Fresh Fruits

The Clambake

The traditional New England–style clambake, in which all the food is steamed in a pit over hot rocks and wet seaweed, is an experience that no American should miss.

Elsewhere in this book (pages 305–306), we tell you how to have a clambake in your own backyard. But, honestly, it can't compare with the New England kind. The atmosphere, if nothing else, makes the difference. So gather up your family and friends, head for the sand hills, and enjoy, no matter how far from New England you live.

All of our coastal states have seafood, including clams, so if you live by the sea, you can enjoy clambakes, too. If you live in one of our interior states and don't have clams, so what? You do have crayfish, and you do have fin fish. The latter, no matter where it's caught, New England or Oklahoma, is very much a part of a clambake.

Or, and this goes also for people everywhere who might not be in the mood for foraging for clambake foods, you might buy your clams and lobster from your local fishmonger. If he's so far inland that he doesn't stock them, he might get them for you, alive and well, thanks to fast planes and modern refrigeration.

---

* If unobtainable, substitute any appetizers of your choice; they need not be canned. Just add a drop of soy sauce to each, and suddenly they've gone Hawaiian!

One thing he won't get for you is seaweed. Use grass and leaves instead.

So, wherever you may live, go anywhere where there is water and be a New Englander for a day. Take lots of people with you. The more the merrier. Besides, there will be many things to be done, and the more hands the better.

You must plan and do certain things ahead of time. First of all, how many people will there be? Let's figure on twelve. You need a menu for twelve that includes something for everybody, no matter what his personal likes or dislikes:

CLAMBAKE MENU FOR 12

Radishes, Olives, Pickles, Green Onions, Celery, Cucumbers, Carrot Sticks
Steamed Clams with Melted Butter
Steamed Fish with Melted Butter
Steamed Lobster with Melted Butter
Steamed Chicken with Melted Butter
Steamed Corn with Melted Butter
Steamed Potatoes with Melted Butter
Lettuce and Onion Salad with Vinegar and Sugar Dressing (page 225)
Salt and Pepper
Lemon
Bread and Butter
Apple Pie (pages 342–343)
Cheddar Cheese
Watermelon
Coffee, Tea, Milk, Beer

That's the menu. Quite a feast. Quite a contemplation. Quite a bit of advance planning and preparation.

What foods can be definitely and successfully foraged for? Will there be any fishermen in your party who can catch fish? How about spearfishermen to dive for lobsters? Let's assume the answers will all be affirmative. You need not, therefore, take along store-bought clams, fish, and lobsters.

But chicken, corn, and potatoes you will have to take along. How many people will eat them? Count up, and that's how many chicken quarters, ears of corn, and potatoes make the journey from home with you.

Stow all the perishables in coolers for the trip to the waterfront. Plus knives, forks, dishes, tablecloths, napkins, coffee pot and pot for melting butter, beer can opener, and probably quite a few other things, too. Like, for example, nosebag lunches to keep the kids happy until the clambake is ready for the come-and-get-it cry.

Let's break down the recipe for the clambake itself—excluding all the fixings—and see what you can prepare in advance:

> 144 clams, preferably steamers, tied 12 to a bundle in cheese-cloth or arranged in throw-away aluminum-foil dishes
>
> 12 fish steaks or fillets
>
> 12 lobsters, each weighing about a pound and a quarter
>
> 12 serving-size pieces of young chicken. Keep the pieces small, cut drumsticks from thighs and cut breasts in half.
>
> 12 ears of corn, husks pulled back, silk removed, washed and husks restored
>
> 12 medium potatoes, scrubbed and still in their jackets

Now you have everything—including swimsuits and towels and maybe a dining fly—and you're at the beach.

Oh yes, you also should take several old pillow cases along. They're excellent receptacles for seaweed foraged in the surf. So are bushel baskets fitted into inflated tire tubes to keep them afloat while foraging for clams. Plus an old broom, a rake, and about a four-foot square piece of canvas or lots of burlap bags.

There are many chores to be done. Divide them according to each person's special skills and talents. The spear-fisherman goes after lobsters; others dig for clams; others gather loads and loads of driftwood for a long-lasting fire; the strongmen round up the rocks; the children, and at least one adult member of the gentle sex to watch over them, harvest seaweed; the skilled fisherman catches fish—but don't let him tell you that it's impossible for him to do other things at the same time.

There is a pit to be dug, a fire to be built, and rocks to be pre-heated. Here's how:

- Scoop out a circular hole in the sand about three feet in diameter and about eighteen to twenty-four inches deep.
- Line it on all sides with rocks. They must be hard, nonporous, heat-holding, and each about the size of a football. Fit them as closely together as possible and make the top as level as can be.
- Sweep the pit clean of all dirt or sand with the broom you brought from home.
- Build a fire as described on page 77. Make sure it is distributed to cover the entire circle of rocks. Keep it burning well, never too high, because its purpose is to heat the rocks, which must be

intensely hot in order for the clambake to work. Keep the fire going for at least two hours. Perhaps for longer but never less until you've had sufficient clambake experience to know when the rocks have reached the necessary temperature.

• When the rocks are hot enough, remove every speck of still-burning wood, ember, coal, and cinder with the broom and rake. You must immediately start cooking.

• Place a six-inch layer of wet seaweed atop the rocks. Spread it carefully to cover every bit of the pit.

• Working very fast to take advantage of the steam, place your foodstuffs on the seaweed in layers—the clams first, next the lobster, then the fish, chicken, corn, and potatoes.

• Wet the canvas or burlap bags and spread over the pit, anchoring down well with a ring of stones and making sure that no gaps remain for steam to escape. It's a good idea to cover the tops of the rocks lining the pit with seaweed to keep them from burning the canvas.

• In about an hour, everything should be ready for the table. A good way to tell is by carefully lifting up an edge of canvas on the side of the pit that's away from the wind and looking at a lobster. If it's red all over, melt plenty of butter and start serving. And eating. And enjoying a feast such as you've never feasted upon before. Unless, of course, you're a New Englander or have been to New England once or twice.

Champagne Picnic

The bubbly stuff, champagne, is generally associated in American minds with special occasions like weddings, golden anniversaries, and New Year's Eve.

Maybe that's because we've always thought of good champagne as the juice of the grape that comes only from the vineyards of France. A mighty costly item and definitely not for everyday use.

But, and somebody should bruit the news about, there are good American champagnes, made from grapes that grow in California and New York vineyards, that are not nearly so expensive.

Another thing that perhaps we are not so aware of as we might be: Advances in food production, processing, and preparation no longer make it necessary to regard certain foods as meant mainly to be eaten on holidays, like turkey at Thanksgiving and ham at Christmas. They're continually on sale, at prices that almost anyone can afford, twelve months of the year.

Put those two facts together, add twentieth-century refrigeration and transportation, and what do you get? Answer: a champagne picnic, complete with roast turkey and baked ham crusted with pineapples and cherries.

Mighty fine fare, and you'll find the recipes in Part III.

So be gay. Be festive. Live it up. Get your gang together and plan a party like they've never had before. You need not spend an arm and a leg. Or even very many fingers, if everyone chips in to divvy up the cost.

Don't stint on anything. Choose a picnic locale that's the nicest you know. Take along everything from soup to nuts to silverware and stemware and decorations. If you break anything, so what? You only live once. While you're at it, take along a movie camera. Load it with color film and record it all for posterity.

A linen, or at least a very nice plastic tablecloth that looks like lace, can completely hide a rough-hewn picnic table; fireproof lanterns can disguise bare bulbs; pretty plastic pads can soften splintery benches.

Set the tables as if you were having a fancy affair at home. Dainty dishes, nice knives and forks and spoons, good glasses—including, don't forget, champagne glasses. Plus punch bowls and candles. A clean beach in the off-season, a hidden meadow beside a clear-running stream—you should be able to take it from there.

It will be a lot of fun, a memorable occasion.

So much so that you'd better count on going early and staying late. Make sure that there is something for everybody. Plan, therefore, on two champagne picnic meals—the works at lunch, a lighter repast in the evening. For the children, not champagne to drink but a fruit punch that looks like champagne and which they will consider very elegant. As for the guy or gal who doesn't like champagne, beg some of the children's punch and spike it neatly with gin. You'll be amazed at how good it is.

In planning such a party, you'll probably need all the coolers you can get, not only for carrying the food to the picnic grounds but also for storing it between meals. Possibly, too, there will be leftovers to transport home again. You'll also need a host of other things, such as two charcoal grills with hoods (one for ham, one for turkey), cutting boards, carving sets, serving platters, and, of course, the two things without which an outdoor feast can never be complete—a pot for making coffee for the grownups and a pot for making cocoa for the kids.

But providing all that is needed is no problem since several families other than your own will be going along. In fact, you should plan a champagne picnic as a joint venture: Mrs. Jones bakes the ham, Mrs. Smith roasts the turkey, someone else this, someone else that. The same for the gear you'll need and the boxes in which to pack it so that nothing will break along the way. And the vehicles in which to carry it all. Including the people.

It should be a happy caravan.

Here are the menus and the punch recipes:

CHAMPAGNE PICNIC MENU

Lunch (Buffet Style)

Champagne
Judy's Punch (page 179)
Gin Punch (page 179)
Smoked Oyster and Mussel Appetizers (page 234)
Tossed Green Salad (pages 228–229)
Pineapple-Cranberry Mold (page 233)
Canned Cranberry Sauce
Baked Ham with Pineapple and Cherries (pages 269–270)
Roast Turkey with Lots of Stuffing (pages 280–281)
Foil-Wrapped Cheese Wedges
Fresh Fruit
Coffee, Tea, Milk, Cocoa, Soda

Champagne Picnic Supper

Leftover Turkey, Ham, and Salad
Frozen Clam Chowder (page 245)
Oyster Crackers
Fresh Fruit
Coffee, Tea, Milk, Cocoa

Here are the drink recipes.

CHAMPAGNE

As many bottles of domestic champagne as you think you'll need. One bottle (4/5 quart) will almost fill seven four-ounce champagne glasses. If you want it more on the sweet side, try pink champagne or a sparkling wine. You can make your own pink champagne by adding grenadine to a bottle of the regular. Chill well in ice bucket before opening.

JUDY'S PUNCH

2 6-ounce cans frozen lemonade
1 1-pint 2-ounce can pineapple juice
1 8-ounce jar Maraschino cherries
3 7-ounce bottles club soda, ice cold
4 cups ice chips

Remove lemonade from home freezer long enough in advance to defrost by time you plan to mix punch at picnic site. There, empty contents into a pitcher and add *ice water* according to container directions. Pour through strainer (to remove pulp particles) into punch bowl and add pineapple juice, cherries and juice, *ice-cold* club soda, and ice chips. Stir well and serve in champagne glasses. Yield: about 30 4-ounce drinks.

GIN PUNCH

Add 1 pint of your favorite gin (feel free to substitute vodka) to the above recipe and stir.

An outing with that kind of banquet at the end of the rainbow should never be a quickie affair. Bring along all that you'll need to make it an unforgettable day.

Depending on where you go, plan on such activities as swimming, volleyball, softball, mother-and-daughter sack races, father-and-son tug-o'-war. Anything that suits your fancy. Maybe even chess, checkers, and horseshoe-pitching.

Be versatile.

You'll find the menu is versatile, too: the ham and turkey can either be cooked at home the day before, refrigerated until time to pack for the picnic, then stowed whole in coolers; or, since you'll be playing games and having fun for hours, cook them in those two hooded charcoal grills we suggested you bring along.

No matter where you decide to cook, the yield will easily be enough to feed twenty. As for the other recipes, you can adapt them to the size of your party simply by increasing the amounts of the ingredients.

So have fun. No one will go hungry. Or thirsty.

Breakfast on the Desert

We have said that the desert is a beautiful place to camp. Sunrise on the desert. A lovely sight to see. And then, of course, breakfast.

It's a wonderful combination, a desert sunrise, a desert breakfast. So much so that dwellers in the few lovely hamlets that dot the desert quite a few years ago came up with a new wrinkle in picnics.

They call it a chuck-wagon breakfast.

Everybody gets up long before sunrise, saddles up, and rides out to a previously chosen vantage point, where a chuck wagon and steaming coffee are waiting and steaks are on the open fire.

Well, you too, the tenderfoot, the first-time visitor who knows not a soul, can have your chuck-wagon breakfast. Complete with beautiful sunrise. Without the chuck wagon, though.

Let's say that you and your family—four in all—check into a Palm Springs motel from which you hope to learn what the desert is like. A good point of departure, yes, but no more. For as old-time desert denizens would say, going no farther than Palm Springs is like going to the ocean and sticking in only your toe.

Get to bed early, leave a call for a couple of hours before sunrise, stow supplies into your station wagon, and ride out. Destination: the Joshua Tree National Monument about forty miles up the road to Twenty-nine Palms. High desert country where the dawn comes up, not like thunder, but like a symphony.

There is a lookout point there from which, they say, you can see across the Mexican border. And you take it all in with all your senses, with all your emotions. Then you pour that grand-tasting first cup of coffee from a Thermos jug that you've brought from home, and you lay out all the fixings and you start to cook your chuck-wagon breakfast on the tailgate of your station wagon. Or on the ground, if you don't have a station wagon.

TAILGATE BREAKFAST

Coffee in a Thermos for First Cup
Fresh-Perked Coffee for Seconds
Milk or Cocoa for the Kids
Easy Baked Beans (page 317)
Two-Step Chuck Fillets (page 257)
Shell-Cooked Eggs
Bakery Rolls and Butter or Margarine
Chilled Oranges

You'll need these supplies:

Camp stove, preferably the Thermos Jet-Air
Charcoal
Ten gallons of water
One canteen for each person
Frying pan
Coffee pot
Two-quart pot with cover
Wide-mouth Thermos jug for beans
Thermos jug for coffee
Thermos jug for cocoa
Cooler
Folding table and chairs (unless you prefer to eat Western style, squatted on your haunches)
Dishes and tableware
Soap pads

This breakfast leaves very little work to be done at the sunrise-site, thanks to advance chores being done back in the motel:

- Immediately on arising in morning, brew a pot of coffee and pour into Thermos jug that has been preheated with hot water.
- Do the same with cocoa.
- Bake beans according to recipe directions the day before, leave in pot in refrigerator until morning, then reheat and transfer to preheated wide-mouth Thermos.
- The day before, flour steaks according to recipe directions and freeze. (If you don't trust the motel refrigerator's freezer compartment to work so fast, prepare two days before.) Just before leaving, transfer to prechilled cooler.
- A day or two before, place two oranges per person in refrigerator to thoroughly chill. Before leaving in morning, wrap them individually in two layers of aluminum foil and stow in cooler with steaks and eggs.

That takes care of all the preliminary food preparations, and away you go to see the sunrise and to cook breakfast over your camp stove.

You'll note in the supply list that we said "preferably the Thermos Jet-Air." It's a wonderful utensil that looks like a camp stove and cooks just like a camp stove. But it doesn't burn the usual fuels.

The Thermos Jet-Air stove (*King-Seeley Thermos Co.*)

It burns wood chips or charcoal, and all you need to fire them is a match and a couple of shreds of paper. Flip a switch to kick up a draft (it works on flashlight batteries), and in a few minutes you're cooking. It's great. And your breakfast will taste even greater. Especially because of where you are. But don't eat the oranges. They come later.

Now to do the dishes. Very simple. You had to cook the eggs in two quarts of water. So use it now to clean up.

Then go exploring or rock hunting, each of you carrying a canteen full of water and two foil-wrapped oranges, which you eat or suck as the urge moves you.

Roam around as long as you like, see all there is to see, feel all there is to feel. Then, if you don't like the desert, maybe you ought to buy a boat.

Picnic Ahoy!

There are many ways of getting to your favorite picnic grounds: auto-
mobile, bicycle, horseback, on foot, airplane. However, the nicest method
we know of is by boat. Not only is it a relaxing way to travel, often it is
also the only means of getting to where you're going.

Imagine cooking and eating out on a grass- and tree-covered back-
bay island or riverbank or on a sea-girt sand beach, inaccessible to all
who travel other than by boat. In this age of crowds, congestion, traffic
tie-ups, and auto fumes, it's a wonderful thought and an even more wonderful reality.

Shore picnicking is made to order for the small boat man who has
no facilities for cooking on board. Just gentle the bow up onto the beach;
unload guys, gals, kids, and gear; drop the hook in the sand or tie a bow-
line around a tree and play out enough line to let the boat drift out into
deep water. Then, when it's time to leave, just haul in, load up, cast off,
and away you go.

Or if you're sure an outgoing tide won't leave you high and dry,
leave the bow right there on the strand and use the foredeck as a table top.
It's a different way to dine.

Those who cruise in galley-equipped boats need not feel left out.
In fact going ashore for a charcoal-cooked picnic lunch or dinner often is
a highly welcome change from galley fare. Maybe even tastes better, too.
If the boat is too big for gentling up to shore to unload, no matter. That's
what dinghies are for. Just drop anchor in safe water, transfer people and
supplies to the dink for the stone's throw row to land, and have a leg-
stretching fling.

For the days when, for one reason or other, you want a more civilized locale for your boat picnic, there are—in just about every state—
public picnic grounds on mainland shores (see layout of Long Island's
Wantagh Marine Park on pages 138–139) which are designed to accom-
modate seafarers, offering just about everything in the way of facilities.
Even charcoal- or wood-burning fireplaces that often work the way they
should—certainly well enough to roast hot dogs or broil a steak.

There are no special things to do when planning a boat picnic, no
special menus to prepare or dishes to cook. Just remember never to overload your boat.

Since you're on the water where they're waiting to be caught, cook
fish—fresh, healthful, easy, tasty. But if you prefer something else, we don't
mind. Just make sure that your menu is properly balanced for good
nutrition.

Tupperware food containers and a boat's bow deck combine to make waterborne picnics a success. (*Tupperware*)

And though you could lug along a camp stove, it's far better to take with you a hibachi or charcoal grill. Not only will everything taste better, you won't have to carry camp-stove fuel—all of it combustible—in your boat. Instead, take along only charcoal.

You can also simplify the shore operation by preparing such things ahead as coffee, juices, and soups and transporting them in Thermos jugs. Also a jug or two of Orange Snapper Punch (page 165). It helps brighten up any picnic.

Dictionaries define a picnic as an excursion in which food is eaten outdoors. Going by that, you can have a picnic without going ashore. Just eat aboard your craft and you're having a picnic.

Don't cook there though unless your boat meets all the safety requirements. Instead, take all your foodstuffs along, ready to be eaten, packed in watertight containers and consisting only of things that either can't spill or that can be drunk or eaten from utensils that minimize the possibility. This warning is applicable mainly in heavily populated areas, because as more and more boats take to the water, the more wake there is to contend with. Come to think of it, it isn't so bad after you get the hang of negotiating the waves. You can have all the fun of waves without having to venture into hazardous ocean waters. Your kids will think it's better than a roller coaster! Not conducive to good eating, though.

PART II

Facts Every Outdoor Cook Should Know

7—Meat, Poultry, and Fish

There are three main things to keep in mind when you buy meat and poultry to be cooked outdoors: quality, grade, and cut. In purchasing fish, there is really only one: freshness.

You must check to be sure that meat, poultry, and fish have not been exposed to contamination, which could result in rapid bacteria growth. The government helps you with meat and poultry. Look for the U.S. Department of Agriculture (USDA) inspection stamp or label on the meat and fowl you buy—a circle enclosing a statement that it has been inspected for wholesomeness and passed—and buy from a butcher on whom you can rely. These are the best assurance you have of getting top quality. With fish, you must depend on the word of the fishmonger—and on your own senses: sight and smell.

Meat that is to be broiled or roasted, with or without a spit, should be naturally tender. The less tender meats are fine for stews cooked in a pot or when wrapped in aluminum-foil packages to which moisture has been added in some form, such as vegetables that will steam when heated. Moist heat tenderizes by breaking down tough and stringy meats and the connective tissues that are sometimes unpleasant to chew.

"Grade" and "cut" are your guides to tenderness.

Beef

For any given cut, the higher the USDA grade the more tender and juicy the meat will be. USDA Prime grade is the most tender, then USDA Choice, then USDA Good. There are lesser grades, but we won't go into

189

them, because generally nothing lower than USDA Good should be considered for barbecuing.

Meat cut from the less active muscles of an animal, such as the rib and loin sections, will always be more tender than those from the active areas of the same animal, such as the shoulder (chuck), flank, and round.

Here is a list of beef steaks in their general order of tenderness, based on cut, not grade. Roasts cut from the same area would have the same tenderness.

> Most tender: tenderloin (filet mignon), porterhouse, T-bone, strip loin, club, sirloin, and rib.
> Moderately tender: sirloin tip, top round, blade chuck.
> Least tender: bottom round, arm chuck, flank.

Follow this guide and you'll be safe in your shopping if money is no object. But in order to get the most tender meat with the least expenditure of money, learn to combine "grade" with "cut" when buying. Then if, for example, you come upon a blade chuck steak from USDA Prime or USDA Choice beef, buy it, because it probably will be just as tender and nice in every way as a rib steak from USDA Good beef.

Lamb, Pork, and Veal

Lamb and pork are usually (but not necessarily always) slaughtered when young and tender, so the grade is not so important for them as it is for beef. The word of a butcher whom you trust is important. He can tell you if the cut came from a young or an old animal. It's up to you to get him to talk.

Although the fat in pork makes it admirably suited for barbecuing, it should be cooked only over coals if the interior meat will be well done before the outer coating is overcooked. Health is the factor here; pork, as you know, must always be well done.

Veal is the meat of a calf, butchered before it develops fat marbling, and therefore dry unless fat is added. Your butcher can do this by wrapping some around the cut. Veal has connecting tissues that generally make for more pleasant chewing and eating if broken down by moist heat.

How a Butcher Can Help You

We have good luck barbecuing USDA Choice chuck steaks, which Arthur Petry, our butcher in Long Beach, Long Island, New York, has been selecting for us for years. If you are fortunate enough to know a good butcher, ask his advice when in doubt about what meat to buy. Specify that you want to cook it outdoors over coals. He'll almost certainly have a special way of butchering meat for this purpose. Perhaps he'll also favor you with a recipe or a barbecuing trick.

Small legs of lamb, for instance, can be slit down the side, opened out into a butterfly shape, and grilled over the coals.

Ask your butcher to cut lamb steaks for you. With an interesting sauce they become a great outdoor delicacy. Ask him to prepare lamb ribs so that you can barbecue them the same way you do pork ribs. Get to know your butcher well. This book will provide you with the recipes, but he can have much to do with the way they turn out.

Cooking Both Indoors and Out

Some of the recipes you will find in this book combine indoor with outdoor cooking. For instance, we simmer lamb shanks on our kitchen stove to tenderize them, then cook them over our charcoal stove in a barbecue sauce to add delicious flavor.

Before barbecuing, pork spareribs can be simmered in this way, too, not to acquire tenderness but to be sure the pinkness will be gone from around the bone by the time they're crunchy done on the outside.

Poultry

When it comes to our feathered eating friends, it's "grade" and "class" that count. Not cut.

For outdoor cooking, you should always use USDA Grade A poultry, whether the poultry is chicken, turkey, duck or whatever. This is the mark of quality, and it is usually the only grade found in the retail market. It is not an indication of tenderness. That is determined by the age, often referred to as the "class," of the bird.

Young tender-meated classes are most suitable for barbecuing, frying, broiling, and roasting. Young chickens may be labeled as young chicken, Rock Cornish game hen, broiler, fryer, roaster, or capon. Young turkeys may be labeled as young turkey, fryer-roaster, young hen, or young tom. Young ducks may be labeled as young duckling, duckling, broiler duckling, fryer duckling, or roaster duckling.

Mature, less tender-meated classes are suitable for stewing, baking, soups, and salads. They may be labeled by an identifying adjective such as mature, old, hen, stewing, fowl, or yearling.

USDA nutritionists say that poultry should be well done. We suggest that you do not buy turkeys too big to be properly cooked on the inside by the time they're nice and brown on the outside. Cooking them unstuffed helps accomplish this.

As with pork ribs, we often simmer poultry pieces on our kitchen stove before placing them on an outdoor fire in order to make sure the pink is gone from around the bone by the time the outside is browned.

Fish

The best fish to cook is the fish that you catch. The best time to cook it is as soon as possible after it comes out of the water.

Unfortunately, however, there comes a time when even the wife of the most ardent fisherman must to market go, and the fish to buy is the fish that her husband was fishing for but did not catch.

For a very good reason.

It is the fish that's in season in waters where you live. Therefore, the commercial fisherman is fishing for it, too. Therefore, it will be the best buy, not only in price but also in freshness. The fishmonger will tell you what the price is, but your eyes and nose will tell you how fresh the fish is.

Here's what to look for:

> Eyes: bright, clear, full, and bulging.
> Gills: reddish pink, free from slime and odor.
> Scales: adhering tightly to the skin, brightly colored with characteristic sheen.
> Flesh: firm and elastic, springing back when pressed, not separating from the bones.

Here's what to sniff for: a fresh, clean smell, free from even a trace of objectionable odor.

Fish spoils easily if not handled with care. It should be wrapped in moistureproof paper or placed in a tightly covered dish and refrigerated the moment it comes from the market. So stored, its odor will not penetrate other foods.

Proper Storage

Buying good-quality meat, poultry, and fish is not enough. You must maintain its wholesomeness, too. The best way to do this is to hurry it home and into the refrigerator before it loses its market-storage chill.

If meat and poultry are wrapped in butcher paper, loosely rewrap in clean, nonabsorbent paper that will let air circulate around it. Wrappings used for prepackaging are constantly being improved, so it's usually all right now to refrigerate fresh meat and poultry in them for one or two days. Some fish, too.

Cured and smoked meats—bacon, frankfurters, sausage, and some types of ham—can usually be stored in their containers. But read the label instructions to make sure.

Refrigerator Storage Times

- Ground meat, poultry, most fish, and variety meats (liver, kidneys, brains, and such) should be used in one or two days.
- Clams, lobster, mussels, oysters, and crayfish should be kept alive until time to cook. It's safest to figure that that won't be more than a day.
- Chops, steaks, and roasts can be refrigerated for from three to five days.
- Use ham slices and half-hams in three to five days, whole hams within a week.
- Although you sometimes can keep bacon, franks, and smoked sausages longer, for best flavor they should be used within a week.
- Cooked meat, poultry, fish, and the broths and gravies in which they were cooked should be cooled quickly by placing in a dish set in ice water, then refrigerated in tight-cover containers and used in one or two days.

The same storage limits apply to your camping or cruising coolers, ice chests, and refrigerators, provided you are able to maintain a temperature of 38 to 42 degrees Fahrenheit. It's a good idea, therefore, to keep a thermometer in your box.

Freezer Storage

Before placing uncooked meat, poultry, and fish in the freezer, wrap it well in good-quality paper constructed for that purpose. All the air should be pressed out, the package closed with securely overlapped edges, tied or sealed with freezer tape, and marked to show content, weight, and date.

Many of the two-step recipes in this book call for all or part of the finished, cooked dish to be frozen. Some of the recipes give special freezing instructions, but, generally, cooked meats and combinations of meats and other foods should be frozen in the same manner as described for uncooked meats, with this exception—a little or all of any broth or gravy in which they were cooked should be poured over them. If they are going on a camping or cruising trip in a portable icebox, they should be packaged in a way that will prevent leakage. Here are two suggestions:

Package these foods in freezer paper, double-fold, leaving a little air space, fasten with freezer tape, then place in a plastic bag, and fasten the bag with a twist of wire designed for that purpose. Or line a Tupperware container with a plastic bag, into which you put your meat dish, including the sauce. But do not fill quite full. Liquids—this means sauces and gravies—expand when they freeze, so you must leave "head room" amounting to approximately 15 per cent of the total area. Put the open container in the freezer, and after its contents are frozen solid, fasten the plastic bag with a twist of wire and put the lid on the container.

Both cooked and uncooked meat, poultry, and fish that you transport in a frozen state in your camp or cruise ice chest should be reheated or cooked as soon as it thaws and while still icy cold.

If you arrive at camp or picnic grounds while steaks or chops are still hard-frozen, speed up defrosting and tenderize at the same time by pounding the meat with a wooden mallet.

Since they make such good and quick outdoor fare, it's a good idea to keep chopped meat patties in the freezer for hurry-up or spur-of-the-moment occasions.

Here's how to package them so you can take them out one at a time:

- Arrange the patties in a single layer on a cookie sheet, unwrapped and without touching each other.
- Place the cookie sheet, unwrapped, in your freezer. It will take from about three to six hours for each patty to freeze, depending upon its thickness and the size, shape, and condition of your freezer. So check frequently.
- The moment the patties are frozen, remove the cookie sheet from the freezer, transfer all of them into one heavy-duty plastic bag, seal it tightly with a wire twist, and place it immediately back into the freezer.

The patties won't stick together, and you can remove them one or two at a time or in any amount you'll need for an unplanned cookout. If possible, let the meat defrost before you cook it.

This easy-to-get-at freezer packaging method need not be confined to hamburger patties. Do the same with small, thin steaks and chops, too. But don't prepare very much meat ahead this way, just what you'll be likely to use in a month.

The Uncertainties of Timing and How to Overcome Them

Even indoors, under ideal conditions, it's difficult to give cooking times that will be accurate. Different types of heat cook at different speeds. Ovens cook differently from broilers, and the many different types of materials used in pots and pans and skillets all diffuse the heat differently.

And people, thank heaven, are not automatons. They do things at different rates of speed, sometimes taking time out from peeling a potato to gossip on the phone, read the newspaper, listen to a symphony, or diaper the baby.

Outdoors, in addition to all that, you must contend with air temperature, wind velocity, heat of the coals, type of fuel, distance of the food from the heat, hood up, hood down, shape of the food being cooked, and miscellaneous other things.

All fish is naturally sweet and tender so you do not have to cook it to get rid of toughness, as you must do with meat. Fish must be cooked just long enough for the protein to coagulate. Not a second longer. The best way to tell when that moment comes is by gently prodding the flesh with the tines of a fork. Start testing at about half the cooking time given in most printed recipes and at the minimum times given in the recipes in this book and you'll be safe.

Another way to tell is simply by looking. When the protein coagulates, the flesh loses its shiny, clear, almost translucent appearance and becomes opaque. White-fleshed fish will become the color of milk.

But what do you do about timing when cooking meat or poultry? You relax.

You let your menu be flexible. You serve the salad before or with the rest of the meal, depending on when the main course gets done. You serve steamed clams, celery, olives, and other things that will whet rather than take the edge off appetites sharpened by the aroma of steaks and birds and such cooking over your outdoor fire.

Plan on your meal being ready a little earlier than you told people it would be, so that you won't keep them waiting too long.

Ideally, roasted meat and poultry should be allowed to cool for fifteen minutes after removal from the fire because it will slice so much more easily and nicely then. But if it's late getting done, slice and serve at once.

Use times given in recipes and in charts as rough guides and rely on tests for doneness such as these:

- Use a sharp knife to cut into the thick part of a steak or chop, next to the bone if there is one, to see the color. Don't overdo this, though, or you'll let too much juice run out.
- Gently move a bird's drumstick. The juices will run clear and drumsticks will move easily in their sockets when it's done.
- The most accurate way to tell when a roast or turkey is done is to use a meat thermometer.

Poultry should be cooked until the thermometer registers 180 ° to 185 ° F.

Pork must be cooked until well done. The thermometer should register 170 ° F. for loins, 185 ° F. for other roast fresh pork; 160 ° F. for cured pork and either a whole or half ham. "Fully cooked" ham can be served as is or heated to 130 ° F.

Spit Roasting Time and Temperature Chart

Variety of Meat	Cut of Meat	Size or Weight	Recommended Heat of Fire*	Approximate Time for Cooking				
				Very Rare	Rare	Medium-Rare	Medium	Well Done
Beef	Standing Rib	3 to 5 lbs.	Med. to Hot	1½ to 2¼ Hrs.	1¾ to 2¼ Hrs.	2 to 2¾ Hrs.	2½ to 3 Hrs.	3 to 4½ Hrs.
	Rolled Rib	6 to 7 lbs.	Med. to Hot	1¾ to 2½ Hrs.	2 to 2¾ Hrs.	2¼ to 3 Hrs.	2¾ to 3¼ Hrs.	3¼ to 5 Hrs.
Pork	Fresh Ham	10 to 16 lbs.	Medium					4 to 6 Hrs.
Poultry	Chicken	3 to 5 lbs.	Medium					2 to 3 Hrs.
	Turkey	10 to 25 lbs.	Medium					3 to 6 Hrs.

* Hot fire, 400° plus; medium, 350°; slow, 250 to 300°.

Grilling Time and Temperature Chart

Variety of Meat	Cut of Meat	Size or Weight	Recommended Heat of Fire*	Approximate Time for Cooking (each side)				
				Very Rare	Rare	Medium-Rare	Medium	Well Done
Beef	Steak	1 inch	Hot	4 Min.	5 to 6 Min.	7 Min.	7 to 8 Min.	10 Min. or More
	Steak	1½ inches	Hot	5 Min.	6 to 7 Min.	8 to 9 Min.	10 Min.	12 to 15 Min.
	Steak	2 inches	Med. to Hot	7 to 8 Min.	8 to 10 Min.	10 to 15 Min.	15 to 18 Min.	20 Min. or More
	Steak	2½ inches	Med. to Hot	10 to 12 Min.	12 to 15 Min.	15 to 17 Min.	18 to 23 Min.	25 Min. or More
Fish	Fillet or Split	Small	Medium					5 to 10 Min.
	Fillet or Split	Large	Medium					10 to 15 Min.
Lamb	Chops or Steaks	1 inch	Medium		4 to 5 Min.	6 Min.	6 to 7 Min.	8 Min. or More
	Chops or Steaks	1½ Inches	Medium		5 to 6 Min.	7 Min.	8 to 9 Min.	10 Min. or More
	Chops or Steaks	2 Inches	Medium		6 to 7 Min.	8 Min.	9 to 10 Min.	12 Min. or More
Lobster	Split	1 to 2½ Inches	Med. to Hot					15 to 20 Min.
Pork	Chops or Steaks	1½ Inches	Low to Med.					20 to 25 Min.
	Spareribs	Whole	Very Low					20 to 30 Min.
Poultry	Chicken	Split	Medium					30 to 45 Min.
	Cornish Hen	Split	Medium					30 to 45 Min.

* Hot fire, 400° plus; medium, 350°; slow, 250 to 300°.

The charts, prepared by the "Char-Broil" outdoor stove division of the Columbus Iron Works, are just about as accurate as it's possible to be in estimating outdoor cooking times.

How to Use a Meat Thermometer

It's wise to always use a meat thermometer when cooking roasts and large birds. The printing on the thermometer will show when each type of meat should be done. The thermometer should be inserted at a slight angle, so that the tip is in the center of a roast but not resting in fat or on the rotisserie rod. It must clear the cooking unit and drip pan if the meat is to turn properly on a spit.

Insert the thermometer into the center of the inside thigh muscle or into the thickest part of breast meat of a large bird. Be sure it does not touch bone.

Placing the Rotisserie Rod

Do it correctly, because the way the rotisserie rod is placed can influence how evenly meat cooks.

For roasts, insert the rod lengthwise through the center of the meat or bird. Make sure one side is not heavier than the other so that it will turn and cook evenly.

For ribs, weave the rod in and out of the bones, forming accordion folds. Make sure they are well balanced so they will turn smoothly and cook evenly, then tighten screws with pliers.

Basting

The length of time you baste meat depends on the sauce being used for basting. If it contains sugar, the meat usually will start turning too dark a color if the sauce cooks more than twenty or thirty minutes.

Controlling the Temperature of Your Charcoal Stove

If you have one of the new outdoor gas stoves (see page 17), you can skip this item, because your heat indicator should work as well as the one on your kitchen range. If you do not, you had better read on.

Most charcoal stoves with hoods have heat indicators built into them. Unfortunately, there is no way of setting them for the temperature you want your cooking fire to be. All the indicators do is tell you what the temperature is. Not very helpful and often very frustrating.

But you can compensate:

- First of all, always let the coals burn down to a good gray color before starting to cook. At night a pink glow will show through the gray ash.
- Never cook over flames. Burned down, gray coals will assure more uniform heat. A single layer will usually do for steaks, chops, hot dogs, and hamburgers.
- Roasting requires two or three layers of coals. You should also keep an additional supply of burned-down coals ready to add to the fire if necessary to keep it burning evenly and at the heat you want. Dry coals left over from an earlier fire are ideal for this purpose.
- With experience, you'll learn just how much to adjust your dampers to control the heat. Open them to get a hotter fire, close them to cool it down.
- If you are cooking something small in a big grill that requires more heat than one layer of coals will provide, build a small enclosure with building bricks and bunch your coals inside it two or three deep or more if needed. Not only will you have a better cooking fire, you'll also conserve charcoal.
- There are thermometers made to be laid on the grill. They can be a help for broiling.
- Depending on the kind of stove you have, you can control the temperature either by raising and lowering the grill or by lowering and raising the fire bed.
- Generally, it's best to place meat (and most other foods, too) four to six inches above the coals. As the coals burn down and lose their heat, you may have to reduce the distance to about two inches. It's safe to lower it almost to the point where you will cause flare-up, but no farther.
- When food needs long, slow cooking so that both the interior and exterior will be done at the same time (pork and poultry that have not been presimmered, for example), you may have to increase the cooking distance to more than six inches. If so, let us warn you, you'll have to take special care to keep your coals burning well. Keep a bucket of second-day coals ready and add them to the fire as necessary.

Always Remember This

Meat will be more moist, more tender, more tasty, and lose less of its vitamins if cooked at a low heat.

8—Other Perishables

Dairy Products, Eggs, Fats and Oils

Dairy products sometimes carry a USDA grade or inspection mark. This is the best assurance you can have that they are wholesome, were packaged under sanitary conditions, and that the label is an accurate description of the contents. Sometimes the date they were sold to the store is stamped on them. This lets you know whether you are starting out with fresh food.

Beyond this, your best bet when stocking up on dairy products, eggs, lard, and salad oils to take on a camping trip or cruise is to buy brands you have found to be reliable from a store you have found to be reliable. After buying these products, take proper care of them so they don't deteriorate unnecessarily.

Milk

Fresh milk should always be refrigerated and should not be exposed to light. It will keep for up to a week.

Nonfat dry milk stored at 75 ° F. or lower will keep inuefinitely. Powdered whole milk should be kept tightly covered in the refrigerator. Check the package label for the length of time it can be kept under different conditions.

Evaporated milk in a can is whole milk with about 60 per cent of

199

the water removed. Sweetened condensed milk has sugar in it and is often substituted for cream in desserts.

Eggs

When you're going to take shell eggs camping, start with the best you can buy: USDA Grade AA, Fresh, Fancy, or if you can't get these, Grade A.

Neither color nor size of the egg influences interior quality, but whether your grocer has kept it in a refrigerated case does. Never buy eggs from a stack of store-temperature eggs, not even if the store is equipped with air conditioning. A plastic egg-carrying container will help reduce breakage, especially if you carefully examine each egg for cracks before packing it.

Because eggs are a high-protein food that can supplement and even replace meat in our diet, the increasing availability of packaged dehydrated dried eggs to campers and boat-galley chefs can be very important to you, provided you can store the product at 50 ° F. or lower.

Mrs. Velma Seat, Food Marketing Specialist at the Oregon State University Extension Service, Corvallis, Oregon (where Inez once worked in the Poultry Disease Laboratory), tells us that a number of large companies and educational institutions are now developing new egg products for the consumer market. These include eggs combined with fruit juice, omelets, scrambled eggs, egg salads, and French toast. Some of the items are dried and can be quickly reconstituted. Maybe by the time this book is published, some of these items will be available to consumers, so begin your camping or cruising trip by exploring your grocer's display shelves.

Buy dried eggs in a container carrying the USDA inspection mark, because it is your assurance that the product was pasteurized, contains wholesome materials, and was packaged under sanitary conditions.

To reconstitute, sift the egg powder if possible (don't pack it down when you measure) and sprinkle over an equal amount of lukewarm water. Stir to moisten the egg, then beat until smooth, scraping mixture from sides of container as you beat until smooth. Two and a half tablespoons of powder mixed with two and a half tablespoons of lukewarm water equals one large egg. One cup powder mixed with one cup lukewarm water equals six large eggs.

Unless the package label states that egg powder is safe to use in dishes that are only slightly cooked—such as soft omelets and custards—don't do it. Use it only for baked or top-of-stove dishes in which it will be cooked until thoroughly done.

Rather than reconstituting the eggs before mixing, when making pancakes, muffins, and such you may combine the dry egg powder with other dry ingredients and add the lukewarm water to other liquids the recipes call for.

Fats and Oils

You can store most firm (hydrogenated) vegetable shortenings at room temperature even after opening them. Salad oils and salad dressings will keep best if refrigerated after opening. Butter, margarine, lard (from animal fat), and meat drippings should be kept very cool, preferably at all times in the refrigerator. Go generally by label instructions to determine how and how long these foods can be kept.

Fresh Fruits and Vegetables

Buy the freshest, best-quality fruits and vegetables you can find to take on trips with you. They will keep longer than poor-quality produce and are therefore more economical in the long run, because you will not have to throw away parts that spoil. Good-quality fruits and vegetables also taste better and are more nutritious than poor quality.

Of course, if you don't take care of what you buy, produce is going to spoil, no matter how good it was when you made your purchase. The USDA Homemaking Department prepared the following storage guide for fruits and vegetables, which should be helpful. Even though it was meant for home kitchens, the general principles can be applied to an outdoor kitchen or boat galley almost as well.

Hold at room temperature until ripe; then refrigerate, uncovered: Apples, Apricots, Avocadoes, Berries and Cherries (sort but don't wash), Grapes, Melons (except Watermelons), Nectarines, Peaches, Pears, Plums, Tomatoes.

Store in cool room or refrigerate, uncovered: Grapefruit, Lemons, Limes, Oranges.

Store in cool room, away from bright light: Onions, mature; Potatoes; Rutabagas; Squash, winter; Sweet potatoes.

Refrigerate, covered: Asparagus; Beans, snap or wax; Beets; Broccoli; Cabbage; Carrots; Cauliflower; Celery; Corn, husked; Cucumbers; Greens; Onions, green; Parsnips; Peas, shelled; Peppers, green; Radishes; Squash, summer; Turnips.

Refrigerate, uncovered: Beans, lima, in pods; Corn, in husks; Peas, in pods; Pineapples; Watermelons.

If you plan to pick up fruits and vegetables along the way (get off the freeways in farming country and you'll see some that are mouth-watering), before you leave home you may find it practical to construct a storage crate out of slats so air can circulate. Give it slatted shelves, put the greenest produce on the bottom shelf and the ripest on top or transfer to your refrigerator or ice chest. Try to keep the box out of the sun and in a fairly cool place.

9—Food Poisoning
Is No Accident . . .
and It's No Fun!

Many people, caught up in the holiday spirit of eating, drinking, and being merry in the yard or while camping, cruising, or picnicking, take a holiday from taking care of their food—sometimes with disastrous results.

It need not happen to you, however. All you have to do is take a few proper common-sense precautions, and you won't be in any greater danger of being poisoned while eating outdoors than you would be while eating indoors at home.

The U.S. Public Health Service has documented records of hundreds of persons who have suffered the consequences of food-borne illness while on an outing and has attributed them all to human carelessness. Its findings were published in a pamphlet appropriately entitled "No Picnic," which contained a series of precautionary recommendations that can apply to all areas of outdoor eating and cooking covered in this book. So we quote:

> Disease-producing bacteria prefer certain types of food, particularly those high in protein and moisture, such as milk, milk products, eggs, meat, poultry, fish, shellfish, cream pies, custards and potato salad. For this reason, we refer to these types of food as potentially hazardous. After preparation, these foods must be kept either hot or cold.
>
> Hot is 140 ° F. or above. Cold is 45 ° F. or below. Temperatures between 45 ° F. and 140 ° F. are unsafe. Disease-producing bacteria grow most rapidly at the middle of this temperature range.
>
> If you have little or no facilities for maintaining these foods hot or cold, DO NOT TAKE THEM! Instead, plan your picnics (or

other outings) around canned, preserved or dehydrated food, fresh fruits and vegetables.

Keep preparation time to a minimum (in other words, for example, don't stop to talk on the telephone in the middle of making a potato salad) and keep foods at a safe temperature during transportation. Disease-producing bacteria multiply quickly—in as little as the few hours normally encountered between the preparation and serving at a picnic (or other outing). Even small numbers of bacteria can grow sufficiently to produce illness.

Bacterial growth in sandwiches can be reduced by using frozen slices of bread together with chilled (45 ° F. or below) fillings. They then should be wrapped tightly in a plastic film wrapper and placed in the cooler. They then will stay cold.

Do not refrigerate in deep containers. Food acts as an insulator and the center of large masses can be warm for long periods of time though the outer edges may be almost frozen. Use shallow pans and fill no more than three to four inches deep.

Remember, refrigeration does not kill disease-producing bacteria. It only slows their growth.

Do not place food in ice unless the ice has been produced from water of drinking quality, and unless the food can be washed (fruit and vegetables) or is sealed in a protective covering. Foods that are not otherwise protected should be sealed in clean plastic containers before placing on ice. (Don't wash dishes in a stream that might contain polluted water.)

Cover the serving area (ground, blanket or table) with a table cloth to provide a clean surface on which to place food. Food should be kept covered except when being prepared or served.

Return leftover potentially hazardous food to the ice-chest immediately after the meal. If there is no ice left, or the food has been at an unsafe temperature for long meal periods, THROW IT OUT! The best plan is to limit food quantities so there will be no leftovers. Don't make the mistake of serving foods at lunchtime, then leaving them unrefrigerated to serve again later in the day.

Buffet or Picnic-Style Serving

To all of which we'd like to add one word—Amen!—and these suggestions for avoiding contamination while foods are displayed in all their splendor and waiting for hungry guests to help themselves at an outdoor buffet or picnic table:

- Set serving dishes containing perishable foods on beds of ice. See page 29 for suggested ways of doing this.

- Put perishables out in small amounts only and replenish serving dishes often.
- If you want to put a golden-brown whole turkey on the table to be admired, by all means do so. But after you've gracefully and modestly taken your bows, removed the stuffing, and carved off enough slices to go around, immediately put the remainder back into the cooler. Ditto with the stuffing. Replenish both, of course, as needed.
- Replace serving tools with clean ones each time you replenish serving dishes. Or wash them.
- If you're using chafing dishes, remember that sauces and gravies that are going to have to stand for a long time should be the kind that can frequently be reheated to the boiling point without curdling. This usually means that those containing egg yolks or cream are out. So, please, no Hollandaise, Newburg, or Stroganoff.
- Cover every serving dish once it's laden. But you need not despair at the thought of hiding all those beautifully cooked and arranged delicacies from sight. Instead: (1) Cover them with see-through plastic, the kind that comes in rolls and clings to the dish, or (2) get yourself an assortment of easy lift-off, transparent covers that will fit over your serving dishes (they're made of both glass and plastic), or (3) design and sew your own serving-dish covers from clear but very heavy plastic that will need almost no reinforcement beyond the stitching. We think the last is nice because it has that personal touch. And that's what cooking and eating and liking are all about.

10—Nutrition

There is a song that includes the line "Goodbye, all my cares and woe." This is a very appropriate phrase, because outdoor cooking and eating are very much part of leisurely living, a time for vacation, a time for forgetting all your care and woe.

But don't let outdoor cooking and eating ever be a vacation from good nutrition, because all that will bring is additional care and woe.

It's just as important to practice good nutrition outdoors as it is indoors—if for no other reason than that there may not be a doctor for miles around.

Federal surveys show that startling nutritional oversights are occurring in all areas of American life. Many quite well-to-do people suffer an assortment of health ailments because of poor eating habits, and many poor people are well because they eat properly balanced meals. The choice for the latter is basic: Pay attention to nutrition or pay money they can't afford to doctors.

The choice with outdoor vacationers is basic, too. Forget about well-balanced meals for a few days and you'll not feel so good as you would if you'd eaten properly. Result: less fun and more grief that you'll probably pass off as stomach upset "due to the water" or some such wrong reason.

Never take a vacation from good nutrition. It's really very simple to abide by the guidelines:

• Include milk in some form in your daily diet. It can be whole

milk, dehydrated milk, nonfat milk, or any milk product—cheese and ice cream, for example. Adults need at least two full cups or the equivalent every day; teen-agers, four or more cups; younger children, three or four cups.
- Include two or more servings of meat, poultry, fish, or eggs in your daily diet.
- Four or more daily servings of fruits and vegetables, including those that provide vitamins A and C plus others, such as potatoes.
- Four or more daily servings of whole grain or of enriched or restored cereal-grain products such as bread, cereals, and spaghettis.
- Maintain variety in meals. Don't eat all your daily servings of any one thing at one sitting. Spread them around among breakfast, lunch, and dinner. Meat does much more good when eaten twice a day rather than just once. This is no problem, because eggs are included in the meat category.

The U.S. Department of Agriculture's Home and Garden Bulletin Number 1 (revised April 1968 edition) categorizes the vitamin content of fruits and vegetables like this:

Sources of Vitamin A. Dark-green and deep-yellow vegetables and a few fruits. In alphabetical order: apricots, broccoli, cantaloupe, carrots, chard, collards, cress, kale, mango, persimmon, pumpkin, spinach, sweet potatoes, turnip greens and other dark-green leaves, winter squash.

Good Sources of Vitamin C. Grapefruit or grapefruit juice, orange or orange juice, cantaloupe, guava, mango, papaya, raw strawberries, broccoli, Brussels sprouts, green peppers, sweet red peppers.

Fair Sources of Vitamin C. Honeydew melon, lemon, tangerine or tangerine juice, watermelon, asparagus tips, raw cabbage, collards, cress, kale, kohlrabi, mustard greens, potatoes and sweet potatoes cooked in jacket, spinach, tomatoes or tomato juice, turnip greens.

Campers and boaters who do not have easy access to meat, poultry, and eggs (and who find the fish unresponsive) need not lack for substitutes. For just such contingencies they should pack along such excellent protein legume stand-ins as dry peas, dry beans, nuts, peanut butter, lentils, and chick peas. To make beans even more nourishing than they are, add a piece of bacon to the pot in which they cook.

As for such other essentials as fats and sugars, no special planning is necessary. Normal eating practices pretty much take care of them automatically.

Here are a few more good nutrition-pointers:

- If you use the bleached varieties of rice and such grain products as flour, spaghetti, bread, and cereals, check the labels to be sure missing nutrients have been replaced in an enriching process.
- Eat the skins of apples and potatoes—after cleaning them, of course. Aluminum foil is fine for wrapping potatoes while they're baking, but, be smart, throw it away after the potato is done and consume that natural casing.
- Store food properly so there is the least possible loss of vitamins. Generally, this means keeping it in a clean, cool or cold place out of bright light.
- Don't overcook; excessive heat robs you of vitamins.
- Don't throw out any of the liquid in which meat and vegetables are cooked. It's loaded with vitamins, so use it in one way or another. It's grand for making soups, sauces, gravies, and omelets.
- Or, perhaps better still, cook meat and vegetables in so little liquid that it all will be absorbed at the moment your food is done. For this kind of cooking, a heavy pot like a dutch oven is best.

11—Planning Menus

Put all we've already said together now and you're ready to plan the menus for your camping trip, cruise, or picnic. Well, almost. First, you'll have to shop for all the things you'll need.

This will be no great problem if you are already in the habit of precise planning and shopping for so many meals for so many days.

But if you aren't, here are some pretty comprehensive estimates to guide you, gotten up by U.S. Department of Agriculture researchers.

In using their guidelines, remember two things:

- Serving sizes given are approximations of what the average American eats at home, not on an outdoor trip. Only you know your family's appetites, which are usually half again as great on the water or in camp.
- Don't include in your menus more buy-ahead perishable foods than you have cold-storage space for.

Meat, Poultry, and Fish

Three ounces of *cooked* lean meat, poultry, or fish per serving.

Meat	*Servings per Pound*
Much bone or gristle	1 or 2
Medium amounts of bone	2 or 3
Little or no bone	3 or 4

209

Poultry (ready-to-cook)	*Servings per Pound*
Chicken	2 or 3
Turkey	2 or 3
Duck and goose	2

Fish

Whole	1 or 2
Dressed or pan dressed	2 or 3
Portions of steaks	3
Fillets	3 or 4

Vegetables and Fruits

For this table, a serving of vegetable is one-half cup cooked vegetable unless otherwise noted. A serving of fruit is one-half cup fruit; one medium apple, banana, peach, or pear or two apricots or plums. A serving of cooked fresh or dried fruit is one-half cup fruit and liquid.

Fresh Vegetables	*Servings per Pound*
Asparagus	3 or 4
Beans, lima (bought in pod)	2
Beans, snap	5 or 6
Beets, diced (bought without tops)	3 or 4
Broccoli	3 or 4
Brussels sprouts	4 or 5
Cabbage	
Raw, shredded	9 or 10
Cooked	4 or 5
Carrots	
Raw, diced or shredded (bought without tops)	5 or 6
Cooked (bought without tops)	4
Cauliflower	3
Celery	
Raw, chopped or diced	5 or 6
Cooked	4
Kale (bought untrimmed)	5 or 6
Okra	4 or 5
Onions, cooked	3 or 4
Parsnips (bought without tops)	4
Peas (bought in pod)	2
Potatoes	4
Spinach (bought pre-packaged)	4

Fresh Vegetables	*Servings per Pound*
Squash, summer	3 or 4
Squash, winter	2 or 3
Sweet potatoes	3 or 4
Tomatoes, raw, diced, or sliced	4

Frozen Vegetables	*Servings per Package* (*9 or 10 oz.*)
Asparagus	2 or 3
Beans, lima	3 or 4
Beans, snap	3 or 4
Broccoli	3
Brussels sprouts	3
Cauliflower	3
Corn, whole kernel	3
Kale	2 or 3
Peas	3
Spinach	2 or 3

Canned Vegetables	*Servings per Can* (*1 lb.*)
Most vegetables	3 or 4
Greens, such as kale or spinach	2 or 3

Dry Vegetables	*Servings per Pound*
Dry beans	11
Dry peas, lentils	10 or 11

Fresh Fruit	*Servings per Market Unit* (*as purchased*)
Apples ⎫ Bananas ⎪ Peaches ⎬ Pears ⎪ Plums ⎭	3 or 4 per pound
Apricots ⎫ Cherries, sweet ⎬ Grapes, seedless ⎭	5 or 6 per pound
Blueberries ⎰ Raspberries ⎱	4 or 5 per pint
Strawberries	8 or 9 per quart

	Servings per Package *(10 or 12 oz.)*
Frozen Fruit	
Blueberries	3 or 4
Peaches	2 or 3
Raspberries	2 or 3
Strawberries	2 or 3

	Servings per Can *(1 lb.)*
Canned Fruit	
Served with liquid	4
Drained	2 or 3

	Servings per Package *(8 oz.)*
Dried Fruit	
Apples	8
Apricots	6
Mixed fruits	6
Peaches	7
Pears	4
Prunes	4 or 5

PART III

Yard, Camp, Wilderness, Boat, and Picnic Recipes

12—About the Recipes

Y, C, W, B, P

There are recipes in this book for every meal of the day, for family-style cooking and eating, and for entertaining; for cooking in the coals, over campfires, on charcoal grills and stoves, on gasoline and LPG camp stoves, and on marine galley stoves. Most of the recipes were created for use in more than one area of outdoor eating. Some can be used, for instance, equally well in a boat galley or on your patio. Some can be used in all five of the areas of outdoor cooking and eating we cover in this book: yard, camp, wilderness, boat, and picnic.

The letters in the upper right corner of each recipe tell you for which category or categories of outdoor eating the recipe is suitable. Y = Yard; C = Camp; W = Wilderness; B = Boat; and P = Picnic.

Some of our designations are general because individual methods and facilities of our readers will be many. The designations will, however, be helpful in narrowing down your search for the right recipes when making up your lists of menus.

Wilderness (W) recipes may require the greatest amount of adapting to your own particular circumstances. If you are camping in the desert, packing your supplies in a jeep-type vehicle, you almost certainly would be carrying more canned goods than if you were hiking in a mountain range or canoeing, where space would be very limited. If you knew there'd be water available in your mountain camp, you'd probably have lightweight dehydrated foods along. You'd therefore have to figure recipe quantities of these foods after they'd been reconstituted and were back to more or less normal size and weight. You might have to do a good deal of substituting one food for another in either dry-desert or water-plentiful mountain camping. You can, however, remove a considerable amount of the juggling

215

and guesswork by planning your menus ahead of time and then buying supplies according to the ingredients needed. It's much easier to do your substituting at home than in a wilderness camp.

Ingredient Substitutions

We have developed versatile recipes in which you can easily substitute another ingredient for one you don't have, such as canned for frozen or canned or frozen for the fresh product and vice versa. Dehydrated foods can be substituted if you reconstitute according to the package instructions. The amounts of reconstituted foods you'd use in a recipe would be roughly the same as canned, frozen, or cooked.

We suggest you do a little experimenting with dehydrated broths, soups, salad dressings, gravies, and other sauces before leaving home to get an idea of how versatile they are and of the ones you might want to include on your food list. They'll come in handy after you run out of your initial supply of food and must start improvising and adapting recipes to what you can forage or buy along the way.

Two-Step Recipes

We planned the cooking procedure for some of our recipes so that they can be partially prepared ahead of time in your home kitchen and finished up later over coals in the yard or at picnic grounds, on a camp stove, over a camp cooking fire, or in your boat galley.

Some of the do-ahead, or step 1, parts of these recipes can be frozen so that they will keep for a day or two in your ice chest before they must be finished up and served. Any additional ingredients needed for step 2 usually won't take up precious camp or galley cooler space.

We show separate times needed for step 1 and step 2 in the upper right corner of these partially do-ahead recipes. As we've said before, many things make cooking times differ. Keep that in mind when using these two-step schedules and you'll find them quite helpful when planning a patio party, picnic, camping trip, cruise, or a family meal in the yard.

Don't overlook these two-step recipes when you are going to cook from start to finish at one time. They work just as well in one operation as they do in two.

One-Pot Meals

The designation one-pot meal in the upper right corner of a recipe should help people who will be cooking over one burner or a small campfire pick out recipes easily that won't require juggling hot pots around when trying to prepare a well-balanced full-course meal.

13—Seasonings and Sauces

Seasonings and sauces are very important, because they combine with wood or charcoal smoke to give the foods you prepare outdoors such a wonderful aroma and flavor.

It's hard to say in outdoor cookery where seasonings leave off and sauces begin. Both add flavor, so we're taking what seems a sensible course and lumping them together in our discussion here.

We've included individual sauces with many recipes in this book. When we don't include a needed sauce, we refer you by page number to one of the recipes at the end of this chapter.

If you're going on camping or cruising trips that will keep you away from your home-base kitchen for more than a few days at a time, you should learn to create your own sauces from whatever you have or can get, no matter how isolated the place you may be. It's very easy. Just start with one thing and add to it. For that matter, many of the things you can start with will do very well all by themselves. You'll see what we mean a little further along. But before you start opening cans and mixing, there are a few general comments we should make:

- Don't overpower a delicately flavored food (such as veal or some white-meated fish and shellfish) with strong seasonings.
- Always add the broths from cooked meats, fish, poultry, and vegetables—whether from the pots or pans you cooked them in or the can you opened—to the sauces you use as marinades or gravies. *This is probably the most important sauce-making secret we can tell you.*
- Familiarize yourself with the characteristic flavors and strengths of different seasonings so that you can read through a list of sauce ingredients and pick out the teaspoon or tablespoon or something with such a powerful kick it will alter the character of a whole cupful of other things. Specifically, such things as horse-

radish, soy sauce, teriyaki sauce, Worcestershire sauce, cayenne pepper, paprika, sesame seed oil, and garlic. If you're not sure how popular these things are with your family or guests, add them a little at a time, tasting as you add—or choose a different sauce recipe.

Here, now, are those suggested easy sauce bases and some of the things you might add to them:

- One of the best of all and the easiest is canned soups. For campers and boating people this is a cinch, because you should carry a supply of them along with you anyway as emergency foods. Try one of these: undiluted tomato soup, cheddar cheese soup, cream of mushroom, cream of celery, and other creamed soups. Add other liquids and other seasonings to them as the food you're cooking seems to require. For that matter, you can use canned soups in making salad dressings, too.
- Catsup and canned tomato sauces and pastes are often a good beginning for a sauce or a good addition to one started with a different base, such as cooking oil, salad oil, olive oil, butter, or margarine, which are excellent sauces to use when basting lean or dry meats. You can add many combinations of liquid and dry seasonings.
- There's wonderful mayonnaise to which you can add so many things, perhaps first combining it with cultured sour cream or cream cheese. You can add crumbled blue or Roquefort cheese, grated cheese of any kind, crushed pineapple, chopped cucumber, chopped apple, or pickle relish. Here's an example of what we mean—Easy Tartare Sauce. Mix together ½ cup mayonnaise and 1 tablespoon pickle relish and serve with fish. For a variation, add ¼ to ½ cup sour cream or 2 tablespoons catsup.
- Herbs, cheeses, garlic powder, anchovy paste, and other things that have pronounced flavors and can be mashed or ground up or blended into pats of butter and then placed individually in small plastic bags, securely fastened, and kept in your home freezer or the coldest part of your cooler or icebox to be spread on meat, poultry, or fish before or after cooking or melted into a can of soup that's to serve as a sauce (or, for that matter, as a soup). An example is Blue Cheese Butter. Blend together with back of spoon 1 tablespoon soft butter, 1 tablespoon blue cheese, and freeze in small plastic bag. Makes a 2-tablespoon pat, just the right amount for spreading on a good-size steak that's going to serve 4 to 6 people.

- In addition to all the dried vegetables and herbs packaged specifically for and labeled *seasonings,* there are increasing numbers of little envelopes containing dehydrated combinations for making soups and salad dressing that add a real gourmet touch to many dishes. Try them at home, if you haven't already, to see which ones work magic for you and take them camping or cruising. Once you open these envelopes, they'll lose quality rapidly unless you keep them in an absolutely airtight container.
- Experiment with wines as seasonings (they are nonalcoholic after cooking) so that you'll be able to substitute the kind you have for one that may be called for in a list of ingredients but that you don't have with you wherever you are. Sherry is one wine you should try not to substitute something else for and vice versa because it's usually chosen for its own very distinctive flavor.
- Fruit-juice crystals make it possible to keep your nutrition balanced and add immeasurably to the flavor of camp fare, especially when you're in the wilderness, where food weight is such an important factor.
- And try seasoning your food with the fruit juices you may, up to now, have thought of only as something to drink, such as apple juice and cranapple juice.
- Finally, a word of caution: Don't marinate food in a metal container if your marinade contains an acid. Chipped or cracked enamelware dishes must be considered in the same class as a metal dish.

Here are some additional sauce recipes to help round out your repertoire of taste treats.

FRUIT JUICE GLAZE   Y, C, B, P

3 ounces undiluted frozen pineapple juice concentrate
3 ounces undiluted frozen orange juice concentrate
1 tablespoon lemon juice
1 tablespoon brown sugar
2 tablespoons honey
½ tablespoon ginger, powdered
1 tablespoon soy sauce

Combine and use as a marinade and glaze for barbecued meat, poultry, and fish.

HAWAIIAN-STYLE SWEET AND SOUR BARBECUE SAUCE
Y, C, B, P

6 tablespoons crushed pineapple in extra heavy syrup (optional)
½ cup soy sauce, preferably imported
¼ cup catsup
1 tablespoon brown sugar
6 tablespoons undiluted frozen lemonade
1 tablespoon mild mustard
½ teaspoon garlic powder

Combine all ingredients, mix thoroughly, and use as a barbecue sauce on meat or poultry. This sauce is especially good with spareribs. Freeze what you don't use for another time.

Variation
To 1 cup of the above sauce add:

   ¼ cup syrup or honey
   ½ cup undiluted frozen orange juice
   ¼ teaspoon paprika

Mix well. This is very good with chicken.

MEAT SAUCE TERIYAKI
Y, C, B, P

¼ cup Teriyaki sauce
¼ cup catsup
1 tablespoon mustard
2 tablespoons finely minced green onion (optional)
¼ teaspoon freshly ground pepper

Mix well and use as a marinade and to baste barbecuing steaks, roasts, and hamburger patties.

SAUCE POLONAISE
Y, C, B, P

1 10-ounce can brown gravy or brown sauce
¼ cup crushed gingersnaps
¼ cup raisins
¼ cup slivered almonds, skins removed, roasted
½ teaspoon sugar
½ cup red wine

Combine ingredients; heat, stirring constantly. Serve over fish. This is especially good on carp.

SPICY COCKTAIL SAUCE   Y, C, B, P

¾ cup catsup
1 tablespoon horseradish
2 tablespoons vinegar
1 tablespoon grated onion
3 drops Tabasco sauce
½ teaspoon Worcestershire sauce

Combine all ingredients, chill, and serve as cocktail sauce with shellfish or as a dip for meat balls.

SPICY MARINADE

Add 2 teaspoons cooking oil and 1 tablespoon olive oil to Spicy Cocktail Sauce recipe and use as a marinade and to baste meat, fish, and poultry.

VINEGAR AND OIL DRESSING   Y, C, W, B, P

2 tablespoons olive oil or salad oil
2 tablespoons wine vinegar
¼ teaspoon salt or to taste
¼ teaspoon black pepper or to taste

Combine in a jar, shake, cover, and set aside but do not refrigerate. When time to serve, shake again, pour over salad vegetables that have been dried off, and toss until they are well coated with dressing. Makes about ¼ cup. This is a versatile, basic dressing that can be used equally well on a tossed salad or to baste a broiling steak. This dressing is best when not held for more than a few days before using. Double the quantities to make ½ cup, for Two-Day Tossed Camp Salad.

Variation
Add 1 clove garlic, crushed, and ½ teaspoon sugar or to taste.

14—Salads

AVOCADO AND ORANGE SALAD   Y, B

2 ripe avocados, peeled and sliced into 12–16 wedges each
Lettuce leaves
2 ripe oranges, peeled, separated into sections, and skin removed
1 cup mayonnaise
½ cup sour cream
2–3 teaspoons sesame seeds

Divide avocado wedges over lettuce leaves on 4 to 6 salad plates. Divide orange sections into same number and arrange on top of avocado. Combine mayonnaise and sour cream; mix well. Divide over salads and top with sprinkling of sesame seeds.

AVOCADO AND GRAPEFRUIT SALAD

Substitute 1 grapefruit for 2 ripe oranges. Substitute 1 cup cottage cheese for mayonnaise and prepare in same way as for Avocado and Orange Salad.

CAESAR SALAD   Y, B
                                   Two-Step Recipe
                                   Step 1: ½ hour
                                   Step 2: ½ hour

You can start things going at an outdoor buffet by serving this salad yourself and then letting the guests, after they've eaten it, help themselves to other foods as the spirit moves them. This is a particularly good way to serve Caesar Salad because it really should be eaten at once and without anything else detracting from it.

Although you wouldn't ordinarily think of serving Caesar Salad on board a boat, prepared in the following two-step manner, it can be done very easily for a special occasion.

222

2 small heads romaine lettuce
1 clove garlic, cut in half
10 tablespoons salad oil
¼ teaspoon salt
¼ teaspoon pepper
¼ teaspoon Worcestershire sauce
½ teaspoon anchovy paste
½ teaspoon creamy mild mustard
6 slices stale white bread
1 egg, very fresh
½ lemon in tightly closed small plastic bag
1 tablespoon crumbled blue cheese in tightly closed small plastic bag
2 tablespoons freshly grated Parmesan cheese in tightly closed small plastic
   bag

Step 1

Cut stem end from romaine lettuce, discard any spoiled or unsightly leaves, and wash under running water, being sure to get rid of all the sand. Shake off moisture, then place leaves in a large, clean linen towel, hold ends securely and shake to remove the remaining moisture. Cut and discard heavy rib from each of the larger leaves. Place leaves in a plastic bag and close tightly.

Combine half the garlic clove in a jar with half of the salad oil, salt, pepper, Worcestershire sauce, anchovy paste, and mustard and shake. Cover tightly and set aside.

Lay slices of stale bread in a flat pile, cut away crusts (save them for another recipe), and cut bread into ½-inch cubes. Put bread cubes into a plastic bag and fasten shut.

Combine second half of garlic clove with remaining salad oil in a small jar, cover tightly, place in a paper bag together with the plastic bag of bread cubes, and set aside.

Assemble the bag of romaine lettuce, the jar of salad oil mixture, the paper bag containing bread cubes, the oil, egg, ½ lemon, and the plastic bags of cheese and put them all together in a bag and refrigerate. If you're afraid of breaking the egg, wrap it in tissue and put it in a jar. Now everything's ready for the second step. Step 1 can be prepared the night before a buffet dinner in your outdoor dining room or just before packing your cooler to take aboard your boat with you.

Step 2

Take bowl of salad ingredients from kitchen or boat refrigerator. Remove the small bottle of oil and bread cubes. Discard clove of garlic and pour the oil from the bottle into a large shallow pan. Spread over the bottom of the pan and scatter the bread cubes over the coating of oil. Put pan in 400° F. oven and toast cubes for about 15 minutes, stirring often or until they are crisp and have a light golden color. Transfer to a covered bowl or jar.

While bread cubes are browning, tear romaine lettuce into bite-size pieces and put them in a large salad bowl.

Carry bowl of lettuce and other salad ingredients (including toasted bread cubes) on a tray to the serving table and mix and serve. Caesar Salad is one of those dishes that is rather special and should be served with a proud flourish!

Shake bottle of oil dressing, pour it over salad, and toss with salad fork and spoon. Add both packages of cheese and toss again. Break the raw egg into the salad bowl, squeeze juice of the lemon directly over egg and then immediately mix the egg into the greens. Keep at it, tossing thoroughly until not a trace of yolk or white remains to be seen. Dump warm, toasty bread cubes into the bowl, mix lightly, and serve at once on individual salad plates. Serves 12 to 16.

Note
If you prefer egg to be slightly cooked, put it in a small pan, cover with cold water, bring the water just to boil, turn off, and immediately remove the egg. If you put the egg in the water just after putting the bread cubes in the oven, it should be ready at the right moment.

COTTAGE CHEESE AND VEGETABLE SALAD

Y, C, B

1 bunch sweet, crisp radishes, cleaned and chopped
1 bunch sweet young green onions, cleaned and chopped, including a little of the green
1 firm cucumber (it must not be watery), peel on, chopped
1 pint creamed cottage cheese
Lettuce leaves

Combine chopped vegetables with cottage cheese, mix well, and serve on lettuce leaves. Serves 4 to 6.

Variation
Add 1 small carrot, very finely minced.

YOGURT AND VEGETABLE SALAD

Substitute plain yogurt for the cotttage cheese in the Cottage Cheese and Vegetable Salad recipe.

Variation
Add 1 small carrot, very finely minced.

FROZEN FRUIT AND SHRIMP SALAD   Y

½ teaspoon lemon juice
1 6½-ounce can nice-quality deveined shrimp, drained and dried off
4 sections ripe, sweet grapefruit
4 sections ripe, sweet orange
1 teaspoon sugar
½ cup mayonnaise
1 3-ounce package cream cheese
1 cup very sweet seedless green grapes
½ cup blanched, slivered almonds, toasted
½ cup whipping cream
Lettuce leaves

Stir lemon juice into shrimp. Skin grapefruit and orange sections, cut each section in half, sprinkle with sugar, and stir. Thoroughly blend mayonnaise and cream cheese together and stir in shrimp, fruit, and nuts. Whip cream, stir gently into mixture, and pour into shallow freezer dish. Stir once before it sets. When almost frozen solid, make cutting indentations so it will be easy to separate later on. Unmold onto pieces of lettuce leaves arranged on decorative aluminum-foil serving dishes. Serve immediately or set over ice, because this salad defrosts very quickly. Serves 6 to 8.

LETTUCE AND ONION SALAD WITH   Y, C, B, P
VINEGAR AND SUGAR DRESSING

½ large head of lettuce, washed, dried, and torn into bite-size bits
1 medium sweet onion, thinly sliced
2 tablespoons white vinegar, or to taste
Granulated white sugar to taste

Combine lettuce, onion, and vinegar, toss and serve. Pass sugar and let each person sprinkle desired amount over salad. Serves 4 to 6.

MANY–COLORED COLE SLAW   Y, C, B, P

¼ cup seedless raisins
2 tablespoons sherry
2 tablespoons orange juice
½ medium cabbage, sliced finely
1 small carrot, grated
½ green pepper, chopped
½ cup mayonnaise
1 teaspoon vinegar
1 tablespoon granulated white sugar
10–12 cherry tomatoes

Marinate raisins in sherry and orange juice overnight. Combine cabbage, carrot, and green pepper and stir in marinated raisins, including the sherry-and-orange-juice marinade. Mix mayonnaise, vinegar, and sugar together, add to vegetables, and stir until they're well coated. Transfer to a clear glass bowl, arrange cherry tomatoes over the top, and serve. Serves 6 to 8.

PICKLED HERRING SALAD   Y, B

1 jar (about 12-ounces) pickled herring in cream sauce
2 large boiled potatoes, peeled and diced
2 red apples, cored and diced with skin left on
2 tablespoons pickle relish
1 tablespoon sugar
2 tablespoons vinegar
Lettuce leaves
4 hard-boiled eggs, shelled and cut in wedges
6 slices pickled beets

Dice herring in as small pieces as possible and, along with the cream sauce in which it comes, combine diced potatoes, apples, pickle relish, sugar, and vinegar and chill for 2 hours. Mound in center of large lettuce leaves, leaving room to arrange egg wedges and beet slices around the edge of mound. Serves 6.

Note
If there is not enough cream sauce to make a nice consistency, add ¼ to ½ cup sour cream or plain yogurt.

POTATO SALAD   Y, P

2 eggs, hard cooked and shelled
4 medium potatoes, cooked in their skins
½ cup chopped celery
½ cup crushed walnuts
1 large onion, chopped
2 tablespoons vinegar
2 tablespoons vegetable oil
½ teaspoon salt, or to taste
¼ teaspoon white pepper
1 large, crisp red apple
2 teaspoons lemon juice
½ cup dairy sour cream
½ cup mayonnaise
Several large lettuce leaves, washed
1 cucumber, peeled and sliced
1 ripe tomato, cut into wedges

Boil eggs, cool, peel, slice, and set aside. Boil potatoes, cool under running
water. Remove skins and cut potatoes in cubes. Combine potato cubes,
chopped celery, crushed walnuts, and chopped onion in a bowl. Mix vinegar, vegetable oil, salt, and pepper together and stir very thoroughly into
the vegetables. Cut apple in quarters—don't peel—remove core, and chop
into small pieces. Pour lemon juice over the bits, mix to coat all sides,
then stir into the bowl of salad. Combine sour cream and mayonnaise and
stir very thoroughly into salad.

　　　　Line a large salad bowl with lettuce leaves. Pile potato salad inside
leaves, press down gently, and smooth the top. Make a circle of egg and
cucumber slices around outer edge of bowl, just inside of where edges of
lettuce leaves stick up. Put one egg slice in center of salad and arrange
tomato wedges around the egg slice, petal fashion. You can tear bits of
lettuce into leaf shapes and put a few around the tomato if you like. Cover
with plastic wrap and keep in refrigerator or icebox until time to serve.
Then place atop a bowl of crushed ice to keep good and cold. Serves 6 to 8.

STUFFED CELERY À LA WALDORF   Y, B, P

1 bunch of celery, washed, drained, and separated
1 8-ounce package cream cheese
½ cup raisins
½ cup slivered almonds, skins left on
1 red apple, peel on, chopped
1 teaspoon lemon juice

This is an easy, colorful way to serve a favorite salad outdoors. Spread celery stalks with cream cheese. Starting at one end of each stalk, press a raisin into the cheese, then a piece of almond, skin edge up. Coat chopped apple with lemon juice, then add a piece of apple, red skin side up. Start over again with a raisin and continue doing this until all stalks are filled. Arrange stalks like the spokes of a wheel on a plate and add a sharp knife so those who don't want a whole stalk can cut off a piece. You can cut each stalk into about 6 pieces before serving, but they won't look nearly so pretty on your buffet if you do. Makes 30 to 40 appetizers.

Note
If any pieces of celery are left after about 20 minutes, set serving plate over ice.

TOSSED GREEN SALAD

Y, C, B, P
Two-Step Recipe
Step 1: ½ hour
Step 2: 5 minutes

½ head of lettuce, washed and excess moisture
   shaken off
½ cup very thinly sliced broccoli, raw, including stem
½ cup very thinly sliced cabbage, including the heart
½ cup slivers of raw asparagus, sliced on diagonal, about ⅛-inch thick
1 small cucumber, skin on, very thinly sliced (must not be watery)
1 medium onion
¾ cup mayonnaise
¼ cup catsup

Step 1
Place first 5 ingredients in Tupperware lettuce crisper or plastic bag, close so it's airtight, and store in your camp ice chest. Be sure onions and catsup are included on your list of general things to take with you if you're going camping or cruising, or on a picnic. If you won't be taking mayonnaise with you for other meals, measure ¾ cup into a small airtight jar or plastic container and store in your ice chest.

Step 2
Just before serving time, tear lettuce into bite-size pieces, slice onion, stir mayonnaise and catsup together. Combine all salad ingredients, toss together until each piece is coated with dressing, and serve. Serves 6 to 8.

TWO-DAY TOSSED CAMP SALAD

Y, C, B, P
Two-Step Recipe

2 large tomatoes
2 small onions
1 head lettuce, washed, dried, and torn into bite-size
    pieces
4 radishes, thinly sliced
1 cucumber, thinly sliced
½ cup Vinegar and Oil Dressing (page 221) in a leak-proof container

Step 1: ½ hour
Step 2: ¼ hour

Step 1
Place all ingredients except the dressing in a plastic bag, fasten, label, and store in cooler or icebox.

Step 2
Slice one tomato and one onion into half of the other salad vegetables. Shake dressing, add half to salad, toss, and serve. Repackage remaining ingredients, return to cooler or icebox, and use second day of camping. Serves 6 to 8.

WATERMELON FRUIT BASKET SALAD

Y, P

1 large watermelon
4–6 cups of mixed fruit (grapes, cherries, blueberries, chopped peaches, sliced bananas, cantaloupe balls)

Cut watermelon in half lengthwise. (Leave a strip of the top half attached to bottom half to be your basket's handle if you're an amateur sculptor.) Cut about 2 cups of melon balls from the melon heart, combine with mixed fruit, and refrigerate. Scoop remaining melon from watermelon and refrigerate, covered. Cut scallops or a zigzag edge on your watermelon basket, carve a design on it (maybe your monogram), or leave it plain. Fill it with chilled fruit salad, cover with plastic wrap, set on a bed of ice, and place it where it can get the attention it deserves on your serving table. Replenish with additional melon balls from your reserve in the refrigerator as necessary. Serve as a dessert or a salad. Either way, it will be beautiful and delicious and, if you keep it cold, will last for two days. Serves 20 or more.

WILDERNESS SALAD   C, W, P

If you find yourself around a cattail-lined swamp in the spring, you've got a delicious salad just waiting to be picked. Find shoots between 1 and 3 inches long and cut them off down near the root. Peel away the outer layers until you come to a yellow-white shoot. This is your salad vegetable; use it alone or with other forage foods such as dandelion, which, incidentally, should be young and tender at the same time of year.

1 cup cattail shoots, sliced into thin bits
1 cup young, tender dandelion leaves and flower buds
½ cup Wilderness Salad Dressing (recipe follows)

Combine all ingredients, toss and serve. Serves 2.

WILDERNESS SALAD DRESSING   W

4 slices bacon
¼ cup vinegar
Dash garlic powder
½ teaspoon salt
½ teaspoon sugar
¼ teaspoon pepper

Fry bacon until crisp, crumble, combine with other ingredients, and heat through. Stir while hot into Wilderness Salad. Makes ½ to ¾ cup of dressing.

CARROT–MUSHROOM SOUP MOLD   Y, B

3 medium carrots, scraped and sliced
2 cups water
¼ teaspoon salt
1 tablespoon unflavored gelatin
¼ cup cold water
1 10½-ounce can condensed mushroom soup

Simmer carrots in the 2 cups of water, salt added, until tender but not mushy. Drain, reserving liquid. Add water or take away to make one cup. Sprinkle gelatin onto ¼ cup of cold water and stir until blended. Bring cup of liquid in which carrot was cooked to a boil and stir it into gelatin mixture. Continue until thoroughly blended, then add can of mushroom soup and cooked carrots. Mix well and pour into a mold. Cover and chill. Unmold as described in Step 2 of Creamed Chicken Salad Mold and serve. Serves 4 to 6.

CREAMED CHICKEN SALAD MOLD   Y, B

Two-Step Recipe
Step 1: 24 hours
Step 2: ¼ hour

½ of 3-ounce package lemon gelatin
½ cup boiling water
⅛ cup strained lemonade
6 pimiento-stuffed olives, sliced
1 green pepper, cut in rings
½ cup grated raw carrot
1 envelope unflavored gelatin
¼ cup cold water
1 10½-ounce can cream of chicken soup
1 3-ounce package cream cheese
1 cup chopped chicken meat
¼ cup crushed pineapple, drained
½ cup chopped celery

Step 1

Mix lemon gelatin until thoroughly blended with boiling water, add strained lemonade, cool but don't let it set, and pour into an ice-cold 1 to 1¼ quart mold. Tip the cold mold so that gelatin runs all over the inside of it. When gelatin is firm enough to hold them in place (again, don't let it completely set), press sliced olives, green pepper rings, and grated carrot into it. Make up your own design or put a sliced olive in center of each green pepper ring and circle the olive slices with a little grated carrot. Refrigerate.

Sprinkle contents of envelope of unflavored gelatin on ¼ cup cold water in a saucepan. When gelatin is softened, turn on heat and stir until it is completely dissolved. Remove from heat and stir into can of undiluted cream of chicken soup. Pour soup into a dish with cream cheese and blend them together until smooth. Add chopped chicken, drained pineapple, chopped celery and stir. Pour into mold on top of lemon gelatin, cover, and refrigerate overnight.

Step 2

To unmold, run hot water into a large bowl or pan, dip mold into the hot water, but don't let the water go over the sides and get on the gelatin. Leave in water no more than 15 seconds, dry off quickly so it doesn't drip, invert serving plate over top of mold, and quickly flip over. Set plate with inverted mold on it on table and gently tap. If it feels as if mold has fallen out, remove mold form; if not, dip a kitchen towel in hot water and hold it over the mold form. Then lift off the form. Serves 4 to 6.

JELLIED FORAGED FRUIT AND FISH SALAD

Y, C, B
One-Pot Meal

½ teaspoon salt
1 medium onion, chopped
1 2–2½-pound fresh-caught fish
5 cups water
1 tablespoon soy sauce
1 teaspoon mustard
½ cup lemon juice, or to taste
¼ cup sugar or to taste (add more if necessary after all ingredients, including fish broth, have been combined)
1–2 cups foraged berries supplemented with any leftover fresh fruit you may have (substitute 1 1-pound can fruit cocktail)
Shredded lettuce or cabbage

Place wire rack in skillet or large pot and add water to a depth of about ½-inch, but not deep enough to touch rack when it simmers. Add salt and onion. Bring water to a simmer and lay fish on rack. Cover, turn heat to low or move skillet or pot to side of fire, and let fish steam for 5 minutes or until flesh flakes easily when tested with tines of a fork. Remove from skillet or pot and carefully flake flesh from bones and skin and set aside. Do not bother trying to flake any flesh that is full of little bones. Return any such flesh along with skin and bones to skillet or pot, add 5 cups of water, and boil for about one-half hour. Strain liquid through clean cloth or several layers of cheesecloth. You will need about 2½ cups. If you have more, simmer to reduce further. If you have less, add sufficient water to make 2½ cups. Combine fish broth with all ingredients except fish flakes and simmer together for 5 minutes. Add fish flakes and pour into a bowl or jar with a tight-fitting lid that won't let any moisture in or out.

Chill salad in icebox or by setting in ice-cold water, which you must change frequently so that it stays ice cold. When very cold, the broth should set into a soft jelly. Spoon over shredded lettuce or cabbage and serve at once. Serves 2 as a complete meal, 4 as an accompaniment to other dishes.

Note
If you substitute canned fruit cocktail, reduce fish broth further and consider the liquid in the cocktail as part of the 2½ cups.

This can be a wilderness recipe if you're camped near cold water.

PINEAPPLE–CRANBERRY MOLD   Y

1 1-pound can whole cranberry sauce
2 11-ounce cans Kabuki Mandarin Orange Segments and Pineapple Tidbits
2 cups boiling water
1 6-ounce box pineapple gelatin
½ cup cold pineapple juice
Juice of ½ lemon
Ice water
1 cup coarsely crushed English walnut meats
Large lettuce leaves

Drain juice from cranberry sauce and canned orange and pineapple mixture. Reserve juice and set sauce and fruit aside. Add boiling water to gelatin, stirring until completely dissolved. Combine cold pineapple juice with lemon juice and juice drained from 2 cans. Add enough ice water to make 1½ cups and stir into dissolved gelatin. Pour ⅔ of gelatin into 2-quart mold and refrigerate. Set bowl containing reserved ⅓ of gelatin where it will stay a little warm so it won't set.

When refrigerated gelatin has set, combine reserved unset gelatin with drained cranberry sauce and drained orange segments and pineapple tidbits, stir in crushed walnuts, and pour into mold on top of firm gelatin. Cover and chill. When it is thoroughly set, unmold as described in Step 2 of Creamed Chicken Salad Mold and invert on bed of large lettuce leaves. Cover with clear glass or plastic bowl and place, over ice, on outdoor buffet or dinner table. This mold goes especially well with roast turkey served either hot or cold. Serves 12 to 15.

REAL FRUIT JUICE GELATIN   Y, C, W, B

1 3-ounce package lemon gelatin
Boiling water as called for in package instructions
1 cup reconstituted orange-juice crystals (substitute fresh juice)
1 3-ounce package slivered almonds (optional)
1 cup foraged berries (optional)
Topping mix

Make gelatin according to package instructions, substituting reconstituted orange-juice crystals for cold water. Stir in slivered almonds and foraged berries when gelatin is partly set. If berries are juicy, reduce amount of orange juice or boiling water to compensate for the amount of juice that might thin the gelatin and keep it from setting. Prepare topping mix according to directions. Serves 4.

Note

You can also use unflavored packets of gelatin with reconstituted fruit-juice crystals. If you have a cooler of some sort or snow or ice water available for setting dishes in to chill, real fruit juice–flavored gelatin can become a tasty and nutritious dessert standby. Gelatin dessert powders are available that don't require chilling to set and become firm; however, we think this dessert needs to be cold to taste good.

FRUIT SALAD GELATIN

Substitute 1 cup or more of drained, mixed fresh fruit or canned fruit cocktail for foraged berries in recipe above. Reserve drained juices and substitute for part of water in making gelatin.

SMOKED OYSTER AND MUSSEL APPETIZERS

Y, C, B, P

1 3⅔-ounce can smoked oysters
1 3-ounce can smoked mussels
2 small onions cut into ¼-inch slices
½ small cucumber cut into ¼-inch slices, peel on
Small round crackers

Put smoked oysters and mussels in a bowl in center of platter. Arrange sliced onions, cucumber and round crackers on the platter and let people decide which they'd prefer to set a piece of the smoked shellfish on before popping into their mouths. Makes about 48 appetizers.

TACOS FILLED WITH GUACAMOLE

Y, B, P
Two-Step Recipe
Step 1: ½ hour
Step 2: ¼ hour

2 ripe avocados, peeled, seeded, and mashed
1 tablespoon lemon juice
1 tablespoon finely minced onion
½ teaspoon salt
⅛ teaspoon pepper
1 1-dozen package pre-folded taco shells

Step 1

Mix mashed avocados, lemon juice, minced onion, salt, and pepper together until very well blended. Put immediately into heavy plastic bag and fasten securely with metal twist so no air can get at the avocado flesh and turn it an unpleasant dark color. Refrigerate until time to use or transfer to cooler.

Step 2

Keep guacamole cool and tightly closed until serving time; then use it to stuff the taco shells. Makes 12.

A Word about Raw Fish

For most Americans, the word would be "Ugh!" That's because our eating habits haven't accustomed us to raw fish, and so we find the very thought of it unpalatable. That's not the case, however, if the raw fish is marinated. Marinating is a form of pickling, pickling can be considered a form of cooking. Sometimes the marinade is a variety of liquids or seasonings, sometimes only one liquid—for example, lemon juice. There's nothing commonplace about the results. When combined on the plate with fruits, nuts, and other things, fish served in this way constitutes delicacies (known as *seviche*) and commands top prices in fancier restaurants and therefore rates being called food fit for gourmets.

The fish can be any at all that has white meat, and it should be freshly caught—which makes these next two recipes perfect for the boat galley. Just remember not to use a metal dish—and that includes chipped or cracked enamelware—for marinating.

AVOCADO SEVICHE   Y, B

1½ pounds any fresh-caught white-meat fish fillets
1½ cups lemon juice
3 avocados
¾ cup orange juice
1 green pepper, cut in julienne strips
1 red pepper, cut in julienne strips
½ medium red onion, thinly sliced
3 green onions (scallions), finely chopped
2 tablespoons catsup
¼ teaspoon chili powder
Salt and pepper to taste

Cut fillets lengthwise into 1-inch strips; then, slicing at an angle, cut the strips into 1-inch pieces. Place in glass bowl, add 1 cup of lemon juice, and stir to make sure fish is thoroughly saturated. Let stand 3 to 6 hours in the refrigerator, but stir and turn about once an hour. When fish is through marinating, put in a colander and rinse well in cold water.

Cut avocados in half lengthwise, discard seeds, and scoop the pulp in small chunks into a mixing bowl, leaving about a ½-inch lining of pulp in the shells. Add to the bowl all other ingredients and toss gently until well mixed. Add marinated fish and again toss gently, just enough to mix in the fish.

Fill each avocado shell with the mixture, spoon over with the liquids from bottom of bowl, trying to coat all avocado pieces in order to keep them from discoloring. Serve at once. Serves 6.

MARINATED FISH   Y, C, B

1½ pounds any fresh-caught, white-meat fish fillets
1 cup lemon juice
1 large red onion, sliced
Radishes
Cucumber slices
Lemon wedges

Cut fish fillets lengthwise into 1-inch strips; then, slicing at an angle, cut the strips into 1-inch pieces. Place in glass or earthenware bowl, add lemon juice, stir to make sure fish is thoroughly saturated. Let stand 3 to 6 hours, the longer the better, but stir and turn about once an hour.

When fish is marinated, transfer to colander and rinse well in cold water. Arrange on serving platter, surround with an alternating border of sliced onion, radishes, cucumber slices, and lemon wedges, and place on appetizer table with picks. Serves 18 to 20.

15—Soups

BOATMAN'S BOUILLABAISSE

Y, C, B, P

This recipe starts with things available in cans such as shrimp and crab meat and stewed tomatoes. Set them on the fire in a big pot and add whatever you catch to it.

2 tablespoons olive oil
2 tablespoons butter or margarine
1 large onion, chopped
1 small clove garlic, minced
1 1-pound can tomatoes
2 cups water
1 8-ounce jar clam juice
½ teaspoon saffron shreds
⅛ teaspoon dried thyme
2 bay leaves
2 pounds mixed fish, cut up and bones removed
6 cups water
1 7½-ounce can minced clams
1 7½-ounce can crab meat
1 4½-ounce can shrimp, cleaned and deveined
Salt and pepper to taste

Heat olive oil and butter or margarine in large pot, add onion and garlic, and cook until tender. Add canned tomatoes, 2 cups water, clam juice, saffron shreds, dried thyme, and bay leaves and simmer for 10 minutes. Add fish and 6 cups of water. (If you don't catch any fish, the soup will be good anyway, but reduce the amount of water you add at this point from 6 to 2 cups.) Continue simmering for 5 minutes, add clams, crab meat, and shrimp. Stir, taste, and add amount of salt and pepper you think it needs, continue cooking for 5 minutes and serve with French bread. Serves 8.

Note
If you dig clams, catch crabs, net shrimp, or otherwise forage up fresh shellfish of any kind, by all means add them to the pot, omitting the canned stuff if you like. This recipe is versatile, as a Bouillabaisse should be. It

began as a fisherman's chowder in the Mediterranean, where commercial anglers, at day's end, threw a bit of everything they caught into the supper pot.

BORSCHT (BEET SOUP)   Y, C, B, P

Cold soups are a perfect way to serve vegetables at an outdoor dining table where you want a beautiful, different, and tasty touch.

2 bunches fresh young beets
2 quarts water
1 8-ounce can tomato sauce
1 teaspoon salt
¼ cup sugar, or to taste
¼ cup lemon juice, or to taste
4 eggs, beaten
1 pint sour cream

Peel beets, cut into quarters and thinly slice. Combine with water, tomato sauce, and salt in a deep pot; cover and simmer 1 hour. Add sugar and lemon juice to taste to make it pleasantly sweet, yet sour. Beat eggs in a bowl with about 1 tablespoon of the hot borscht until well mixed, then stir into the pot and beat well. Allow to cool and then store in refrigerator to chill.

Beat in about a cup of sour cream and serve cold with more sour cream as topping to individual tastes. (Some people, Dan for instance, prefer borscht without cream.) Serves 6 to 8.

Note
Serve this beautiful pink soup in your best tureen, set in a bowl of ice. Or a large Thermos jug full makes an excellent picnic companion.

CABBAGE SOUP WITH BEEF

Y, C, P
One-Pot Meal

3 pounds lean beef stew meat
2 1-pound 12-ounce cans whole peeled tomatoes
1 can water
3 medium carrots cut in half, crosswise
½ teaspoon powdered ginger
1 tablespoon vinegar
2 tablespoons lemon juice
4 tablespoons brown sugar or to taste
1 bay leaf
6 small wedges of cabbage
Grated Parmesan cheese
French bread

Put everything except the last three items in heavy, large (at least 5-quart) pot. Bring to a boil, stir, then raise grill far enough above coals—or move pot to one side—so that boil is reduced to a simmer. Lay cabbage wedges over top of brew, cover tightly, and continue simmering for 2 hours. If you can't keep simmer uniform and low, remove lid every half hour or so, invert it, and lay cabbage wedges on it while you stir contents of pot, checking bottom carefully to be sure dinner's not sticking.

When the meat is tender, dip out a bowl of soup for everyone. Pass grated Parmesan cheese for sprinkling over top. Serve French bread with soup and again with carrots, cabbage, and meat. Serves 6 to 8.

Variation
Remove cooked meat from pot, cover with a commercial barbecue sauce, or use the following recipe for Barbecue Sauce Made with Cabbage Soup, and string on skewers or place in a long-handled two-sided grill and brown over coals, basting frequently, while you serve and eat the soup.

BARBECUE SAUCE MADE WITH CABBAGE SOUP

¼ cup soup from Cabbage Soup with Beef
⅛ cup undiluted frozen lemonade
⅛ cup honey
1 teaspoon creamy mild mustard

Combine all ingredients and use as a sauce when barbecuing meat.

CHICKEN SOUP WITH
DILL MATZOH BALLS

Y
Two-Step Recipe
Step 1: 1½ hours
Step 2: 1 hour

Frozen or refrigerated chicken broth for 6 to 8
    prepared with Barbecued Chicken in Oriental
    Sauce (pages 276–277)
½ cup lukewarm water
⅓ cup melted butter or margarine
½ teaspoon salt
1 pinch white pepper
3 large eggs, lightly beaten
½ teaspoon dried dill weed
1 cup matzoh meal
Carrots (set aside after preparation of broth)

Step 1
The first step of this recipe, making the broth, is done at the same time as the first step of Barbecued Chicken in Oriental Sauce. You don't have to do anything about it now except remove and discard the solidified fat from the top of the broth and, if the broth was frozen, defrost it overnight in the refrigerator or by warming on the stove over very low heat.

Step 2
Add water, melted butter, salt, and pepper to eggs and mix well. Stir dried dill into matzoh meal until it is thoroughly mixed in, then combine with egg mixture. Mix well, cover, and refrigerate for 20 minutes.

Pour chicken broth into large dish in which it can be both heated and served. Bring to a boil, drop matzoh mixture by rounded spoonful into it, and cook uncovered at low boil for 20 minutes.

Cut carrots that were cooked when chicken broth was prepared into thin strips or circles and add to boiling soup. Serve at once. Serves 6 to 8.

CHICK PEA SOUP

Y, C
One-Pot Meal

½ pound chick peas
6 cups water
2 13¾-ounce cans chicken broth (substitute like amount of reconstituted
  dehydrated chicken broth)
½–2 cups leftover meat
3 large stalks celery, chopped
1½ cups onion, chopped
2 whole carrots (remove before serving)
1 pinch rosemary
1 pinch pepper
Salt to taste
¼ teaspoon garlic powder
2 tablespoons vinegar
2–4 cabbage leaves torn into bite-size pieces

Soak chick peas overnight in 6 cups of water. Add all other ingredients
except cabbage leaves and simmer for 2 hours on back of fire. Add cabbage
leaf bits to pot during the last half hour of cooking. Serves 4 to 6.

CANNED CHICK PEA SOUP

Substitute 2 1-pound cans chick peas for dried variety in above recipe,
combine all ingredients, and cook for 30 minutes. Eliminate 6 cups of
water.

EASY CREAM OF SPINACH SOUP

Y, C, B

1 cup water
1 10-ounce package frozen spinach, chopped (substitute 1 16-ounce can)
1 10½-ounce can condensed cream of chicken soup
1 cup sour cream (substitute ½ cup canned milk)
Salt and pepper to taste
Pinch of dried basil

Bring water to a boil, add spinach, and cook 1 minute beyond time it is
completely defrosted. Rub the spinach through a strainer (use a sieve if
you're at home and have one), reserving juice. Pour undiluted chicken
soup into pot, blend with spinach juice, return spinach, stir, and bring to
a boil. Slowly stir some of soup into sour cream, then stir the mixture back
into soup. Add seasonings, reheat but do not boil, and serve at once.
Serves 4 to 6.

DANDELION FISH SOUP   Y, C, W

1 pound fish or head and other trimmings from filleted fish
1 medium onion, chopped (substitute dried onion flakes)
½ teaspoon salt
½ clove garlic, fincly minced
6 cups water
¼ teaspoon black ground pepper
1 pinch of saffron (optional)
1 pinch of sage
¼ teaspoon dried dill weed
3 or 4 young, tender dandelion leaves, torn into bits

Combine all ingredients except dandelion in skillet or saucepan and simmer for about 40 minutes. Strain through strainer (reserve fish to flake for use in other dishes such as fish cakes or omelet). Return broth to saucepan, add dandelion leaves and enough water to make 4 to 6 servings, cook for an additional 5 minutes, and serve. Serves 4 to 6.

Variation
Add 1 spray of mint leaves and 1 teaspoon lemon juice.

Cooking in Camp
If you don't want to reserve fish flakes, add them to the soup.

LOBSTER AND SHRIMP BISQUE   Y, C, B

4 tablespoons butter
4 tablespoons flour
3 cups milk
½ cup chicken broth, strained
Salt and pepper to taste (use white pepper if you have it)
2 tablespoons sherry (optional)
1–1½ cups cooked lobster meat cut in small pieces
½ cup small cooked shrimp, de-veined
½ cup heavy cream (substitute canned milk)
1 tablespoon finely chopped parsley
Dash of paprika

Melt butter in top of double boiler (or in a saucepan) and stir in flour until well blended. Over simmering water, gradually add milk, stirring constantly. When sauce is smooth, stir in chicken broth and cook until thickened. (Use a wire whisk for stirring if you have it.) Season with salt and pepper to taste, stir in sherry, add lobster and shrimp, and continue cooking until they are heated through. Remove from fire, stir in cream, pour into tureen or other bowl, decorate with a sprinkle of chopped parsley and dash of paprika, and serve. Serves 6 to 8.

LOBSTER AND SHRIMP SAUCE

To above recipe add ½ to 1 cup sliced and fried mushrooms and serve over rice or noodles.

Variation
Add sliced blanched and roasted almonds.

LOBSTER AND SHRIMP CURRY

Blend 2 tablespoons cold water into 1 teaspoon curry powder and add to Lobster and Shrimp Sauce.

Note
To make a thin soup or sauce, use 2 tablespoons flour instead of 4.

Substitute crab or a nicely flavored white-meat fish for one or both of the shellfish used in bisque or sauce.

If you are serving bisque at home in the yard, it will taste even better if you "age" it for a few hours, covered, in the refrigerator, then reheat just to simmering over hot water. This is a very perishable soup so, unless you have adequate refrigeration facilities, it should be eaten at once when prepared in camp or aboard a boat.

MANHATTAN CLAM CHOWDER

2 dozen chowder clams
5 cups cold water
3 slices bacon, chopped
1½ cups chopped onion
1 cup chopped celery
½ cup chopped green pepper
1 cup chopped carrot
2 ripe tomatoes, chopped
7 cups of broth from clams
Salt and pepper to taste
1 cup tomato juice or to taste
1½ cups chopped raw potato

Discard any clams that don't close tightly when you tap them. Scrub clam shells with wire brush and rinse several times under running water. Put clams in a large pot containing 5 cups cold water, cover, and bring almost to a boil. Keep at a very low simmer for 3 to 6 minutes. As the steam forces the shells open, use tongs to remove clams from pot and let them cool just enough to handle. You can hold them in your left hand wearing a clean padded kitchen glove, while using your ungloved right hand to cut through the tough muscle holding clam to shell. To get rid of any clinging sand, dip the shucked clam into a dish holding 2 cups of cool, clear water. Reserve this water and pour it into the pot when you are through opening clams. You should also catch liquid that runs out of the clams as you pull them open and cut the muscle. Pour this liquid also into the pot. Chop shucked clams, put in a dish, cover, and refrigerate immediately. (The clams are taken out of the steaming pot and then removed as quickly as possible from their own hot shells to stop the cooking process. Chowder clams are not very tender anyway, and any unnecessary cooking will toughen them even more.)

Strain clam broth twice through 2 or 3 thicknesses of cheesecloth before using.

Put bacon in a heavy pot, add onion, celery, and green pepper, and sauté until lightly browned. Add chopped carrot and tomatoes and cook for an additional 5 minutes, stirring frequently to blend juices and bacon fat with vegetables. Put clam broth in a saucepan or pot, add contents of frying pan, and stir in salt and pepper to taste. Stir in tomato juice a little at a time and tasting as you go, because too much will overpower the flavor of the clam broth. Add potatoes, bring chowder to a boil, turn heat down to low simmer, and cook for about 30 minutes or until all vegetables are soft but not mushy. The flavor of clam chowder is improved if you cool and refrigerate it for several hours or overnight. To serve, reheat only the amount that will be eaten immediately, add chopped clams (save some if you're not serving all of the soup), simmer for no more than 3 minutes, and serve with toast, French bread, or crackers. Makes approximately 12 servings.

FROZEN CLAM CHOWDER

Chill Manhattan Clam Chowder quickly; ladle in 1-cup amounts into plastic bag–lined freezer dishes. When frozen solid, remove bags, seal with a twist of metal, put them into a heavy paper bag, label, and store in freezer. Chowder can be quickly defrosted and heated in a heavy pot to which you've added 2 or 3 tablespoons water. Freeze clams separately and add after soup is hot, continuing to heat just until clams are defrosted and cooked through. Or, instead of freezing clams, add minced canned clams to defrosted soup when it's hot.

CAMP OR GALLEY CLAM CHOWDER

Substitute canned vegetable soup for vegetables listed in Manhattan Clam Chowder ingredients if they are unavailable. Or substitute canned or dehydrated vegetables for any or all of those listed in chowder ingredients.

QUICK NEW ENGLAND   Y, C, B, P
CLAM CHOWDER

1 dozen medium chowder clams (substitute 2 7½-ounce canned minced clams)
4 slices lean bacon, chopped
1 cup of the broth clams were steamed in (substitute canned broth)
2 cups of milk
½ cup instant mashed potato flakes
Salt, pepper, and onion powder to taste
½ cup heavy cream (substitute canned milk)
1 tablespoon chopped parsley (substitute 1 teaspoon dried flakes)
1 tablespoon butter

Steam and chop clams as in Manhattan Clam Chowder. Cook bacon until lightly browned in cooking-serving dish. Add clam broth, milk, and potato flakes and heat to boiling. Season to taste, add clams, and cook at low simmer for 3 minutes. Turn off heat, stir in cream, and serve with sprinkling of parsley and a small dab of butter in each bowl. Serves 4 to 6.

OYSTER CHOWDER

Prepare in the same way as preceding recipe but using oysters instead of clams.

SALMON AND FLOUNDER IN MUSHROOM SOUP

Y, C, B

2 10-ounce cans cream of mushroom soup
½ cup milk
1 cup chicken broth, your own, canned, or reconstituted dried
1 pound boneless flounder meat, cut into chunks (substitute any fish, fresh
 or canned)
1 1-pound can salmon
2 tablespoons sour cream (optional)

Combine soup, milk, and broth in a pot and heat to simmering point. Add flounder meat and simmer for 5 to 8 minutes, stirring frequently, until it cooks. Add salmon, stir until it breaks up and is heated through, mix in sour cream and serve. Serves 6 to 8.

Variation   *One-Pot Meal*
Add 1 16-ounce can peas to preceding recipe.

SPLIT PEA SOUP

Y, C, B
One-Pot Meal

1 1-pound box quick cooking split peas
4 quarts of liquid in which New England Boiled Dinner
 (page 271) was cooked
Ham bone from New England Boiled Dinner (optional)

Combine all ingredients, adding water if necessary to make 4 quarts of liquid. Simmer, stirring frequently, on camp or galley stove or on back of evening campfire for 1 hour or until peas are soft and soup is a nice consistency. Cool and refrigerate. Reheat to serve. Serves 6. This soup made with liquid from New England Boiled Dinner will be satisfying and nourishing enough to serve with bread and butter as a one-pot meal for either breakfast or lunch.

TUNA SOUP   Y, C, W, B, P

1 tablespoon butter, margarine, or cooking oil
1 small onion, minced (substitute onion flakes)
1 10½-ounce can condensed cream of celery soup
1 soup can water or fish, chicken, or beef broth
1 7-ounce can light meat tuna, including the oil
1 teaspoon dried parsley flakes

Heat butter, margarine, or oil in saucepan, add minced onion, and cook until tender. Stir in remaining ingredients, heat to boiling point, lower to a simmer, and continue cooking for 5 minutes. Serve 2 to 4.

WISHBONE SOUP   Y, C
One-Pot Meal

Leftover carcass (or carcasses, if very small birds are
   used) of poultry or wild bird, including wishbone and some breast meat
2¾ quarts cold water
½ pound red kidney beans
1 8-ounce can tomato sauce
3 slices raw bacon, chopped
2 beef bouillon cubes or 2 envelopes powdered broth
1 tablespoon molasses
1 medium onion, chopped
1 1-pound 12-ounce can tomatoes
2 stalks celery, chopped (substitute ¼ teaspoon celery salt)

Cut any meat off of carcass, cube, and set aside. Put carcass in a very large pot, cover with water, add all other ingredients, and bring to a boil. Turn heat down to a simmer and cook until beans are soft—3 or 4 hours. Add cubes of meat the last 20 minutes. Add more water any time soup starts getting too thick. Serves 6 to 8 when eaten with other things. Serves about 4 as a one-pot meal if there is some meat left on carcass.

16—Meats

BEEF

BEEF PATTIES   Y, C, B, P

1 pound lean ground beef (chuck is good)
½ cup toasted bread crumbs
1 small onion, grated
¼ cup sour cream
1 pinch sweet basil
Salt and pepper to taste

Combine all ingredients, shape into patties about ¾ of an inch thick, and broil 4 inches from cooking coals 5 to 10 minutes to a side or until browned on both sides and cooked, but not dry, on the inside. These patties are also good cooked in a frying pan. Serves 4.

Variation
Brush both sides with Blue Cheese Butter (page 218) before serving.

MEAL IN A BURGER

Y, C, B, P
Two-Step Recipe
Step 1: ½ hour
Step 2: ½ hour

One of the easy and delicious ways to cut out pots and pans, and even plates, yet serve a well-balanced meal, is to stuff hamburgers with sautéed mixed vegetables. Serve the vegetables with your dinner the night before, but fix more than you need.

8 plump stalks fresh green asparagus
2 stalks of broccoli (about 1-inch diameter stem)
4 large stalks of celery
1 tablespoon butter or margarine
1 tablespoon olive oil
1 tablespoon cooking oil
1 large onion, sliced
1 3-ounce can sliced mushrooms, drained
Salt and pepper to taste
2 pounds lean chopped beef
2 ounces (approximately) cheddar cheese, thinly sliced
2 tablespoons soy sauce
2 tablespoons catsup

Step 1
Cut asparagus, broccoli, and celery in ¼-inch thick diagonal slices. Heat fats in a large, heavy frying pan. Add vegetables, salt and pepper to taste, and cook on medium heat, stirring frequently until crisp-tender (about 10 minutes). Turn off heat, cover, and let stand in their own steam for an additional 5 minutes.

Serve one-half of vegetables with your dinner, refrigerate the second half. You've painlessly completed the first step of an outdoor Meal in a Burger recipe.

Step 2
Divide meat into 8 patties, 5 to 6 inches in diameter. (You can make the patties smaller but they will be hard to stuff.) Divide cheese slices over 4 of the patties, leaving a 1½ inch margin of meat. Cover cheese on each pattie with 1 to 2 tablespoons of vegetable mixture. Top with remaining meat patties, press edges together, and flatten tops slightly with a spatula. Mix soy sauce and catsup together into a sauce and brush both sides of the patties with it. Put the patties in a long-handled grill, fasten shut, and place 4 to 6 inches above burned-down cooking coals. Broil 5 to 10 minutes to a side, basting several times with sauce, or until meat is nicely browned and cooked through.

Serve on rolls or with bread and sliced tomatoes. Serves 4.

For the Nautical Cook
Fry patties on your galley stove or carry them to the beach to charcoal broil.

Variation
Saute 4 slices of lean chopped bacon with vegetables. Instead of using fresh vegetables described in step 1, use any leftovers you may have on hand.

HAMBURGERS ON TOASTED BUNS

Y, C, B, P
Two-Step Recipe
Step 1: ¼ hour
Step 2: ¼ hour

1½ pounds chopped beef, lean
1 5-gram packet instant mix for beef or chicken broth
½ teaspoon salt
⅛ teaspoon pepper
2 tablespoons grated Parmesan cheese (optional)
1 teaspoon oregano
6–8 hamburger buns
1 large onion cut into 6–8 slices
Catsup
Pickle relish

Step 1
Mix chopped beef and next 5 ingredients together (broth mix is added dry), form into 6 to 8 patties, and refrigerate until time to use them or transfer to camp or cruiser icebox. If to be carried very far, they should be frozen overnight in freezer first.

Step 2
Cook in two-handled, greased grill, 4 to 6 inches above burned-down cooking coals or in a frying pan over a camp stove until nicely browned on both sides and done to the degree each person likes. This should take from 5 to 10 minutes to a side. Split buns in half and toast them, using a second hinged, long-handled grill if you have it. Serve hamburgers on the buns with onion slices, catsup, and relish. Serves 4 to 6.

To Cook over Camp Stove or in Boat Galley
Fry hamburgers in frying pan or broil if galley stove has broiler.

TOMATOES STUFFED WITH CORNED BEEF HASH

Y, C, B
One-Pot Meal

4–6 ripe but firm tomatoes
1 12-ounce can of corned beef hash
4–6 slices of cheese

Slice tops from tomatoes, remove insides, invert, and drain. Chop insides, press gently in strainer to remove most of liquid, and combine with corned beef hash. Fill tomato shells with mixture, putting any that's left over into a small casserole. Top stuffed tomatoes with cheese, arrange in a shallow baking pan, pour about ¼ cup of water in bottom of pan, and bake for 30 minutes in 325 ° F. oven. Or cook, covered, in a dutch oven. Serves 2 to 4.

GREEN PEPPERS STUFFED WITH CORNED BEEF HASH

Slice tops from green peppers, remove seeds and membrane, and parboil for 5 minutes. Remove from water, invert for 2 or 3 minutes to drain, stuff, and bake in the same way as in preceding recipe.

SCANDINAVIAN MEAT BALLS   Y, B

2 cups of your own rye bread crumbs
½ pint plain yogurt
2 pounds ground beef
2 eggs
1 cup chopped onion
2 teaspoons salt
¼ teaspoon pepper
¼ teaspoon nutmeg
¼ cup butter or margarine
2 tablespoons flour
1½ cups beef broth
½ cup sour cream (optional but very nice when added)

Combine rye bread crumbs with yogurt in large mixing bowl and let stand 5 minutes. Add meat, eggs, onion, salt, pepper, and nutmeg and mix well. Shape into balls about 1½ inches in diameter. Melt butter in heavy skillet, add meat balls, and brown on all sides. Remove meat balls to serving bowl and keep warm. Add flour to skillet drippings and stir until brown. Heat beef stock to boiling, add all at once to pan, stirring constantly until thick and smooth. (If you are limited to one burner, sprinkle flour into cold broth, stirring constantly until well blended and smooth. Add to drippings, stirring constantly as you pour, and continue stirring until gravy thickens and cooks until it does not taste starchy.) Turn off heat, stir in sour cream, and pour over meat balls. Serves 8 to 10.

MEAT BALLS AS APPETIZERS

With toothpicks as spears, meat balls make an excellent addition to the buffet table. They can be dipped in Spicy Cocktail Sauce (page 221) or some other sauce.

MEAT CAKES   Y, C, B

2 pounds chopped beef
½ teaspoon salt
1 pinch black pepper
¼ teaspoon garlic powder
⅛ teaspoon powdered ginger
1 pinch thyme
¼ teaspoon rosemary leaves
¼ cup undiluted cream of mushroom soup (optional)
¼ cup dry bread crumbs (optional)

Combine all ingredients. Mix well, form into 8 patties, and cook 4 inches above coals, 5 to 10 minutes to a side, depending on how well done you prefer them. Serve with sliced onion. Serves 6.

To Cook in Boat Galley
Fry in frying pan or broil if galley stove has broiler.

MEAT LOAF   Y, C, B

1½ pound chopped meat
3 small firm ripe tomatoes, finely chopped
1 medium onion, chopped
1 large celery stick, grated
½–1 cup leftover cooked carrot or sweet potato, mashed
½ small, very firm raw zucchini, grated
1 cup seasoned bread crumbs
1 egg, lightly beaten
1 teaspoon salt
Pepper to taste

Combine all ingredients, put in a lightly greased loaf pan, and bake for 50 minutes or until done in 375 ° F. oven. Or divide in half and bake in two small pans or wrapped in foil for 30 to 40 minutes in reflector oven. Serves 4 to 6.

Note
Spoon part of the fat off the top of the juices left in the pan, then pour the juices over slices of meat loaf when you serve them. Or use juices in place of all or part of the water needed to reconstitute dried eggs when making scrambled eggs for the next day's breakfast. Use some of the fat from the meat loaf pan to fry the scrambled eggs in.

POT ROAST AND BEAN SOUP

Y, C, B
Two-Step Recipe
Step 1: 2½ hours
Step 2: ½ hour

6½ pounds rolled boneless roast
1 15-ounce can tomato sauce
2 15-ounce cans of water
3 tablespoons molasses
2 tablespoons vinegar
½ teaspoon garlic powder
¼ teaspoon coriander powder
¼ teaspoon powdered ginger
3 bay leaves
1 large onion, chopped
3 stalks celery, chopped
1 1-pound can small white beans
1 1-pound can vegetarian beans in tomato sauce
1 1-pound 4-ounce can chick peas

Step 1
Put meat in a heavy pot that will hold at least 5 quarts, add next 10 ingredients, cover, and simmer for 2 hours or until tender, turning meat at least once during that time. If sauce thickens, add 1 cup water. Remove meat from pot, set in a cool bowl, and set that bowl in ice water to chill quickly. Wrap, label, and freeze until you want to transfer it to your camp or boat icebox, or defrost to slice for a cold buffet on the patio. Chill sauce quickly, pour into a plastic bag–lined container that has a tightly fitting lid. Freeze, then fasten bag with metal twist, and cover with lid. Don't forget to take the sauce when you pack meat for camping or cruising.

Step 2
Plan on using part of the meat the second day away from home. It should still be partly frozen, if your icebox was properly packed, but not too hard to slice easily. Cut 3 or 4 slices from each end of the roast (making a total of 6 to 8). Pour sauce from plastic bag into large pot, add canned beans and chick peas and enough water to make a good, rich soup. Simmer for 20 minutes or until everything is bubbling hot and well blended. Add sliced meat and continue cooking for 5 minutes. Dip soup from pot and serve. Leave meat in pot to stay warm, then serve with any remaining beans and chick peas. Serves 6 to 8.

Note
Use remaining meat the following day.

BARBECUE–BRAISING ECONOMY CUTS OF BEEF

Y, C, P

1 2½–3-pound boneless chuck of beef roast, defrosted but still icy or slightly frozen
2 tablespoons wine vinegar
2 tablespoons soy sauce
1 tablespoon mustard
2 tablespoons honey
1 6-ounce can tomato paste
2 large onions, thinly sliced
1 clove garlic, finely minced
4 tablespoons water

Wipe roast with a damp cloth. Combine the rest of the ingredients except water, mix well, and spread over all sides of roast, which is lying in center of large, double sheet of *heavy-duty* aluminum foil. (You may have to lay the meat diagonally in order to have enough foil edge to seal properly. This placement of the meat will mean you'll have 4 sealed edges—plus a fold in the center of the package—instead of the customary 3 seals.) When you seal the edges, leave one small opening, pour the water through this opening, then seal it, too.

Lay the package on the grill 4 to 6 inches above a hot, compact bed of coals (a minimum of 3 pounds of charcoal briquettes) and cook for half an hour. Turn and cook second side of package for half an hour. Remove grill, turn package again, and lay it directly on the coals. Leave it alone for half an hour, then turn over (if the package is leaking, lay it on an extra double thickness of foil), and again leave it for half an hour. You will have cooked the roast all together for a total of 2 hours when it is finished.

Remove the package of meat from the fire, cut a hole in the foil, and carefully pour gravy into a serving dish. Open the package, slice the meat, and serve with the gravy. It should be very tender and just a little rare, with enough that is well done for those who prefer it that way. Serves 4 to 6.

ROLLED BEEF ROAST ON A SPIT

Y, P

1 5–7 pound boned and rolled beef roast, USDA Choice or Prime
Salt and pepper to taste
1 clove of garlic cut in several pieces (optional)

Prepare and cook in the same way as Standing Rib Roasted on a Spit (page 255). If the meat is lean and lacks marbling, ask your butcher to fasten strips of suet to the outside when he ties it. Tell him how you plan to cook the roast, and he will know the best way to prepare it for you.

In addition to the seasonings already listed, you might want to rub a little ginger or rosemary into the meat or marinate it in a barbecue sauce. See page 220.

STANDING RIB ROASTED ON A SPIT   Y, P

1 4–6 pound standing rib roast
Salt and pepper to taste
1 clove of garlic cut in several pieces (optional)

Wipe meat with a damp cloth and rub with salt and pepper. This delicious roast really needs no additional seasoning, but, if you are fond of garlic, insert pieces in several different places in the outer layer of fat. Melted fat will mingle with garlic flavor to ooze over the roast as it turns on the spit.

You can conserve juice by fastening aluminum foil over the two cut ends of the roast. Remove it for last half hour of cooking time.

Insert spit for best balance possible, fasten tightly, insert meat thermometer so that it's in center of thickest meat but does not touch spit or fat. It will also have to clear all parts of the barbecue grill as it turns. Be sure the dripping pan is under the roast, and that coals are burned down for cooking and positioned for indirect heating—usually at the back of your fire bed, but check printed instructions.

If your stove has a heat indicator, cook roast at 300–325 ° F.; if it does not, lower fire bed so that you are cooking with a medium hot heat. Your roast should be cooked to a succulent medium rare in 2 to 3 hours, but check your meat thermometer for accuracy. If the meat is rare, it will read 140 ° F., if medium, 160 ° F., and if well done, 170 ° F.

Use drippings in pan to make gravy.

BARBECUED LEFTOVER ROAST BEEF   Y, C, W
SLICES WITH BEANS

6 1-inch thick slices of cooked medium to rare roast beef or game
2 tablespoons oil, preferably olive
1 18-ounce can baked beans
1 cup catsup

Spread oil over both sides of beef slices and lay on grill 3 or 4 inches above cooking coals. Open can of beans, empty into saucepan and set on side of fire to be warming. Cook meat 8 to 10 minutes or until nicely browned, turn with spatula, and spread beans carefully over browned side of meat slices. Divide catsup over beans with a spoon, taking care not to knock them off meat into fire. Cook another 10 minutes or until second side is browned the way you like your meat to be. Use spatula to lift each piece carefully onto warm plates. Serves 6.

Note

If you don't want to dirty a saucepan to warm beans, open the can but leave the top in place and set on side of grill. Handle can with a hot-pot lifter while spooning beans onto meat.

FRIED CHUCK FILLET STEAKS   Y, C, B, P

8 chuck fillets, USDA Choice
½ cup flour
⅛ teaspoon finely ground rosemary
Salt and pepper to taste
⅛ teaspoon onion powder
⅛ teaspoon garlic powder
2 tablespoons cooking oil

Pound fillets with wooden mallet. Combine flour, rosemary, salt, pepper, onion powder, and garlic powder in heavy paper bag and shake steaks, a few at a time, in the mixture. They should be well coated. Heat cooking oil in skillet until sizzling hot but not smoking, add steaks, a few at a time (don't crowd or they won't be nice), and fry until crisp and brown on one side. Turn and repeat on the other side. Add more oil to the pan as you go if necessary. Serves 4 to 6.

SWISS STEAK

If steaks are a lower grade than USDA Choice or a tougher cut than chuck fillet, turn them into Swiss steak. Prepare as above, then place in dutch oven or large pot, add 2 cups of water combined with 1 envelope of gravy mix. Add sliced or dried onion, cover, and let cook on low heat for 40 minutes or until steak is tender and gravy is thick. Check frequently, especially during last 20 minutes, and stir gravy from bottom of pot before it has a chance to stick and burn.

TWO–STEP CHUCK FILLETS

Freeze steaks in a single layer immediatley after flouring them. Cook the next day in the yard with eggs for a cookout breakfast, or take them with you on a picnic, all ready to cook in a skillet or on a large griddle (if there's a large number of people). Properly packaged in an insulated bag, they'll keep well and stay cold for several hours. If you're going to be traveling for a long time, they should be packed in an icebox or refrigerator. Cut Fried Chuck Fillets recipe in half to serve 4 for breakfast with eggs.

TWO–STEP SWISS STEAK

Prepare and freeze as in Two-Step Chuck Fillets, but cook in liquid as in Swiss Steak.

STEAK BARBECUED IN VINEGAR AND OLIVE OIL   Y, C, B, P

2½–3 pounds steak, 1½–2 inches thick
½ large onion cut into small pieces
1 clove garlic, minced
1 teaspoon salt
½ teaspoon pepper
1 tablespoon olive oil
2 tablespoons wine vinegar

Cut slashes in fat deposits and make openings between layers of meat. Poke pieces of onion and garlic into these slashes and openings until pieces are used up. Combine salt, pepper, oil, and vinegar and rub all over steak. Refrigerate for at least half an hour before cooking and for several hours if going camping, cruising, or picnicking. Lay on barbecue grill 4 to 6 inches over a good hot bed of cooking coals and cook 10 to 12 minutes to a side for medium-rare steak. Brush while cooking with any of the mixture that may have been left in dish in which steak was refrigerated. Serves 4 with enough left over to make Leftover Steak and Peppers for following day's lunch.

To Cook in Boat Galley
Cook in large frying pan or in broiler if you have one.

LEFTOVER STEAK AND PEPPERS   Y, C, B

1 tablespoon butter or margarine
1 tablespoon cooking oil
3 Italian frying peppers, sliced
2 stalks celery, sliced diagonally
6 mushrooms, sliced
1 medium onion, sliced
1 tablespoon corn starch
1½ cups beef or chicken broth (substitute 2 bouillon cubes and water)
1 teaspoon soy sauce
1 teaspoon sherry
Pepper to taste
1–2 cups leftover barbecued steak, sliced in small pieces

Heat butter or margarine and cooking oil in heavy skillet, add vegetables, and saute, stirring frequently for 6 to 8 minutes. Blend corn starch into beef or chicken broth and stir until smooth. Add soy sauce, sherry, and pepper to taste and stir into vegetables. Cook, stirring frequently, until sauce thickens. Add sliced steak, turn down heat to low, and continue cooking until steak is hot. Serve over rice or bread. Serves 4.

Note
If you're going camping or cruising, slice the peppers, celery, mushrooms, and onion before leaving home, seal them in a plastic bag or an airtight Tupperware container, and carry in your portable icebox or other cooler.

LEFTOVER BEEF AND PEPPERS

Slice leftover pot roast or oven roast and cook in Leftover Steak and Peppers.

PORK AND PEPPERS

Substitute slivers of cooked pork for leftover steak.

SHERRIED STEAK   Y, C, W, P

1 cup sherry
2 teaspoons oregano
3 pounds steak of your choice, 1½ inches thick
Salt and pepper to taste

Combine sherry and oregano. Cut and discard excess fat from steak. Place steak in shallow dish just large enough to hold steak when laid flat. Pour marinade over it, brushing on each side to assure an even coating. Marinate in refrigerator for 3 hours, turning every hour and brushing occasionally.

Broil 4 to 6 inches from hot coals, 8 to 10 minutes to a side for medium-rare steak. Baste occasionally with marinade. Season with salt and pepper. Serves 4 to 6.

BARBECUED STEAK SANDWICHES   Y, C, B, P

2 pounds steak, ½–¾ inch thick
1 teaspoon salt
⅛ teaspoon pepper
1 teaspoon olive oil
1 tablespoon cooking oil
¼ teaspoon Worcestershire sauce
1–1½ tablespoons catsup
½ teaspoon sugar
8 large thick slices of French bread or 4 submarine rolls, sliced lengthwise
2 tomatoes, sliced
1 sweet onion, sliced

Wipe steak with damp cloth and lay it in a dish. Combine salt, pepper, olive oil, cooking oil, Worcestershire sauce, catsup, and sugar and pour over steak. Marinate in refrigerator for at least an hour before cooking in the yard. If you are taking the steak on a camping or cruising trip, line the dish with freezer paper before adding steak and marinade. Put in freezer. When frozen solid, wrap securely, sealing edges of paper, and put the package in a plastic bag. Fasten shut with wire twist as a double insurance against liquid leaking out when steak defrosts.

Broil steak 4 to 6 inches above burned-down cooking coals until it's done the way you like it in a sandwich. Cut into strips, lay them on half of the bread, cover with sliced tomatoes and onions and second half of bread. Makes steak sandwiches for 4.

TWO-STEP CAMP AND GALLEY STEW

Y, C, B
One-Pot Meal
Two-Step Recipe
Step 1: 2½ hours
Step 2: ½ hour

Step 1: Frozen Base
7 pounds lean beef stew meat
7 large carrots, whole and unpeeled
3 stalks celery, chopped
2 onions, chopped
½ large head cabbage, cut into small pieces (optional)

Put meat in freezer until it becomes stiff enough to slice easily, then cut each chunk across the grain into pieces about ½ inch thick. Spread over bottom of a large, shallow pan and cook uncovered in 300 ° F. oven for 45 minutes or until nicely browned on top. Turn and continue cooking until second side is brown, about 30 minutes.

While meat cooks, put remaining ingredients in 5-quart or larger pot, cover with water, and simmer. When meat is through cooking in oven, remove from pan and discard any fat that has rendered out. Take carrots out of stew pot, replace with meat, and continue simmering for 1 hour. Run cold water over carrots, slip off skins, cut the carrots in slices approximately ¼ to ½ inches thick, and return them to stew pot for the last few minutes of cooking.

Do not season, because the ingredients you will be adding later may provide sufficient spices.

Chill stew quickly by setting pot in a sinkful of ice water, then divide into 2-cup square-cornered freezer containers suitable for packing in portable ice chest or galley refrigerator. The yield is about 6 2-cup containers to which the following variety of additions can be made later to create a number of different dishes.

Step 2
Camp and Galley Stew Number 1
1 2-cup container frozen base prepared at home
1 1-pound can small whole white potatoes, drained
1 10½-ounce can cream of mushroom soup
Salt and pepper to taste
Heat and serve. To thin, add a little milk or water. Serves 2 to 4.

Camp and Galley Stew Number 2
1 2-cup container frozen base prepared at home
1 1-pound 4-ounce can beans
Salt and pepper to taste
Heat and serve. To thin, add a little water or tomato juice.
Serves 2 to 4.

Camp and Galley Stew Number 3
1 2-cup container frozen base prepared at home
4–6 crumbled ginger snaps
1–2 teaspoons brown sugar
1 6-ounce can tomato paste
Salt and pepper to taste
Heat and serve. To thin, add a little water or tomato juice.
Serves 2 to 4.

LAMB

Some Authoritative Advice on Preparing
Lamb Shish Kabobs and Stew

The American Sheep Producer's Council has this to say about preparing
lamb shish kabobs:

> For charcoal broiling, some people like to alternate the lamb
> squares with bay leaves. As they begin to glow from the heat, they
> impart a savory flavor to the broiled meat. Some use bacon squares,
> mushrooms, tomato wedges and various vegetables, as well as fruits
> of various kinds threaded alternately with the lamb squares. Since
> fruits and vegetables usually cook more quickly than the meat, they
> are often prepared on separate skewers.
> When broiling over coals, broil all sides until deep brown in color,
> lifting the skewers to roll in sauce, or brush with sauce, frequently.

Arabs—from the home of the shish kabob—say it's considered a
must there to alternate onion and tomato with the meat because even
though the vegetables may overcook, they flavor the meat.

LAMB STEW   Y, C, P

The ingredients in this recipe have been reduced considerably from the original for which Oregon lamb producers used 900 pounds of lamb and cooked their stew in a big iron kettle over one hundred years old. It was a fragrant success at a very large patio party. We think you'll like it too. Our thanks for this recipe and the one that follows, Soy Marinade for Shish Kabobs, to Mrs. Velma Seat, Food Marketing Specialist, Oregon State University Extension Service.

10–12 pounds lamb brisket, neck meat, and riblets cut into 1-inch chunks
    with fat trimmed off
Salt and pepper to taste
3–4 pounds chopped onions
4 cloves garlic, minced
2 pinches allspice
2 pinches cumin
2 pinches ground cloves
2 pinches oregano
2 pinches cinnamon
2 tablespoons Worcestershire sauce
2 quarts sherry or Sauterne (substitute water for all or part of wine)
Cooked rice for 12

Cook lamb in skillets until pink color is gone, stirring occasionally. Drain off excess fat, add salt and pepper, onions and garlic, and cook with meat for 10 to 15 minutes until meat and onions are nicely browned. Transfer to large Dutch oven or other heavy baking dish, add remaining ingredients, and cook in 300 ° F. oven for 3 hours or until meat falls off bones. Serve over rice with a tossed green salad. Serves 12 to 16.

Note
Stew can be cooked in Dutch oven or other heavy pot on top of stove or to one side of a grill over a campfire, covered. Stir occasionally.

SOY MARINADE FOR SHISH KABOBS   Y, C, P

¾ cup soy sauce
1 tablespoon curry powder
¼ teaspoon powdered ginger or approximately ½ teaspoon diced fresh
    ginger root
1 clove minced garlic

Combine ingredients. Pour over boneless cubes of lamb cut from shoulder or leg. Let stand overnight in refrigerator.

LAMB SHANKS, SIMMERED THEN BARBECUED

Y, C, B
Two-Step Recipe
Step 1: 1½ hours
Step 2: ¾ hour

8 small lamb shanks
2 leaves fresh basil
1 medium onion
3 carrots, peels left on
3 stalks celery
1 tablespoon salt
¼ teaspoon pepper
4 tablespoons mint jelly
1 tablespoon spicy brown mustard ⎫
3 tablespoons Teriyaki sauce   ⎬ *Sauce*
½ cup catsup   ⎭

Step 1

Put all except sauce ingredients in very large pot (or divide into 2 pots), cover with water, and bring to a boil. Cook at a very low simmer for 50 to 60 minutes or until shanks are fork-tender. Re-arrange the shanks after first 25 minutes of cooking, putting those that were on top on the bottom of the pot. Combine sauce ingredients, stir until well blended. Remove shanks from pot, wipe off any scum, coat each one thoroughly with sauce and refrigerate in a covered bowl. Or, if to be taken on a camping trip or aboard your boat to cook in the galley, freeze shanks in single-layered packages, no more than 3 shanks to a package. Reserve remaining sauce in a tightly closed jar. Set vegetables aside for making Boiled Vegetables in Celery Sauce (page 320) and reserve broth in which they and the shanks were cooked for future soup making.

Step 2

To brown shanks over coals, defrost shanks if frozen and lay on grill 4 to 6 inches above a hot bed of cooking coals. Turn frequently and baste with reserved sauce until nicely browned on all sides. Serve at once. Serves 4 to 6.

To brown shanks in oven, the shanks, if frozen, should be defrosted. Place in a shallow pan, mix reserved barbecue sauce with water to make ¼ inch in bottom of pan, and pour around shanks. Cover for first 20 minutes and bake for 35 to 45 minutes in 400 ° F. oven or until shanks are nicely browned and tender. Baste and turn as necessary.

SHOULDER LAMB CHOPS WITH GRAVY AND POTATOES

C, B
Two-Step Recipe
Step 1: ½ hour
Step 2: ½ hour

6 lean shoulder lamb chops (substitute 10 loin chops)
1 tablespoon lemon juice
Salt to taste
¼ cup mint jelly
1 16-ounce can small whole potatoes
1 15½-ounce can beef gravy

Step 1
Rub both sides of lamb chops with lemon juice and salt to taste. Arrange chops in broiler pan and broil, about 2½ inches from source of heat, at 550 ° F. for 5 minutes. Spread chops with half of mint jelly and broil another 5 minutes, watching that they don't burn. Turn chops over, broil second side for 5 minutes, spread with remaining mint jelly, and again broil for 5 minutes. Arrange in single layers on feezer paper. Pour liquid from broiler pan, cool, spoon fat from top, and pour over chops. Wrap chops in 2 or 3 single-layered packages and freeze until time to transfer to camp or boat ice box.

Step 2
Grease large shallow baking pan lightly with butter or margarine. Cut canned potatoes in ½-inch slices and spread over bottom of pan. Pour any liquid out of freezer packages of meat into canned gravy. Mix and spread over potatoes. Top with chops and bake for 30 minutes at 350 ° F. or until chops are tender and everything is bubbling hot. Serves 4 to 6.

LAMB STEAKS ROSEMARY

Y, C, P

2 tablespoons red wine
1 tablespoon olive oil
¼ teaspoon garlic powder
⅛ teaspoon rosemary
Salt and pepper to taste
4 lamb steaks, about ¾-inch thick

Combine first 5 ingredients, mix well, and rub into both sides of lamb steaks. Place in a dish and marinate in refrigerator for at least 1 hour. Arrange in a long-handled hinged grill and barbecue, 4 to 6 inches above cooking coals, about 10 minutes to a side or until well done and nicely browned. Baste occasionally with any sauce left in bottom of marinating dish. Serves 4.

LIVER

CHOPPED CHICKEN LIVER   Y

1 pound chicken livers
2 tablespoons butter
1 tablespoon cooking oil
1 cup chopped onion
½ teaspoon salt
⅛ teaspoon pepper
4 hard-cooked eggs, shelled

Wash and dry livers. Put butter and cooking oil in heavy skillet. When butter melts and blends with the oil, add chopped onions and cook until tender but not brown. Remove onions with slotted spoon and set aside. Fry livers in same oil, 2 or 3 minutes to a side, or until they are just cooked through but not dry. Do not let oil smoke and don't crowd livers in the pan. When done, combine livers with onions in a bowl and mash together with a fork. Add salt and pepper and thoroughly mix in. If you find it difficult to blend liver and onion together into a thick paste using fork, put them through meat grinder, using medium blade.

Mash or grind hard-cooked eggs into the liver mixture and put the mixture in a bowl and serve as an appetizer to spread on crackers or sliced cucumbers. Makes spread for about 60 crackers.

Variation
Double amount of hard-cooked egg if you like a mild flavor.

For chopped liver in the shape of a chicken, press into a lightly greased chicken mold and unmold on serving plate. Use a piece of pimiento for the comb, slivered almonds with the skin left on for beak, legs, and feet and any bit of food you have that resembles an eye. If you don't have a chicken-shaped mold, look at a picture of a chicken and form liver into the best facsimile you can.

LIVER AND BACON KABOBS   Y, C, P

½ pound chicken or calves liver
1 tablespoon mild mustard
4–6 slices lean bacon cut into 1½-inch long pieces
1 medium onion cut in wedges

Wash liver and dry on absorbent towels. Cut two sections of chicken livers apart or, if you're using calves liver, cut it into 14 to 18 pieces of fairly uniform size. Put the liver pieces in a small dish and smear the mustard over all sides.

String the pieces of liver on skewers with a piece of bacon at each end and a slice of onion wedge in between. You will have to run the skewers through the chicken livers in more than one place to hold them securely.

Place the skewers about 4 inches above hot coals. Turn frequently. The bacon will be cooked and the liver cooked through in about 15 minutes. If you like liver to be pink inside, don't cook that long. Makes 14 to 18 appetizers. Serves 2 as main course of a meal.

LIVER, BACON, AND ONIONS   Y, C, W, B

2 serving size slices of liver, ¾-inch thick
½ cup milk (optional)
2 medium onions sliced
4 slices bacon, cut in 1-inch pieces
1 tablespoon cooking oil

Soak liver overnight in milk. If liver is frozen, rub milk over surface of pieces and turn them once or twice as they defrost. Fry onions and bacon in cooking oil until onions are a light, golden color. Stir frequently. Push to side, add liver to pan, and cook until nicely browned on one side. Turn over, pile bacon and onions on top of cooked side, and continue cooking until second side is brown and liver is cooked the way you like it. Carefully slice into it with a sharp knife to check, because liver should not be overcooked. Serve with salad and potatoes. Serves 2.

PORK

BARBECUED PORK CHOPS IN   Y, C, P
MUSHROOM SAUCE

6 pork chops
Pepper to taste
½ cup water
1 10½-ounce can undiluted cream of mushroom soup

Arrange chops in long-handled grill, sprinkle with pepper, and cook 4 to 6 inches above cooking coals for 10 minutes to a side or until nicely browned and almost cooked. Remove from grill, lay chops on sheets of heavy-duty aluminum foil, 2 to a sheet. Add water to mushroom soup, stir until smooth, and spread over chops. Wrap and seal chops with the foil and lay packages on grill 4 to 6 inches above coals. Cook for 20 minutes, turning over after 15. Serves 4 to 6.

BARBECUED SPARERIBS   Y, P

Spareribs are hard to cook thoroughly over coals. The safest way to prepare them is to simmer the ribs before you barbecue them. You can do this
the day before. Then marinate the ribs overnight in a barbecue sauce and
heat and brown them at the same time in just 20 to 30 minutes over the
coals when you serve them the next day. Or if you're going on a picnic,
freeze the ribs in a single layer and covered with barbecue sauce. Carry
them to the picnic site in a cooler and place on a grill over cooking coals
while still icy cold.

1 rack of spareribs, cut into 2- or 3-rib pieces
1 teaspoon salt
1 cup Hawaiian-Style Sweet and Sour Barbecue Sauce (page 220)

Place sections of rib compactly in bottom of heavy pot, add just enough
cold water to cover. Add salt, cover pot, bring to a boil, then turn down to
very low simmer, and continue cooking for 10 minutes (5 minutes if ribs
are very small). Drain, spread barbecue sauce over all sides, and marinate
in refrigerator or freeze in single-layered packages. Save sauce in which
ribs are marinated or frozen and use it to baste ribs as they brown over the
coals. Serves 2 to 4.

FRIED PORK CHOPS AND APPLE   Y, C, B
                                              Two-Step Recipe
8 pork rib chops, small, bone in   Step 1: ½ hour
½ cup flour combined with ½ teaspoon salt   Step 2: ¾ hour
2 tablespoons milk
1 large egg
½ cup dry bread crumbs
½ teaspoon salt
4 tablespoons cooking oil
2 apples
Cinnamon, nutmeg, and sugar for sprinkling on apple

Step 1
Wipe chops with a damp cloth, dry off, and shake, about 2 at a time, in
paper bag containing flour. Beat milk and egg together. Combine bread
crumbs and salt in a paper bag. Dip each chop in milk and egg batter, then
shake it in bag of crumbs until well coated. Lay on sheets of freezer paper,
two or three to a sheet, and let stand for 5 minutes to dry. Fold paper
around them and seal in single-layer packages. Refrigerate to be completed

and served outdoors at home within 24 hours or freeze until time to transfer to camp or cruiser icebox.

Step 2

If you froze chops, cook them when defrosted but still icy cold. Heat 2 to 3 tablespoons cooking oil in skillet until sizzling but not smoking. Add chops, 2 or 3 at a time, and fry slowly so they will be well done, until golden brown on one side. Turn over and repeat on second side. While pork chops cook, core and cut apples into ½-inch slices. Heat 1 tablespoon cooking oil in a second skillet if you have one or in a saucepan or heavy pot. Cook apple slices in the hot oil until lightly browned on both sides. Serve atop pork chops. Let each person sprinkle cinnamon, nutmeg, and sugar as he likes over fried apples. Serves 4 to 6.

LOIN OF PORK WITH SAUERKRAUT AND CARAWAY SEEDS

Y, C, B

1 3–4 pound loin of pork
1 15-ounce can sauerkraut
1 tablespoon caraway seeds

Place meat thermometer in thickest part of meat where it is not touching bone. Place meat, fat side up, in a shallow roasting pan and cook for 1½ hours at 350 ° F. in a charcoal oven to one side or in front of charcoal cooking coals or in camp or galley oven. At end of 1½ hours of cooking, spread sauerkraut and juice from can over top of roast and sprinkle with caraway seeds. Continue cooking until thermometer registers 170 ° F. (loin of pork is the one cut of fresh pork that does not need to be cooked until it reaches 185 ° F.), basting occasionally with juices from pan. It should take about 1 hour more of cooking. If sauerkraut becomes brown and starts to dry out, cover with aluminum foil. Serves 6 to 8.

TWO–STEP LOIN OF PORK WITH SAUERKRAUT AND CARAWAY SEEDS

C, B

Cook loin of pork at home as in preceding recipe. Freeze and take to camp or cruising in icebox. Reheat when still icy cold or a little frozen. Place in a shallow pan or a Dutch oven, pour 2 cups of apple juice around pork, cover, and heat in 325 ° F. oven or over medium heat if in Dutch oven for 30 to 60 minutes or until meat is thoroughly reheated. Baste occasionally.

PORK OR LAMB SHISH KABOB   Y, C, P

¼ cup undiluted frozen lemonade
½ cup crushed canned pineapple
1 tablespoon honey
1 teaspoon mustard
1 tablespoon soy sauce
¼ teaspoon ginger
2 pounds cubed meat cut from young, lean shoulder of pork or lamb
1 large onion cut in wedges
2 medium green peppers, cleaned and cut in pieces
2 medium very firm tomatoes cut in wedges

Combine lemonade, pineapple, honey, mustard, soy sauce, and ginger and, for a richer flavor, marinate cubed meat overnight in the mixture. Alternate meat cubes, onion, pepper pieces, and tomato wedges on skewers and cook over charcoal fire that has burned down to a hot pink and gray. Turn often. Baste frequently with sauce and cook slowly so that meat very gradually turns brown. Check pork to be sure cubes are done all the way through before eating. Serves 4 to 6.

BAKED HAM WITH PINEAPPLE   Y, P
AND CHERRIES

Baked ham, decorated with pineapple rings and maraschino cherries, looks about as fine on an outdoor buffet as anything you could put there. Cold and sliced, it tastes wonderful with many different combinations of food.

1 7-pound precooked half ham
2 1-pound 4¾-ounce cans pineapple slices (18 to 20 slices)
1 8-ounce jar maraschino cherries
½ teaspoon powdered cloves
¼ cup honey
4 tablespoons frozen lemonade concentrate
4 tablespoons brown sugar
1 teaspoon mustard
2 tablespoons pineapple juice from can of slices
1 teaspoon cherry juice from jar of maraschino cherries

Leave the skin on ham. Put ham in a large, heavy pot and add cold water until it comes two-thirds of the way up the sides of the pot. Turn heat on high. When the water starts to boil, turn it down immediately so that the water stays just under a simmer for 5 minutes. Turn off heat; turn ham over and let it stand in hot water for 20 minutes. Remove from water and, when cool enough to handle, remove skin.

Drain pineapple slices and maraschino cherries. Set fruit aside and reserve juices. Combine cloves, honey, lemonade concentrate, brown sugar, mustard, pineapple juice, and cherry juice and mix until well blended. Spread sauce all over ham, including cut side. Dip pineapple slices in remaining sauce and use wooden picks to fasten over every bit of the ham. Fasten 1 maraschino cherry in center of each pineapple slice, again using wooden picks.

Finish cooking ham either in your outdoor oven, if it has a hood, or in your kitchen range. Place in a shallow pan and bake in 400 ° F. oven for about 40 minutes, basting frequently with remaining sauce and pan drippings. Watch closely to be sure sauce doesn't scorch. You can add a little water to pan if necessary. Ham is done as soon as glaze is lightly browned. If it is to be eaten hot, serve at once; if cold, cool quickly over ice and refrigerate until time to serve. If the ham is going to a picnic with you, carry it in an ice chest. Before carving, remove fruit and place in a serving bowl. Serves 10 to 14.

Note
You can use the liquid in which ham steamed for making split pea soup.

If you prefer ham that's very salty and the label states that it is fully cooked, you can forget about pre-simmering. Just cook the ham in your oven, as described, until it's heated through (130 ° F. on your meat thermometer) and the glaze is nicely brown.

HAM STEAK WITH FRUIT SAUCE

C, B
Two-Step Recipe
Step 1: ½ hour
Step 2: ½ hour

1 1-pound 4¾-ounce can pineapple slices
¼ cup undiluted frozen lemonade concentrate
½ teaspoon mustard
1 teaspoon molasses
1 1½-ounce package seedless raisins
¼ teaspoon ground cloves
4 precooked ham steaks ½–¾-inch thick

Step 1
Open can of pineapple slices and pour ½ cup of the juice from it into a saucepan. Add lemonade concentrate, mustard, molasses, raisins, and ground cloves and cook on medium heat until mixture comes to a boil. Turn down to a simmer and cook, stirring frequently, for 15 minutes or until mixture is reduced by about one-half. Arrange ham steaks in broiler

pan about 3 inches from source of heat and broil at 400 ° F. for 10 minutes. Turn steaks over, put 2 pineapple slices on each steak. Remove raisins from sauce with slotted spoon and set aside. Divide sauce over each piece of pineapple-covered ham and broil at 400 ° F. for 5 minutes. Remove ham from broiler, divide raisins into center of the pineapple slices and put steaks in single layer in one or two shallow dishes in which they can be reheated. Wrap and freeze. When ready to go camping or on a boat cruise, transfer to portable icebox and take them with you to use for dinner no later than second night away.

Step 2
Cook ham steaks while they are still very cold. Pour ½ cup of water around them, put in 400 ° F. oven and bake for 20 minutes or until steaks are very hot. Check frequently to be sure they don't turn too dark a color. Serves 4.

NEW ENGLAND BOILED DINNER

Y, C, B
One-Pot Meal

1 precooked smoked half ham (have butcher cut
   steaks off, leaving a 4-pound piece)
6 whole carrots, scraped
6 whole potatoes, peeled
½ head cabbage, cut in wedges
6 small onions, whole
Garlic powder to taste
Pepper to taste

Freeze steaks for another meal. Cut away any skin and fat and cover 4-pound piece of ham with cold water. Cover and bring to a boil. Taste water; if it is quite salty, discard and recover ham with hot water. Add all other ingredients and simmer for 45 minutes or until vegetables are tender. Serves 6.

Note
If you are going to be in camp another day, reserve liquid and make Split Pea Soup (page 246) with it over grill at the edge of the campfire.

WILDERNESS NEW ENGLAND BOILED DINNER

If you don't have a piece of smoked ham, substitute what bacon or salt pork you can spare and boil with dehydrated vegetables. Eat as a soup so none of the rich liquid will be wasted.

SAUSAGE AND SAUERKRAUT SUPPER

Y, C, B
One-Pot Meal

1 16-ounce can sauerkraut
1 10-ounce can beef broth
1 10½-ounce can condensed cream of potato soup
3 4-ounce cans Vienna sausage, cut in 1-inch slices

Soak sauerkraut in 1 quart water for 1 hour, then discard water, or pour 2 quarts of water through the sauerkraut. Combine all ingredients, heat through, and serve with bread. Serves 4.

VEAL

CHOPPED VEAL AND GREEN PEPPER

Y, C, B
One-Pot Meal

1 tablespoon olive oil
2 tablespoons cooking oil
3 medium onions, chopped
3 large stalks celery, chopped
3 green peppers, cut in ½-inch slices
2 pounds chopped veal
6 ounces seedless raisins
1 1-pound can baked beans
Salt and pepper to taste

Combine olive and cooking oil in large, heavy pot. Heat to sizzling, add onions, celery, and green peppers, and sauté until crisp-tender. Remove with slotted spoon and set aside. Add chopped veal to pot and stir fry until there is no pink color remaining. Add raisins, baked beans, and salt and pepper to taste. Return vegetables to pot and continue cooking, stirring constantly, until everything is well blended and very hot. Serve with bread and butter. Serves 6.

VEAL BALLS IN TOMATO–SAUERKRAUT SAUCE

Y, C, B
One-Pot Meal

2 10½-ounce cans tomato soup, undiluted
1 1-pound 11-ounce can sauerkraut
1 teaspoon onion salt
¼ teaspoon pepper
1½ pounds chopped veal or other chopped meats

Pour undiluted tomato soup into a large saucepan or Dutch oven. Pour 2 quarts cold water through sauerkraut. Discard water but do not drain. Add sauerkraut to tomato soup. Turn heat on medium and bring to a boil. Turn down to slow simmer and cook for 5 minutes, stirring frequently. Mix onion salt and pepper into chopped veal and roll into balls 1¼ to 1½ inches in diameter. Drop into sauerkraut and soup mixture, cover, and simmer slowly for 40 minutes or until meat balls are cooked. Add water if mixture becomes so thick that it starts to stick to the bottom of pan and burn. Serve with rolls and butter. Serves 4 to 6.

CANNED MEAT BALLS IN TOMATO–SAUERKRAUT SAUCE

Substitute 2 cans of meat balls for those in preceding recipe. Add to tomato-sauerkraut mixture and cook just until meat balls are heated through.

VEAL CHOPS BRAISED IN FRUIT COCKTAIL

Y, C, B

1 tablespoon cooking oil
1 tablespoon butter or margarine
6 thick veal chops, about 1½ inches
½ teaspoon salt
½ teaspoon black pepper
½ teaspoon ground ginger
½ teaspoon spicy mustard
1 tablespoon honey
Juice of 1 lemon
1 tablespoon brown sugar
1 1-pound 14-ounce can fruit cocktail in extra heavy syrup
2 tablespoons water
1 tablespoon corn starch

Heat oil and butter or margarine in heavy skillet but don't let them smoke. Season chops with salt, pepper, and ginger and cook on low to medium heat until brown on both sides. Add mustard, honey, lemon juice, and brown sugar to can of fruit cocktail and pour over chops.

Cover with a heavy lid and simmer until they are well done, about 40 minutes. Turn chops once while cooking.

About 15 minutes before time for meat to be done, mix 2 tablespoons water with corn starch. When mixture is smooth, stir ½ cup of fruit sauce from meat into it 1 tablespoon at a time. Pour sauce into skillet and carefully stir. Leave the lid off and stir occasionally until done. Serve with sauce. Serves 4 to 6.

Note
If you have a place to keep meat warm, finish cooking, then remove it from skillet while cooking sauce.

VEAL PARMESAN

Y, C, B
Two-Step Recipe

1½ pounds Italian-style veal cutlets (about 12 cutlets)
2 tablespoons milk
1 large egg
½ cup dry bread crumbs
½ cup grated Parmesan cheese
½ teaspoon salt
½ teaspoon paprika
2 tablespoons oil
1 tablespoon butter or margarine
½ pound Mozzarella cheese, thinly sliced (do not use pre-sliced)
1 1-pound 15-ounce jar marinara sauce

Step 1: ½ hour
Step 2: 1 hour

Step 1
Pound cutlets until they are thin and flat. Lightly beat milk and egg together. Combine crumbs, grated Parmesan cheese, salt, and paprika. Dip each chop into egg mixture, coat with crumb mixture, and lay on waxed paper to dry for at least 5 minutes. Heat oil and butter or margarine in heavy skillet until sizzling hot but not smoking. Add a few cutlets at a time (don't crowd) and fry until golden brown on one side. Turn with spatula and repeat on second side. Cool cutlets, wrap in freezer paper in single-layered packets, and freeze until such time as you want to take them camping or on a cruise, carrying them, of course, in your portable icebox. You might also want to finish preparing them at a later date to serve on your patio.

Variation
Some people prefer to shake their veal chops, a few at a time, in a paper bag containing about ½ cup of seasoned flour before dipping in beaten egg. This procedure, if you don't mind taking the extra time for it, does make the batter adhere to the meat a little better.

Step 2
Place cutlets, while still very cold or even partially frozen, in shallow, lightly greased pan (or pans), divide sliced Mozzarella cheese over them, and top with marinara sauce. Cover and bake in 325 ° F. oven for 45 minutes or until veal is very tender and sauce has a nice consistency. Serves 6 to 8.

To Cook Step 2 in a Galley without an Oven
Arrange cutlets in one or more large skillets or saucepans—the heavier the better—and, after covering with cheese and marinara sauce, pour ¼ cup water around cutlets. Cover tightly and steam until cutlets are hot and cheese and sauce are bubbly hot. Placing insulated metal disks under the pans will help keep cutlets from burning on the bottom. Cook at low to medium heat.

VEAL CORDON BLEU WITH CRANAPPLE

Prepare breaded veal cutlets as in step 1 of Veal Parmesan recipe. In step 2, substitute 2 or 3 cups of cranapple juice and 6 slices of boiled ham for the marinara sauce. When you are ready to complete step 2, top 6 of the cutlets with the 6 slices of ham. Divide the Mozzarella cheese over them and top with the remaining 6 cutlets. Pour 2 cups of cranapple juice into pan. Cover and bake for 30 to 40 minutes or until veal is tender and juice is absorbed. Check frequently and add more juice if pan gets dry before veal is very tender and cheese melted.

VEAL CUTLETS À LA HOLSTEIN

Prepare breaded veal cutlets as in step 1 of Veal Parmesan recipe, but don't cook them. Get them ready for frying, then wrap and freeze. Take them camping or cruising in your icebox and, when defrosted but still icy cold, fry as described in step 1 of Veal Parmesan recipe. Substitute 6 to 8 soft fried or poached eggs for Mozzarella cheese and marinara sauce and serve one egg atop each veal chop.

VEAL STEW

Y, C, B
One-Pot Meal

2 pounds veal stew meat cut in small cubes
½ cup flour
2 tablespoons cooking oil
1 1-pound can sauerkraut
1 8-ounce can tomato sauce
1 6-ounce can tomato paste
4 tablespoons brown sugar, or to taste
2 onions, chopped
2 carrots, sliced
4–6 apples, cored and sliced
6 cups of water

Dredge veal stew meat in flour. Heat oil in large, heavy saucepan or pot, add stew meat, and lightly brown on all sides. Add all other ingredients, bring to a boil, turn down to simmer, and cook for 1½ to 2 hours or until meat is tender and gravy is well blended.

POULTRY

BARBECUED CHICKEN IN ORIENTAL SAUCE

Y, C, B, P
Two-Step Recipe
Step 1: 1½ hours
Step 2: ½–¾ hour

2 2½–3 pound young chickens cut into serving-size
   pieces
12 cups cold water
3 medium carrots, scraped
1 medium onion
¼ teaspoon celery salt
1 pinch pepper
1 tablespoon salt
1 pinch saffron
⅛ teaspoon paprika
¼ cup soy sauce, preferably imported
1½ tablespoons honey
2 tablespoons wine
¼ teaspoon powdered ginger
¼ teaspoon garlic powder
¼ cup orange juice
2 tablespoons lemon juice

Step 1
Combine first 7 items in a pot (6 quart or larger), put on medium heat,
bring to a boil, turn down to a low simmer, and continue cooking for
15 minutes or until chicken meat is just done. (Don't overcook as chicken
will be heated again over coals.) While chicken is cooking, combine remaining ingredients, mix together into well-blended sauce, and set aside.

Remove chicken from broth into large shallow pan. Continue cooking broth until it has the strength you like in chicken soup. Spread sauce
over each piece of chicken. Cool quickly and freeze in single-layer containers for future use or refrigerate in covered dish for use no later than
next day. Before covering whichever type of container you use, pour any
remaining sauce over chicken pieces.

When transporting to camp or boat, put freezer packages in a
tightly closed plastic bag or other plastic container to prevent the defrosting broth from leaking out.

Strain broth, cool quickly, and freeze or refrigerate for making
Chicken Soup with Dill Matzoh Balls (page 240). Wipe off carrots and
refrigerate in covered dish for use in soup or to serve as a vegetable in a
later meal.

Step 2

Remove chicken pieces from dish or other containers, reserving any sauce that does not cling to them to use for basting. (If chicken is frozen, defrost overnight in refrigerator, in portable cooler en route to camp or picnic grounds, or in galley icebox. Finish preparing chicken before it gets warm.) Arrange chicken pieces in long-handled hinged grill and place 4 to 6 inches above burned-down cooking coals. Turn often, brush with sauce remaining in dish, and cook until both sides are nicely browned. Serves 6 to 8.

To Cook in Galley Stove

Cook in 350 ° F. oven for 30 to 45 minutes, basting occasionally, or until chicken is nicely browned. If your galley stove has a good broiler, brown chicken there. Whether cooking in oven or broiler, turn chicken at least once and watch closely to be sure sauce does not burn.

BARBECUED CHICKEN MARINARA

Y, C, B, P
Two-Step Recipe
Step 1: 1 hour
Step 2: ½–¾ hour

1 3–3½-pound young chicken
1 teaspoon salt
2 stalks celery
1 large onion
1 1-pound 15-ounce jar marinara sauce

Step 1

Put chicken in a pot, cover with water. Add salt, celery, and onion and bring to a boil. Turn down to a simmer and cook 20 minutes or until chicken is just barely done. Remove chicken from pot. Cool enough to handle, cut into serving pieces, and place in dish for marinating.

Add one cup of the broth in which chicken was cooked to marinara sauce, mix well, and pour over chicken. Marinate in the refrigerator until one-half hour before you are ready to serve.

If you are going to take this chicken dish picnicking, camping, or cruising, lay chicken in a single layer in a shallow pan (square-cornered for convenient packing), surround with marinara sauce, cover, and freeze.

Step 2

Remove chicken pieces from sauce, after defrosting if frozen, arrange in a long-handled hinged grill, and place 4 to 6 inches above burned-down cooking coals. Turn often, basting with sauce remaining in marinating dish, and cook until both sides are nicely browned. Serves 4.

To Cook in Galley

Heat in your galley oven, at 400 ° F. for 30 to 40 minutes, or brown in the broiler if your galley stove has one.

CREAMED CHICKEN, MUSHROOMS, AND PEAS

Y, C, B, P
One-Pot Meal

1 cup leftover chicken meat (substitute 1 5-ounce can boned chicken)
1 10½-ounce can condensed cream of mushroom soup
¼ cup water
¼ cup canned milk
1 cup slivered almonds, toasted
½ cup leftover peas or other vegetable, cooked
Dash nutmeg
1 3-ounce can sliced mushrooms (optional)
8 slices toast

Combine chicken meat in a saucepan with cream of mushroom soup, water, and milk and stir over medium heat until soup is no longer lumpy. Add almonds, peas, nutmeg, and mushrooms and heat, stirring frequently, until mixture is well blended and heated through. If too thick, add water or milk. Serve on toast. Serves 4.

Variation
Serve with rice or potatoes.

CHICKEN AND RICE AND RAISINS

Y, C, W, B

3 cups water, mixed with 1 teaspoon salt
1 cup brown rice
½ cup raisins
1 tablespoon cooking oil
1 clove garlic
1 pound raw chicken or game-bird meat, skinless, boneless, and finely diced
Salt and pepper to taste

Bring salted water to a boil, stir in the rice, cover, move to side of fire (or turn down low if cooking on camp stove or in boat galley), and cook until all liquid is absorbed and rice is tender, about 45 minutes. After about 30 minutes of that time has gone by, do two things: Stir in the raisins and, in a separate skillet, bring the oil to a sizzle, add garlic, stir-fry until golden brown, and then discard. Now add meat to the oil and stir until it turns color with no signs of red. Finally add stir-fried meat to rice and raisins, add seasoning, stir for a minute or two to mix well, and serve at once. Serves 4 to 6.

CANNED OR LEFTOVER POULTRY AND RICE AND RAISINS

Substitute canned or leftover poultry (including game bird) meat for raw chicken meat. If it's already cooked, just heat long enough to brown slightly in garlic-flavored oil. Otherwise, proceed as in preceding recipe.

FRIED CHICKEN   Y, C, P

2 2–2½ pound fryers, washed, dried, and cut up
1½ cups flour
1 teaspoon salt
⅛ teaspoon pepper
Cooking oil

Dredge chicken pieces in flour into which salt and pepper have been mixed.

Put about ½ inch of cooking oil in each heavy skillet (you won't be able to serve everyone at once unless you use at least two) and heat to very hot but below the smoking point—just so chicken pieces will sizzle when added. The chicken must not be crowded in the pans. It must be cooked slowly but at a high enough heat that the flour does not become soggy. The way to achieve this is to turn each piece frequently, using tongs, not a fork, and cooking it for 20 to 30 minutes. When done, the meat around the bone should be completely cooked with no suggestion of pink remaining, and the outside should be a hard golden brown crust that has kept the grease from the chicken meat. Serves 4 to 6.

Note
This fried chicken is good served cold in your yard or on a picnic.

ROAST TURKEY WITH LOTS OF STUFFING

Y, P

Two-Step Recipe
Step 1: ¾ hour
Step 2: 4½ hours

12-pound turkey
1 pound bacon, cut in small pieces
2 or 3 cups chopped onion
2 or 3 cups chopped celery
3 or 4 cups cooked and peeled chestnuts (if you can't get them already prepared, substitute shelled walnuts)
5 8-ounce packages Pepperidge Farm herb-seasoned bread crumbs
2 cups water
1 pound butter
3 cups canned beef broth

Step 1
Wash turkey inside and out in cold water, thoroughly dry, cover loosely, and refrigerate.

Start bacon cooking in a heavy pot, add chopped onion and celery, and cook on low to medium heat, stirring frequently, until vegetables are tender. Break up chestnuts slightly and add to mixture. Transfer to a dish, cool, and refrigerate.

Step 2
Combine bacon, vegetable, and nut mixture with bread crumbs in large mixing bowl. Heat water, cut butter into pieces, add to hot water, and stir until it melts. Turn off heat, add broth, and pour over ingredients in mixing bowl. Mix together until bread crumbs are thoroughly moistened. Stuff bird loosely with mixture and skewer openings shut. Or leave your bird un-stuffed. It will cook more quickly if you do. Refrigerate unused stuffing.

Fasten turkey securely on the skewer of your outdoor stove, making sure that it is evenly balanced, with wings and legs tied against the body. Or place it in a pan or on a grill, positioning it according to printed instructions that came with your particular outdoor stove. Insert meat thermometer and cook turkey until it is well done, at 300 ° F. This will probably take from 3 to 4 hours, depending on whether your bird is stuffed and other factors. Check timing charts that came with your stove and be guided by them, too. No matter how short or long it takes, your bird is done when the thermometer registers 185 ° F. Baste with butter or margarine if you like, but it shouldn't be necessary. If any part gets too brown, fasten foil over it.

One hour before you think the turkey will be done, remove drippings from pan. Mix enough hot water with the least fatty part of the drippings to make 1 cup (2 cups if none of the stuffing went inside the bird) and stir this liquid into stuffing left in the mixing bowl. Press stuffing into 1 or 2 lightly greased loaf pans and cook in the oven of the outdoor stove if there is room and you are keeping the hood down, or in the oven of your kitchen range, for 45 minutes (at 300 ° F.) or until lightly browned.

Let turkey stand for 15 minutes before carving—unless eating it while nice and hot means more to you than nice-looking slices of meat. Serve with cranberry sauce and a tossed salad. Serves 12 to 14.

COLD ROAST TURKEY

Prepare as above, remove stuffing, and chill in refrigerator before slicing.

WHOLE, UNSTUFFED CHICKENS IN ORANGE–LEMON SAUCE
Y, P

2 2½-pound roasting chickens
½ 6-ounce can undiluted frozen orange juice
½ 6-ounce can undiluted frozen lemonade
4 tablespoons honey
¼ teaspoon paprika
¼ teaspoon ground ginger
½ teaspoon salt

Wash chickens and dry with lint-free absorbent towel. Place, back up, in shallow roasting pan, and put in 350 ° F. outdoor oven where it will not be directly over the coals. (If you cook on a spit, place pan beneath birds to catch drippings.)

Combine rest of items and mix well. When chicken has cooked for 1¼ hours, pour about ¼ of the sauce over it, baste after 10 minutes, and turn over. Baste every 5 minutes thereafter until chicken is done, approximately 20 to 30 minutes. After using up juices in the two cans, baste with sauce in the dripping pan. If sauce starts to turn brown in the bottom of pan, add water as necessary.

Spoon a little sauce over each serving. Serves 8.

WHOLE, UNSTUFFED DUCK IN ORANGE–LEMON SAUCE

Use fork tines to pierce skin of 3- or 4-pound duck in several places. Put duck in cold water to cover. Bring water to a boil, turn down to a low simmer, and cook for 10 minutes. From then on, follow preceding chicken recipe and cook either in a pan or on a spit over coals.

FRANKFURTERS

BOILED FRANKFURTERS ON BUNS   Y, C, B, P

8 frankfurters
8 frankfurter buns
Mustard
Pickle relish

Add frankfurters to simmering water and cook for 5 to 8 minutes or remove pan from fire, cover, and let frankfurters stand in water for 8 to 10 minutes. Remove from water, place each one on half of a frankfurter bun (either toasted or plain), spread with desired amount of mustard and pickle relish, top with second half of bun and serve at once. Serves 4.

BARBECUED FRANKFURTERS ON BUNS   Y, C, P

8 frankfurters
8 frankfurter buns, sliced lengthwise but not quite through, so that the halves remain attached
Mustard
Pickle relish
Chopped onions (optional)

Arrange frankfurters in long-handled, hinged grill and cook 4 to 6 inches above burned-down but very hot cooking coals. They are ready to eat when both sides are the color and degree of crispness you like. Lay one frankfurter in each slit bun and spread with mustard, pickle relish, and chopped onions in the desired amounts.

BARBECUED MARINATED FRANKFURTERS

Slash each frankfurter diagonally in 4 to 6 places, then marinate for 1 hour in Fruit Juice Glaze (page 219) or another sauce of your choice and broil as above, basting occasionally with sauce.

FRANKFURTERS BARBECUED WITH BACON

Wrap one slice of raw bacon diagonally around each frankfurter and cook as in Barbecued Frankfurters on Buns.

CHILI–BAKED FRANKS AND BEANS   Y, C, B

4 cooked frankfurters, sliced lengthwise
¼ cup grated sharp cheese
1 3½-ounce can French fried onion rings
1 15-ounce can red kidney beans
1 8-ounce can tomato sauce
½ cup mayonnaise
1 teaspoon chili powder

Lay franks in a shallow baking dish. Sprinkle with cheese, top with half
the French fried onion rings, and cover the rings with the kidney beans.
Combine tomato sauce, mayonnaise, and chili powder. Mix well and pour
over ingredients in dish. Top with remaining onion rings and bake in
350 ° F. oven for 40 minutes or until bubbling hot all the way through.
Serves 4.

FRANKFURTERS WITH SAUERKRAUT   Y, C, B, P
One-Pot Meal

1 dozen frankfurters
1 1-pound 11-ounce can sauerkraut
½ teaspoon caraway seeds (optional)
1 dozen frankfurter buns
Mustard

Put frankfurters in a pot with the sauerkraut, add caraway seeds, bring to
a boil, turn down to a simmer, and cook for 5 minutes. Serve frankfurters
together with sauerkraut in buns with mustard. Serves 4 to 6.

LEFTOVER SAUERKRAUT

Rinse leftover sauerkraut several times in clear water, chop, and combine
with hamburger meat and bread crumbs to make meat balls. Or mix into
a gravy and serve with meat.

FRANKS IN A BISCUIT BLANKET   Y, C

1 cup prepared biscuit mix
⅓ cup milk
8–10 frankfurters

Combine prepared biscuit mix with milk, stir together, and roll out in sheet
approximately ¼ inch thick. Cut in 8 to 10 strips about 1 inch shorter
than the frankfurters are long. Roll up each frankfurter in one of these

strips, leaving both ends exposed, and wrap loosely, allowing plenty of expansion room, in a lightly greased piece of aluminum foil. Cook foil-wrapped franks on top of grill, 4 to 6 inches above burned-down coals for 15 minutes or until dough is cooked. Check one for doneness before opening all the packages. Eat plain or dunk in catsup to which you can add a little soy sauce if you like. Serves 4 to 6.

POTATO–FRANKFURTER MIXTURE WITH EGG AND VEGETABLES

Y, C, B
One-Pot Meal

2 slices bacon, diced
4 frankfurters, sliced crosswise
2 large cooked potatoes, diced
¼ cup chopped cheddar cheese
1 tablespoon butter or margarine
1 tablespoon cooking oil
¼ medium green pepper, sliced
1 small sweet onion
½ cup powdered whole egg
½ cup lukewarm water
½ teaspoon wine vinegar
½ teaspoon Worcestershire sauce
1 pinch pepper

Fry bacon and frankfurter slices together in large skillet or big, heavy pot. Remove from pan and brown diced potatoes in the grease. Turn with a spatula, fry other side, then stir in cheese, and heat until it melts. Remove contents of pan and mix together with bacon and frankfurter slices. Add butter and margarine to skillet or pot, heat, add green pepper and onion, and lightly sauté. Reconstitute egg with lukewarm water (see page 200), stir in remaining ingredients, and pour into pan with sauteed pepper and onion. Cook on medium heat. Turn over when one side is done, top with potato-frankfurter mixture, cover tightly, and cook 2 or 3 minutes longer or until egg is done and everything is nice and hot. Serve at once. Serves 4 to 6.

Note
Add other vegetables you may have or substitute them for green pepper and onion.

17—Fish and Shellfish

Most fish and shellfish recipes are interchangeable. Pick a recipe suitable for the type of fish you have. A delicately flavored recipe calling for lobster meat, for instance, would also be good if you made it with crab or delicately flavored finny fish such as flounder, sole, and halibut. Oyster, clam, and mussel recipes are interchangeable. And so it goes.

If you don't find a fish or shellfish recipe you want here, look in Chapter 15, "Soups"; Chapter 18, "Meat and Fish Combinations"; and Chapter 23, "How to Prepare and Cook Wild Game."

BARBECUED FISH FILLETS IN CLAM SAUCE

Y, C, P

4 medium-size flounder (or other white-fleshed fish) fillets at least ½ inch thick
1 8-ounce can minced clams
½ cup butter
2 tablespoons finely minced onion
1 pinch white pepper

Wash fillets by dipping in cold water and dry on lint-free absorbent towels. Drain clams, reserving liquid. Melt butter, lightly sauté onions in it, and stir in pepper and reserved clam juice. Heat, then spread half of mixture over both sides of fillets. Barbecue 4 to 6 inches above cooking coals 4 or 5 minutes to a side or until fish flakes easily when gently tested with fork.

Add clams to remaining half of sauce, divide over barbecued fillets, and serve. Serves 4.

285

FILLETS WITH CANNED   Y, C, B
CLAM AND CRAB

1 pound fresh-caught fish fillets
1 8-ounce can minced clams and the broth in which they were canned
1 7½-ounce can Alaska king crab

Dip each fillet into a pan of cold water to clean, then put into a heavy saucepan that has a heavy, tight-fitting lid. Open canned clams and crab and drain any liquid off into a measuring cup. Add water to make ¾ cup of liquid. Pour into the dish of fish, add clams and crab, and cook at medium heat until liquid just starts to boil. Turn down to simmer, gently stir, cover, and cook for 5 minutes. Remove pan from heat but don't take off the cover. Let stand for 10 minutes, steaming in its juices before serving.

FRIED CATFISH IN   Y, C, B
PINEAPPLE SAUCE

¼ cup soy sauce
2 pounds skinless catfish fillets, cut in 1 x 2-inch pieces
½ cup flour
¼ teaspoon pepper
3 tablespoons cooking oil
1 1-pound 4½-ounce can pineapple tidbits
1½ tablespoons corn starch dissolved in ¼ cup cold water

Spread soy sauce over all sides of catfish pieces and marinate for 30 minutes, turning once.

Season flour with pepper, dry off pieces of catfish, and dredge with the mixture. Heat cooking oil in skillet until sizzling hot but not burning, add fish pieces, and cook until they are golden brown on all sides and flake easily when tested with a fork.

While fish cooks, pour pineapple tidbits, including juice from can, and corn starch and water into saucepan; heat, stirring almost constantly, until mixture comes to a boil. Turn down heat and cook until sauce thickens. Pour over fried catfish and serve with rice. Serves 4 to 6.

PAN–FRIED AND OVEN–FRIED FISH FILLETS

Y, C, B, P
Two-Step Recipe
Step 1: ¼ hour
Step 2: ½ hour

6 large fish fillets, ¼–½ inch thick (1¼–1½ pounds)

⎡ ¼ cup flour
⎨ ½ teaspoon salt or to taste   Mix together in paper bag.
⎣ 1 pinch pepper or to taste
1 egg
1 tablespoon water
1 cup flavored bread crumbs in a paper bag
2 tablespoons oil
2 tablespoons butter or margarine

Step 1

Wash and dry fillets, then shake, one at a time, in bag of seasoned flour until each one is coated with mixture. Combine egg and water, beat together lightly, dip each fillet into mixture, then shake it in bag of flavored crumbs until well coated. Wrap, two fillets to each single-layered package, and freeze ready to defrost and cook in the yard or pack, still frozen, in your ice chest for a picnic, a camping trip, or cruise in your boat.

Step 2

To Pan Fry

Heat oil and butter in a large skillet until hot but not smoking. Add defrosted fish and cook until golden brown on first side. Turn and repeat on second side. Fish should be cooked so that it flakes easily when tested with a fork by the time two sides are browned. Serve at once with lemon wedges or Easy Tartare Sauce (page 218). Add a salad and potatoes for a satisfying meal. Serves 4.

To Oven Fry

Melt oil and butter, pour into large shallow baking pan (or cookie sheet with slightly raised edges). Lay fillets in the oil, press down gently, and move about to coat them. Turn over and repeat so oils cover second side, too. Leave fillets in pan and bake in pre-heated 350 ° F. oven for 15 minutes or until lightly browned and fish flesh flakes easily when tested with a fork. It's not necessary to turn fillets. Serve same way as suggested for pan-fried fish. Serves 4.

CRUNCHY STEAMED COD Y, B

1½ pounds cod fillets, ¾–1 inch thick and skinless
Liquid from 2 3-ounce cans Broiled in Butter sliced mushrooms (to be used
  in making Cauliflower and Mushrooms in Wine Sauce, page 321)
½ cup sherry
¼ cup flavored bread crumbs
2 tablespoons butter or margarine, very cold
4 lemon wedges

Wash fish by dipping into salted water and dry on lint-free absorbent towels.
    Combine mushroom liquid with sherry and pour into bottom of
shallow baking pan. Place a rack in pan (use one made of perforated metal,
not wire) and lay fish fillets on it, skinned side down. Sprinkle bread crumbs
evenly over fish. Dot with butter. Place in 400 ° F. oven and bake for 20
to 25 minutes or until crumbs are light brown and fish flakes easily when
tested with a fork. Reserve liquid in pan for making sauce for Cauliflower
and Mushrooms in Wine Sauce and return fish to oven to keep warm while
you make it. Garnish with lemon wedges and serve with cauliflower dish
and sliced tomatoes. Serves 4.

Note
This recipe and Cauliflower and Mushrooms in Wine Sauce should be prepared at the same time.

BAKED FISH STEAKS AND Y, C, B
STEAMED BEER

6 fish steaks, about ¾ inch thick
Bread crumbs to cover
¼ pound margarine
Beer
2 bay leaves, crumbled
Salt and pepper to taste

Spread steaks on rack of shallow broiler pan, cover liberally with bread
crumbs, and dot freely with margarine. Heat beer, add crumbled bay leaves
and salt and pepper, and pour to a depth of about ¼ inch or less—making
sure it does not reach the rack—into pan. Bake in 400 ° F. oven for 20
minutes or until crumbs are nut brown and fish flesh flakes easily when
tested with a fork.

Note
Men in particular go for this, usually adding herbs of their choice to the
beer. A good one to try is pieces of cinnamon stick.

BARBECUED SALMON STEAKS   Y, C, W

½ cup brandy or dry vermouth (optional, substitute 2 tablespoons vinegar)
¾ cup melted butter or margarine or cooking oil
⅓ cup lemon juice
3 tablespoons chopped chives
1 teaspoon soy sauce or salt to taste
⅛ teaspoon garlic salt
Pepper to taste
½ teaspoon marjoram
2 pounds salmon steak

Mix together all ingredients except salmon steak and marinate the fish in the mixture for at least 1 hour before cooking. Turn fish occasionally and be sure all surfaces are covered by the sauce. Place fish in well-greased hinged grill and barbecue 4 to 6 inches above cooking coals until both sides are nicely browned (5 to 7 minutes to a side) and fish flakes easily when tested with a fork. While cooking, baste with any sauce left in the marinating dish.

FISH STEAKS IN ZESTY SAUCE   Y, C, P

4 fish steaks, ¾–1 inch thick
2 tablespoons cooking oil
3 tablespoons catsup
2 tablespoons lemon juice
1 tablespoon wine vinegar
1 teaspoon mustard
½ teaspoon Worcestershire sauce
3 drops Tabasco sauce
1 clove minced garlic
1 tablespoon grated onion
¼ teaspoon salt
1 pinch of paprika, or to taste

Wash fish by dipping in cold water and dry thoroughly on lint-free absorbent towels. Combine all other ingredients, mix well, and marinate the fish in the mixture for 30 minutes. Remove fish and retain sauce. Place fish in a long-handled, hinged wire grill, fasten securely, and place about 4 inches above cooking coals. Cook 4 to 6 minutes to a side, basting frequently with sauce or until fish flakes easily when gently tested with a fork. Serves 4.

Note
To increase smokiness of flavor, add hickory or other hardwood chips to the fire, after first soaking them in water for at least 1 hour.

FISH LAULAUS
Y, C, B, P

This recipe came to us from the Chun King Kitchens.

½ pound fresh spinach leaves
4 fillets (approximately 1 pound) of sole, flounder, or ocean perch, each
    about 6 inches long
Salt and pepper to taste
Onion or garlic salt to taste
Juice of 1 lemon
1 tablespoon soy sauce
1 10-ounce package Chun King frozen fried rice, thawed or 1 13½-ounce
    can Chun King fried rice
4 squares of heavy-duty aluminum foil, 12 x 12 inches

Wash spinach leaves well, cutting off tough stems and singling out the largest leaves. Drain.

One at a time, place fish fillets between two pieces of plastic wrap or waxed paper. With a mallet or the side of a heavy knife, pound each fillet lightly until it is flattened to approximately 4 inches across the widest part. Sprinkle fish with seasonings, lemon juice, and soy sauce. Divide fried rice over 4 fillets and wrap fish around rice to make a fat roll.

Place 4 or 5 good-sized spinach leaves in the center of each square of foil. Set each fish roll on spinach leaves and wrap leaves around fish, adding extra spinach leaves to each as needed to completely cover fish. Wrap foil around spinach in tight bundles, sealing ends tightly to prevent juices from leaking out during cooking.

Place bundles on barbecue grill about 6 inches above gray cooking coals and cook for 25 to 40 minutes, turning frequently. Or place in baking pan and cook in 350 ° F. oven for 25 to 30 minutes. Test one bundle to see if done before opening them all. They're ready to eat if the fish separates easily into flakes when gently probed with a fork. Serves 4.

Note
These fish bundles can be part of the menu at a luau.

Fish Laulaus (*Kitchens of Chun King*)

FISH WITH CARAWAY SEEDS   Y, C, W, B

4 fillets or fish steaks
2 tablespoons caraway seeds
2 tablespoons butter or margarine (substitute cooking oil or bacon grease)
Salt and pepper to taste

Spread caraway seeds over both sides of fillets or steaks. Heat butter or margarine to sizzling but not smoking hot in large skillet and fry fish until golden brown on both sides. Fish is ready to eat if flesh flakes easily when gently prodded with tines of a fork. Season to taste with salt and pepper. Serves 2 to 4.

Don't Believe What They Say about Carp

When fishing regulations don't permit you to go after the familiar game fish, you will often still be permitted to take carp because it is considered by many as the trashiest of all trash fish—full of bones and tasting strongly of the muddy water in which it swims.

It's a traditional joke among sportsmen to say the only way to prepare carp is to plank it, then throw away the carp and eat the plank. But we've discovered that sticking to eating traditions can deprive one of a lot of pleasure and that there are ways to make carp taste good.

Start by skinning the fish. Then rip as much of the flesh away from the bones as you can. Use this flesh and discard everything else.

FRIED CARP BITS   Y, C, W, B, P

2 cups raw pieces of carp flesh
Salt and pepper to taste
½ cup flour
3–4 tablespoons cooking oil

Wash fish pieces in cold water and dry with lint-free absorbent towel. Mix salt and pepper into flour in a heavy paper bag. Add fish pieces and shake until each one is thoroughly coated with flour. Heat oil in skillet (use a heavy one if you have it) until it is sizzling but not smoking, add fish, and fry until crunchy, golden brown. Serves 2.

Note
Many Europeans are fond of carp and often serve it with a strongly flavored sauce. See Sauce Polonaise (pages 220–221).

FISH, RICE, AND VEGETABLE WITH A TOMATO TOUCH

Y, C, W, B
One-Pot Meal

1 10¾-ounce can condensed tomato soup
1 can water
1 cup rice, preferably brown
4 tablespoons soy sauce
½ pound fresh-caught fish, steamed or simmered and then flaked and liquid reserved (substitute 7-ounce can of tuna fish)
1 16-ounce can peas or carrots

Stir soup and water together in a saucepan according to directions on can. Bring to a boil, stir in the rice and the soy sauce, cover, move to side of fire, and cook slowly until all liquid is absorbed, stirring occasionally, 40 to 45 minutes. Add fish and peas or carrots and liquid from can. Stir well for a few minutes until everything is good and hot, then serve at once. Serves 2 to 4.

Note
If liquid in pan of rice is absorbed before rice is tender, add as much of the liquid reserved from cooking fish as necessary.

FRIED MACKEREL POACHED IN RED WINE

Y, C, B, P

1 pound mackerel cut in small strips
½ cup flour
¼ teaspoon salt
⅛ teaspoon pepper
2 tablespoons cooking oil
2 tablespoons butter
½ cup red wine

Carefully dredge pieces of mackerel in flour in which salt and pepper have been mixed. Heat cooking oil and butter in large heavy skillet. When oils start to show tiny bubbles and are very hot but not smoking, add pieces of fish to the pan and fry until crispy brown on both sides. Pour off oil, add wine, and heat for 3 minutes, gently stirring. Remove fish and serve at once. Serves 4.

Note
These delicious bits of fish also can be served with picks as a hot hors d'oeuvres.

QUICK PEPPER–POT FISH
AND BROCCOLI

Y, C, B
One-Pot Meal

2 10½-ounce cans pepper-pot soup
1½ cans water
½ 10-ounce box frozen broccoli (substitute canned, chopped broccoli)
1½ pounds fish, bones and skin removed

Combine soup and water in a pot and heat. Break up frozen broccoli (the easy way is to cover with a linen towel and pound with a wooden mallet) and add to soup. Wash fish and add it, too. When soup comes to a boil, cook for 2 minutes, remove from heat, cover with a tight-fitting lid, and let stand until protein in fish coagulates (8 to 10 minutes). Stir and serve at once with slabs of bread or baked potatoes. Serves 4 to 6.

SALMON BISCUIT ROLL

Y, C, W, B

1 1-pound can of salmon
1 10-ounce can cream of celery soup, undiluted
1 cup cooked minced vegetables (leftovers or canned)
2 cups biscuit mix
1 cup milk
1 tablespoon lemon juice

Drain salmon, reserving liquid, flake, add ¼ can of celery soup and the minced vegetables, and stir.

Combine biscuit mix and ⅔ cup milk, turn out on lightly floured board, and knead about 12 strokes. Roll out into a 9 x 12 rectangle, spread with salmon mixture, and roll up lengthwise, jelly-roll fashion. Lay seam-side down on a baking sheet or directly on the shelf of a reflector oven and bake in preheated 400 ° F. oven for 25 to 30 minutes or until lightly browned.

Add milk to reserved salmon liquid to make ½ cup, combine with remaining celery soup, and heat. Stir in lemon juice and serve with slices of salmon biscuit roll. Serves 4 to 6.

TUNA LOAF WITH CHEESE   C, B

2 6½-ounce cans tuna
1 chicken bouillon cube dissolved in ½ cup hot water
1 teaspoon undiluted orange juice concentrate (optional)
1 teaspoon honey
1 pinch paprika
1 teaspoon ground ginger
1 egg, lightly beaten
2 cups soft stale bread crumbs
½ cup leftover vegetables, cooked
¼ pound sliced cheese

Combine all ingredients except cheese and mix until bread crumbs are moist. Put half of the mixture in greased loaf pan and spread with half of the cheese. Add remaining mixture and top with second half of cheese. Bake in pre-heated oven at 350 ° F. for 45 minutes or until lightly browned. Serves 4 to 6.

Note
Brown leftover slices of loaf in a skillet, pour beaten egg around, and cook for the next day's breakfast. Or chill and slice for second day's lunch, either in or out of a sandwich.

DR. KRAEMER'S FOIL–BAKED FISH   Y, C, W, P

1 2-pound fresh-caught fish, dressed and cut into 2 chunks
2 tablespoons butter or margarine
Garlic salt and pepper to taste
1 large onion, sliced
1 teaspoon chopped parsley (substitute dried flakes to taste)
Lemon juice

Place each fish chunk on a double square of heavy-duty aluminum foil. Divide butter or margarine, seasonings, sliced onion, and chopped parsley over the two chunks. Fold foil into two packages and seal so butter or margarine won't leak out when it melts. Lay packages 4 to 6 inches above burned-down cooking coals on grill and cook for 15 to 20 minutes, turning frequently, or until fish flakes easily away from the bone when gently tested with a fork. Serve at once with lemon juice. Serves 2.

Note
You can bury foil packages in coals instead of placing them on the grill, but test to see if they are done after about 10 minutes. Thin fish, such as flounder, will be done about 5 minutes sooner than timings given above.

POACHED WHOLE FISH   Y, C, W, B, P

1 3–4 pound whole dressed fish
Boiling water
2–4 bouillon cubes or dehydrated gravy mix (optional)

Place dressed fish in a dish that's a little deeper than the fish is thick. (It could be your frying pan or something fashioned of 2 thicknesses of foil and supported by rocks or pieces of wood.) Pour boiling water over to completely cover, place an airtight cover over the dish so steam can't escape, and let stand for 15 to 20 minutes (a thick fish might need 25 but test at 15 to see if the flesh separates into flakes when gently poked with fork). It should be done in 15 minutes, but if it's not, add more boiling water and re-cover or place over fire and poach for 5 minutes more. In high altitudes you'd better let it poach at the edge of the fire for the entire time. You can add bouillon cubes to steaming water, or mix dehydrated gravy and pour over cooked fish, or you can eat it plain with a little butter or margarine. Serves 4.

How to Prepare Your Own Seashell Dishes   Y, C, B, P
for Many Uses

Some of the most beautiful dishes to be had anywhere for any price are seashells. If you live or vacation on or near the seashore, you can usually have all you want for free. If you have an abundance of them, they're great for outdoor eating because, when through, you can toss them in the garbage, just like a paper plate. Except they're much prettier and more satisfying to use than paper.

You can stuff seashells with food, bake, and serve for main course or appetizer.

You can use them for nuts, candies, and so on.

You can serve salads in them.

Here's how you clean them:

Clam and Scallop Shells from Live Shellfish
Scrub with a wire brush before opening clams and rinse several times under cold, running water. (The recipe for Manhattan Clam Chowder, page 244, tells how to steam them open.) After you have removed clam or scallop, if there is meat and muscle clinging to shells that won't come loose, boil them in water to which soda has been added. If you are baking shells immediately after opening clams, you don't need to bother about bits of flesh unless they are unsightly. But the shells must be thoroughly cleaned before subsequent use.

Crab Shells
After the crab has been removed, scrub the shell with a brush or soapless metal pot scrubber. Place it in a pot, cover with water, add 1 teaspoon baking soda, and boil for 20 minutes.

Mussel Shells
Mussel shells, though small, can be very effective when both sides are used and they are served tightly closed. Whatever food may be inside is then a surprise, as is the lovely, rainbow-hued lining of this much overlooked shell. West Coast mussels cannot be eaten at certain times of the year. Consult local health authorities before using any you may gather in that area.

Scrub mussels thoroughly, using a stiff brush, under cold running water. Pull and scrape away the beardlike appendage and put mussels to soak for 2 hours in a pot of clean cold water. Discard any that float.

Lay mussels on a rack in a pot, add 2 cups of water, and bring to a boil. Turn down to a simmer and cook until all the mussels have opened. Remove meat from shells and use in the same way as you would clam meat. Strain the broth through several layers of cheesecloth and use in soups and sauces. Save the shells and use as dishes.

CLAMS ON THE HALF–SHELL   Y, C, B, P

12 littleneck or cherrystone clams per person, ice cold and raw
Salt and pepper to taste
Lemon wedges

Pry clams open with a clam knife, lay on a bed of crushed ice, and serve with salt and pepper and lemon wedges.

Note
If you find it difficult to pry clams open with a knife, try one of the openers (a slicer attached to a board) being sold now in many department stores.

You can also steam them open and eat them just slightly cooked after chilling them for a few minutes arranged on the half-shell on a bed of crushed ice.

CLAMS ON THE HALF–SHELL WITH
SPICY COCKTAIL SAUCE

Serve ¼ cup of Spicy Cocktail Sauce (page 221) with each serving of 12 clams. Add a dash of cayenne pepper (or to taste) to the sauce if you like it very hot.

CHOWDER AND STEAMER CLAMS
ON THE HALF-SHELL

There's no rule saying you can only eat cherrystones and littlenecks on the half-shell. Our daughter prefers chowder clams (maybe because she digs them herself), and steamers, too, can be eaten on the half-shell if you like them that way. Either pry them open with a knife or steam them open the easy way.

STEAMED CLAMS   Y, C, B, P

12 steamer clams per person, thoroughly scrubbed and washed
¼ cup (or less) melted butter per person
Salt and pepper to taste
Lemon wedges

Steam the clams with a clambake as described on pages 305–306, or put about an inch of water in a large pot, add scrubbed steamer clams, cover, and bring water to a simmer. Let the water continue to simmer until clams open. Serve immediately or cook from 3 to 5 minutes longer if you prefer your clams well cooked. The longer you cook, the tougher the clams will become.

Serve, in the shell, with hot melted butter, salt and pepper, and lemon wedges. Although 12 steamers are usually considered a serving, some people are satisfied with 6, while others will eat them as long as they last.

Note
Although steamers are the nicest, other types of clam can be served this way, too.

STUFFED CLAMS   Y, B

12 clams steamed open (see above)
2 tablespoons olive oil
1 large tomato, chopped
1 large onion, chopped
1 stalk celery, chopped
1 8-ounce can tomato sauce
¼ cup toasted bread crumbs
¼ cup grated Parmesan cheese
Garlic salt to taste
Paprika to taste
Butter for dotting

Chop clams and set aside. Heat olive oil in heavy skillet, add tomato, onion, and celery, and lightly sauté until just tender. Add tomato sauce and simmer for 10 minutes. Add chopped clams and stir. Lightly grease clam shells, fill with clam mixture, sprinkle with bread crumbs, then with grated Parmesan cheese and last with garlic salt and paprika to taste. Dot with butter and arrange stuffed clam shells in shallow, ovenproof tray and brown tops under 550 ° F. broiler flame. Makes 12 appetizers.

STUFFED MUSSEL SHELLS   Y, P

1 tablespoon olive oil
1 tablespoon butter or margarine
½ cup uncooked white rice
1 cup mussel liquid reserved when preparing mussel shells, page 297 (substitute canned clam liquid)
½ cup water
1 teaspoon honey
1 teaspoon lemon juice
½ teaspoon salt
¼ teaspoon cinnamon
¼ teaspoon freshly grated lemon peel
2 tablespoons pinon nuts or pistachio nuts, shelled
2 tablespoons white seedless raisins, chopped
½ cup sour cream
32 large mussel half-shells saved from making other recipes (substitute about 24 2–3 inch clam shells)

Heat olive oil and butter or margarine in heavy saucepan, add rice, and cook, stirring several times, for 3 minutes. Add all other ingredients except sour cream and mussel shells. Stir, turn down to a simmer, cover, and cook for 15 to 20 minutes or until rice is tender and all liquid is absorbed. Cool, stir in sour cream, fill matching mussel shells with the mixture, and press them together. Wipe off outside of shells and refrigerate until time to serve. Arrange on a bed of mixed green and blue coarsely crushed ice or pass around in a shell-shaped dish and return to ice box or refrigerator between servings. Makes 16 appetizers.

Variation
Add chopped steamed or canned mussel or clam meat to taste.

RED OR WHITE CLAM SAUCE FOR SPAGHETTI

Y, C, B

All of you who have eaten spaghetti in a tomato sauce—and who hasn't?—will discover that pasta takes on new meaning when it is topped with a thin, delicately light clam sauce. It's made with wine; the color you use determines the color of the sauce.

¼ cup olive oil
2 tablespoons butter
½ medium onion, finely chopped
½ clove garlic, finely chopped
1 tablespoon finely chopped parsley
1 8-ounce can minced clams
1 cup dry, either red or white, wine
Freshly ground black pepper to taste

Combine olive oil and butter in a heavy skillet, heat until they start to sizzle. Add onion, garlic, and parsley and sauté gently until golden. Stir in the minced clams, including their juices. Simmer for 2 or 3 minutes, then add wine, and simmer for another 3 minutes. Top with freshly ground pepper. Should make enough sauce for 2 to 4 servings of spaghetti.

SHELLFISH BAKED IN SEASHELLS

Y, B

3 slices good-quality, day-old bread, thinly sliced
1 tablespoon butter or margarine
2 tablespoons cooking oil
2 tablespoons butter or margarine
¼ cup minced onion
¼ cup chopped green pepper
3 tablespoons flour
1 cup milk
½ teaspoon salt
¹⁄₁₆ teaspoon pepper
¼ teaspoon Worcestershire sauce
1 tablespoon lemon juice
3 large hard-cooked eggs, minced
½ pound cooked shellfish, chopped
1 cup cooked peas (substitute cooked, diced potato, zucchini, okra, celery, carrots, mushrooms, or cooked corn kernels)
1 cup grated cheese (substitute 1 cup fine dry buttered crumbs)
Paprika

Toast bread to light golden color in toaster and slice into ¼-inch cubes. Leave crusts on. Heat 1 tablespoon butter or margarine in heavy skillet; add toast cubes and stir in the hot, melted butter until crisp. Toast should remain light gold. If either it or the butter gets hot enough to turn dark brown, the flavor will not be so good.

Remove toast cubes from pan, add cooking oil and 2 tablespoons butter or margarine, heat to sizzling point, add minced onion and chopped green pepper, turn heat down to medium, and cook, stirring until onion and green pepper start to soften. Remove them with a slotted spoon, add flour, stirring constantly, and cook for about 2 minutes. Heat milk just below simmering point and add all at once to flour and butter paste. Stir constantly with a wire whisk until sauce is smooth and thickened. Turn off heat. Add salt, pepper, Worcestershire sauce, lemon juice, eggs, shellfish, peas, and toasted bread cubes. Spoon mixture into buttered shells, sprinkle cheese and a dash of paprika over them, and bake in 350 ° F. oven for 20 to 25 minutes or until cheese browns. Serves 12 as hot hors d'oeuvre; serves 4 to 6 as main course.

18—Meat and Fish Combinations

Everybody Gather Round, Cook Your Own, and Love It

If you've never enjoyed a fondue feast, at least you've seen pictures of one on television commercials. It's the rage, it's the thing to do.

Everybody gather round, dip a piece of French bread on a fork into a bowl of hot cheese or a bite-size cube of beef into bubbling oil, and enjoy, enjoy. That's a fondue, imported to America from Europe, where the French and the Swiss think they invented the idea.

But what they don't know is that they imported it from the Orient, where the Chinese have cooked that way for thousands of years, a fact of which we were very much unaware until Dan wrote *The Hong Kong Cookbook* with a great Chinese chef, Arthur Lem. We think the Chinese way is perfectly suited to outdoor eating in your yard, patio, or on a picnic.

The recipe that follows isn't for just one dish or for an appetizer; it's for the entire meal, and it's called (among other things) Dar Bin Loo. The authentic Chinese recipe can be found in *The Hong Kong Cookbook*. We're giving you our simplified version, using ingredients that you can usually get at the supermarket and that can be easily cooked outdoors.

This is the recipe we specifically had in mind when, in Chapter 1, we suggested you sometimes set a 4½ x 5 foot heavy-duty sheet of plywood on benches and circle it with plastic-covered cushions so that you can eat (Oriental style) sitting on the ground. The Dar Bin Loo is great fun this way, and it's easy to get up on your knees and reach into the middle of the table to the cooking bowl.

THE OUTDOOR DAR BIN LOO   Y, P

It's nice to have chopsticks or fondue forks for this meal, but you can get by with regular forks. You'll be cooking directly on the table, so you'll need one or two hibachis or one or two good electric plates or other small table-top stove operated by a fuel that can produce enough heat to keep water simmering.

½ pound cooked chicken meat, cut into bite-size pieces
½ pound cooked pork cut in tiny slices about ⅛-inch thick
½ pound raw steak, fat removed, cut in tiny pieces about ⅛-inch thick
2 pounds flounder fillets (fresh or frozen) cut in generous bite-size pieces
2 1-pound bags frozen shrimp, defrosted
1 small bunch celery, washed and sliced in ⅛-inch pieces
1 to 2 10-ounce packages raw spinach, washed (don't skimp on the spinach, because it's a big favorite when cooked this way)
1 8½-ounce can water chestnuts, thinly sliced
½ pound raw mushrooms washed and sliced very thin
About 3 quarts chicken broth (we prefer canned College Inn unless you make your own) divided into two casseroles that can be placed directly over flame
1 cup soy sauce mixed with 1 teaspoon sesame oil, divided into 12 small individual sauce bowls
1 cup mustard, divided into 12 small individual sauce bowls
Instant rice for 18 (substitute chicken or beef broth for water; cook according to package instructions and keep hot over boiling water until ready to use)

Since your indoor stove probably heats liquid faster than will the table stoves you're using outdoors, heat chicken broth to a boil indoors in the two flameproof casseroles, carry them out, and set them on the two outdoor table stoves. If charcoal, it should be burned down and very hot; other types of stove should be turned to whatever heat will keep the broth simmering. Now you're ready for the Dar Bin Loo.

Call your guests to the table, sit them down, and tell them to select whatever food they'd like to cook and to use their chopsticks or fondue forks to put it in the simmering liquid. (We find it best to cook the spinach in one bowl, leaving the other one free for everything else.) Nothing takes much more than 3 to 5 minutes to cook. You're on your own when it comes to deciding whether to have each guest spear his own morsel or spoon everything out with a slotted spoon and serve it, pot luck, over individual servings of rice. Arriving at a method is all part of the Dar Bin Loo.

After everyone has eaten his fill of solid food, finish off with a bowl of soup in each bowl. It will be unbelievably delicious by the time all that assortment of meat, fish, and vegetables has been cooked in it! Add just a little spinach broth because its flavor can overpower everything else if you use too much.

LEFTOVER DAR BIN LOO CASSEROLE

Remove any unused perishable foods to the refrigerator the minute you finish eating. Cook them and any leftover vegetables the next day with rice in a casserole. Use frozen shrimp or canned mushroom soup for a sauce. Carry it to your outdoor dining room and serve a relaxing one-pot "day after" dinner.

Clambake on Saturday; Paella on Sunday

One of the easiest ways to entertain ten or twelve people is to divide them into two groups. Entertain twice but do all your planning and most of your preparation just once. Have one group in on Saturday; have the other group in on Sunday. Whip up a clambake for six on the first day, serve up a paella—partially prepared with the clambake—for the second six on the second day.

Clambakes are native to, and peculiar to, the New England coastal states. Paella is native to, and peculiar to, coastal Spain. Both meals are traditionally prepared by coastal people with whatever ingredients are available at the moment. Both lend themselves perfectly to two-in-a-row yard or patio serving, especially since the clambake no longer needs to be done over hot stones, with seaweed for steam, the way the Indians taught the Pilgrims to do it. Today, all you need is a five-gallon covered container, be it a fancy store-bought steamer or a five-gallon galvanized can that once housed pretzels. This is much quicker and much easier than digging and using a pit.

All you do is load your container with the ingredients that go into a clambake, add some salt water, poke a couple of vent holes in the lid if you're using a pretzel can, and let it steam for 20 minutes. Then try to beat off the mob when you serve up the steamed clams and melted butter, the steamed corn and melted butter, the steamed lobster and melted butter! And every one of them part of the next day's paella!

Nor does it matter that you live far from the sea, far from the clams, far from the lobster, because modern transportation, modern refrigeration, and, if need be, modern food processing make clams and lobster almost as easily available to many interior families as they are to the family that lives in Bangor, Maine.

If your fish market doesn't stock them, it may very well be able to swiftly get them for you. If for some reason it can't, lobster is available in frozen food sections of every supermarket, and the clams, shell and all, are not far away on the canned goods shelves.

Here are the recipes, interspersed with instructions on how one abets the other.

YARD OR PATIO CLAMBAKE WITH PAELLA PRELIMINARIES

Y, C, P
One-Pot Meal

Water
1 tablespoon salt or to taste (liquid from clams will add salt, too)
7 1-pound live lobsters
6 medium baking potatoes
8 ears of corn, husked
6 pieces of fish, raw, in a cheesecloth bag
6 dozen small clams, preferably softshell (5 dozen divided into 6 thin aluminum dishes or cheesecloth bags and 1 dozen refrigerated and saved, raw, for the Sunday paella)
1–1½ pounds melted butter
2 lemons cut in wedges

Pour water until 2 inches deep into steamer pot or pretzel can, then add salt. Pick up lobsters by the back of the neck (or with tongs if you fear for your fingers) and put them into the pot. Add each of the other ingredients in the order listed, making sure you do not include the 1 dozen clams to be refrigerated for Sunday's paella. (If there's not room in pot or can for potatoes, you can wrap them in foil and bake in the coals. Put them in before placing can or steamer over fire and they should be ready at about the same time as the clambake.) Cover steamer pot or pretzel can (if the latter, poke 2 or 3 vent holes in the lid), place on charcoal grill over a deep, hot bed of cooking coals that will hold their heat for an hour. Then go have a drink with your guests, but don't go so far away that you can't see the clambake, because you have to watch for it to start steaming. When the steam escapes from the vent holes in a steady stream, you should start your timing. (Be sure a good, strong stream of steam is coming out before you start timing or you might open your clambake too soon and some of the food would not be cooked.) Twenty minutes from then is when the clambake is ready to serve.

Start by serving each of the guests a container of clams with a dish of melted butter and a lemon wedge. Dining must be very informal so that you can be dipping into your own clams while preparing the other food from the steamer pot or can for eating or storing in the refrigerator ready for making into Sunday's paella.

Set 2 ears of corn aside.

Lay each lobster on its back and split the body in two lengthwise. Remove the stomach and whatever is left of the intestinal vein, which may contain sand, and discard. You'll want to have a large chopping board, a good knife or cleaver, a paper bag for discards, and poultry shears ready at hand for this job. Place the coral roe and green fat in a separate serving bowl for those who recognize what good eating they are. Remove claws and use poultry shears to cut what's left into chunks, shell and all.

Set aside 6 large claws and 6 good-sized chunks of meat for Sunday's paella. Send someone into the kitchen to place these things and the two ears of corn you set aside in the refrigerator.

Pile remaining lobster claws and chunks into center of a large serving platter. Surround with fish and corn, put potatoes into a bowl, and serve everything with more melted butter, lemon wedges, and salt and pepper.

Strain the clambake broth, reserve 4 cups of it for Sunday's paella (refrigerate as soon as it cools), pour what remains into a pitcher, and place on the table for those who prefer it to, or along with, beer.

You need add very little to complete your clambake dinner for 6, as well as much of the following day's paella. You'll want bread, of course. And a green salad. Prepare enough green salad for both occasions. And you can also prepare a Watermelon Fruit Basket Salad (page 229), which will serve for both dinners.

You can increase the quantities for the clambake on Saturday and the paella on Sunday, serving 8, 10, or 12 each day if you like—but we recommend that you keep the numbers down to 6 and 6 for the first time, just to get the feel of it.

You can change quantities and ingredients as you like and prepare and serve the pretzel can clambake at a beach or other picnic grounds. At the seashore, substitute sea water for the plain water and salt in the recipe.

PATIO PAELLA

Y
One-Pot Meal

Sunday's paella can be just a little bit more formal than was Saturday's clambake. You, the hostess, will be able to serve everything at once and sit down and stay with your guests. Candles burning in wine bottles would set the right mood.

The paella gets its name from the two-handled iron frying pan that is pretty much a fixture in every Spanish household. If you don't have one (they're available in quite a few American stores), use some other large top-of-the-stove cooking utensil with a tight-fitting lid in which you can also serve your paella. It should measure about 15 inches across the top. If you don't have anything that big, you can manage by substituting two smaller ones.

1 teaspoon saffron shreds
2 tablespoons water
½ cup olive oil
6 small pieces frying chicken, cut into 1-inch lengths
2 cloves garlic
4 medium onions, chopped
¼ cup diced bacon
¼ pound pepperoni
2 large green peppers, seeded and sliced
6 medium tomatoes (firm, not too juicy) cut into small wedges
1 5-ounce can pimientos, drained and cut into ½-inch slices
2 cups raw rice
1 10-ounce package frozen peas, broken apart but not defrosted
Kernels cut from 2 ears of corn reserved from clambake (substitute 1 12-ounce can corn)
1 6½-ounce can cleaned and deveined shrimp
½ teaspoon celery salt
2 teaspoons salt or to taste
⅛ teaspoon freshly ground black pepper
4 cups clambake broth (substitute canned clam juice)
6 chunks lobster meat (substitute canned or frozen shellfish meat) reserved from Saturday's clambake
6 large lobster claws reserved from Saturday's clambake
12 clams reserved from clambake, uncooked in the shell
1 cup chicken broth (substitute water)

One hour before you start preparing paella, combine saffron shreds and water and set aside to soak.

Put olive oil in paella pan and heat until it is just starting to sizzle but not smoking. Add chicken pieces and lightly brown on all sides over medium heat. Don't let the oil burn. Remove chicken with slotted spoon and set aside. Put garlic, chopped onions, bacon, and pepperoni in pan and stir fry until all are lightly browned. Remove with slotted spoon, discard garlic, and set other ingredients aside. Stir-fry green peppers in the paella pan for about 3 minutes. Add tomatoes and pimientos and stir fry for 2 minutes more. Remove everything from the pan with a slotted spoon, leaving the drippings, and set aside.

Put rice and saffron and water mixture in the paella pan and stir until rice is pretty uniformly yellow and well coated with oil. Stir in everything previously cooked in the pan except chicken. Add frozen peas, corn kernels, shrimp and stir into mixture. Add celery salt, salt, and pepper to clambake broth, stir, and pour over rice mixture. Top with pieces of chicken, cover, and simmer 20 minutes on low to medium heat. When 20 minutes is up, arrange lobster meat, lobster claws, and clams on top of rice with chicken meat. Cover and continue cooking until rice is tender and clams have opened (about 15 minutes). If rice dries out before it is tender and clams are opened and very hot, add cup of chicken broth and continue cooking until it is absorbed.

Place paella pan on your patio table with a green salad, bread, and a bottle of wine and watch your guests go to town! Serves 6.

ITALIAN BOILED DINNER   Y, P
One-Pot Meal

Here's a recipe for a zesty one-pot meal that's made to order for that mob scene that occurs when your relatives drop in for dinner on the same day your teen-age son brings all his friends in for a snack after a hard day on the diamond, gridiron, surfboard, or whatever. You'll need an 8 to 10-quart pot to cook it and plenty of fuel for the fire. This is one of those times when it's easiest—and one of those recipes that makes it possible—to cook everything on your outdoor cooking fire. If your little barbecuer won't handle the heavy pot, improvise, using a slit trench or the cinder-block arrangement described on page 12. Just remember to rub soap on the outside of your pot.

2 carrots, peeled and diced
1 onion, chopped
2 large marrow bones, each halved
Salt and pepper to taste
1 bay leaf
1 3–4 pound lean, boneless roast
2 links Italian sausage
1 4-pound young chicken (or 2 2½ pounders)
2 bunches carrots (it's not necessary to peel them first), cut in half cross-
    wise
2 stalks celery, sliced
10–12 medium onions, quartered
12 large potatoes, cut up (you can leave the skins on them, too)
1 large cabbage, cut in eight wedges
2 small yellow turnips, peeled and cut up

Fill your pot half full with hot water, add diced carrots, chopped onion, marrow bone, salt, pepper, and bay leaf. Cover and simmer 15 minutes. Add the roast and continue simmering for 1½ hours. Now add sausage and chicken and cook another ½ hour, still at a simmer, or until meats are tender. Put all remaining vegetables into the pot and simmer 30 minutes or until they are tender.

If pot is not large enough to hold everything, the beef, chicken, and sausage can be removed and kept warm while the vegetables are cooking.

When vegetables are done, arrange carved meat, chicken, and sausage on large platter, surround with vegetables, moisten with stock, and serve, Serves 14 to 18.

Note
A treat for the youngest (or the oldest) is the marrow spread on bread like jelly.

MINESTRONE SOUP FROM LEFTOVERS

To make minestrone soup with broth and meat and vegetable leftovers from preceding recipe, all you need do is add a can of beans or lentils, some frozen dark-green leafy vegetable, heat, and sprinkle with grated Parmesan cheese. It's ready to serve with toasted French bread for a snack before the hangers-on go home.

19—Eggs

BOILED EGGS

Y, C, W, B, P

The secret of cooking eggs in the shell so they're tender is *not* to boil them. This means longer cooking, but it doesn't need to mean longer use of your camp stove burner if you do it this way:

Put 4 eggs, straight from the cooler in a large, heavy pot and cover with about 2 quarts of cold water. Heat over medium fire, uncovered, until water starts to move but hasn't begun to boil. Remove pot from fire, cover with a heavy lid, and let stand. Remove individual eggs according to the way individual people like them cooked: very soft, remove and serve in 4 to 5 minutes; medium, remove and serve in 10 minutes; well done, remove and serve in 15 minutes.

Hard-cooked eggs that you're going to chill and make into salads or carry with you to eat later should be cooked in the following manner:

Cover eggs with cold water and bring to a simmer over medium heat. Don't let them boil. Turn down heat, or reduce it by moving pot to side of fire, and continue cooking at a very low simmer for 20 minutes. Put eggs in cold water and leave them there to chill. Changing the water once or twice will speed up the process.

Don't feel badly if your eggs are hard to peel; it probably means they're fresher than the kind you used to buy before the hen house and the farmer became mechanized.

And don't worry about the green discoloration that sometimes appears around the yolk of a hard-boiled egg. It's a harmless chemical reaction. Cooking eggs at a low temperature and cooling them promptly helps prevent it.

Don't waste your egg-boiling water. It may seem extravagant to use 2 quarts of water for boiling eggs if you're picnicking in the desert or cruising on a boat. It's not if you save the water to make your coffee (assuming, of course, the egg shells were very clean) or use it to wash the dishes.

310

CLAM SCRAMBLE   Y, C, B

1 8-ounce can minced clams
1 small envelope dehydrated beef broth (about 5 ounces)
½ cup water
1 tablespoon soy sauce or salt to taste
1 tablespoon flour
Scrambled Eggs for Four (page 313)
1 tablespoon green pepper, finely chopped
1 tablespoon finely chopped celery
2 tablespoons finely chopped green onion, including some of green part

Drain clams, reserving liquid, and set clams aside. Combine liquid with dehydrated beef broth, water, and soy sauce. Blend in flour and cook, stirring constantly until mixture comes to a boil and thickens. Set aside where it will keep warm.

Make Scrambled Eggs for Four, adding minced clams and chopped vegetables to egg mixture before cooking it. Serve with sauce and thick slices of bread for a hearty lunch. Serves 4.

Note
One-quarter cup reconstituted dehydrated vegetables can be substituted for chopped green pepper, celery, and onion.

DEVILED EGGS   Y, C, B, P

6 hard-cooked eggs (see page 310)
½ teaspoon salt
1 tablespoon mustard
1 tablespoon minced onion
3 tablespoons mayonnaise
Paprika

Cut eggs in half lengthwise. Remove yolks, mash them, and add salt, mustard, onion, and mayonnaise. Mix until well combined and then fill egg white cavities with the mixture. Sprinkle with paprika, wrap carefully, and chill. Keep cold until time to serve and then either place over ice on table or leave outside refrigerator or icebox for only a short time.

Variation
Add small amount of finely chopped parsley, pickle, or pimiento to yolk mixture. For a more tart, slightly moister filling, add 1 tablespoon vinegar.

EGGS POT POURRI   Y, C, B

3 tablespoons oil
2 garlic cloves, crushed
1 large onion, diced
2 large stalks celery, diced
1 cucumber, diced
6–8 radishes, sliced
1 cup sherry
1 tablespoon honey
1 Eight Egg Omelet (see next recipe)

Preheat heavy skillet, add oil and garlic, and stir for 30 seconds. Then add diced onion and sauté over medium heat for about 2 minutes. Add celery, cucumber, and radishes and stir for about 2 minutes more. Add sherry and honey, stir well, reduce heat to low, cover, and let simmer while you prepare the Eight Egg Omelet. When done, divide omelet on warm plates, top with vegetable mixture, and serve. Serves 4.

EIGHT EGG OMELET   Y, C, W, B

8 eggs (fresh or reconstituted dried eggs)
Salt and pepper to taste
6 tablespoons milk or other liquid (water, wine, beer, broth)
3 tablespoons butter (you can use margarine instead, but an omelet is one
    dish that tastes much better with butter)

Beat eggs with a fork until yolks and whites are well mixed but not thoroughly blended. Stir in salt, pepper, and milk. Melt butter in a large skillet, tipping pan so it flows around sides. When butter is sizzling hot but not smoking, pour in egg mixture and cook on medium heat. Lift edges of egg as bottom of omelet becomes cooked to let raw mixture run underneath. When all egg mixture has coagulated, serve at once. Do not overcook. Serves 4 to 6.

CLEAN–OUT–YOUR–COOLER OMELET

You can add bits of meat, fish, vegetable, and cheese to the omelet mixture before cooking. And you can serve it with a sauce made from leftover soups and gravies. Or make a plain omelet, then fold it around a stuffing made all or in part from whatever is left in your cooler that's suitable.

SCRAMBLED EGGS FOR FOUR

Use the same ingredients as in Eight Egg Omelet (page 312) but mix yolks and whites together until they are well blended and stir the eggs frequently as they cook, rather than letting them set as you do an omelet.

FRANKFURTER AND EGG   Y, C, B

2 tablespoons butter or margarine
2 frankfurters, cut in ¼-inch slices (crosswise)
4 eggs (substitute reconstituted dried eggs)
10 drops Worcestershire sauce

Melt butter or margarine in skillet, add pieces of frankfurter, and lightly sauté. Beat eggs and Worcestershire sauce together, pour over frankfurters, and scramble. Serves 2 to 4.

MATZOH BRIE   Y, C, W, B

3 tablespoons butter or margarine
1½ cups crumbled matzohs or other plain crackers
4 eggs, lightly beaten with 1 tablespoon water (substitute reconstituted dried eggs)
Salt and pepper to taste
Jam or marmalade

Heat butter or margarine in skillet to sizzling hot and spread over bottom and lower sides. Combine remaining ingredients, except jam, pour into skillet, and cook as you would an omelet. Serve with jam or marmalade. Serves 4.

ONE EGG AND BACON   Y, C, W, B

1 slice bacon, chopped
1 egg

Fry bacon in small, heavy frying pan. When almost done, break egg over the top of it. Continue cooking for 1 minute, then cover with a tight fitting lid and remove from fire. Let set for 4 to 5 minutes without removing lid. At the end of that time, the white should be completely coagulated and the yolk softly cooked.

SHRIMP OMELET   Y, C, B

1 4½-ounce can tiny shrimp, cleaned and deveined
Reserved shrimp liquid and milk to make ¼ cup
Salt and pepper to taste
6 eggs, lightly beaten
2–3 tablespoons butter or margarine
⅛–¼ pound thinly sliced cheese

Drain shrimp, reserving liquid. Add enough milk to the liquid to make
¼ cup, season with salt and pepper, and stir into beaten eggs. Melt butter
in skillet, and when it is sizzling hot but not smoking, pour in egg. Cook on
medium heat, lifting edges of cooked egg to let raw egg run underneath.
When almost all of egg is cooked, spread cheese over it, top with shrimp,
cover, and continue cooking on low heat just until cheese melts and shrimp
is warm. Serve at once. Serves 4.

STIR–FRIED EGGS AND MEAT   Y, C, W, B

1 tablespoon oil
2 cloves garlic
1 small onion, diced
½ pound leftover meat or game, diced (substitute canned meat)
Salt and pepper to taste
4–6 eggs, lightly beaten (substitute dried eggs)

Preheat frying pan, add oil, and bring to a sizzle. Add garlic, brown, and
discard. Add onions and stir-fry until translucent. Add meat in small pieces,
season to taste, and stir fry until meat turns color with little or no traces
of red. Add eggs and stir fry until well blended with meat. Serves 4.

STIR–FRIED EGGS WITH   Y, C, W, B
LEFTOVER STEW

3 tablespoons cooking oil
1–2 cups leftover stew, meat, and vegetables cut into small pieces
4–6 eggs (substitute reconstituted dried eggs), lightly beaten

Heat oil in large frying pan, add small pieces of meat and vegetables from
stew, and lightly brown. Add eggs, stir fry until almost cooked. Then
add any leftover stew gravy and continue cooking just long enough to heat
it. Serve at once. Serves 4 to 6.

20—Legumes

Basic Cookery Methods for Beans and Other Legumes

If packages containing beans and other legumes such as lentils and chick peas don't give specific instructions for preparing, you will have to assume they must be soaked overnight and then cooked until tender.

Dry Beans

Don't figure on cooking ordinary dry beans unless you'll be in one place long enough and have enough fuel for your fire to do it. Beans need to be soaked overnight in plenty of water (at least double the quantity of the beans because they swell up when soaked), drained, then slowly simmered with a little salt and onion in the water for 2 or 3 hours or until beans are very tender. Add water as necessary and drain again when cooked. Slow cooking is the secret of good beans. You can serve the simmered beans just as is, adding salt and pepper to taste. You can use them in any of the recipes in this book calling for canned or leftover beans, or you can bake them after adding whatever combinations of tomato sauce, catsup, mustard, molasses, brown sugar, vinegar, chili powder, and bacon or salt pork appeal to you. Keep them in a slow oven for at least an hour to give all the flavors a chance to blend. Just watch that the beans don't become too dry and add water or tomato juice as needed.

If you're on the move all day, every day, you can soak enough beans for 2 or 3 days' eating (some people could eat them every day and never get enough): One night simmer them at the side of the campfire; the second night keep them cool; add them to recipes the next 2 or 3 days.

Chick Peas

This dried legume, overlooked by many Americans, particularly as a food to take camping, is very nutritious, delicious, and versatile. Prepare chick peas for use in recipes in the same way you do dry beans, use them in the same way as you do beans, and, for an interesting flavor change, try substituting them for beans in some of the recipes in this book.

Lentils
The lentil, one of the oldest foods known to man, is another nutritious and versatile dried legume many of us have forgotten. It too can be prepared and used in the same way as the bean and substituted for beans in recipes in this book. It does not have to be cooked quite so long as do beans and chick peas to become tender.

BEAN AND VEGETABLE PATTIES   Y, C, P

1 1-pound 4-ounce can red kidney beans, drained and mashed
1 6-ounce can tomato paste
2 large slices light pumpernickel bread, crumbled (substitute any nourishing bread)
2 ounces crushed peanuts
1 small carrot, peeled and grated (substitute green pepper, celery, or onion)
12 1-inch squares of cheddar cheese, about ½ inch thick

Mix all ingredients except cheese. Form into small patties ¼ to ½ inch thick. Place one cheese square in center of each pattie and cover with a dab of mixture. Place over coals on pancake griddle or large frying pan and cook until patties are just firm enough to lift with spatula. Then place directly on wire grill, where they will get brown and smoke-flavored. Cook for 5 to 10 minutes on each side. Makes 10 to 12 patties, serving 6 to 8 people.

BEANS WITH PRUNES AND CELERY   Y, C, B, P
                                         Two-Step Recipe
2 tablespoons cooking oil   Step 1: ½ hour
6 stalks celery, cut in ¼-inch slices   Step 2: ¼ hour
4 medium onions, cut in ¼-inch slices
1 1-pound can beans in barbecue sauce
4–6 dried prunes, pitted and chopped in small pieces

Step 1
Heat cooking oil in heavy saucepan or large skillet, add celery and onions, and sauté until tender-crisp. Add beans and prune pieces and cook until thoroughly heated through. Serve as a side dish with sliced barbecued steak or hamburgers. Chill for later use on boat, picnic, or at camp.

Step 2
Reheat in saucepan over coals or on galley or camp stove. Serves 4 to 6.

EASY BAKED BEANS   Y, C, B, P

1 1-pound 4-ounce can kidney beans
2 tablespoons dark molasses
½ cup catsup
1 tablespoon bacon grease

Combine all ingredients, mix well, and bake in 350 ° F. oven for 30 to 40 minutes or until well blended and a nice consistency. Or heat in pot on top of stove for 5 to 10 minutes, stirring frequently, until well blended and very hot. Serves 4.

EASY BAKED BEANS WITH BACON

Spread slices of bacon over top of beans before dish goes in oven. Remove as soon as beans are hot and bacon is cooked the way you like it.

EASY BAKED BEANS WITH HAM

Stir 1 cup of cooked, cubed pieces of ham into beans before putting them in oven.

EASY BAKED BEANS WITH FRANKFURTERS

Cut 1 frankfurter for each person to be served, crosswise, in ½-inch slices. Stir some of slices into beans and spread some over top before putting in oven.

FRIJOLES REFRITOS CON QUESO   Y, C, W, B
(REFRIED BEANS WITH CHEESE)

2 cups leftover beans, drained of excess liquid
2 tablespoons butter or margarine
1 tablespoon cooking oil
Grated cheese

Mash beans with a fork, mix with butter or margarine, and form into 4 thin patties. Heat oil in frying pan and cook patties in it until brown on both sides. Sprinkle with grated cheese and continue cooking until cheese melts. Serves 4.

21—Vegetables

Charcoal Broiled Foil-Wrapped Vegetables

There are some distinct advantages to be gained from cooking vegetables in foil bundles instead of in a pot of water, whether the bundles are buried in the charcoal or wood campfire coals, laid on top of the coals, or placed around the outer edges of a grill on which you're barbecuing some meat. Chief among the advantages are these four:

• Prime hot grill space that otherwise might be taken up by a pot full of boiling vegetables is freed for broiling meat.

• Individually packaged, sealed bundles of vegetables stay piping hot for 10 to 15 minutes after they are removed from the heat.

• You don't have to wash up a messy pot (assuming you have a pot wherever you may be cooking); instead, you discard some pieces of foil. You can even eat out of the foil if you want to instead of dirtying a plate.

• And what could be more important than the fact that vegetables cooked in foil, either in the coals, on top of the coals or above the coals, have an interestingly delicious and different flavor from those cooked in more traditional ways.

There's a wide variety of foil-baked vegetable recipes in the following pages. After trying them, you'll undoubtedly want to experiment with your own combinations so just pick one of the methods we describe, use it as a pattern, and cook away. The illustration will help you wrap vegetables so the juices won't leak out. Remember when you're wrapping to leave a little extra space in your package for any steam that develops to spread out in; otherwise, it'll force an escape through the sealed edges, taking a lot of flavor and juice along with it.

318

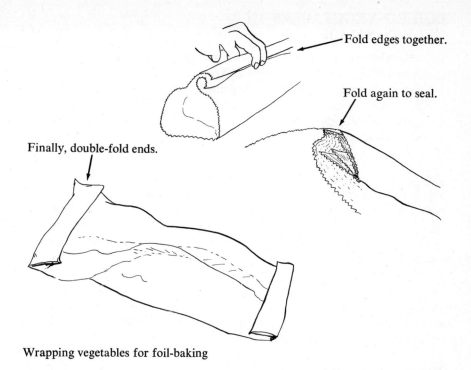

Fold edges together.

Fold again to seal.

Finally, double-fold ends.

Wrapping vegetables for foil-baking

BAKED EGGPLANT   Y, C, B

4 small eggplants, cut in two lengthwise
salted water to cover
¼ cup butter
½ cup chopped onion
½ cup sliced mushrooms
3 tablespoons flour
½ cup plain yogurt
Salt and pepper to taste
1 cup bread crumbs
Butter for dotting

Place eggplant halves in pot, cover with salted water, and simmer about 10 to 15 minutes or until tender. Remove pulp, taking care to leave ¼-inch shells intact. Dice pulp. Melt butter in skillet. Add pulp, onion, and mushrooms and sauté 5 minutes. Sprinkle with flour and cook 2 minutes more. Stir in yogurt until thick and smooth. Add salt and pepper and fill the shells with the mixture. Top with bread crumbs, dot with butter, and bake in 350 ° F. oven until brown. Serves 8.

BOILED VEGETABLES IN   Y
CELERY SAUCE

Carrots, celery stalks, and onions reserved when preparing Lamb Shanks,
   Simmered Then Barbecued (page 263)
1 4-ounce can broiled in butter mushrooms
1 10½ ounce can celery soup, undiluted
1 canned pimiento, chopped
1 tablespoon sherry (optional)
¼ cup table cream or sour cream (optional)

Peel carrots, pull most of strings from celery, and then cut the 3 reserved
vegetables into small pieces. Drain mushrooms, reserve liquid, and mix it
with celery soup until smooth. Combine all ingredients except cream in
double boiler or saucepan and heat to boiling. Turn down to simmer and
cook for 2 or 3 minutes, stirring constantly. Turn off heat, stir in cream,
and serve at once. Serves 4 to 6.

Note
Don't add sherry if serving with Lamb Shanks, Simmered Then Barbecued,
because the pronounced flavor of the sherry will detract from the flavor
of the sauce in which the shanks are barbecued.

BROCCOLI WITH APPLE   Y, C, B

½ bunch of fresh broccoli (substitute frozen)
1 raw apple, cored and sliced (substitute dried, reconstituted)
¾ cup orange juice (substitute reconstituted crystals)
1 tablespoon brown sugar
1 tablespoon butter or margarine

Combine all ingredients except butter or margarine and cook 15 to 20
minutes or until broccoli is tender. Brush on butter and serve at once.
Serves 4.

CAULIFLOWER AND MUSHROOMS IN WINE SAUCE   Y, B

1 10-ounce box frozen cauliflower
2 3-ounce cans Broiled in Butter mushrooms (reserve liquid for Crunchy Steamed Cod, page 288)
Liquid used for steaming cod (page 288)
2 egg yolks, lightly beaten and at room temperature

Cook cauliflower according to package instructions. Drain, add mushrooms, and reheat.

Add liquid from cod to egg yolks. If liquid is hot, add first ½ cup 1 tablespoon at a time. Beat in remaining liquid. Heat on low flame. Cook, stirring constantly, until sauce thickens. Don't cook beyond this moment. Pour over cauliflower and mushrooms and serve at once with Crunchy Steamed Cod. Serves 4.

CAULIFLOWER AU GRATIN BLUE   Y, B

¼ cup water
1 10-ounce package frozen cauliflower
¼ cup milk
1 tablespoon butter or margarine
2 ounces blue cheese, crumbled

Bring water to a boil in an all-purpose casserole dish, add cauliflower, return to a boil, cover, and simmer about 10 minutes. Remove cover, reduce heat to lowest possible, and continue cooking until water has almost completely evaporated. Add milk, butter or margarine, and cheese, in that order. Cover and simmer, stirring 2 or 3 times, until cheese is thoroughly melted and cauliflower is tender. Serves 4.

CHINESE–STYLE VEGETABLES   Y, C, B

2 medium onions
5 large stalks celery
3 large green peppers, seeds removed
1 tablespoon butter or margarine
2 tablespoons cooking oil
2 tablespoons soy sauce
2 tablespoons sherry
1 tablespoon honey
1 teaspoon lemon juice

Wash and slice vegetables on the diagonal. Heat butter or margarine and cooking oil in large heavy skillet or saucepan, add vegetables, and sauté lightly, stirring frequently (about 5 minutes). Combine soy sauce, sherry, honey, and lemon juice. Stir into sautéed vegetables, cover, and continue cooking on low heat for 5 minutes or until they are crisp-tender. Serve with meat balls or bite-size pieces of meat. These vegetables go well with left-over roast beef or pork or steak, cut into slivers and added with the sauce. Serves 4.

CHINESE–STYLE VEGETABLES COOKED ON THE COALS

Combine all ingredients after slicing vegetables (soften butter if necessary); mix well until vegetables are well coated with seasonings and oils. Divide onto four squares of heavy-duty foil. Wrap and seal, leaving space for steam to expand. Lay packages on top of coals and cook for 15 to 25 minutes, turning once or twice.

COLORFUL CORN   Y, C, W, B

1 tablespoon butter or margarine
1 12-ounce can whole kernel corn
2 tablespoons finely chopped green
  pepper
½ medium carrot, finely grated
⅛ teaspoon pepper
Salt to taste
½ teaspoon brown sugar

Substitute suitable combination of reconstituted dehydrated vegetables.

Spread butter over bottom of heavy saucepan. Mix other ingredients and add to pan. Turn on low heat and bring to a simmer. Cover and cook for 10 minutes. Turn off heat, but do not remove cover until ready to serve, which should be within 10 minutes. Serves 4.

CORN ON THE COB COOKED   Y, C, W, P
IN COALS

4 ears of corn
2 tablespoons salt
2 quarts water
2 teaspoons butter or margarine
Pepper to taste

Pull back husks and remove silk. Add salt to water and soak corn in the mixture for half an hour. Rub each ear of corn with ½ teaspoon butter and sprinkle with pepper to taste. Pull husks back in place, without shaking off drops of water, and wrap each ear in foil. Bury the ears in a hot bed of cooking coals and cook 6 to 8 minutes if ears are young and fresh, 8 to 12 minutes for older corn. Check one ear to see if done. Serves 4.

To Cook Corn on Grill over Coals
Lay foil-wrapped corn on grill 4 to 6 inches above cooking coals and cook, turning several times, for 10 to 15 minutes.

BACON, CORN, AND EGGS

Follow preceding instructions but, instead of rubbing corn with butter, wrap 1 strip of bacon diagonally around each ear. Don't salt because the bacon grease will take care of that, but add other seasonings to taste, such as garlic powder or onion powder and freshly ground black pepper. Wrap in foil and cook in the coals while you scramble your eggs on the grill. Then sit down to a deliciously different breakfast. Cook at least 5 minutes longer than in the preceding recipe so bacon will be well done.

FORAGED ASPARAGUS AND   C, W, P
DANDELIONS ORIENTAL STYLE

½ pound wild asparagus, washed and sliced ¼-inch thick on the diagonal
1–1½ cups young dandelion leaves, 1–3 inches long, and flower buds
1 tablespoon butter or margarine
1 tablespoon cooking oil
1½ tablespoons soy sauce
1 teaspoon corn starch
1 cup chicken or beef broth
Pepper to taste

Sauté asparagus and dandelion leaves and flower buds in butter or margarine and cooking oil mixed together in skillet. When asparagus is tender but still crisp, turn off heat. Combine soy sauce and corn starch and blend until smooth. Add chicken broth, pour into skillet of vegetables, and cook, stirring constantly, until sauce thickens. Add pepper to taste and serve at once. Serves 4.

Note
You can do this in your yard, too, merely by substituting domestic asparagus for the wild and confining your foraging to the dandelions in all likelihood growing on your lawn or, if not there, certainly somewhere close by.

FRESH ZUCCHINI–TOMATO MIX   Y, C, B

1 teaspoon butter
3 tablespoons water
1 small, very firm zucchini sliced ¼-inch thick, then quartered
1 fresh, firm, ripe tomato, chopped
1 small onion, chopped
1 fresh mint leaf, finely chopped (optional)
Salt and pepper to taste

Spread butter over bottom of a small saucepan; add water and rest of
ingredients. Bring to boil, turn to low boil, cover, and cook just until all
liquid disappears and zucchini is tender but still firm and almost crunchy.
If necessary, add water, but only a few tablespoons at a time. Serves 2.

ZUCCHINI AND TOMATO COOKED   Y, C, B
ON THE COALS

Spread 1 teaspoon butter over each of 2 squares of heavy-duty aluminum
foil. Divide vegetables onto the squares, sprinkle each half with 1 tablespoon water, salt and pepper to taste, and add ½ teaspoon of butter. Seal
tightly, leaving a little air space for steam expansion, and place on top of
cooking coals. Cook for 15 to 25 minutes, turning once or twice.

MASHED POTATO AND CARROT   Y, C, B, P
BUNDLES   *Two-Step Recipe*
                                                 Step 1: ¾ hour
8 small carrots   Step 2: ¼ hour
2 tablespoons butter or margarine
2 teaspoons honey
Salt and pepper to taste
⅛ teaspoon nutmeg, or to taste
¼ teaspoon cinnamon, or to taste
Mashed potato flakes for 4, including butter and milk called for on pack-
    age
4 tablespoons minced green onion, including some of the green top (sub-
    stitute minced parsley)

Step 1
Simmer carrots until soft. Add butter or margarine, honey, salt and pepper
to taste, nutmeg, and cinnamon and mash or beat with an electric beater
until well blended and pureed.

    Prepare mashed potatoes for 4 according to package instructions
and stir in minced green onion.

Divide carrot puree over 4 sheets of lightly greased, heavy-duty foil. Top with potatoes. Wrap packages so they are sealed and refrigerate until time to reheat or transfer to camp or boat icebox.

Step 2
When the meat you're serving is almost done, scatter foil packages of vegetables over coals (leave plenty of spaces for heat to get through to meat), leave 5 minutes, then turn over and cook for 5 minutes on second side. Open one package before serving to be sure carrots and potatoes are heated through. Serve in foil, which can, unless you object to eating out of it, do double duty as a dish.

To Heat in Camp or Galley Oven
If you don't have a bed of coals, put packages of carrots and potatoes in hot oven for 15 to 20 minutes or until heated through.

MIXED VEGETABLES BAKED IN COALS

Y, C, W, B, P
Two-Step Recipe
Step 1: ¼ hour
Step 2: ¾ hour

You will need the following for each person to be served:

1 ¼-inch slice from large onion
1 square-foot piece of heavy-duty aluminum foil
1 small tomato, not more than 2½ inches in diameter, rubbed with 1 teaspoon butter or margarine
½ small zucchini, not more than 1½ inches in diameter, rubbed with 1 teaspoon butter or margarine
2 or 3 slices of celery, ¼–½ inch thick
Salt and pepper to taste

Step 1
Lay onion slice in center of aluminum foil. Arrange other vegetables on top of onion slice, season, and wrap foil envelope-style, folding edges 3 times and sealing tightly. Refrigerate until time to cook in yard or take camping, cruising, or picnicking. Packets can go unrefrigerated for a few hours during transportation, provided they are kept cool, but they will taste better if they can be refrigerated or kept in an icebox until cooking time.

Step 2
Bury packets in coals that are well started and forming ash but not necessarily burned down enough for cooking meat. If packets are not completely surrounded by hot coals, try to turn them several times during cooking process. If coals are very hot and packets are completely surrounded, the

vegetables will be done in 15 to 25 minutes. Test one before opening other packets. Serve one packet to each person. If unopened and protected from the breeze, they will stay warm for at least 15 minutes.

Note
Packets can be laid on top of grill and cooked, 4 to 6 inches above a hot bed of burned-down coals, for 20 to 35 minutes.

To Cook in Camp or Boat Oven
Put packets in hot oven and bake 35 to 40 minutes. Test 1 package before opening others.

POTATOES AND ONIONS IN BUTTER HERB SAUCE

Y, C, W

1 1-pound can whole potatoes (11 to 12 small potatoes) or like amount
    raw potatoes, peeled and sliced about ¼ inch thick
4–6 heavy-duty aluminum foil squares approximately 1-foot square
1 large onion, sliced
¼ cup butter or margarine or 2 tablespoons bacon drippings
Salt and pepper to taste
1 clove garlic, finely minced
1 teaspoon dry oregano, finely minced.

Drain potatoes and divide over the aluminum foil squares. Divide all other ingredients evenly over potatoes and wrap securely, sealing edges. Lay directly on burned-down coals for 10 to 20 minutes. Turn over and cook for an additional 10 to 20 minutes, depending on the heat of your coals. If you have coals enough to completely bury packages, the potatoes and onions will be ready in a total of 10 to 20 minutes and won't need turning. Serves 4 to 6.

POTATOES BAKED IN THE COALS

Y, C, W, P

For Moist Potatoes with Soft Skins
Pierce each potato on two sides with the tines of a fork. Nest in a square of heavy-duty aluminum foil. Add 1 teaspoon of water. Wrap, seal, and bury in the coals of your cooking fire.

For Crisp-Skinned, Drier Potatoes
Wrap potatoes in foil without piercing skin or adding any moisture. Wrap, seal, and bury in the coals of your cooking fire.

For Charred Skins
Cook your potatoes the way some of us did as kids: bury them, without any wrapping at all, in the coals and brush away the soot before you eat them.

Timing Potatoes Baked in the Coals
It usually takes from 30 to 60 minutes for medium to large potatoes to bake, depending on size and heat of coals. Take one out and test it before removing and unwrapping the rest.

QUICK HOME FRIES   Y, C, W, B

1 cup Kraft instant potato slices
2 tablespoons butter, margarine, or bacon grease
2 heaping teaspoons dehydrated minced onions
Salt and pepper to taste
Garlic powder to taste

Boil potato slices in water to cover. Heat butter, margarine, or bacon grease in skillet, add dehydrated onions, and sauté while potatoes cook. When potatoes are tender, drain and add to sautéed onions. Stir in seasonings. Cover and cook for 15 minutes, turning with a spatula every 5 minutes. Serves 2 to 4.

Note
You can serve these potatoes at night but make extras, then reheat the leftovers in the morning to serve with bacon and eggs for a real stick-to-the-ribs meal.

STRING BEANS WITH APPLES   Y, C, W, B

1 slice bacon, chopped
1 15-ounce can string beans (substitute frozen or reconstituted dehydrated string beans)
1 beef bouillon cube
½ cup dried apples

Sauté chopped bacon in saucepan. Drain string beans. Reserve liquid, add enough water to make one cup, dissolve beef bouillon cube in the mixture, and add to saucepan. Add dried apple, cook until soft, add string beans, and cook until most of liquid is absorbed. Serves 4.

SUCCOTASH   Y, C, W, B

1 10-ounce package frozen baby lima beans, cooked according to package
directions (substitute 1 16-ounce can)
1 16-ounce can whole-kernel, dry-style corn
2 tablespoons butter
Salt and pepper to taste

Combine all ingredients, heat through, and serve. Serves 4 to 6.

SUCCOTASH AND POTATOES
COOKED IN THE COALS

Add one 16-ounce can of potatoes, sliced or chopped, to combination of
ingredients in Succotash recipe. Divide over 4 to 6 heavy-duty aluminum
squares that have been lightly greased and seal. Bury in coals or lay on
top of coals or on grill over fire and cook just until very well heated
through. Serves 4 to 6.

SWEET AND SOUR RED CABBAGE   Y, C, B

1 small head red cabbage
4 tablespoons butter or margarine
1 tablespoon lemon juice
1 tablespoon vinegar
¼ cup chicken broth
1 tablespoon granulated sugar
1 tablespoon brown sugar
½ teaspoon salt
1 large tart apple, peeled, cored, and sliced
⅓ cup red currant jelly (substitute any berry jelly)

Remove any damaged leaves from cabbage, cut out the core (slice it and
eat raw with salt as an appetizer), remove tough part of stalk, discard, and
shred cabbage. Combine all other ingredients, except apple and jelly, in a
heavy saucepan. Heat and stir until sugars and butter melt and blend into
liquids. Add cabbage, bring to a boil, turn down to simmer. Cover and
cook for 15 minutes, stirring occasionally. Add apple and jelly and cook
for another 30 minutes. Taste. If it is too sweet, add a little more lemon
juice; if too sour, add more sugar. Almost all liquid should be absorbed
when the cabbage finishes cooking. If it's not, remove lid, stir, and cook
until most liquid evaporates. If the pan gets dry at any time before it is
done, add about ¼ cup of water as needed. Serves 6 to 8.

SWEET POTATOES BAKED IN COALS   Y, C, W, P

4 medium sweet potatoes, washed (leave moisture on skin) and wrapped in heavy-duty foil

Bury foil-wrapped sweet potatoes in coals that are well started and forming ash but not necessarily burned down enough for cooking meat. If potatoes are not completely surrounded by hot coals, try to turn them several times during cooking process. If coals are very hot, potatoes should be done in 25 to 40 minutes, but test one after it's been cooking for 20 minutes. Serves 4.

BAKING SWEET POTATOES ON TOP OF CHARCOAL GRILL

Sweet potatoes can be cooked, either wrapped or unwrapped, by laying them on the grill 4 to 6 inches above burned-down cooking coals. Medium potatoes will take 40 to 50 minutes to cook this way. If you don't have meats cooking on the grill at the same time, you can hasten cooking by lowering the grill. If everything else is done and potatoes are not (it's very difficult to estimate time accurately when cooking sweet potatoes, particularly in this way), lay them directly on the coals and turn frequently.

SWEET POTATO SURPRISE   Y, B

1 17-ounce can small whole sweet potatoes or yams in heavy syrup
2 tablespoons butter
1 tablespoon honey
1 teaspoon lemon juice
¼ cup brown sugar
1 tablespoon butter
½ cup coconut
6 to 8 maraschino cherries
2 tablespoons maraschino cherry juice

Combine sweet potatoes, 2 tablespoons butter, honey, lemon juice, and 2 tablespoons of brown sugar in a saucepan and heat, stirring frequently. Pour potatoes into a lightly greased, shallow baking dish. Spread 1 tablespoon butter over them, sprinkle with remainder of brown sugar, then coconut. Spread maraschino cherries uniformly over top of sweet potatoes and sprinkle two tablespoons of cherry juice over the dish. Put in 400 ° F. oven until top of dish is lightly browned. Serves 4.

Foil-Baked Sweet Potato Surprise
Fashion dish of two thicknesses of heavy-duty foil, grease well with butter or margarine, arrange sweet potatoes in it, top with other ingredients, cover with foil, and cook on top of grill, 4 inches above coals for 20 minutes or until very hot and butter and brown sugar topping are well blended. Remove top carefully so as not to spoil appearance and serve from foil.

TOP–OF–STOVE CANDIED SWEET POTATOES

Y, C, B

3 tablespoons butter
2 17-ounce cans small whole sweet potatoes or yams in heavy syrup
1 cup light brown sugar, lightly packed

Spread butter over bottom of large, heavy pot or skillet. Add sweet potatoes and liquid from cans. Sprinkle brown sugar over them. Simmer, uncovered, for 40 minutes. Serves 6 to 8.

22—Desserts and Breads and So Forth

BISCUIT–MIX BREAD
Y, C, W, P

2 cups biscuit mix such as Bisquick
½ cup water (approximate)

Add just enough water to the biscuit-mix flour to make a workable dough, knead it a few times to mix well, and shape into a loaf. Dust loaf with flour and place it in the center of a large sheet of well-greased heavy-duty aluminum foil. Wrap, leaving plenty of room for expanding dough, and make a tiny hole for escaping steam. Place package of dough on your grill over the edge of your cooking coals and turn it every five minutes. The bread is done when it can be easily pierced with a straw (try it after 15 minutes, poking the straw right through the foil) and no dough clings to it.

If you like a crunchy crust, place bread in the middle of the grill for the last three minutes. Serves 10 to 12.

Note
This bread is worth trying a second time if it doesn't come out right at first.

BISCUIT–MIX TWISTS
Y, C, W, P

2 tablespoons sugar
⅛ teaspoon cinnamon
1 cup biscuit mix
¼ cup milk

Stir sugar and cinnamon into biscuit mix. Add milk, stir (should make a soft dough). Divide into 4, give one portion to each of 4 people to complete preparations, and cook.

Roll each portion between floured hands into a rope. Roll dough rope around a skewer in a spiral, tucking each end under and squashing to hold. Cook over coals, turning frequently until lightly browned and cooked through. It takes practice, but it's worth it.

Eat as is in the fingers or brush with butter while still hot and sprinkle with sugar. Serves 4.

331

CAMP PANCAKES

Y, C, W, B, P

2 cups biscuit mix
2½ tablespoons dried egg (sift if you have the equipment for it)
5 tablespoons dried skim milk powder
1¾ cups water, cool but not cold
Oil for frying pan

Combine dry ingredients, add water, and beat until fairly smooth. Brush a very small amount of oil onto frying pan, heat, and, when hot but not smoking, ladle in enough batter to make whatever size pancakes you like without crowding them. Let each cake spread out before adding batter for the next. When bubbles appear on top and bottom is golden brown, turn pancakes and cook second side. Serve with butter or margarine and syrup, jelly, honey, or a dust of sugar. Makes about 18 medium-sized pancakes.

QUICK–MIX PANCAKES

You may prefer to pack along one box of biscuit mix instead of both biscuit mix and pancake mix. But if you have the space for the extra box, such premixed pancake flours as Krusteaz require the addition of nothing but water. They can be whipped up in almost no time at all. (Check label for storage instructions.)

FLAVORED PANCAKES

Add ½ teaspoon, or to taste, of almond, orange, vanilla, or lemon extract when you add the liquid to pancake mixture. (Remember to add any extracts you want to use to your camp list of food staples.)

BERRY PANCAKES   Y, C, W, B, P

Stir 1 cup of cleaned wild berries (less will do if you don't have a cupful) into Camp Pancakes or Quick-Mix Pancakes batter for making 18 medium-sized pancakes. Keep berries stirred evenly through the batter as you ladle it into pan.

DRIED FRUIT PANCAKES

Chop dried fruit into small bits and cook as in Berry Pancakes.

PANCAKE DESSERT

Any of the preceding pancakes can be turned into a delicious and tempting dessert. Spread with jam or jelly, roll up, and eat them in your fingers around the fire—in the yard, at the campsite, in the wilderness, at a picnic, or on the deck of your boat. Put the same thing in a dish and top with a scoop of ice cream or whipped topping of any kind and top that with shaved chocolate or a few small berries.

PANCAKE TRAIL SANDWICH   C, W, P

If you have some breakfast pancakes left over because someone didn't feel like eating so early in the morning, spread them with peanut butter, top with any leftover cooked bacon you may have (crumbled), roll up, wrap in foil, and let the finicky eater carry them in his pocket until he's suddenly ravenously hungry.

Pancake Trail Sandwiches can be filled with many different types of leftovers you might have on hand from the night-before's dinner. If the filling isn't perishable, the sandwiches can be carried in hikers' pockets for a no fuss, no fire-building lunch.

QUICK PRUNE BREAD   Y, C, W, B, P

Prunes and other dried fruits are a real boon to the camper. They keep well without refrigeration, they can be compactly packed in many different shapes (even dried prunes now come without pits), and they are loaded with satisfying nutrition.

We are indebted to the U.S. Department of Agriculture for this recipe, which adds prunes to a quick bread. You can easily whip it up in the evening and let it bake in your camp oven while you relax around the fire. If you don't have prunes, substitute another dried fruit.

Serve it for a late evening dessert or save to eat, with eggs, for breakfast. If you want to make a quick getaway in the morning, boil and chill your eggs at night, make up a thermos of coffee and another of hot chocolate for the children, then pack up your camp stove, grill, and kitchen supplies. In the morning, you have little to do but eat a quick, satisfying meal, which even the camp cook can relax over and enjoy. If you're in a terrific hurry to beat the rest of the crowd to first place on the highway line of traffic, you can share the driving and eat this breakfast in the car.

1 egg, beaten
1 teaspoon vanilla
1 teaspoon baking soda
1½ cups chopped prunes
1 cup boiling water
½ cup honey
2¼ cups flour
⅔ cup sugar
1 cup chopped walnuts (substitute other nuts of your choice)
Flour and butter or margarine to spread inside pan

Mix together beaten egg, vanilla, baking soda, and prunes. Then slowly stir in boiling water. Cover, let stand 20 minutes, then stir in honey. Combine flour and sugar and stir into prune mixture. Add walnuts. Mix well and pour into a greased, floured loaf pan about 8 x 8 and not more than 2 inches deep. Bake for 1 hour in a 325 ° F. camp oven or for approximately the same length of time in a moderately hot reflector oven. Serves 4 to 6.

CAMP MARMALADE   Y, C, W, B

Save orange and lemon peels, put them on a string, and, when you're in camp, hang them from a tree branch to dry. Soak them in water and scrape away the pith before using in marmalade or as seasonings.

Skin of 1 medium orange cut into tiny bits
1 pinch grated lemon skin
1 teaspoon lemon juice
⅓ cup sugar
1¼ cups cold water

Simmer all ingredients together for about 40 minutes or until they boil down to about ⅓ cup of syrup. Cool to thicken and serve on toast.

STICK–TO–THE–RIBS OATMEAL

Y, C, W, B
One-Pot Meal

This is a high-energy one-pot hurry-up breakfast that will leave campers feeling satisfied even though they don't have any bacon and eggs.

2 cups instant oatmeal
½ cup raisins or chopped dried fruit
½ cup nuts, crushed
Milk or cream to serve with the oatmeal

Cook oatmeal according to package instructions, adding fruit and nuts as soon as it's absorbed the water you added. Serve with milk or cream.

RICH CINNAMON OATMEAL

Stir 1 tablespoon butter or margarine and cinnamon and sugar to taste into the preceding recipe. Serve with milk or cream.

CARAMEL SPREAD FOR CRACKERS

Y, C, W, P

1 15-ounce can sweetened condensed milk
Water to cover can in pot
Crackers

Put can of sweetened condensed milk (unopened) in a pot of water to cover and simmer over side of your evening campfire for three hours. Add water as necessary to keep can completely covered. Open and spread the thick, caramel flavored creamy substance over crackers (it's especially good on graham crackers) for a wonderful bedtime snack in camp or for the end of a yard or picnic barbecue.

Note
You can cook this spread on your indoor stove at home, but it takes too much fuel to cook on a gasoline or LPG stove in camp.

It's also good eaten with a spoon, like a pudding, but it has more the consistency and the taste of a caramel candy.

WHIPPED TOPPING MADE FROM NONFAT DRY MILK POWDER

Y, C, W, B, P

2 tablespoons lemon juice
½ cup cold water
½ cup nonfat dry milk powder
2 or 3 tablespoons sugar
½ teaspoon vanilla

Combine lemon juice and cold water in a bowl that will hold at least one quart. Chill for an hour, add dry milk powder, and beat until mixture thickens. Add sugar, continue beating until soft peaks form, stir in vanilla, and serve as topping on desserts such as wild berries.

WILD BERRY SYRUP

Y, C, W, B, P

1 cup wild berries (use more berries if you have them)
½ cup water
1 cup sugar
1 teaspoon lemon juice (optional)

Clean leaves and stems out of berries, wash, crush, and combine in a sauce-pan with other ingredients. Slowly bring to a boil, stirring often, and cook until sugar is thoroughly dissolved and all ingredients are well blended. Serve, hot or cold, over pancakes, ice cream, or rice pudding. Makes ¾ to 1 cup syrup.

Note
There is nothing to stop you from substituting tame berries—the kind you buy in stores—for the wild.

BLUEBERRY AND ICE CREAM DESSERT

Y, P

1 quart blueberry ice cream
1 pint large ripe blueberries
8 small sprigs of 2 or 3 mint leaves, washed and dried on absorbent towels

Serve ice cream in glass dishes (heavy pyrex or stemware, depending on table setting), divide blueberries over it, and top with a mint sprig stuck wherever it will be most effective. Serves 8.

BRANDIED PEACH SUNDAES   Y, B

4–6 peach halves, canned
1 cup peach juice from can (if you don't have a cupful, add orange juice or lemonade)
2 tablespoons brandy
1 pint peach ice cream

Put peach halves in a bowl. Combine juice and brandy and pour over the peach halves and refrigerate. When time to serve, put one peach half for each person in a glass dessert dish, put a scoop of ice cream on top of it and divide brandied juice over all the dishes. Serves 4 to 6.

CANNED PEAR WITH CREAM CHEESE   Y, C, B

1 16-ounce can pear halves
1 3-ounce package cream cheese
⅛–¼ cup canned milk
4–6 large ripe strawberries or grapes (fresh, frozen, or canned)

Drain and refrigerate canned pears. Whip cream cheese, adding just enough canned milk to make a thick sauce. Cover and refrigerate. When time to serve, divide pear halves into 4 to 6 dessert dishes, top with whipped cream cheese, place a strawberry or grape on top of each. Serves 4 to 6.

GRAPEFRUIT HALVES   Y, C, B
BAKED IN HONEY

2 grapefruit, cut in half, crosswise
4 tablespoons honey
½ cup water
Maraschino cherries (optional)
Mint leaves (optional)

With a sharp knife, cut around each grapefruit section, just inside layer of skin. Place grapefruit halves in a shallow baking pan or casserole and spread 1 tablespoon honey over each. Pour ½ cup of water into bottom of pan and bake for 15 to 20 minutes in 350 ° F. oven or moderately hot reflector oven.

     If serving in the yard, decorate top of each grapefruit half with 1 to 3 maraschino cherries and 3 fresh mint leaves. Serves 4.

Note
This dish is nice as a dessert or for a special patio breakfast.

STRAWBERRY SHORTCAKE   Y, C, W, B, P

1 pint sweet, ripe strawberries, from the market or foraged
Sugar to taste (optional)
6 sponge cake shortcake cups, packaged (substitute pound cake or biscuits
    made from a mix)
½–1 cup heavy whipping cream (substitute topping mix), whipped
6 mint sprigs (optional)

Wash berries, add sugar, and slightly crush. Place one shortcake cup in
each of 6 dishes, divide berries over them, and top with whipped cream.
Stick a mint sprig into the top of each dessert. Serves 6.

BLACKBERRY, RASPBERRY, OR
ANY KIND OF BERRY SHORTCAKE

Substitute any ripe berry for strawberries and prepare as in preceding recipe.

NUT AND RAISIN RICE PUDDING   Y, C, B

1 15-ounce can rice pudding
1 cup seedless raisins or any wild fruit or berry
½ cup crumbled pistachio or piñon nuts, or toasted, slivered almonds
1–1½ cups evaporated milk milk or whipped cream

Stir all but last ingredient together and serve with evaporated milk or
whipped cream. Serves 4.

Cakes Made with Vegetables

Just a spoonful of sugar could make the medicine go down for Mary
Poppins' charges, and you can apply the same principle to cake and
vegetables! If some of your children or even your husband hasn't learned
how good vegetables are, bake vegetables into a cake, using one of the
delicious recipes that follow, and take it camping, picnicking, or cruising
or serve it right in your own backyard. Everybody will come back for
seconds. Is there an easier way to sneak added nutrition into vacation-time
fare?

Wrap whole, uniced cakes in foil, plastic wrap, or plastic bag or,
best of all, put in a plastic Tupperware cake carrier for their camping or
cruising trip. If there's room, keep in icebox or refrigerator. Serve them
plain or iced with a canned or dry frosting mix.

MOTHER DOWD'S CARROT CAKE   Y, C, W, B, P

(Mrs. Dowd is the mother of TV personality Mike Douglas, and this is one of her marvelous recipes from *The Mike Douglas Cookbook,* by Mike and Dan.)

3 cups sifted flour
1 teaspoon baking soda
1 teaspoon baking powder
1 teaspoon salt
2 teaspoons cinnamon
1½ cups cooking oil
1½ cups sugar
4 eggs
½ cup chopped nutmeats
2 cups finely grated or ground carrots

Preheat oven to 350 ° F. Sift together dry ingredients and set aside. Beat oil and sugar together. Add eggs, one at a time, beating well after each addition and continue beating until light and lemon colored. Add dry ingredients, nuts, and carrots and mix until well combined. Pour into greased 10-inch tube pan. Bake 1 hour or until done. Remove from pan to cool. Serves 16.

Note
Serve plain, with a frosting of your choice, or cover with a canned frosting or dry frosting mix.
        Wrap whole or slice and wrap separately in foil and take with you whatever your destination. It will keep quite a while. Or use a Tupperware cake carrier, and it will keep even longer.

CHOCOLATE–SAUERKRAUT CAKE   Y, C, B, P

The recipe for this flavorsome, dark, moist cake came to us from the New York *Daily News,* where Dan is a copy editor.

⅔ cup butter or margarine
1½ cups sugar
3 eggs
1 teaspoon vanilla
2¼ cups sifted flour
½ cup unsweetened cocoa
1 teaspoon baking powder
1 teaspoon baking soda
¼ teaspoon salt
1 cup water
⅔ cup rinsed, drained, and chopped sauerkraut

Put butter or margarine into a large mixing bowl, cream until fluffy, and gradually beat in the sugar. Beat in the eggs one at a time, then add the vanilla.

Sift together the flour, cocoa, baking powder, soda, and salt. Stir ⅓ of this dry mixture into mixing bowl containing creamed butter mixture. Stir in ⅓ of water and continue to alternate in this way until both dry ingredients and water are all mixed in. Stir in the sauerkraut and divide batter between 2 8-inch greased and floured cake pans. Bake in 350 ° F. preheated oven for 30 minutes or until cake springs back at the touch of a finger and starts to leave the edges of the pans. Remove from oven, cool for 10 minutes in pans, and then turn out on racks to complete cooling.

Wrap cake well or pack in a Tupperware cake carrier and take it camping or cruising just as it is. Or cover it with the following frosting for a special treat on a picnic or to serve in your outdoor dining room.

MOCHA WHIPPED CREAM

2 tablespoons sugar
2 teaspoons instant powdered coffee
1½ teaspoons unsweetened cocoa
1 cup heavy cream
2 tablespoons rum (optional)

Combine sugar, instant powdered coffee, and unsweetened cocoa in a small bowl. Mix well and set aside.

Put heavy cream in a large bowl and beat until it starts to thicken. Continue beating as you gradually add contents of small bowl, then beat in the rum. When soft peaks form, spread between layers and over top and sides of two-layer cake. Refrigerate until time to serve.

TOMATO SOUP SPICE CAKE   Y, C, B, P

This is a nourishing cake you can bake at home, then cover with a canned frosting at camp or in your boat galley before serving. Or frost with Cream Cheese Cake Frosting (page 342) and serve at home in your yard.

2 cups all-purpose flour (sift, then measure)
4 teaspoons baking powder
1 teaspoon nutmeg
1 teaspoon cinnamon
1 teaspoon ground cloves
½ teaspoon ginger
½ cup butter (take out of refrigerator half an hour before using)
1¼ cups sugar
2 eggs (take out of refrigerator half an hour before using)
1 teaspoon baking soda
1 10¾-ounce can condensed tomato soup
¼ cup water
Canned or Cream Cheese Cake Frosting

Turn oven on to preheat at 350 ° F. Stir first 6 ingredients together in bowl and set aside. Grease inside of 2 9 x 1½-inch layer-cake pans lightly with butter or margarine, sprinkle a little flour over butter, shake pans to completely cover bottoms and sides, then turn upside down to get rid of excess flour.

Using a spoon, blend butter and sugar together in a mixing bowl, then beat (on medium speed if you're using an electric mixer) until mixture is thoroughly blended and creamy. Add one egg and beat until fluffy. Add second egg and beat for about 2 minutes more or until mixture is very light and fluffy.

Mash lumps in baking soda, stir thoroughly into tomato soup, add water, and mix until blended and smooth.

Alternating between flour mixture that you set aside and tomato soup mixture, stir both into butter, sugar, and egg mixture as follows:

Sift about ⅓ of flour mixture into butter mixture and beat (on low speed if using electric mixer) just until flour disappears. Add ½ tomato soup mixture and beat (again on low speed) until it is blended in and no longer. Repeat process with second third of flour mixture, then last half of tomato mixture, and finish with last third of flour mixture. In each step of this part of cake making, beat just until ingredients are blended and no longer.

Divide batter between the two cake pans. Put the pans in center of preheated oven, where they do not touch, and bake at 350 ° F. for 25 to 30 minutes. Insert cake tester or thin-bladed knife into center of cake.

If it comes out dry, cake is done. Let cakes stand 10 minutes in pans, then run a thin-bladed knife around edges to loosen. Place a rack over top of each pan, invert, and give a gentle jerk to shake cake out of pan onto rack. Cool on rack, then transfer to a plate for frosting. Or wrap and freeze until such time as you want to serve in yard or take camping or cruising in your boat. Serves 12 to 16.

CREAM CHEESE CAKE FROSTING   Y, C, B

1½ cups confectioners sugar
1 8-ounce package cream cheese
1 tablespoon lemon juice
¼ cup coconut

Blend sugar into cream cheese with spoon or use electric mixer on low speed. Add lemon juice and stir in thoroughly. Frost bottom layer of cake. Set top layer in place and frost top and sides. Sprinkle coconut over entire cake. Serve at once or cover and refrigerate. Covers a 2-layer 9-inch cake.

Farm-Foraged Apples

A wonderful time for camping is in the fall of the year, when the leaves are turning and apple trees bend beneath the weight of the ripening crop. It's harvest time, and who can resist those crisp, brightly shining apples? Some of them may be blown down by the wind and bruised, and the farmer may invite anyone around to pick up and take all he can carry. Instead of helping yourself only to have them rot because you don't eat them fast enough, better that you cut out the bruises and make an apple pie and a jar of applesauce.

They're both easily carried, highly nutritious camp and cruise companions.

APPLE PIE   Y, C, B, P

½ cup seedless raisins
2 tablespoons slivered, blanched almonds
6 cups peeled, thinly sliced apples
2 tablespoons honey
1 tablespoon lemon juice
2 tablespoons sugar
½ teaspoon cinnamon
½ teaspoon nutmeg
Pie crust mix for 8-inch or 9-inch pie
2 tablespoons instant blending flour
1 tablespoon soft butter

Mix raisins and almonds into apple slices. Mix honey and lemon juice together and stir into apple mixture, completely coating all the apples. Mix sugar, cinnamon, and nutmeg together. Stir apple mixture as you sprinkle the sugar and spices into it.

Make pie crust mix recipe for 8-inch or 9-inch pie according to instructions on packages. Keep your hands cool when handling the dough and work in the shade. Roll out dough and fit bottom crust into pie pan according to recipe instructions. Fill with fruit, sprinkle with flour, dot with butter, and cover with top crust. Make a few slashes in the top and flute around the edges to seal crusts together. Cover fluting with aluminum foil, which should be removed 10 minutes before pie is done so fluting will brown without burning. Bake for 40 minutes or until done in oven preheated to 400 ° F. Serve hot or cold. Serves 6 to 8.

Note
Either ice cream or cheese go very well with apple pie.

Variation
Substitute wild berries for raisins.

CAMP APPLESAUCE   Y, C, W, P, B

4 pounds apples
½ cup water
1–3 tablespoons lemon juice, or more if desired
½ cup white, granulated sugar (substitute honey to taste)
½ cup brown sugar (substitute maple syrup)
⅛ teaspoon ground cinnamon
⅛ teaspoon ground nutmeg

Wash and quarter apples, cutting out any bruised spots and the core. Don't bother peeling. Put apple pieces in heavy saucepan with all other ingredients, cover tightly, and bring to a boil. Turn heat down to simmer and continue cooking until soft. Stir occasionally to be sure apples are not sticking. If they dry up before juice in apples is released, add a little water. The less water you must add, the better the flavor will be. Taste and adjust seasoning; more sugar if too tart, more lemon if too sweet, more cinnamon or nutmeg if too bland.

Force apple pulp through a colander or large strainer and serve with whipped cream or a topping mix. Serves 8.

EASY BUTTERSCOTCH PIE   Y, C, B

1 3¼-ounce package butterscotch pudding mix
Milk called for in recipe on box
Graham Cracker Pie Crust (see next recipe)
Whipped topping mix

Cook butterscotch pudding mix according to instructions on package. Cool, fill pie shell, completely cover, and store in ice chest where no moisture will drip on it until time to serve.

Make whipped topping according to package instructions or whip skimmed milk powder or if you're so lucky as to have whipping cream, whip that and decorate top of pie before serving. Serves 8.

GRAHAM CRACKER PIE CRUST   Y, C, B

¼ cup butter or margarine
1½ cups graham cracker crumbs
¼ cup sugar
½ teaspoon cinnamon

Mix all ingredients together well and pat evenly against bottom and sides of baking pan. Make sure it clings, then either chill or bake for 15 minutes or until it becomes more or less crisp and adheres together well. Fill with pudding mix and serve either hot or cold. It's nice decorated with whipped topping mix if you have it.

CAMP COFFEE   C, W

6 cups ice-cold water (melted snow or clear, cold water from a mountain
    stream)
7 heaping teaspoons ground coffee
Egg shells (all that you have available)
Whisky or brandy (optional)

Put water in a pot, add coffee, and bring to a boil. Add egg shells and salt, move to the edge of the fire, and simmer for about 15 minutes. Remove from fire, add ½ cup of cold water, let stand for two or three minutes or until grounds have settled. Serve.

Though camp coffee has plenty of punch on its own, on crisp mornings it can be laced with a little whisky or brandy for a quick warmer-upper.

23—How to Prepare and Cook Wild Game

by Norman and Priscilla Strung*

Although there are many recipes designed specifically for the preparation of wild game, domestic recipes for pork, beef, lamb, and poultry work equally well on wild counterparts.

Chicken recipes work for pheasant, grouse, quail, rabbit, and squirrel.

Wild duck and goose can be cooked the same as domestic duck and goose, and domestic turkeys were developed from the wild strain of Merriam turkey which inhabits many of our states.

Red-meated animals like moose, deer, and elk are comparable to beef. Antelope, mountain goat, and mountain sheep come close to lamb and are delicious when eaten with mint sauce.

Javalinis, peccaries, and wild hogs are pigs and should be cooked like pork, as should bear. All are subject to trichidna and so should be thoroughly cooked, with no pink meat. Bear liver is poisonous, due to an abundance of Vitamin A in excess of human tolerance.

If you use a meat thermometer on domestic meats and poultry, the same settings would work for their wild equivalents.

* With a good deal of hard-earned know-how and a large freezer, the Strungs are able to live almost entirely off the land, hunting and fishing for their meat, growing most of their vegetables and foraging for wild fruits. They do a lot of outdoor cooking, even at home, often serving one or more of the following recipes to friends and friends of friends who have heard of the Strungs and wander in from all over the United States. They also use some of these recipes when camping or on wilderness trips, preparing some ahead, cooking some on the trail or in camp.

Getting Rid of the "Wild" Flavor

When cooking wild meat, if you don't like "wild" flavor, remove as much fat from the animal as possible. This fatty tissue is the source of most complaints about strong meat, particularly if the meat has been frozen for a while. For additional ways to tame the flavor, see the corning recipe on page 348 and the one for Sauerbraten on page 350.

If you want to make hamburger from some cuts of meat, try adding beef suet in place of natural fat. That way your wildburgers will always be juicy and tasty.

Most wild animals have some sort of musk gland that should be removed if possible. Usually, but not always, it's on the inside of the hind legs. On antelope it's below the ear.

More important than removing the musk gland is to keep all the animal's hair off the meat. One hair left on a skinned deer can add an unwanted flavor. The reason for this is that the musk secretion is spread through the animal's hair by the foliage it passes through.

Once you understand the meat comparisons and replacement of fat, you're ready to forge ahead with your favorite kitchen recipe, which now has added attraction: the distinctive, different, and delicious flavor of wild meat.

If you have a cold icebox available, you'll have much more tender and tasty game (birds and small animals or pieces of venison) if you dress it and store in the icebox for 24 to 36 hours before cooking.

Norman hangs his game in the cool, fresh Montana breezes to age it, but he knows just how to prepare each different kind and where and how to hang it so flies, insects, and marauding animals will leave it alone. Besides which, contamination that might attack vulnerable food is at a minimum in this remote region.

HOW TO DRESS AND COOK OPOSSUM

To prepare opossum for roasting the way you would a turkey, dip it in hot water (close to but not boiling) for one minute, then scrape off its hair with a dull knife. Avoid cutting the skin.

Cut it from throat to anus, remove entrails, and cut off head and tail.

Wash thoroughly, inside and out, with hot water and cut away any fat you can reach. Cover with cold salt water and let it stand overnight.

Before cooking, again wash the opossum thoroughly with hot water. Fill body cavity with your favorite stuffing and cook as you would a turkey (approximately 20 minutes to the pound or until thermometer registers 185 ° F.), basting every 15 minutes.

To prepare an opossum for cutting into pieces and cooking on a spit, you should skin it. When you do this, remove the musk glands at the small of the back and inside the forelegs and cut away excess fat.

Skewer the pieces and cook over the coals as you would any other meat, basting with barbecue sauce.

PREPARING PORCUPINE

Porcupine has long been renowned as a survival food because it's one of the few animals that can be killed by unarmed persons. Beyond the survival aspects, this animal is just plain good eating, especially when broiled over coals.

To prepare for cooking, skin porcupine from the quill-less belly and up. Once skinned, remove the tiny scent glands on the inside of the forelegs and the thin layer of fat that surrounds the body cavity.

Next, section the porcupine as you would a frying chicken and soak the pieces in salt water for two hours. Remove from the salt water, put in a pot, cover with cold water, and bring to a boil. Turn down to a simmer and continue cooking for 35 minutes. Remove from the boiling water and dry off each piece.

Brush the cooked porcupine pieces with butter seasoned to taste with paprika, salt, and pepper and broil over coals until nicely browned (20 to 25 minutes).

The average porcupine will serve 2 to 4 people.

CORNED MEAT   Y, C, W, B

Corning is an excellent method of preparing any wild, red meat—moose, deer, bear, elk, antelope, goat, sheep—that is tough to eat or strong to the taste. Since corned meat keeps so well, it's an ideal dish for the camp or wilderness cook, as well as the backyard picnicker who wants to serve something different. The secret to successful corned meat lies in the marinade, adequate corning time, and long, slow cooking of the meat after the corning process is completed.

The following recipe makes about 4 gallons of marinade and is sufficient for any size piece of meat it will completely cover.

2 tablespoon pickling spice
4 bay leaves
1 teaspoon black pepper
1 teaspoon whole cloves
2 pounds salt (3 cups)
⅞ cup sugar
1 ounce sodium nitrate
¼ ounce sodium nitrite
3½ gallons warm water
1 large lemon, cut in six slices
1 medium onion, minced
1 large garlic clove, minced
Raw meat

Mix first 8 ingredients well, then slowly add to 3½ gallons of warm water in a large crock (don't use a metal container), stirring as you pour. Add lemon, onion, and garlic and stir again. Add meat, cover, and place in your refrigerator or somewhere where the temperature will remain between 33 and 40 degrees for 15 days. Stir and turn every second day. Once corned, meat will keep well in a cool place.

Corned wild meat should be cooked in the same way as corned beef. Place it in a pot, cover it with water, and bring to a boil. Once a scum forms, reduce the heat to simmer, remove the scum, and cook slowly for five hours or until the meat is tender.

Note
Buy sodium nitrate and sodium nitrite at a drug store.

STRUNG'S JERKY   Y, C, W, B

Jerky is one of the finest wilderness rations ever devised by man. It tastes quite good if prepared correctly, and two thin strips with a glass of water will satisfy any appetite. Although Indians originally prepared jerky over an open fire, cooking it on a kitchen range well in advance of a proposed trip is a lot more practical and convenient.

Begin with any red meat, wild or domestic. Once done, jerky tastes like jerky whether you used sirloin or flank, so a cheaper cut of meat is the most sensible.

4 pounds meat cut into pieces approximately 1 x 2 x 8
2 teaspoons salt
4 teaspoons powdered barbecue seasoning
2 teaspoons chili pepper and curry powder mixture (optional)

Cut away all fat, gristle, and tendon from the strips of meat. Combine seasonings in a salt shaker. Pound the meat and, as you pound, sprinkle with the seasonings. (There should be about ½ teaspoon of the combination spread across each side of each strip of meat.)

Place the strips directly on the oven rack, turn to 150 ° F., and leave them there until all the moisture is gone, usually about 7 hours. The strips should feel like dry leather when done and should be supple enough to bend a little without breaking.

Jerky can be eaten as is (chewed slow and long) or used as a base for soups, stews, and pemmican. It's also a delicious and different party snack when you're serving a crowd in the backyard. It will literally keep for years without refrigeration.

PEMMICAN

Pemmican is really one cut above jerky, since it's a well-balanced meal in a portable meat ball. We've had great success using wild game jerky with this recipe given to us by a Crow Indian woman.

3–4 cups jerky pieces
½ pint dried, chopped fruit (raisins are fine but anything works)
¼ pint chopped nuts
¼ pint hot animal fat (preferably beef or pork as wild fat tastes bad)

Powder the jerky by pounding with a clean hammer until you have 1 pint that looks like dried hamburger. Add remaining ingredients and mix well. Before the mixture fully cools, shape into golf-sized balls. The fat will harden and the pemmican will keep its shape. Pemmican doesn't keep as well or as long as jerky, due to the fat souring (about a month in the relatively cool Montana summer), but it's ideal for the average high mountain camping trip. Like jerky, it can be eaten as is (one ball to a meal) or cooked in soups or stews.

SAUERBRATEN   Y, C, W, B

Here's a delicious German recipe that will successfully mask the most objectionable taste in wild meats. The cut of meat you use isn't important, so it's a good recipe to use for meat on the rib cage, forelegs, and neck that might normally go to waste.

2 tablespoons sugar
2 cups vinegar
2 cups water
2 medium onions
1 sliced lemon
3 bay leaves
10 peppercorns
10 whole cloves
2 tablespoons salt
4 pounds meat
½ cup flour
2 tablespoons cooking oil

Combine all ingredients except meat, flour, and cooking oil in a large dish. (Don't use metal.) Bone and dice the meat into 2-inch square pieces and marinate in the mixture for at least 36 hours. Stir at least once a day.

Remove meat from the liquid, dry with a towel, and dredge in flour. Brown all sides of the meat in cooking oil for about 20 minutes. Strain marinade, add 2 cups of the liquid to the browned meat. Cover and cook over very low heat for 3 to 4 hours or until so tender it literally falls apart.

Use cooking liquid as a base for thick, brown gravy and serve over dumplings with red cabbage and black bread. Serves 8 to 12.

SHEPHERD'S STEW   Y, C, W

If you need to prepare a hearty campfire meal in a hurry, this is the recipe for you. Prepare the following for each person who will be eating.

½ pound diced wild meat (substitute hamburger or other ground meat)
1 small carrot, cut in thin slices
1 small potato, cut in thin slices
½ teaspoon dried minced onion
1 square foot heavy aluminum foil
Salt and pepper to taste
1 bouillon cube dissolved in ½ cup hot water

Combine meat, carrot, potato, and onion in center of square of foil and sprinkle with seasonings. Pour broth over mixture, fold foil around it, seal leaving some space for steam expansion, and bury package in coals. Cook 20 to 30 minutes in hot fire.

Pour juices into cup and drink as a hot broth. Eat stew directly out of foil package.

WILD MEAT SCALLOPINI   Y, C, B

2 pounds meat
½ cup all-purpose flour
2 tablespoon paprika
½ teaspoon salt
¼ teaspoon pepper
3 tablespoons fat
1 4-ounce can mushrooms
1 bouillon cube
1 8-ounce can tomatoes
¼ cup chopped green peppers
½ cup wine
Grated Parmesan cheese

Tenderize meat thoroughly by pounding with a mallet and cut into bite-size pieces. Combine flour, paprika, salt, and pepper and dredge meat in the mixture. Heat fat until it starts to sizzle but isn't smoking. Brown meat in the hot fat, then remove to a baking dish.

Drain canned mushrooms, add water to liquid to make 1 cup, and heat until it boils. Dissolve bouillon cube in mushroom liquid and pour over meat. Bake in 350 ° F. oven for 45 minutes.

Combine tomato sauce, green peppers, mushrooms, and wine in

saucepan and simmer for 30 minutes while the meat is baking. Pour over meat during the last 15 minutes of baking time and baste with the sauce once or twice. Serve with noodles and sprinkle with grated Parmesan cheese. Serves 6.

Note
Meat can be cooked in Dutch oven.

TRADITIONAL DEERHUNTER'S SCRAPPLE

Y, C, W

When a buck is killed, the dish served that night should be scrapple.

4 cups beef bouillon
1 cup cornmeal
1 teaspoon salt
1½ pound finely chopped deer liver
½ pound finely chopped deer heart
1 onion, finely chopped
¼ pound butter or margarine
½ cup flour
3 tablespoons butter or margarine

Bring broth to a rapid boil and slowly add cornmeal. Stir constantly until mixture returns to a full boil. Add salt, reduce heat. Cover and cook slowly for 5 to 7 minutes.

Fry chopped deer liver, heart, and onions in butter, stirring frequently, until meat is an even color (5 to 7 minutes). Stir into cornmeal. Pour mixture into a shallow baking pan and chill until it becomes firm.

Slice scrapple into ¼-inch slices, roll in flour, and fry in butter until both sides are golden brown. Serves 4.

ROAST SQUIRREL

Y, C

Squirrels are one of the most widely distributed game animals in the United States and one of the best eating. They can be fried, broiled, or spitted over a campfire—or cooked into a meat pie. But the best way to eat them is when they're stuffed and roasted.

Before preparing squirrels for cooking, skin and clean them and soak for an hour in salt water, then dry them thoroughly.

3 squirrels
¼ cup lemon juice (substitute 2 tablespoons vinegar)
¾ cup cooking oil
2 cups bread crumbs
½ cup milk
1 4-ounce can mushroom pieces
½ teaspoon salt
1 dash pepper
1 small onion, grated
1 teaspoon Worcestershire sauce
¼ teaspoon tabasco sauce
¼ cup olive oil or bacon fat
1 dash paprika

Prepare squirrels as described above, then combine lemon juice and cooking oil and rub into them.

Mix together the bread crumbs, milk, mushrooms, salt, pepper, onion, and Worcestershire and tabasco sauces to make a moist stuffing and fill the squirrels with it. Skewer shut, brush with olive oil or bacon fat and sprinkle with paprika.

Arrange in a shallow baking pan and cook in 325 ° F. oven for 90 minutes or until tender and well done. Baste as necessary.

REMOVING FISHY TASTE FROM WILD DUCK

Here's a way to eliminate the fishy taste from wild ducks that have been feeding on minnows or fish grass (you can tell by the smell when you clean them) that will, at the same time, give them a unique, fresh flavor and aroma.

Cut the peels from 3 oranges into strips ¼ inch wide by 1½ inches long. Poke holes (approximately 1 per square inch) deep into the breast of a medium to large dressed duck and force the strips of peel into them.

Cut the peels from 3 more oranges into 1-inch wide strips and cover the duck with them.

Stuff the duck and cook it as you normally would do, but remove the larger strips of peel for the last 25 minutes of baking.

ROAST QUAIL   Y, C, W, B

Dress quail as you would a chicken, but be very careful when removing entrails not to break the gall bladder. Feathers can be plucked after dipping the bird into hot water to loosen them, but the bird should be nicer if you dry-pluck it and singe to get rid of hair-like bits of feather after you are through. Hang the carcass up to cool before refrigerating.

When it comes to flavor, few birds can match the little quail. It can be spitted and cooked over the coals, split and broiled, stuffed and roasted, or cooked in any other way you'd prepare a small chicken.

4 quail
4 large canned oysters
2 tablespoons melted butter or margarine
½ cup flour, seasoned with salt and pepper to taste
8 slices of bacon (optional)

Prepare quail as described above. Stuff each one with an oyster, brush with melted butter or margarine, and dredge with flour.

If the birds are lean or if you've removed the fat, roll them in a blanket of 2 strips of bacon. Bake in a 350 ° F. oven for 15 to 20 minutes or until done, basting frequently. Serves 4.

BURGUNDY BAKED TROUT   Y, C, W, B

2 1½–2 pound trout, dressed
⅛ pound butter or margarine
1¼ cup dry red wine
1 large green pepper, sliced crosswise
1 large onion, sliced
2 medium tomatoes, sliced
Salt and pepper to taste
Paprika to taste

Place fish in a baking pan, dot with butter, and pour wine over them. Cover with green pepper, onion, and tomato slices. Sprinkle with salt, pepper, and paprika and seal top of pan with aluminum foil. Bake in 325 ° F. oven for 25 to 35 minutes or until flesh flakes easily away from the bone when touched with a fork.

Variation
Bake fish individually in aluminum foil packages. You can substitute canned tomatoes and their juice for fresh tomatoes and wine.

CRACKLING FRIED TROUT   Y, C

8 small trout, 5–7 inches long
1 egg, beaten
½ cup cracker crumbs
Cooking oil for deep frying
Salt and pepper

Clean the trout but leave them whole. Dip in beaten egg, then in cracker crumbs. Don't use trout that are longer than 7 inches.

Heat oil to about 375 ° F. and add trout—in a basket if you have one. Cook until the tail is as crisp as a potato chip, dry off the oil on absorbent paper towels, sprinkle with salt and pepper to taste, and eat. Bones and all, if you like.

If the fish are soft and moist inside, you haven't cooked them long enough. If they curl up in the fat, the fat isn't hot enough. Serves 4.

SPICY TROUT TWISTS   Y, C

4 ¾–1½ pound trout
½ cup cracker crumbs
½ cup corn meal
1 tablespoon salt
½ teaspoon black pepper
½ teaspoon garlic
½ teaspoon oregano
1 tablespoon dried parsley
1 egg
½ cup milk
Cooking oil for deep frying

Clean the trout, peel off the skin with a sharp knife and, using your fingers, rip the flesh from the bone. Start at the back and rip down until you've reduced all the fish into ragged strips about ½ inch wide.

Combine crumbs, meal, and seasonings in a paper bag and shake to mix well. Stir egg and milk together, dip pieces of fish into the mixture, and then drop them one by one into the paper bag. Shake until each piece is coated, then spread them out to dry for a few minutes.

Heat oil to about 375 ° F; it should be very hot but not smoking. Drop pieces of fish gently into the oil (use a deep fry basket if you have one) and fry for 3 to 5 minutes or until they are flaky inside. Save oil for future use. Serves 4 to 6.

Note
Fish bits can be served as party snacks with cocktail sauce.

BAKED PIKE
Y, C, B

This recipe works well on any member of the pike family.

8 1-inch thick pike steaks
2 cups tomato juice
Juice of 2 lemons
½ teaspoon celery salt
Tartare sauce

Lay fish steaks in a shallow baking pan and pour tomato and lemon juice around them. Sprinkle with celery salt. Cover pan with aluminum foil and bake for 25 to 40 minutes at 325 ° F. or until fish flakes easily when touched with a fork.

Serve with rice and a garnish of tartare sauce. Serves 4 to 6.

Index

Abalones, foraging for, 122, 123, 124
Accessories, outdoor cooking, 24–26
Acorns, 125
Air Force Survival Manual, U.S., 116–117, 123
Air mattresses, 89
Alcohol stoves, 46, 147
Aluminum foil
  cooking with, 79, 108, 318–330
    See also specific recipes
  firebox bottom lining, 25
  griddles, 108
  hoods for charcoal grills, 14, 25
  pots and pans, 26, 108
  reflector oven, 47, 48, 101
Aluminum pots, 151
Animals, *see* Wild game
Apartment houses, and outdoor cooking, 3–4
Appetizers
  Meat Balls as, 251
  Smoked Oyster and Mussel, 234
Apple(s)
  Broccoli with, 320
  Fried Pork Chops and, 267–268
  Pie, 342–343
  String Beans with, 327
Applesauce, Camp, 343
Asbestos flame regulators, 149
Asparagus
  and Dandelions Oriental Style, Foraged, 323
  wild, 127
Auto-Fire charcoal cooker-lighter-heater, 21–23, 46
Avocado
  and Grapefruit Salad, 222
  and Orange Salad, 222
  Seviche, 235–236
Awnings, 4
Axes, 59, 102

Back-packing, wilderness, 88, 94–95, 111
Bacon
  and Corn and Eggs, 323
  Easy Baked Beans with, 317
  Frankfurters Barbecued with, 282
  and Liver and Onions, 266
  and Liver Kabobs, 265–266
  and One Egg, 313
  use in wilderness cooking, 90
Bacteria, disease-producing, 28, 203–205

Baked Beans
  Easy, 317
    with Bacon, 317
    with Frankfurters, 317
    with Ham, 317
Baked Eggplant, 319
Baked Fish Steaks and Steamed Beer, 288
Baked Ham with Pineapple and Cherries, 269–270
Baked Pike, 356
Baked Trout, Burgundy, 354
Barbecue-Braising Economy Cuts of Beef, 254
Barbecue Sauce
  Hawaiian-Style Sweet and Sour, 220
  Made with Cabbage Soup, 239
Barbecued Chicken
  Marinara, 277
  in Oriental Sauce, 276–277
Barbecued Fish Fillets in Clam Sauce, 285
Barbecued Frankfurters
  with Bacon, 282
  on Buns, 282
Barbecued Leftover Roast Beef Slices with Beans, 255–256
Barbecued Marinated Frankfurters, 282
Barbecued Pork Chops in Mushroom Sauce, 266
Barbecued Salmon Steaks, 289
Barbecued Spareribs, 267
Barbecued Steak
  Sandwiches, 259
  in Vinegar and Olive Oil, 257
Barracudas, 123, 124
Basting, timing for, 197
Bean(s), 315–317
  Chili-Baked Franks and, 283
  Easy Baked, 317
    with Bacon, 317
    with Frankfurters, 317
    with Ham, 317
  nutrition in, 207
  with Prunes and Celery, 316
  Refried with Cheese, 317
  Soup and Pot Roast, 253
  use in wilderness cooking, 89, 90
  and Vegetable Patties, 316
  See also Legumes
Bear liver, 120, 345
Bears, 120, 348

Beef
  Barbecue-Braising Economy Cuts of, 254
  Barbecued Leftover Roast Beef Slices with Beans, 255–256
  Barbecued Steak Sandwiches, 259
  basting time, 197
  Cabbage Soup with, 239
  controlling charcoal-stove temperature, 197–198
  cooking time, 194–195, 196, 197
  facts about, 189–191, 192–198
  freezer storage, 193–194
  Fried Chuck Fillet Steaks, 256
  grades and cuts, 189–190
  Green Peppers Stuffed with Corned Beef Hash, 251
  Hamburgers on Toasted Buns, 250
  Leftover, and Peppers, 258
  Leftover Steak and Peppers, 258
  low-heat cooking, 198
  Meal in a Burger, 248–249
  Meat Balls as Appetizers, 251
  Meat Cakes, 252
  Meat Loaf, 252
  meat thermometers, 197
  Patties, 248
  placing rotisserie rod, 197
  Pot Roast and Bean Soup, 253
  refrigerator storage time, 193
  Rolled Beef Roast on a Spit, 254–255
  Scandinavian Meat Balls, 251
  Sherried Steak, 259
  Standing Rib Roast on a Spit, 255
  Steak Barbecued in Vinegar and Olive Oil, 257
  storage, 192–194
  Swiss Steak, 256
  Tomatoes Stuffed with Corned Beef Hash, 250
  Two-Step Camp and Galley Stew, 260–261
  Two-Step Chuck Fillets, 257
  Two-Step Swiss Steak, 257
Beer, Steamed, Baked Fish Steaks and, 288
Beet Soup (Borscht), 238
Benches, for yards, 9
Bernard's Kamp Pack, 90
Berries, wild, 126, 129–131, 333, 336
Berry Pancakes, 333
Berry Shortcake, 338
Berry Syrup, Wild, 336
Birds, edible wild, foraging for, 118, 119
Biscuit Blanket, Franks in a, 283–284
Biscuit-Mix Bread, 331
Biscuit-Mix Twists, 331
Biscuit Roll, Salmon, 294
Bisque, Lobster and Shrimp, 242–243

Blackberries, 126
Blackberry Shortcake, 338
Blue Cheese Butter, 218
Blueberry and Ice Cream Dessert, 336
Boating (boat cooking)
  eating utensils, 152–153
  emergency rations, 155–156
  entertaining, 164–165
  fire prevention, 140–142
  food supplies, 161–163
  fuels, 144–149
  galley equipment, 157–158
  garbage disposal, 156
  housekeeping, 153–155, 156
  meal planning, 158–163
  menus, 160–161
  oven utensils, 152
  ovens, 150
  picnics, 183–185
  planning ahead, 136–140
  pots and pans, 151–152
  refrigeration, 150–151
  seasickness, 164
  storage, 153–155
  stoves, 142–150
  water supply, 155
  wet- and rough-weather cooking, 163–164
Boatman's Bouillabaisse, 237–238
Boiled Dinner
  Italian, 308–309
  New England, 271
    Wilderness, 271
Boiled Eggs, 310
Boiled Frankfurters on Buns, 282
Boiled Vegetables in Celery Sauce, 320
Borscht (Beet Soup), 238
Bottles, use aboard boats, 154
Bouillabaisse, Boatman's, 237–238
Brandied Peach Sundaes, 337
Bread(s)
  Biscuit-Mix, 331
  Biscuit-Mix Twists, 331
  Quick Prune, 333–334
Breakfasts, wilderness, 91
Bricks, stoves made of, 12
Briquettes, 17, 21, 23–24
Broccoli
  with Apple, 320
  Quick Pepper Pot Fish and, 294
Broiling, campsite, 79–80
Broths, use in seasonings and sauces, 217
Buckets, 60
Burgundy Baked Trout, 354
Butane camp stoves, 43, 44
Butchers, 189, 190–191
Butter
  Blue Cheese, 218

Herb Sauce, Potatoes and Onions in, 326
Butterscotch Pie, Easy, 344

C rations, 90
Cabbage
  Red, Sweet and Sour, 328
  Soup
    Barbecue Sauce Made with, 239
    with Beef, 239
Caesar Salad, 222–224
Cake(s)
  Berry Shortcake, 338
  Chocolate-Sauerkraut, 340
  Frosting, Cream Cheese, 342
  made with vegetables, 338
  Mother Dowd's Carrot, 339
  Tomato Soup Spice, 341–342
Camp and Galley Stew, Two-Step, 260–261
Camp Applesauce, 343
Camp Coffee, 344
Camp Marmalade, 334
Camp or Galley Clam Chowder, 245
Camp Pancakes, 332
Camp Salad, Two-Day Tossed, 229
Campanians, 27, 70–71
Campers (vehicles), 37
Campers' Creed, text of, 85
Campfires, 38–39, 74–78, 97–102
  building, 74–77, 97–102, 103
  cooking on, 77–78
  extinguishing, 84
  holding, 101
  keyhole lay, 98, 99
  laying and starting, 77
  log-cabin, 99–100
  reflector oven, 101
  small stoves, 101–102
  squaw, 101
  starting, 77
    on a wet day, 103
  tepee, 100
  timing cooking oven, 78
  winter, 100–101
  wood for, 75–76
  woodcutting, 102, 115
Camping (camp cooking), 34–85
  adding variety to, 78
  aids, 58–60, 110–111
  broiling, 79
  checking equipment, 84
  cleanup time, 82–89
  commercial campgrounds, 35, 43
  cooking fire, 77
  desert, 112–115
  equipment needs, 60–62, 109–111
  fire regulations, 37
  foil cooking, 79

food packaging, 56–58
food staple needs, 62–63, 109–110
foraging, 116–135
furniture, 56
gas lanterns, 58
KOA Ranch Kamps, 35
meal planning for, 63–65
menus for, 65–67
nosebag lunches, 72–73
oven cooking, 78
ovens and stoves, 37, 38–49
public campgrounds, 36–37
refrigeration, 49–54
smoke cooking, 80–82
steaming, 80
stowing and loading gear, 71–72
timing open-fire cooking, 78
transportation, 37–38
utensils, 54–56
See also Campfires; Campsites; Wilderness cooking; specific recipes
Campsites
  camping, 36–37
  desert, 113–116
  wilderness, 95–96
  See also Campfires
Can openers, 60
Candied Sweet Potatoes, Top-of-Stove, 330
Candles
  citronella, 10
  as fire starters, 21
Canned Chick Pea Soup, 241
Canned fruits and vegetables, serving portions of, 211, 212
Canned heat, 19, 147
Canned Meat Balls in Tomato-Sauerkraut Sauce, 273
Canned or Leftover Poultry and Rice and Raisins, 279
Canned Pear with Cream Cheese, 337
Canned soups, as sauce bases, 218
Canoeing, 86, 88, 94–95
Caramel Spread for Crackers, 335
Caraway Seeds, Fish with, 292
Carp Bits, Fried, 292
Carrot and Mashed Potato Bundles, 324–325
Carrot Cake, Mother Dowd's, 339
Carrot-Mushroom Soup Mold, 230–231
Cast-iron pots, 151
Catfish in Pineapple Sauce, Fried, 386
Catsup, 218
Cattails, 127
Cauliflower
  au Gratin Blue, 321
  and Mushrooms in Wine Sauce, 321
Celery
  Sauce, Boiled Vegetables in, 320

Celery (*cont.*)
à la Waldorf, Stuffed, 228
Chairs
　camp folding, 56
　for yards, 9
Champagne picnic, 176–178
Char-Broil gas cooker, 18
Charcoal-broiled foil-wrapped vegetables,
　318–330
Charcoal stoves
　Auto-Fire, 46
　camp-cooking, 46
　cooking at home, 4, 13–17
　extinguishing the fire, 24
　hibachi, 15–16, 46
　hoods for, 13–15
　starting the fire, 19–24
　temperature control, 197–198
Charts (maps), boating, 137–140
Cheese, Tuna Loaf with, 295
Chick Pea Soup, 241
　Canned, 241
Chick peas, 315
Chicken(s)
　cooking time, 196
　facts about, 191
　Fried, 279
　Liver, Chopped, 265
　Marinara, Barbecued, 277
　and Mushrooms and Peas, Creamed,
　　278
　in Orange-Lemon Sauce, Whole Un-
　　stuffed, 281
　in Oriental Sauce, Barbecued, 276–277
　and Rice and Raisins, 278
　Salad Mold, Creamed, 231
　serving size, 210
　Soup with Dill Matzoh Balls, 240
　See also Poultry
Chili-Baked Franks and Beans, 283
Chimneys, 10
Chinese-Style Vegetables, 321–322
　Cooked on the Coals, 322
Chocolate-Sauerkraut Cake, 340
Choice-grade meat, 189–190
Chopped Chicken Liver, 265
Chops
　Barbecued Pork, in Mushroom Sauce,
　　266
　cooking time, 196
　defrosting, 194
　Fried Pork, and Apple, 267–268
　Shoulder Lamb, with Gravy and Po-
　　tatoes, 264
　storage, 193
　Veal, Braised in Fruit Cocktail, 273
Chowder and Steamer Clams on the
　Half-Shell, 298
Chuck Fillet Steaks, Fried, 256

Chuck Fillets, Two-Step, 257
Chuck-wagon (tailgate) breakfast, 180–
　182
Chugwater, Wyoming, KOA Ranch
　Kamp in, 35
Cinder blocks, stoves made of, 12
Citronella candles, 10
Clam and Crab, Fillets with Canned, 286
Clam Chowder
　Camp or Galley, 245
　Frozen, 245
　Manhattan, 244–245
　Quick New England, 245
Clam Sauce for Spaghetti, Red or White,
　300
Clam Scramble, 311
Clam shells, use as dishes, 296
Clambake(s), 173–176, 304–306
　New England–style, 173–176
　with Paella Preliminaries, Yard or
　　Patio, 305–306
　pit for, 175–176
Clams
　Chowder and Steamer, on the Half-
　　Shell, 298
　foraging for, 121–122, 124
　on the Half-Shell, 297
　　with Spicy Cocktail Sauce, 297
　Steamed, 298
　Stuffed, 298–299
Clean-Out-Your-Cooler Omelet, 312
Cleaning (hygiene, sanitation)
　boating (boat cooking), 153–155, 156
　camping (camp cooking), 30, 82–84,
　　108
　food poisoning and, *see* Food poison-
　　ing
　foraging and, 119
　garbage disposal, 83
　policing area, 83
　water purification, 177
Coal stoves, boating, 144–147
Coat hangers
　camping hooks made of, 60
　grill hood made of, 14
Cocktail Sauce
　Clams on the Half-Shell with, 297
　Spicy, 221
Cod, Crunchy Steamed, 288
Coffee, Camp, 344
Cold Roast Turkey, 281
Cole Slaw, Many-Colored, 226
Coleman Company, Inc.
　coolers (ice chests), 51, 52
　dining fly, 10
　gas cooker, 17, 18
　propane stoves, 41, 42
　stove-top camp oven, 47
　three-burner gasoline stove, 39

Collapsible saws, 102
Colorful Corn, 322
Columbus (Iron Works) gas cooker, 17,
    18
Commercial campgrounds, 35, 113
Conchs, 124
Condensed milk, 200
Cone shells, 124
Containers, food-storage, 29, 57–58
Contour maps, 87
Cooking
    emergency measures in the wilderness,
        105–108
    fire, *see* Campfires
    high-altitude, 104–105
    timing, outdoors, 194–196
    utensils, 26, 54, 152–153
        See also specific kinds
    in wet and rough weather (boating),
        163–164
        See also Boating (boat cooking);
            Camping (camp cooking); Des-
            ert camping; Wilderness cooking
Cookouts, *see* Picnics and cookouts
Coolers (ice chests), 28–29, 49–54
    loading, 53–54
        See also Refrigeration
Copper-bottomed stainless-steel pots, 151
Coral reefs, 124
Corn
    and Bacon and Eggs, 323
    on the Cob Cooked in Coals, 322–323
    Colorful, 322
Corned Beef Hash
    Green Peppers Stuffed with, 251
    Tomatoes Stuffed with, 250
Corned meat, wild game, 348
Cornish hen, cooking time for, 196
Cottage Cheese
    Avocado and Grapefruit Salad with,
        222
    and Vegetable Salad, 224
Coverings for food, 29
Crab(s)
    and Clam, Canned, Fillets with, 286
    foraging for, 122
    shells, use as dishes, 297
Crackers, Caramel Spread for, 335
Crackling Fried Trout, 355
Cranapple, Veal Gordon Bleu with, 275
Cranberry-Pineapple Mold, 233
Crayfish, 121, 122, 173
Cream Cheese
    Cake Frosting, 342
    Canned Pear with, 337
Cream of Spinach Soup, Easy, 241
Creamed Chicken
    and Mushrooms and Peas, 278
    Salad Mold, 231

Crunchy Steamed Cod, 288
Curry, Lobster and Shrimp, 243
Cutting tools, camping, 59
Cypress spurge, 134

Dairy products, care of, 199–200
Dampers, stove, 45
Dandelion(s), 126–127, 242, 323
    and Asparagus Oriental Style, For-
        aged, 323
    Fish Soup, 242
Dar Bin Loo, 302–303
    Casserole, Leftover, 304
Decorations for yard dining, 11
Deerhunter's Scrapple, Traditional, 352
Dehydrated foodstuffs, 89, 90, 109
    See also specific kinds
Desert camping, 112–115
    breakfast, 180–182
    campground and campsite selection,
        113–114
    refrigeration, 115
    vehicle and gasoline, 114
    water, 114, 116
Desert cooler (ice chest), 53
Dessert, Pancake, 333
Desserts, 331–344
Deviled Eggs, 311
Dill Matzoh Balls, Chicken Soup with,
    240
Dining flies, 9, 10
Dinners, wilderness, 92
Disease-producing bacteria, 28, 203–205
    See also Food poisoning
Dishes, 26, 29, 153
    seashell, 296–297
Dr. Kraemer's Foil-Baked Fish, 295
Dried eggs, 200
Dried foodstuffs, 89, 90, 109
    See also specific kinds
Dried fruit, 212
Dried Fruit Pancakes, 333
Dried vegetables, 211
Dry beans, 315
    See also Beans; Legumes
Dry ice, 53
Dry Milk Powder, Nonfat, Whipped Top-
        ping Made from, 336
Duck
    facts about, 191
    in Orange-Lemon Sauce, Whole, Un-
        stuffed, 281
    serving size, 210
    wild, removing fishy taste from, 353
Dude ranches, 35
Dutch oven, 54–55

Easy Baked Beans, 317
    with Bacon, 317

Easy Baked Beans (*cont.*)
  with Frankfurters, 317
  with Ham, 317
Easy Butterscotch Pie, 344
Easy Cream of Spinach Soup, 241
Easy Tartare Sauce, 218
Eating utensils, 26, 54
  boat cooking, 152–153
  seashell, 296–297
  See also specific kinds
Economy Cuts of Beef, Barbecue-Brais-
    ing, 254
Egg(s)
  and Bacon and Corn, 323
  Boiled, 310
  care and storage of, 199, 200
  Clam Scramble, 311
  Clean-Out-Your-Cooler Omelet, 312
  Deviled, 311
  Eight Egg Omelet, 312
  Frankfurter and, 313
  Matzoh Brie, 313
  One Egg and Bacon, 313
  Pot Pourri, 312
  Scrambled, for Four, 313
  Shrimp Omelet, 314
  Stir-Fried
    with Leftover Stew, 314
    and Meat, 314
  and Vegetables, Potato-Frankfurter
      Mixture with, 284
Eggplant, Baked, 319
Eight Egg Omelet, 312
Electric charcoal-fire igniters, 21
Electric plates, 19
Electric skillets, 19
Electric stoves, 19, 144, 145
Electricity, use on boats, 144
Emergency cooking measures, wilderness,
    105–108
Emergency rations
  boating, 155–156
  wilderness, 90
Enamelware, 151
Entertainment
  boating, 164–165
  picnic, 179
Ergot, 129
Evaporated milk, 199–200
Evaporation
  cooling food by, 97
  water supply from, 118

Fats, cooking, care of, 199, 201
Fencing, reed, 5, 6
Fillets with Canned Clam and Crab, 286
Fire
  hazards and regulations, 37, 97, 98,
      140–142

  prevention, boating and, 140–142
  starters, 19–24
Fireplaces, outdoor, 11–23
  See also Campfires
Firewood, 75–76
Fish
  Baked Pike, 356
  Barbecued Salmon Steaks, 289
  Burgundy Baked Trout, 354
  with Caraway Seeds, 292
  cooking time, 195, 196
  Crackling Fried Trout, 355
  Crunchy Steamed Cod, 288
  Dr. Kraemer's Foil-Baked, 295
  facts about, 192, 193
  Fillets
    with Canned Clam and Crab, 286
    in Clam Sauce, Barbecued, 285
    Pan-Fried and Oven-Fried, 287
  Fried Carp Bits, 292
  Fried Catfish in Pineapple Sauce, 286
  Fried Mackerel Poached in Red Wine,
      293
  and Fruit Salad, Jellied Foraged, 232
  Laulaus, 290
  Marinated, 236
    raw, 235–236
  and meat combinations, *see* Meat and
      fish combinations
  Poached Whole, 296
  poisonous, 122–123, 124
  Quick Pepper-Pot, and Broccoli, 294
  and Rice and Vegetable with a Tomato
      Touch, 293
  Salmon Biscuit Roll, 294
  serving sizes, 209, 210
  Soup
    Boatman's Bouillabaisse, 237
    Dandelion, 242
    Salmon and Flounder in Mushroom,
        246
    Tuna, 247
  Spicy Trout Twists, 355
  Steaks
    and Steamed Beer, Baked, 288
    in Zesty Sauce, 289
  storage, 193
  Tuna Loaf with Cheese, 295
  See also Fishing; Shellfish; specific fish
Fishing
  bait, 121
  equipment, 111, 121
  foraging, 121–125
  precautions, 122–125
  in tropical waters, 123–125
Flash points of fire-starters, 20
Flavored Pancakes, 332
Floodlights, 9–10

Flounder and Salmon in Mushroom Soup, 246
Flower boxes, 6–7
Fluids, fire-starting, 19–21
Foam rubber, use on boats, 154
Foil-Baked Fish, Dr. Kraemer's, 295
Foil cooking, 79, 108
    See also Aluminum foil; Foil-wrapped, charcoal-broiled vegetables; specific recipes
Foil-wrapped, charcoal-broiled vegetables, 318–330
Fold-away furniture, 9
Food
    foraging, *see* Foraging
    poisoning
        facts about, 28, 203–205
        fish and shellfish, 122–123
        wild game, 119–120, 122–123
        wild plants, 125
        See also Refrigeration; specific foods
    storage, wilderness cooking, 96
Foodstuffs (food staple needs)
    boat cooking, 154–155, 161–163
    camp cooking, 62–63, 89–90
    picnics and cookouts, 168–170
    wilderness cooking, 89–90, 109–110
    See also specific foods, foodstuffs
Foraged Asparagus and Dandelions Oriental Style, 323
Foraged Fruit and Fish Salad, Jellied, 232
Foraging, 116–135
    fish and shellfish, 121–125
    plants
        edible wild, 125–129
        poisonous, 129–135
    poisonous creatures, 120, 122–123
    precautions, 119–120, 122–125
    in tropical waters, 123–125
    for water, 116–118
    wild game, 118–120
Frankfurter-Potato Mixture with Egg and Vegetables, 284
Frankfurters
    Barbecued
        with Bacon, 282
        on Buns, 282
        Marinated, 282
    in a Biscuit Blanket, 283–284
    Boiled, on Buns, 282
    Chili-Baked, and Beans, 283
    Easy Baked Beans with, 317
    Egg and, 313
    with Sauerkraut, 283
Franks and Beans, Chili-Baked, 283
Franks in a Biscuit Blanket, 283–284
Freezer jells, 50

Freezing (frozen) food
    camp cooking and, 49–54, 64–65, 68
    freezer storage, 193–194
    packaging, 193–194
    refrigerator storage times, 193
    serving portions, 211, 212
    See also Refrigeration
Fresh Zucchini-Tomato Mix, 324
Fried Carp Bits, 292
Fried Catfish in Pineapple Sauce, 286
Fried Chicken, 279
Fried Chuck Fillet Steaks, 256
Fried Mackerel Poached in Red Wine, 293
Fried Pork Chops and Apple, 267–268
Fried Trout, Crackling, 355
Fries, Quick Home, 327
Frijoles Refritos con Queso, 317
Frosting, Cream Cheese Cake, 342
Frozen Clam Chowder, 245
Frozen food, *see* Freezing (frozen) food
Frozen Fruit and Shrimp Salad, 225
Fruit
    Basket Salad, Watermelon, 229
    care of, 201–202
    Cocktail, Veal Chops Braised in, 273
    dried, 212
    and Fish Salad, Jellied Foraged, 232
    -juice crystals, use of, 219
    Juice
        Gelatin, Real, 233–234
        Glaze, 219
    juices, use as seasonings, 219
    nutritional values, 207, 208
    Salad Gelatin, 234
    serving portions, 210, 211–212
    See also specific fruits, recipes
Fuels, boating, 141, 144–149
Furniture (furnishings)
    camping, 56
    terraces, 4
    yards, 7–11
"Fuzz sticks," 75–76

Galley and Camp Stew, Two-Step, 260–261
Galley (boat cooking) equipment, 156–158
Galley or Camp Clam Chowder, 245
Game, *see* Wild game
Garbage cans, 156
Garbage disposal, 83, 108, 156
    See also Cleaning
Gas
    lanterns, 58
    lighting fixtures, 10, 58
    stoves, 17–18
        camp cooking, 41–44

Gasoline
  desert camping and supply of, 114
  precautions on boats with, 141, 144
  stoves, 39–41
  warning against starting fires with, 20
Gimbal-hung stoves, 143, 147
Gin Punch, 179
Glaze, Fruit Juice, 219
Good-grade meat, 189–190
Grades, meat and fowl, 189–190, 191
Graham Cracker Pie Crust, 344
Grain products, nutrition in, 207, 208
Grapefruit
  and Avocado Salad, 222
  Halves Baked in Honey, 337
Grasses, edible and inedible, 129
Green Pepper and Chopped Veal, 272
Green Peppers Stuffed with Corned Beef
    Hash, 251
Green Salad, Tossed, 228–229
Grilling time and temperature chart, 196
Grills
  charcoal, 13–17
  long-handled, hinged, 25
  See also Stoves
Guacamole, Tacos Filled with, 234–235

Ham
  Baked with Pineapple and Cherries,
    269–270
  cooking time for, 193, 195, 196
  Easy Baked Beans with, 317
  New England Boiled Dinner, 271
    Wilderness, 271
  Steak with Fruit Sauce, 270–271
  See also Pork
Hamburgers
  cooking outdoors at home, 3, 4
  stuffed with sautéed mixed vegetables
    (Meal in a Burger), 248–249
  on Toasted Buns, 250
Hangers (saplings), 76
Hardwood plank cooking, 106
Hardy, Ed, 39, 42
Hares, wild, 119
Hatchets, 59
Hawaiian luaus, 172–173
Hawaiian-Style Sweet and Sour Barbecue
    Sauce, 220
Hemlock, 128, 129
Hepatitis, 122
Herbs, use of, 218
Herring Salad, Pickled, 226
Hibachis, 15–16, 46
Hickory wood chips, 81
High altitudes, cooking in, 104–105
Hiking, 86, 88, 94, 95
Hinged grills, long-handled, 25
Holding fire, 101

Home, cooking outdoors at, 3–33
Home Fries, Quick, 327
Homestrand galley stoves, 145, 148
Honey, Grapefruit Halves Baked in, 337
Hoods for charcoal grills, 13–14
Hooks, hanging, 60
Horseback riding, 86, 88–89
Humus, 97
Hunting, 118–120
  See also Foraging; Wild game

Ice, 115
  See also Coolers; Ice chests; Dry ice;
    Refrigeration
Ice chests (coolers), 28–29, 49–54
  loading, 53–54
Ice Cream and Blueberry Dessert, 336
Insect repellents, 58
Interior Department, U.S., 36
Iodine, water purification with, 117
Italian Boiled Dinner, 308–309

Jellied alcohol (Sterno) stove, 19, 46, 147
Jellied Foraged Fruit and Fish Salad, 232
Jellied fuel stoves, 19, 147, 148
Jellies, fire-starting, 19–21
Jellyfish, 123
Jerky, Strung's, 348–349
Joshua Tree National Monument, 180
Judy's Punch, 179

K rations, 90
Kabobs, Liver and Bacon, 265–266
Kampgrounds of America (KOA), 35
Kerosene
  stoves, 148
  use as fire starter, 20
Kettle stoves, 16
Keyhole lay, 98, 99
Kindling, campfire, 76
Knives, 111

Lamb
  Chops, Shoulder, with Gravy and Po-
    tatoes, 264
  cooking time, 196
  facts about, 190, 191
    shish kabobs and stew, 261
  or Pork Shish Kabob, 269
  Shanks, Simmered Then Barbecued,
    263
  Soy Marinade for Shish Kabobs, 262
  Steaks Rosemary, 264
  Stew, 262
Lanterns, camping, 58
Lard, care of, 199, 201
Laulaus, Fish, 290
Leftover Beef and Peppers, 258
Leftover Dar Bin Loo Casserole, 304

Leftover or Canned Poultry and Rice and Raisins, 279
Leftover Roast Beef Slices with Beans, Barbecued, 255–256
Leftover Sauerkraut, 283
Leftover Steak and Peppers, 258
Leftover Stew, Stir-Fried Eggs with, 314
Legumes
    Beans
        Easy Baked, 317
        with Prunes and Celery, 316
        and Vegetable Patties, 316
    chick peas, 315–316
    dry beans, 315
    Frijoles Refritos con Queso (Refried Beans with Cheese), 317
    lentils, 316
Lem, Arthur, 12
Lentils, 316
Lettuce and Onion Salad with Vinegar and Sugar Dressing, 225
Lighting (illumination) for yards, 9–10
Liquefied petroleum gas (LPG), 17, 41–42, 44, 144, 148–149
    stoves, 41–44
Liquid fire-starters, 19–21
Liver
    and Bacon
        Kabobs, 265–266
        and Onions, 266
    Chopped Chicken, 265
Lobster
    cooking time for, 193, 196
    and Shrimp
        Bisque, 242–243
        Curry, 243
        Sauce, 243
Log-cabin campfire, 99–100
Loin of Pork with Sauerkraut and Caraway Seeds, 268
    Two-Step, 268
Luaus, 172–173, 290
Lunches, wilderness, 91

McCluskey, Ross, 23
Mackerel Poached in Red Wine, Fried, 293
Manhattan Clam Chowder, 244–245
Many-Colored Cole Slaw, 226
Maps
    boating, 137–140
    wilderness camping, 87, 88
Marinades
    Fruit Juice Glaze, 219
    Meat Sauce Teriyaki, 220
    raw fish, 235, 236
    Soy, for Shish Kabobs, 262
Marinas, 140
Marinated Fish, 236

Marinated Frankfurters, Barbecued, 282
Marmalade, Camp, 334
Martenhoff, Jim, 81
Mashed Potato and Carrot Bundles, 324–325
Masonry cookers, 11–13
Matches, 61
Matzoh Balls, Chicken Soup with Dill, 240
Matzoh Brie, 313
Mayonnaise, 218
Meal in a Burger, 248–249
Meat
    Balls
        as Appetizers, 251
        Leftover Sauerkraut in, 283
        Scandinavian, 251
        in Tomato-Sauerkraut Sauce, Canned, 273
    Cakes, 252
    cooking, 119–120
    diseases, 119–120
    and fish combinations
        Dar Bin Loo, 302–303
        Leftover Dar Bin Loo Casserole, 304
        Patio Paella, 306–308
        Yard or Patio Clambake with Paella Preliminaries, 305–306
    foraging for, 118–120
    Loaf, 252
    patties, freezing and packaging of, 194
    precautions, 119–120
    Sauce Teriyaki, 220
    serving sizes for, 209
    thermometer, use of, 197, 198
    See also Wild game; specific meats
Menus
    boat cooking, 152, 158–161
    breakfast (picnic), 180
    camping trip, 65–67, 78–79
    champagne picnic, 178
    chuckwagon (tailgate) breakfast, 10
    clambake, 174
    luau, 173
    nutritional, 206–208
    outdoor cooking at home, 31–33
    picnics and cookouts, 170, 171, 173, 174
    planning, 209–212
    teen-ager picnic, 170
    wilderness cooking, 92–94
    winter picnic, 171
Mess kits, 110
Milk
    care and use of, 199–200
    containers, use in refrigerating food, 50
    serving for nutrition, 206–207

Minestrone Soup from Leftovers, 309
Mixed Vegetables Baked in Coals, 325–326
Mocha Whipped Cream, 340
Mold(s)
  Carrot-Mushroom Soup, 230
  Creamed Chicken Salad, 231
  Fruit Salad Gelatin, 234
  Pineapple-Cranberry, 233
  Real Fruit Juice Gelatin, 233–234
Morays, 124
Mother Dowd's Carrot Cake, 339
Motorboat cruising, *see* Boating (boat cooking)
Mountain streams, cooling of food in, 97
Mushroom(s)
  and Cauliflower in Wine Sauce, 321
  and Peas and Creamed Chicken, 278
  Soup
    -Carrot Mold, 230–231
    Salmon and Flounder in, 246
  wild, 125, 131
Mussel(s)
  foraging for, 122, 123
  and Oyster Appetizers, Smoked, 234
  Shells, Stuffed, 299
  shells, use as dishes, 297

National Association of Engine and Boat Manufacturers, 140
National Campers and Hikers Association, 85
National Fire Protection Association (NFPA), 20, 141
Nested utensil sets, 55, 110
New England Boiled Dinner, 271
  Wilderness, 271
New England Clam Chowder, Quick, 245
New England–style clambake, 173–176
Nonfat Dry Milk Powder Whipped Topping, 336
Nosebag lunches, 72–73
Nutrition
  camp cooking and, 64
  facts about, 206–208
  vitamin sources, 207–208
  wilderness cooking, 87, 90
Nut(s)
  acorn, 125
  edible wild, 128, 129
  and Raisin Rice Pudding, 338

Oatmeal
  Rich Cinnamon, 335
  Stick-to-the-Ribs, 335
Oil and Vinegar Dressing, 221
Oilfish, 123
Oils, use and care of, 199, 201

Omelets
  Clean-Out-Your-Cooler, 312
  Eight Egg, 312
  Shrimp, 314
One Egg and Bacon, 313
One-pot meals
  Canned Meat Balls in Tomato-Sauerkraut Sauce, 272
  Chick Pea Soup, 241
  Chopped Veal and Green Pepper, 272
  Creamed Chicken, Mushrooms, and Peas, 278
  Fish, Rice, and Vegetable with a Tomato Touch, 293
  Frankfurters with Sauerkraut, 283
  Italian Boiled Dinner, 308–309
  Jellied Foraged Fruit and Fish Salad, 232
  Manhattan Clam Chowder, 244–245
  Potato-Frankfurter Mixture with Egg and Vegetables, 284
  Quick Pepper-Pot Fish and Broccoli, 294
  Salmon and Flounder in Mushroom Soup, 246
  Sausage and Sauerkraut Supper, 272
  Split Pea Soup, 246
  Stick-to-the-Ribs Oatmeal, 335
  Veal Balls in Tomato-Sauerkraut Sauce, 272
  Veal Stew, 275
  Wishbone Soup, 247
  Yard or Patio Clambake with Paella Preliminaries, 305–306
Onion(s)
  and Lettuce Salad with Vinegar and Sugar Dressing, 225
  and Potatoes in Butter Herb Sauce, 326
  use as cooking utensils, 107
Opossum, dressing and cooking, 346–347
Orange and Avocado Salad, 222
Orange-Lemon Sauce
  Whole, Unstuffed Chickens in, 281
  Whole, Unstuffed Duck in, 281
Orange Snapper lunch, 165
Outdoor Dar Bin Loo, 302–303
Oven cooking, campsite, 78
  See also Campfires; Ovens
Oven-Fried and Pan-Fried Fish Fillets, 287
Ovens
  do-it-yourself, 49
  Dutch, 54–55
  marine, 150
  reflector, 47–49, 101
  stove-top, 46–47

utensils, 152
See also Campfires; Stoves
Overhangs, installation of, 4–5
Oyster(s)
Chowder, 246
foraging for, 121, 122
and Mussel Appetizers, Smoked, 234

Pack horses, 88–89, 94
Packing of wilderness gear, 94–95
Paella, 304
Patio, 306–308
Yard or Patio Clambake with, 305–306
Pancake(s)
Berry, 333
Camp, 332
Dessert, 333
Dried Fruit, 333
Flavored, 332
Quick-Mix, 332
Trail Sandwich, 333
Pan-Fried and Oven-Fried Fish Fillets, 287
Pans, *see* Pots and pans
Paper dishes, 153
Paper (newspaper) burners, 19
Paper (newspaper) fire starters, 21
Parachute cord, 111
Parmesan Veal, 274
Patio or Yard Clambake with Paella Preliminaries, 305–306
Patio Paella, 306–308
Patties
Bean and Vegetable, 316
Beef, 248
chopped meat, care and packaging of, 194
Pea Soup
Chick, 241
Canned, 241
Split, 246
Peach Sundaes, Brandied, 337
Pear with Cream Cheese, Canned, 337
Pemmican, 349
Pepper-Pot Fish and Broccoli, Quick, 294
Peppers
Leftover Beef and, 258
Leftover Steak and, 258
Pork and, 258
Perishable food and foodstuffs, care of, 64–65
eggs, 199, 200
fats and oils, 199, 201
food poisoning, 203–205
fruits and vegetables, 201–202
milk and dairy products, 199–200

See also Food poisoning; Refrigeration
Petroleum gas stoves, 17, 41–44
Pickled Herring Salad, 226
Picnics and cookouts, 166–185
boat and shore, 183–185
champagne, 176–178
clambakes, 174–176
desert breakfast, 180
equipment and supplies, 167–168
food poisoning, 203–205
food to take, 168
luau, 172–174
menus, 170–173, 178
punch recipes, 179
stove, 181–182
tailgate breakfast, 180–181
for teen-agers, 168–170
in winter, 170–172
Pie(s)
Apple, 342–343
Crust, Graham Cracker, 344
Easy Butterscotch, 344
Pike, Baked, 356
Pine nuts, 128
Pineapple-Cranberry Mold, 233
Pit cooking, 12
Planking (plank cooking), 106, 107
Plants
edible wild, 125–129
externally poisonous, 131–135
internally poisonous, 129–131
precautions against poisons, 129–135
Plastic
bags, use of, 57, 58, 61, 154
tarpaulin, 103–104
Poached Fried Mackerel in Red Wine, 293
Poached Whole Fish, 296
Poison ivy, 131–134
Poison oak, 131–134
Poison sumac, 133–134
Poisonous creatures to avoid, 120, 122–124
Poisonous fire starters, 20–21
Poisonous plants, 129–135
Porches, cooking on, 4, 5, 11
Porcupine, preparing and cooking, 347
Pork
Barbecued Spareribs, 267
Chops
and Apple, Fried, 267–268
in Mushroom Sauce, Barbecued, 266
cooking time, 195, 196
facts about, 190, 191
or Lamb Shish Kabob, 269
Loin of, with Sauerkraut and Caraway Seeds, 268
Two-Step, 268

Pork (*cont.*)
　and Peppers, 258
　Sausage and Sauerkraut Supper, 272
　See also Ham
Pot Pourri Eggs, 312
Pot Roast and Bean Soup, 253
Potato and Carrot Bundles, Mashed, 324–325
Potato-Frankfurter Mixture with Egg and Vegetables, 284
Potato Salad, 227
Potatoes
　Baked in the Coals, 326–327
　and Onions in Butter Herb Sauce, 326
　Quick Home Fries, 327
　and Succotash Cooked in Coals, 328
Pots and pans, 26, 55, 108, 151
Poultry
　Barbecued Chicken
　　Marinara, 277
　　in Oriental Sauce, 276–277
　Canned or Leftover Poultry and Rice and Raisins, 279
　Chicken and Rice and Raisins, 278
　Cold Roast Turkey, 281
　cooking time, 195, 196
　Creamed Chicken, Mushrooms, and Peas, 278
　facts about, 189, 191–192, 193, 195, 196
　Fried Chicken, 279
　Roast Turkey with Lots of Stuffing, 280–281
　serving sizes, 209, 210
　storage, 193
　thermometers, 197
　Whole, Unstuffed Chickens in Orange-Lemon Sauce, 281
　Whole, Unstuffed Duck in Orange-Lemon Sauce, 281
Powdered milk, 199
Prime-grade meat, 189
Princess Manufacturing Corp. stoves, 149
Propane gas stoves, 41, 42
Protein, nutrition in, 207
Prune Bread, Quick, 333–334
Prunes and Celery, Beans with, 316
Public campgrounds
　improved, 36
　unimproved, 36–37
Pudding, Nut and Raisin Rice, 338
Punch
　Gin, 179
　Judy's, 179
　Orange Snapper, 165

Quail, Roast, 354
Quick Home Fries, 327
Quick-Mix Pancakes, 332

Quick New England Clam Chowder, 245
Quick Pepper-Pot Fish and Broccoli, 294
Quick Prune Bread, 333–334

Rabbits, wild, 119
Rainwater, 117
Raisin and Nut Rice Pudding, 338
Ranch camps, 35
Raspberries, 126
Raspberry Shortcake, 338
Raw fish, marinated, 235
Real Fruit Juice Gelatin, 233–234
Red bricks, stoves made of, 12
Red Cabbage, Sweet and Sour, 328
Red or White Clam Sauce for Spaghetti, 300
Redwood furniture for yards, 8
Reed fencing, 5–7
Reflector ovens, 47–49, 101
Refried Beans with Cheese, 317
Refrigeration
　boat cooking, 150–151
　camp, 49–54
　desert camping, 115
　food poisoning and, 204
　fresh fruits and vegetables, 201–202
　storage times (meat, poultry, and fish), 193
　wilderness cooking, 97–98
Rhubarb leaves, 129
Rib Roast on a Spit, Standing, 255
Rice
　Pudding, Nut and Raisin, 338
　and Raisins
　　Canned or Leftover Poultry and, 279
　　Chicken and, 278
Rich Cinnamon Oatmeal, 335
Rid-Jid dining group furniture, 8
Roast Beef Slices with Beans, Barbecued Leftover, 255–256
Roast on a Spit, Rolled Beef, 254–255
Roast Quail, 354
Roast Squirrel, 352–353
Roast Turkey
　Cold, 281
　with Lots of Stuffing, 280–281
Roasts
　charcoal stove for, 198
　cooking time, 196
　rotisserie rod placement, 197
　thermometers for, 197
　See also specific meats, recipes
Rocks, cooking on, 106
Rods, fishing, 111
Roll-around grill, Coleman, 17, 18
Ronson stoves, 19, 43, 44
Roofs, 4
Rolled Beef Roast on a Spit, 254–255
Rope, 111

Rose berries (rose hips), 126
Rotisserie rod, placing of, 197
Rucksack packing, 94–95
Rust removers, stove, 45

Sailing (sailboats), 143
See also Boating (boat cooking)
Salad(s)
　Avocado
　　and Grapefruit, 222
　　and Orange, 222
　　Seviche, 235–236
　Caesar, 222–224
　Carrot-Mushroom Soup Mold, 230
　Cottage Cheese and Vegetable, 224
　Creamed Chicken, Mold, 231
　Dressing(s)
　　Vinegar and Oil, 221
　　Vinegar and Sugar, 225
　　Wilderness, 230
　Frozen Fruit and Shrimp, 225
　Fruit, Gelatin, 234
　greens, use in wilderness cooking, 91
　Jellied Foraged Fruit and Fish, 232
　Lettuce and Onion, with Vinegar and
　　Sugar Dressing, 225
　Many-Colored Cole Slaw, 226
　Marinated Fish, 236
　oils, care of, 199, 201
　Pickled Herring, 226
　Pineapple-Cranberry Mold, 233
　Potato, 227
　Real Fruit-Juice Gelatin, 233–234
　Stuffed Celery à la Waldorf, 228
　Tossed Green, 228–229
　Two-Day Tossed Camp, 229
　Watermelon Fruit Basket, 229
　Wilderness, 230
　Yogurt and Vegetable, 225
Salmon
　Biscuit Roll, 294
　and Flounder in Mushroom Soup, 246
　Steak, Barbecued, 289
Sand, use in cleaning utensils, 108
Sandwich, Pancake Trail, 333
Sauce(s)
　Barbecue, made with Cabbage Soup,
　　239
　Blue Cheese Butter, 218
　Easy Tartare, 218
　Fruit Juice Glaze, 219
　Hawaiian-Style Sweet and Sour Barbe-
　　cue, 220
　Oil and Vinegar Dressing, 221
　Polonaise, 220
　Shrimp and Lobster, 243
　Spicy Cocktail, 221
　Teriyaki Meat, 220
Sauerbraten, 350

Sauerkraut
　-Chocolate Cake, 340
　Frankfurters with, 283
　Leftover, 283
　Loin of Pork with Caraway Seeds
　　and, 268
　and Sausage Supper, 272
　-Tomato Sauce
　　Canned Meat Balls in, 273
　　Veal Balls in, 272–273
　Two-Step Loin of Pork with Caraway
　　Seeds and, 268
Sausage and Sauerkraut Supper, 272
Saws, 59, 102
Scallopini, Wild Meat, 351–352
Scallops
　foraging for, 122
　shells, use as dishes, 296
Scandinavian Meat Balls, 251
Scorpions, 125
Scrambled Eggs for Four, 313
Scrapple, Traditional Deerhunter's, 352
Sea Swing canned-heat stove, 147, 148
Seashells
　dishes, preparation of, 296–297
　Shellfish Baked in, 300
Seasickness, 164
Seasonings, 217–221
Seaweed, 128
Seeds, wild edible, 129
Sharks, 124, 125
Shellfish
　Baked in Seashells, 300–301
　Barbecued Fish Fillets in Clam Sauce,
　　285
　Clams
　　Chowder and Steamer, on the Half-
　　　Shell, 298
　　on the Half-Shell, 297
　　Steamed, 298
　　Stuffed, 298–299
　foraging for, 121–123
　Lobster
　　cooking time for, 193, 196
　　See also Shrimp, and Lobster
　precautions, 122–123
　Red or White Clam Sauce for Spa-
　　ghetti, 300
　Shrimp
　　and Frozen Fruit Salad, 225
　　and Lobster
　　　Bisque, 242–243
　　　Curry, 243
　　　Sauce, 243
　　Omelet, 314
　Stuffed Mussel Shells, 299
　Soup
　　Boatman's Bouillabaisse, 237

Shellfish, Soup (*cont.*)
  Lobster and Shrimp Bisque, 242–243
  Oyster Chowder, 246
  See also Clam Chowder
  See also Fishing
Shelters, wet-weather, 103–104
Sherried Steak, 259
Shish Kabobs
  lamb, preparation of, 261
  Lamb or Pork, 269
  Soy Marinade for, 262
Shortcake
  Berry, 338
  Blackberry, 338
  Raspberry, 338
  Strawberry, 338
Shoulder Lamb Chops with Gravy and
    Potatoes, 264
Shovels, 59
Shrimp
  and Frozen Fruit Salad, 225
  and Lobster
    Bisque, 242–243
    Curry, 243
    Sauce, 243
  Omelet, 314
Skewers, 55–56
Sleeping bags, 89
Smoke-cookers, 12
Smoke Cooking (Kramer and Sheppard),
    80
Smoke cooking, camp, 80–82
Smoked Oyster and Mussel Appetizers,
    234
Snakes, 120
Snails, poisonous, 124
Snow, as food cooler, 97
Soap, 108
Soup(s)
  Boatman's Bouillabaisse, 237–238
  Borscht, 238
  Cabbage, with Beef, 239
  Camp or Galley Clam Chowder, 245
  canned, as sauce bases, 218
  Chick Pea, 241
  Chicken, with Dill Matzoh Balls, 240
  Dandelion Fish, 242
  Easy Cream of Spinach, 241
  Frozen Clam Chowder, 245
  Lobster and Shrimp Bisque, 242–243
  Manhattan Clam Chowder, 244–245
  Minestrone, 309
  Oyster Chowder, 246
  Pot Roast and Bean, 253
  Quick New England Clam Chowder,
    245
  Salmon and Flounder in Mushroom,
    246
  Split Pea, 246

Tuna, 247
Wishbone, 247
Soy Marinade for Shish Kabobs, 262
Spareribs, Barbecued, 267
Spice Cake, Tomato Soup, 341–342
Spicy Cocktail Sauce, 221
  Clams on the Half-Shell with, 297
Spicy Trout Twists, 355
Spiders, 120
Spinach Soup, Easy Cream of, 241
Spits (spit cooking), 16, 17
  emergency (wilderness), 106
  roasting time and temperature chart,
    196
  Rolled Beef Roast on a Spit, 254–255
  Standing Rib Roast on a Spit, 255
Split Pea Soup, 246
Spread for Crackers, Caramel, 335
Squaw fire, 101
Squirrel, Roast, 352–353
Squirrels, 119, 352–353
Standing Rib Roast on a Spit, 255
Starters, *see* Fire starters
Steak(s)
  Barbecued in Vinegar and Olive Oil,
    257
  cooking time, 196
  defrosting, 194
  Fried Chuck Fillet, 256
  order of tenderness, 190
  and Peppers, Leftover, 258
  planked, 106, 107
  Sandwiches, Barbecued, 259
  Sherried, 259
  storage, 193
  Swiss, 256
    Two-Step, 257
  Two-Step Chuck Fillets, 257
Steamed Beer, Baked Fish Steaks and,
    288
Steamed Clams, 298
Steamed Cod, Crunchy, 288
Steamer and Chowder Clams on the
    Half-Shell, 298
Steaming, campsite, 80
Sterno stoves, 19, 46, 147
Stew
  Shepherd's (wild game), 351
  Stir-Fried Eggs with Leftover, 314
  Two-Step Camp and Galley, 260–261
  Veal, 275
Stick-to-the-Ribs Oatmeal, 335
Stinging nettle, 134, 135
Stir-Fried Eggs
  with Leftover Stew, 314
  and Meat, 314
Stonefish, 124
Storage, 26–27
  boat cooking, 153–155

camp cooking, 56, 71–72
containers, 29, 57, 58, 61, 154
dairy products, eggs, fats, and oils, 199–202
freezer, 193–194
meat, poultry, and fish, 192–194
refrigerator storage times, 193
sheds, 26–27
wilderness cooking, 96
Storm windows, 4
Stove-top oven, 46–47
Stoves
   accessory equipment and storage, 24–27
   boat cooking, 142–150
   camp cooking, 37, 38–49
   charcoal, 13–17, 19–24, 46
   electric, 19
   extinguishing charcoal fires, 24
   gas, 17–18, 41–44
   gasoline, 39–41
   hibachi, 15
   kettle, 16
   liquefied petroleum, 41–44
   masonry, 11–13
   on-the-table, 19
   outdoor-cooking-at-home, 4, 11–23
   paper burners, 19
   precautions, 44
   reflector ovens, 47–49, 101
   small, wilderness cooking, 101–102
   starting charcoal fires, 19–24
   wood, 44–45
   See also Ovens; specific makes
Strawberries, 126
Strawberry Shortcake, 338
String Beans with Apples, 327
Strung, Norman, 86, 345
Strung, Priscilla, 345
Strung's Jerky, 348–349
Stuffed Celery à la Waldorf, 228
Stuffed Clams, 298–299
Stuffed Mussel Shells, 299
Succotash, 328
   and Potatoes Cooked in the Coals, 328
Sundecks, 4, 5, 11
Sundaes, Brandied Peach, 337
Swan Valley, Montana, KOA Ranch Kamp in, 35
Sweet and Sour Barbecue Sauce, Hawaiian Style, 220
Sweet and Sour Red Cabbage, 328
Sweet Potato Surprise, 329–330
Sweet Potatoes
   Baked in Coals, 329
   baking on top of charcoal grill, 329
   Top-of-Stove Candied, 330
Swiss army knives, 111

Swiss Steak, 256
   Two-Step, 257
Syrup, Wild Berry, 336

Tablecloths, 9
Tables for yards, 7–8, 9
Tacos Filled with Guacamole, 234–235
Tall field buttercup, 134, 135
Tarpaulin, plastic, 103–104
   pitching, 104
Tartare Sauce, Easy, 218
Teen-ager picnics, 168–170
Temperature
   of charcoal stove, control of, 197–198
   and time charts, 196
Tepee fire, 100–101
Teriyaki Meat Sauce, 220
Terraces, apartment-house, outdoor cooking on, 4, 11
Thermometer, *see* Meat, thermometer, use of
Thermos stoves, 40–41, 181–182
Timing
   food cooked over open fire, 78
   high-altitude cooking, 104–105
   outdoor cooking, 194–196
   refrigerator storage, 193
   temperature and time charts, 196
Tinder for campfire, 75–76
Tomato and Zucchini Cooked on the Coals, 324
Tomato-Sauerkraut Sauce
   Canned Meat Balls in, 273
   Veal Balls in, 272–273
Tomato Soup Spice Cake, 341–342
Tomato-Zucchini Mix, Fresh, 324
Tomatoes Stuffed with Corned Beef Hash, 250
Tools, outdoor cooking, 25, 55, 59
Top-of-Stove Candied Sweet Potatoes, 330
Topping from Nonfat Dry Milk Powder, Whipped, 336
Tossed Camp Salad, Two-Day, 229
Tossed Green Salad, 228–229
Traditional Deerhunter's Scrapple, 352
Trail rods, 111
Trailers, camping, 37
Transportation
   and campsites, 3
   and wilderness cooking, 88–90, 94–95
Tropical waters, avoiding trouble in, 123–125
Trout
   Burgundy Baked, 354
   Crackling Fried, 355
   Twists, Spicy, 355
Tularemia, 119

Tuna
  Loaf with Cheese, 295
  Soup, 247
Tupperware, 29, 57–58, 154, 184, 193
Turkey
  Cold Roast, 281
  cooking time, 196
  facts about, 191
  with Lots of Stuffing, Roast, 280–281
  serving portions of, 210
Twists
  Biscuit-Mix, 331
  Spicy Trout, 355
Two-Day Tossed Camp Salad, 229
Two-Step Camp and Galley Stew, 260–261
Two-Step Chuck Fillets, 257
Two-Step Loin of Pork with Sauerkraut
  and Caraway Seeds, 268
Two-Step Swiss Steak, 257

Umbrellas, yard, 9
Underwriter's Laboratory (UL), 19
USDA grade labels, 189–190, 191
Utensils
  boat cooking, 151–153
  camp cooking, 54, 56
  wilderness cooking, 105–106, 107,
    110–111
  See also specific kinds

Veal
  Balls in Tomato-Sauerkraut Sauce,
    272–273
  Chopped, and Green Pepper, 272
  Chops Braised in Fruit Cocktail, 273
  Cordon Bleu with Cranapple, 275
  facts about, 190
  Parmesan, 274
  Stew, 275
Vegetable(s)
  Asparagus and Dandelions Oriental
    Style, Foraged, 323
  and Bean Patties, 316
  Boiled, in Celery Sauce, 320
  Broccoli with Apple, 320
  Cabbage, Sweet and Sour Red, 328
  cakes made with, 338
  care and storage of, 201–202
  Carrot and Mashed Potato Bundles,
    324–325
  Cauliflower
    au Gratin Blue, 321
    and Mushrooms in Wine Sauce, 321
    charcoal-broiled foil-wrapped, 318–319
    Chinese-Style, 321–322
    Cooked on the Coals, 322
  Corn
    and Bacon and Eggs, 323

on the Cob Cooked in Coals, 322–323
    Colorful, 322
  and Cottage Cheese Salad, 224
  Eggplant, Baked, 319
  Mixed, Baked in Coals, 325–326
  nutritional values, 207–208
  Potato-Frankfurter Mixture with Egg
    and, 284
  Potatoes
    Baked in the Coals, 326–327
    and Onions in Butter Herb Sauce,
      326
    Quick Home Fries, 327
  serving portions, 210–211
  String Beans with Apples, 327
  Succotash, 328
    and Potatoes Cooked in the Coals,
      328
  Sweet Potato Surprise, 329–330
  Sweet Potatoes
    Baked in Coals, 329
    baking on top of charcoal grill, 329
    Top-of-Stove Candied, 329
  and Yogurt Salad, 225
  Zucchini
    and Tomato Cooked on the Coals,
      324
    -Tomato Mix, Fresh, 324
Vehicles, camping, 37, 114
Vinegar
  and Oil Dressing, 221
  and Olive Oil, Steak Barbecued in, 257
Vitamins, food sources of, 207–208
Volcanic fire rock, 17

Wantagh Marine Park, 138, 140
Washington wood- and coal-burning
  stove, 146–147
Water (water supply)
  boat cooking, 155
  desert camping, 114–115
  digging for, 118
  foraging for, 116–118
  locating, 117–118
  purification of, 117
  wilderness cooking, 89
Water hemlock, 128, 129
Watercress, 128
Watermelon Fruit Basket Salad, 229
Waterways, navigable, 137
Weather, 87
  See also Wet weather
Weight of wilderness gear, 89, 94–95
Wet weather
  shelters for, 103–104
  starting fires in, 103
Whipped Cream, Mocha, 340

Whipped Topping Made from Nonfat Dry Milk Powder, 336
White or Red Clam Sauce for Spaghetti, 300
Whole, Unstuffed Chickens in Orange-Lemon Sauce, 281
Whole, Unstuffed Duck in Orange-Lemon Sauce, 281
Wild asparagus, 127
Wild Berry Syrup, 336
Wild duck, removing fishy taste from, 353
Wild game
corning, 348
diseases of, 119–120
duck, wild, removing fishy taste from, 353
foraging for, 118–120
getting rid of "wild" flavor, 346, 353
Jerky, Strung's, 348–349
opossum, dressing and cooking, 346–347
Pemmican, 349
porcupine, preparing, 347
precautions, 119–120
preparing and cooking, 119–120, 345–346, 347
Quail, Roast, 354
Sauerbraten, 350
Scallopini, Wild Meat, 351–352
Scrapple, Traditional Deerhunter's, 352
Shepherd's Stew, 351
Squirrel, Roast, 352–353
Wild Meat Scallopini, 351–352
Wild plants
edible, 125–129
poisonous, 129–135
See also specific plants
Wilderness cooking, 86–115
cleaning up, 108
cook and campsite, 95–96, 113
cooling of food, 96–97
desert camping, 112–115
emergency cooking measures, 105–108
fire for cooking, 97–102, 115
food storage, 96
foraging for food and water, 116–137
high-altitude cooking, 104–105
nutrition, 87, 90
packing gear, 94–95
planning meals, 90–92

sample menus, 92–94
starting fire on wet days, 103
vehicle and gasoline, 114
water, 114–115, 116–118
weight of gear, 88–89
wet-weather shelter, 103–104
what to bring, 88–90, 109
wood supply, 102, 115
Wilderness New England Boiled Dinner, 271
Wilderness Salad, 230
Dressing, 230
Wilson, Peter, 140
Wine
Burgundy Baked Trout, 354
Clam Sauce for Spaghetti, Red or White, 300
Fried Mackerel Poached in Red, 293
Sauce, Cauliflower and Mushrooms in, 321
used for seasonings, 219
Winter fire, 100–101
Winter picnic, 170–172
Wiring, electric cookers, 19
Wishbone Soup, 247
Wood
ash, use in washing dishes, 108
-burning stoves, 44–45, 144–147
campfire, 75–76, 81
desert cooking, 115
tools for cutting, 59
wilderness cooking, 102
Wrought-iron furniture, 4, 9

Yacht Safety Bureau, 141
Yard or Patio Clambake with Paella Preliminaries, 305–306
Yards, cooking in, 4–33
fencing, 5, 6–7
flower boxes, 6–7
furnishings, 7–11
menus, 31–33
stoves, 4, 11–23
Yogurt and Vegetable Salad, 225

Zesty Sauce, Fish Steaks in, 289
Zucchini
and Tomato Cooked on the Coals, 324
-Tomato Mix, Fresh, 324